LA LATINA
GRACE RAMIREZ

A COOK'S JOURNEY THROUGH LATIN AMERICA

FOOD PHOTOGRAPHY BY GARTH BADGER

RANDOM HOUSE
NEW ZEALAND

Abuela, esto es para ti

Grandma, this is for you

CONTENTS

Biography
6

My Latin Heart on a Plate
8

Food From the Gods
276

Ingredients List
278

Photo Credits
280

Map
281

Acknowledgements
282

Index
284

GRANOS Y SOPAS
Grains & Soups
10

AVES Y HUEVOS
Poultry & Eggs
32

DEL MAR
From the Sea
56

CARNES
Meats
84

PARA RELLENAR
Dishes with Fillings
108

ARROCES
Rice
140

ENSALADAS Y VEGETALES
Salads & Vegetables
158

SALSAS, ADEREZOS Y MÁS
Sauces, Condiments & More
182

ALGO DULCE
Something Sweet
212

BEBIDAS
Drinks
242

FIESTAS
Feasts
264

Chef and television personality Grace Ramirez combines her love of cooking and food with a strong and proud Latin heritage. While Grace was born in Miami, her family is from Venezuela, her mother has lived in Mexico, Costa Rica, Colombia, Brazil, Chile, Argentina and Uruguay, and her stepfather is from Peru. She has spent most of her adult years in New York and more recently in New Zealand, and all of these culinary influences can be tasted in her cooking.

Grace began her career in the pioneering days of food television, directing and producing one of the biggest shows on The Food Network, *Throwdown with Bobby Flay*. She was later selected from over 60,000 people to appear as a contestant on the US series of *MasterChef*, hosted by Gordon Ramsay. Shortly afterwards Grace was awarded a scholarship to the prestigious French Culinary Institute in New York City and worked at the restaurant Eataly under chefs Mario Batali and Lidia Bastianich.

She currently spends half her year in New Zealand, where she has been a judge on *My Kitchen Rules* and regularly volunteered for the Garden to Table programme that teaches children how to grow and prepare healthy, seasonal food. Grace also gives back to the Latin community as an ambassador for Nuestros Pequenos Hermanos (NPH International), a not-for-profit organisation that helps orphaned, abandoned and at-risk children across South America.

From her bases in New York City and New Zealand, Grace continues to travel the world in search of new cooking experiences and inspiration. *La Latina* is her first cookbook.

www.chefgraceramirez.com

MY LATIN HEART ON A PLATE

My culinary roots go back to Abuelita Vincy, my great-grandmother. At the turn of the 20th century, her parents moved from France via Curaçao to Coro, a little town in West Venezuela between the Sierra de San Luis mountains and the coastal desert of Parque Nacional los Médanos. Those were testing times. My great-grandmother was forced to marry at 15 to help take care of her siblings. She went on to have nine children of her own, and it was hard for her and my great-grandfather Moises to make ends meet. Although Moises was a public accountant, his earnings weren't enough to support such a big family, and there were many nights when the family went to bed hungry.

One Sunday evening, Vincy got on her knees and prayed to Gregorio de la Rivera, a spirit called upon by locals to bring back lost objects. That same night, a neighbour knocked on her door with a hen under his arm and asked whether she had lost it. Immediately she said yes — it was clearly a miracle — and graciously thanked the man. Although Vincy's first instinct was to kill the hen and make a meal out of it, she kept it instead, using its eggs to buy another chicken, then later a goat and a pig. The rest, as they say, is history.

No matter how bare her cupboards, Abuelita Vincy always saw them as half full. She believed in the 'superpoderes' — superpowers — of the kitchen, with which she could magically create daily meals to feed her entire family from even the most modest of ingredients. She bequeathed this legacy to two of her three daughters, my great-aunt Morela and my own grandmother, Mary. Both could miraculously produce a sumptuous feast out of five simple ingredients — just like Abuelita Vincy.

Fast forward to 2008: although I had a busy career as a television producer, I wasn't feeling truly fulfilled. I wanted to become a chef but didn't know how to start. Sensing this, Abuela Mary (my grandmother) sat me down, took my hand in hers, looked into my eyes and said, 'Te los paso, ahora te toca a ti, ya no me pertenecen' — 'I'm passing on to you my gift of cooking, I don't need it any more.' From that moment on, food took over my life: I started working at the Food Network as a director, and later became a US *MasterChef* contestant; although I didn't win, it led me to win a scholarship to the French Culinary Institute in New York. All of a sudden, I went from simply knowing my way around a kitchen to being able to cook effortlessly. I went from home cook to chef, and I like to think it was the 'superpoderes' passed down through the generations that helped me the most. As by now Abuela Mary had developed a respiratory disease that made her lose her palate, it was clearly my responsibility to keep her recipes alive and the family tradition going — which is what I've tried to do ever since, and hope that I have accomplished with *La Latina*.

Food is at the heart of what it means to be Latina. Latin Americans are warm, loud and festive, but above all else we are passionate about food: Peru's national ceviche obsession, mastering the perfect repulge on the Argentinean empanada, the just-enough-but-not-too-much pressing for the ideal Cuban sandwich, or the perfect pabellón criollo beloved by my native Venezuela. It also means friends and family, sharing each other's food over deafening roars of laughter and passionate conversation around a huge table. This passion is also why I chose to write a cookbook about Latin American food. This is where I'm from, where my roots are, and the place I will always go back to. My food and my kitchen take me home.

After living in five different countries, I've realised that many people think of Latin America as just one big Mexico, but in reality it is very different. I was fortunate enough to spend most of my teenage summers travelling all around with my mother, and got to know the people and the soul of this region. I made wonderful friends along the way who have become like family, and I am grateful to them for sharing so many of their recipes with me. I fell in love with Mexico, but can't deny the passion I feel for Peru, Argentina, Brazil and all the rest of the countries in Hispanic America; especially Venezuela, where my family is from.

How can I showcase all of these cultures in just one cookbook? To say that it was a challenge is like saying that Latinos think soccer is 'just another sport'. Different families make the same dish differently, depending on the country and on how their grandma or mom made it — as in the case of the heated debate about how to make arroz con pollo (chicken and rice). The recipes in this book are my take on the food of Latin America, drawn from my great love and respect for what is traditional. Throughout the process, I have felt a profound sense of responsibility to every country, from the smallest island in the Caribbean to vast Brazil with its extensive cuisine. In some cases I have used my French culinary training to simplify a recipe; in others I have allowed myself a little creative licence in adapting a few recipes to my taste. Plenty of times I have had to substitute ingredients that are hard to find outside their home country, while trying to maintain the links with tradition.

La Latina is my journey; it is a collection of my memories, the places I've been, the friends I've made and the family recipes I love. *La Latina* is also a gift to Abuela Mary, Abuelita Vincy, my mother and all the strong women in my life who have the 'superpoderes'. I hope that this book inspires you and passes on to you a bit of that magic dust.

Con todo mi amor — all my love,
Grace Ramirez

GRANOS Y SOPAS

GRAINS & SOUPS

CARAOTAS DE MI MADRE
Mom's Black Beans

FEIJOADA
Black Bean & Meat Stew

FRIJOLES REFRITOS
Refried Beans

FAINÁ
Chickpea Flat-bread

ESPINACA CON GARBANZO Y CHILE
Spinach with Chickpeas & Chilli

POZOLE ROJO
Red Hominy Stew

CHUPE DE CAMARONES
Prawn Chowder

CREMA DE AUYAMA
Creamy Butternut Squash Soup

CALDITO DE POLLO DE LA ABUELA
Grandmother's Chicken Soup

Venezuela

CARAOTAS DE MI MADRE

Mom's Black Beans

500 g dried black beans
100 g good-quality bacon or chorizo, cut into 1 cm dice
¼ cup olive oil
1 onion, peeled and chopped
1 leek, white part only, sliced
1 red capsicum, de-seeded and chopped
4 cloves garlic, peeled and chopped
2 bay leaves
1 tsp epazote (optional)
1 tbsp ground cumin
approx. 1.5 litres water or stock to cover

My mother is not always a great cook — she can be waaaay too adventurous and sometimes adds too many flavour combinations that don't quite go together. My abuela (grandma) says she hasn't had the 'gift' passed down to her; it was only passed down to me. What Mom can make, however, is some tasty black beans and delicious lentils. Black beans, also known as turtle beans, have lots of different names in different countries, and everyone has their method of cooking them. Soaking versus not soaking is the biggest debate. I used to swear by it, but a Mexican friend told me he never soaks and his beans are perfect; they just take a bit longer. So here is a non-soaking recipe, with my mom's flavours. Leave out the bacon/chorizo and use vegetable stock for a vegetarian version.

**Prepare: 15 minutes; cook: 1½–2 hours (can vary considerably)
Serves: 6 as an appetiser**

If you really want to soak the beans, do it! It will speed up the cooking process. Cover beans with plenty of cold water and leave for at least 2 hours. Drain beans and set aside.

Heat a large saucepan over a medium heat, then add bacon or chorizo and fry for 5 minutes or until slightly crisp. Add oil and stir to combine, then add onion, leek and capsicum and fry gently for 5 minutes or until softened. Add garlic and fry gently for a further minute.

Add beans, bay leaves, epazote (if using) and half the cumin to the saucepan. Add enough water or stock to cover the ingredients by about 10 cm. Bring to the boil, then simmer over a medium-low heat, stirring occasionally, for 1½ hours or until the beans are tender; sometimes they are ready in 1 hour. Check beans every 30 minutes or so; if they are drying out but are still not tender, add 1 cup warm water or stock at a time and continue to cook until done. They should always have plenty of liquid on top of them (it's better to have more liquid than needed that can be strained off than have the beans dry out). You can also cook the beans in a pressure cooker; they take about half an hour.

When beans are tender, remove from the heat and stir in remaining cumin. Set aside to cool, then taste and if necessary adjust the seasoning with salt and freshly ground black pepper.

Chef's note: Use the stock from making shredded beef (see page 105) or shredded chicken (see page 42), or buy good-quality beef or chicken stock. Beans are very moody, depending on the brand, where they come from, and the age, altitude and water hardness. They sometimes go soft really quickly, and sometimes they take ages. Adding baking soda will help increase the tenderness, but don't add more than ¼ teaspoon because that may over-soften them and turn them mushy. I only add baking soda if my beans are not even slightly tender after an hour. If you do use baking soda, check your beans for tenderness every 15 minutes. The cooked beans freeze very well, so make a big batch and freeze them in small containers. If you have sofrito (see page 186) in the freezer, add the frozen cubes directly to the pan after the bacon/chorizo is fried.

Brazil

FEIJOADA

Black Bean & Meat Stew

GF

500 g dried black beans
500 g smoked pork:
    mix of bacon slab, loin,
    ribs and ham hocks, cut
    into chunks or pieces
250 g chorizo, cut into
    slices 3 cm thick
250 g sausages, cut into
    slices 3 cm thick
250 g corned silverside
    or brisket, cut into
    slices 2 cm thick
2 tbsp olive oil
2 onions, peeled and
    finely chopped
6 cloves garlic, peeled and finely
    chopped
2 bay leaves

Feijoada is considered Brazil's national dish. It's often shared with friends on Saturday or Sunday afternoons at gatherings that evolve into long sessions of eating and gossiping, and this appetising and filling soulfood is at the centre of convivial family reunions in Brazil. This rich and unpretentious dish incorporates a mélange of meats, cooked low and slow in a flavourful broth. A carnivore's dream dish! Bear in mind that you don't want to rush a feijoada, or attempt to whip it up 2 hours before your guests arrive. This recipe takes time and is best made a day ahead so that the flavours have time to meld together. Use any kind of meat combo that will stand up well to slow-cooking — beef, smoked pork ribs or loin, bacon, your favourite sausages and chorizo; if you're feeling adventurous, it's traditional to add pigs' feet.

Prepare: 15 minutes; soak: overnight; cook: 2 hours
Serves: 6

Soak beans in cold water overnight, making sure they are completely covered.

Drain beans and place in a large saucepan of clean cold water. Bring to the boil over a medium heat, then simmer for 30 minutes until slightly tender.

Add meats to the beans, bring to the boil over medium heat, cover and simmer for about 1½ hours, until beans are cooked and meat is falling off the bone and tender. Add water as necessary so that it doesn't go dry. Season to taste with salt and freshly ground black pepper.

While beans and meat are cooking, heat olive oil in a small frying pan over medium-low heat. Add onion and fry gently until translucent. If necessary add a little more olive oil, then add garlic and turn the heat to low. Fry garlic and onion slowly for about 5 minutes, being careful not to burn or brown the garlic, or it will become bitter. Add this mixture to your beans along with the bay leaves.

For a nicer presentation, add chorizo and sausages whole 1 hour into cooking and when they are cooked through (approximately 20 minutes), remove them from the bean stew and set them aside. Slice them and return them to the stew shortly before you are ready to serve; that way they won't fall apart.

Serve feijoada with perfect white rice (see page 144), slices of orange, and very finely sliced kale or silverbeet fried in olive oil with finely chopped onion and garlic.

Mexico

FRIJOLES REFRITOS

Refried Beans

GF

1 tsp avocado oil
1 spring onion, white part only, sliced
1 fresh red chilli, finely chopped (optional)
425 g can black beans or home-made black beans (see page 15)
¼ tsp ground cumin
1 tsp brown sugar or shaved panela (unrefined cane sugar; optional)

Garnish
queso fresco (see page 208)
1 spring onion, green part only, sliced on an angle
1 fresh red chilli, sliced (optional)

Refried beans can be made with black beans or pinto beans. They make a great dip, or you can add a thick layer to your favourite tortillas, quesadillas, tacos or tostadas. They are also great alongside or under huevos divorciados (divorced eggs; see page 41). When slicing the spring onion for the beans, remember to save the green part for the garnish.

Prepare: 5 minutes; cook: 5 minutes
Serves: 4 as an appetiser

In a medium-sized saucepan, heat avocado oil over a medium-low heat. Add white spring onion and red chilli (if using), and fry gently until light golden brown. Add black beans, cumin and brown sugar (if using), and continue to cook over a medium-low heat until warmed through, stirring occasionally. Remove from heat and mash the beans with a fork or hand-held blender. Season to taste with salt and freshly ground black pepper.

Garnish with crumbled queso fresco, green spring onion and red chilli, if desired, and serve with tortilla chips as a dip or with your favourite taco.

Chef's note: For an extra layer of flavour, feel free to add crema agria (see page 211), sour cream or cheese and mix it in when you are re-frying your beans.

Uruguay

FAINÁ

Chickpea Flat-bread

olive oil, to cover dish
300 ml water, at room temperature
100 g chickpea flour
1 tsp salt

Fainá is a nutty, nutritious and delicious flat-bread made with chickpea flour. It's a great appetiser, and I love dipping it into chimichurri (see page 202), but it is most often served as an accompaniment to pizza — sounds weird, right? In fact, topping a pizza slice with a piece of fainá is a common practice in Uruguay and Argentina, where this flat-bread is hugely popular. When pizza and fainá are paired this way, it's called 'pizza a caballo' — 'horseback pizza'. It's easy to double the recipe and cook it in two pans.

Prepare: 5 minutes; cook: 10 minutes
Makes: one 20 cm x 28 cm piece

Preheat oven to 230°C. Cover bottom of 20 cm × 28 cm baking dish with olive oil, then place in oven while preparing dough. Pour water into a large bowl. In a separate bowl, combine flour and salt. Slowly whisk flour mixture into water until fully incorporated.

Carefully remove heated baking dish from oven, and pour in batter. Return to the oven and bake for 10 minutes until golden brown. Remove from oven and cool slightly before serving.

Mexico

ESPINACA CON GARBANZO Y CHILE

Spinach with Chickpeas & Chilli

GF

1 tbsp olive oil
2 cloves garlic, peeled and sliced
1 red chilli, sliced
300 g washed baby spinach (1 large bag)
400 g can chickpeas, drained (reserve ¼ cup of liquid)
1 tsp salt
¼ tsp ground coriander
¼ tsp paprika
pinch of ground cumin
flaky sea salt

I was once craving a carnitas taco (pork taco) in Mexico — and my friend took me to a vegetarian joint instead! I was furious at first, but then got served this dish in a taco. It's packed with flavour and goodness, perfectly healthy yet so filling and divine. You can serve this as a side or a main. Place this yumminess inside a corn tortilla or on top of rice; whatever you prefer.

Prepare: 5 minutes; cook: 10 minutes
Serves: 4–6 as a side

In a large frying pan, heat olive oil and gently fry garlic with half the sliced red chilli until garlic is light golden brown. Add spinach, chickpeas, chickpea liquid, salt, ground coriander, paprika and cumin. Let spinach wilt, and season to taste with flaky sea salt and freshly ground black pepper. Garnish with the remaining red chilli.

Chef's note: If serving in a taco, place inside a corn or flour tortilla (see pages 113 and 115), topped with pico de gallo (see page 193) and queso fresco (see page 208). You can add more heat using habanero chilli oil (see page 188).

Mexico

POZOLE ROJO

Red Hominy Stew

GF

For the pork
1 kg pork shoulder, cut into 4 pieces
1 small onion, peeled and quartered
2 cloves garlic, smashed
½ tsp whole black peppercorns
1 bay leaf
1 tbsp salt

For the guajillo purée
50–60 g dried guajillo chillies
½ cup diced onion
2 tbsp avocado oil
1 clove garlic, smashed

For the soup
1 cup canned pozole, drained

Garnish
1 avocado, flesh diced
2 limes, cut into wedges
½ purple or white cabbage, shredded
1 bunch baby or regular radishes, sliced
habanero chilli oil (optional; see page 188)
1 fresh chilli, sliced or finely chopped (optional)

Pozole is a traditional pre-Christopher Columbus soup or stew. The word 'pozole' means hominy, which are the dried, puffy corn kernels found in the soup. To get them puffy, dried corn kernels are treated using a special process called nixtamalization that makes the corn more digestible, then cooked until soft and puffy. Pozole is a celebratory meal, prepared for special occasions such as quinceañeras (a girl's fifteenth birthday), weddings, New Year celebrations or baptisms. Most Mexican home cooks will therefore take the time to do the nixtamalization process at home rather than buying canned pozole corn. Here, I share with you my home-made, fool-proof version. If you can't find canned pozole corn, don't worry — just make the stew without it and you will still become a fan.

Prepare: 45 minutes; cook: 1½ hours
Serves: 4–6

In a large stockpot, cover pork with water. Add onion, garlic, peppercorns, bay leaf and salt. Bring to the boil, then reduce heat to a simmer and cook, uncovered, for about 1 hour until pork is fork-tender. Skim fat off occasionally.

Using kitchen scissors, cut stem tops off dried guajillo chillies. Cut down the length of each pepper and open up to reveal the seeds. Remove the seeds and ribs of the peppers; if you wish, use them to make chilli salt (see page 193) or as a garnish; otherwise, discard. Cover peppers with water, bring to the boil and simmer for about 20 minutes.

Meanwhile, gently fry onion with avocado oil until well caramelised, about 10 minutes, then remove from the heat. When guajillo is ready, blend it with ½ cup of its poaching liquid, the caramelised onion and the garlic, until puréed. Set aside.

Once pork is tender, remove from liquid. Pull meat apart with two forks or your hands, and set aside. Strain and reserve the liquid and discard solids. Return liquid to the pot, and add the guajillo purée, shredded pork and pozole. Simmer for about 5 minutes before serving. Taste and adjust seasoning with salt and freshly ground black pepper.

Place garnishes in little bowls on the table, so that everyone can add whatever toppings they prefer.

Peru

CHUPE DE CAMARONES

Prawn Chowder

GF

6 cloves garlic, peeled and chopped
2 tbsp olive oil
1 tsp sriracha or other hot sauce, to taste (optional)
8 large prawns, unpeeled
350 g medium prawns, peeled and deveined
1 yellow capsicum, de-seeded and diced
1 red capsicum, de-seeded and diced
1 onion, peeled and diced small
1 medium carrot, diced
1 tbsp tomato paste
4 cups octopus poaching liquid (see page 68) or fish stock
1 tomato, de-seeded and diced
½ cup long-grain rice
1 small Agria potato, peeled and cut into 2cm dice
1 sweetcorn, husks removed and cut into 4
375 ml can evaporated milk
½ cup defrosted frozen or fresh peas
4 poached or fried eggs (optional)

Garnish (optional)
chopped mint or parsley
guajillo chilli flakes
lime or lemon wedges

This Peruvian rockstar is originally from Arequipa, a town to the south of Lima near the bottom of Peru. Arequipa was once Peru's capital, so a lot of very traditional and important dishes come from this region. Peruvians claim that the most buttery and tasty prawns in the world come from the rivers near Arequipa. This is not an everyday soup; chupes have an explosive combination of flavours from the local chillies and other ingredients and are considered to be a special weekend meal. This is an easier version, using readily available ingredients, and minus the Peruvian chillies. Don't worry, the magic is still there. It's not a stew; it's not a soup — it's a chupe.

Prepare: 30 minutes; cook: 45 minutes
Serves: 4

In a large stockpot, gently fry garlic in olive oil over a medium-low heat. Add hot sauce (if using) and large prawns. Gently cook prawns for about 2 minutes on each side, then add medium prawns. Continue to cook for about 2 more minutes, then remove from the heat. Transfer large prawns to one bowl and medium prawns to another, and set aside.

To the same pot, add capsicum, onion, carrot, tomato paste and 2 tablespoons octopus or fish stock. Gently cook for about 2 minutes on a medium heat. Add tomato and stir to combine.

Add rice, potato, sweetcorn and remaining stock. Bring to the boil, cover and simmer for 20 minutes, until rice is cooked. Add evaporated milk, peas and medium prawns, bring back to the boil and turn off the heat. Add eggs (if using). Cover and let it stand for 5 minutes before serving.

Season to taste with salt and freshly ground black pepper, and garnish with large prawns, chopped mint or parsley, guajillo chilli flakes and lime or lemon wedges (if using).

Venezuela

CREMA DE AUYAMA

Creamy Butternut Squash Soup

GF

1 kg butternut squash
3 tbsp olive oil
3 cloves garlic, peeled
1½ cups chopped onion
1 cup chopped leek, white part only
4–6 cups good-quality chicken stock

Garnish
1 tbsp pumpkin seeds, toasted
1 tbsp coconut milk
guajillos, dried whole chillies, chopped, or chilli flakes, to taste (optional)
sea salt, to taste

When I look back at my childhood, the first thing that comes to mind is memories in and around the kitchen and there is always some type of soup or chupe (chowder) simmering in the background. I can close my eyes and smell bay leaf, peppercorns, cumin, onion, garlic. We always used to begin a lunch meal with some kind of soup — even if it was 40°C outside. My grandma would say that it would cool us down and give us energy. La crema de auyama was my favourite. This is actually a dairy-free soup, but the consistency is more like a cream than a light soup.

Prepare: 15 minutes; cook: 1 hour
Serves: 4

Preheat oven to 150°C. Halve butternut squash and remove seeds. Drizzle squash with 2 tablespoons of olive oil and season generously with salt. Place on a baking dish lined with non-stick baking paper and roast for 20 minutes. Add garlic cloves to the dish and continue to roast for 10–15 minutes more, until squash is fork-tender and garlic is lightly roasted.

Meanwhile, place a stockpot over a medium heat and add remaining olive oil. Add onion and leek, along with 1 tablespoon of chicken stock, and sweat until translucent. The stock will help release some of the moisture from the vegetables. Once vegetables are soft, turn off heat and let it sit until the butternut squash is ready.

When squash is completely soft, remove from the oven. Use a spoon to scoop squash flesh out and add it to the stockpot, mashing it a bit with a fork or potato masher. Add 4 cups of stock and let everything come to the boil, stirring occasionally. Turn the heat off once it boils, and blend in a food processor until smooth. Return to the stockpot and season to taste with salt. Add more stock if it's too thick. When ready to serve, bring the soup back up to the desired temperature.

Garnish with toasted pumpkin seeds, ¼ tablespoon of coconut milk per serving, chilli (if using) and sea salt.

Chef's note: People ask me what kind of stock to use. Since I make a lot of shredded chicken, pork or other meat, I usually have home-made stock in my fridge or freezer. If you don't, just use a good-quality bought stock — preferably those in the refrigerated section of large supermarkets or specialist stores; they taste home-made and are not full of preservatives. This is the base of your soup, and the better the stock the better the soup.

Venezuela

CALDITO DE POLLO DE LA ABUELA

Grandmother's Chicken Soup

GF

12 cups water
1 kg chicken portions (ideally with bones and skin)
1 leek, white part only, sliced
1 onion, peeled and roughly chopped
1 carrot, peeled and roughly chopped
1 stalk celery, roughly chopped
1 capsicum, de-seeded and roughly chopped
12 parsley stems (reserve leaves for garnish)
4 cloves garlic, peeled and mashed
2 bay leaves
pink Himalayan salt, to taste

Garnish
chopped parsley and coriander leaves
1 spring onion or handful of chives, chopped
lime wedges

My grandmother believes that anything can be cured with this chicken soup — anything! It is the cure for the common cold, sore muscles or heartbreak. If someone is really sick, then you step your game up and kill the chicken yourself. In this case, Grandma says, 'Make sure to use the chicken's feet, because that's where the magical powers lie.' Grandma is always right.

Prepare: 15 minutes; cook: 45 minutes
Serves: 6–8

In a large stockpot bring all ingredients except salt to a boil, then reduce the heat and simmer until chicken is cooked through, about 45 minutes. The time will vary depending on what cut of chicken you use; if using breast meat, it will cook much faster. Skim scum off frequently while simmering. Remove chicken, remove and discard the skin and bones, shred the meat with two forks or your hands, and return it to the pot. Adjust seasoning, especially salt.

Add the garnishes just before serving.

Chef's note: The chicken bones and skin will add more flavour, though you will have to skim more frequently. Skinless chicken breasts cook more quickly but add less flavour. If using only the breast, reduce your stock by half. You can also add some chopped Agria potatoes or chunks of fresh sweetcorn for the last 20 minutes of cooking.

AVES Y HUEVOS

POULTRY & EGGS

HUEVOS VERDES
Very Green Eggs

PERICO
Colourful Scrambled Eggs

HUEVOS DIVORCIADOS
Divorced Eggs

POLLO DESMENUZADO
Shredded Chicken

LA REINA PEPIADA
The Curvy Arepa Queen

TACOS DORADOS DE POLLO
Golden Tacos Filled with Chicken

POLLO EN ADOBO DE CHILE ANCHO
Ancho Adobo Chicken

CHILAQUILES CON POLLO
Chicken Chilaquiles in Green Sauce

CODORNIZ CON NARANJA Y ARROZ VERDE
Stuffed Quail with Green Rice & Oranges

PATO EN SALSA DE GUAYABA
Duck Breast with Guava & Wild Berry Sauce

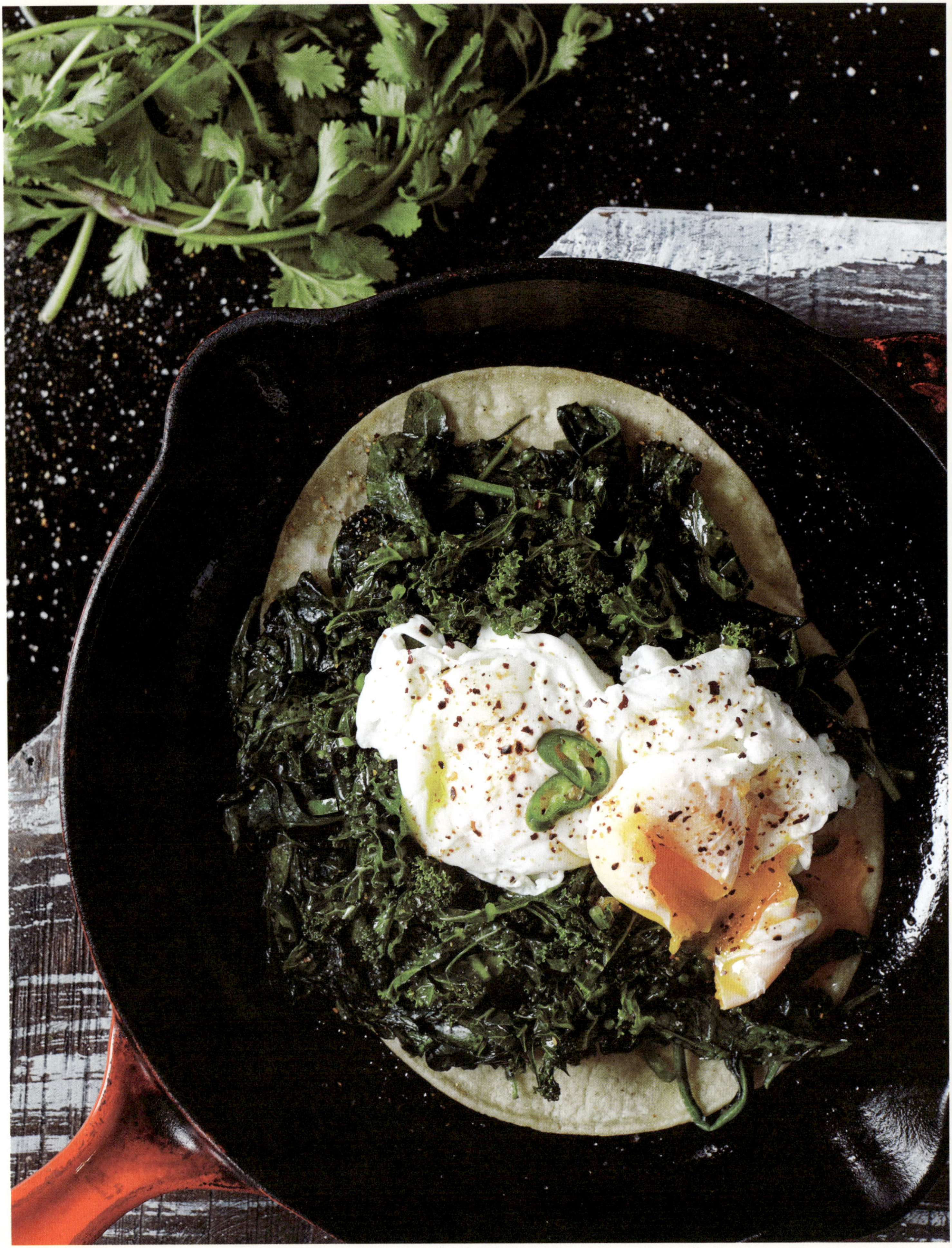

Mexico

HUEVOS VERDES

Very Green Eggs

GF

4 corn tortillas (see page 115)
4 large eggs
1 tbsp white vinegar
1 packed cup shredded kale
2 tbsp olive oil
1 tsp lime juice
½ tsp flaky sea salt
1 jalapeño or green chilli, halved, de-seeded and sliced (optional)
6 cups baby spinach, washed

Garnish
handful of coriander leaves
chilli salt, to taste (see page 193)
1 tbsp grated queso fresco (optional; see page 208)
1 green chilli, thinly sliced (optional)

The ideal way to start your day is with a healthy, nutritious and delicious breakfast, and this meal has all that and more. Although it looks like a Sunday brunch type of recipe, it's actually very quick and simple to prepare. What do we have on hand? Eggs, spinach, kale? Great, let's put it on a tortilla!

Prepare: 10 minutes; cook: 10 minutes
Serves: 2

Preheat oven to 100°C. Wrap tortillas well in foil and place in oven to warm.

To poach the eggs, crack each egg into a separate small bowl. Fill a saucepan with water and add white vinegar (you need 1 tablespoon of vinegar for each litre of water; the vinegar helps the eggs to coagulate). Let water come to a simmer and swirl it with a wooden spoon. Drop eggs in, one at a time, making sure that the water is swirling gently to help the egg whites stay wrapped around the yolks. Cook to your liking.

Meanwhile, marinate the kale with 1 tablespoon of olive oil, lime juice and sea salt. Set aside.

In a deep frying pan, heat the other tablespoon of olive oil over a medium heat. Add jalapeño or green chilli (if using), fry for about 1 minute and then add spinach and a pinch of salt. Fry gently until spinach is just wilted. Transfer to a bowl and set aside.

To assemble, place tortillas in the frying pan or on a plate, and top with spinach, kale and eggs. Garnish with coriander and chilli salt, and grated queso fresco and green chilli if desired.

Chef's note: To make this an even easier meal, you can fry or scramble the eggs instead of poaching them, and you can quickly heat the tortillas in a pan on the stovetop or in the microwave.

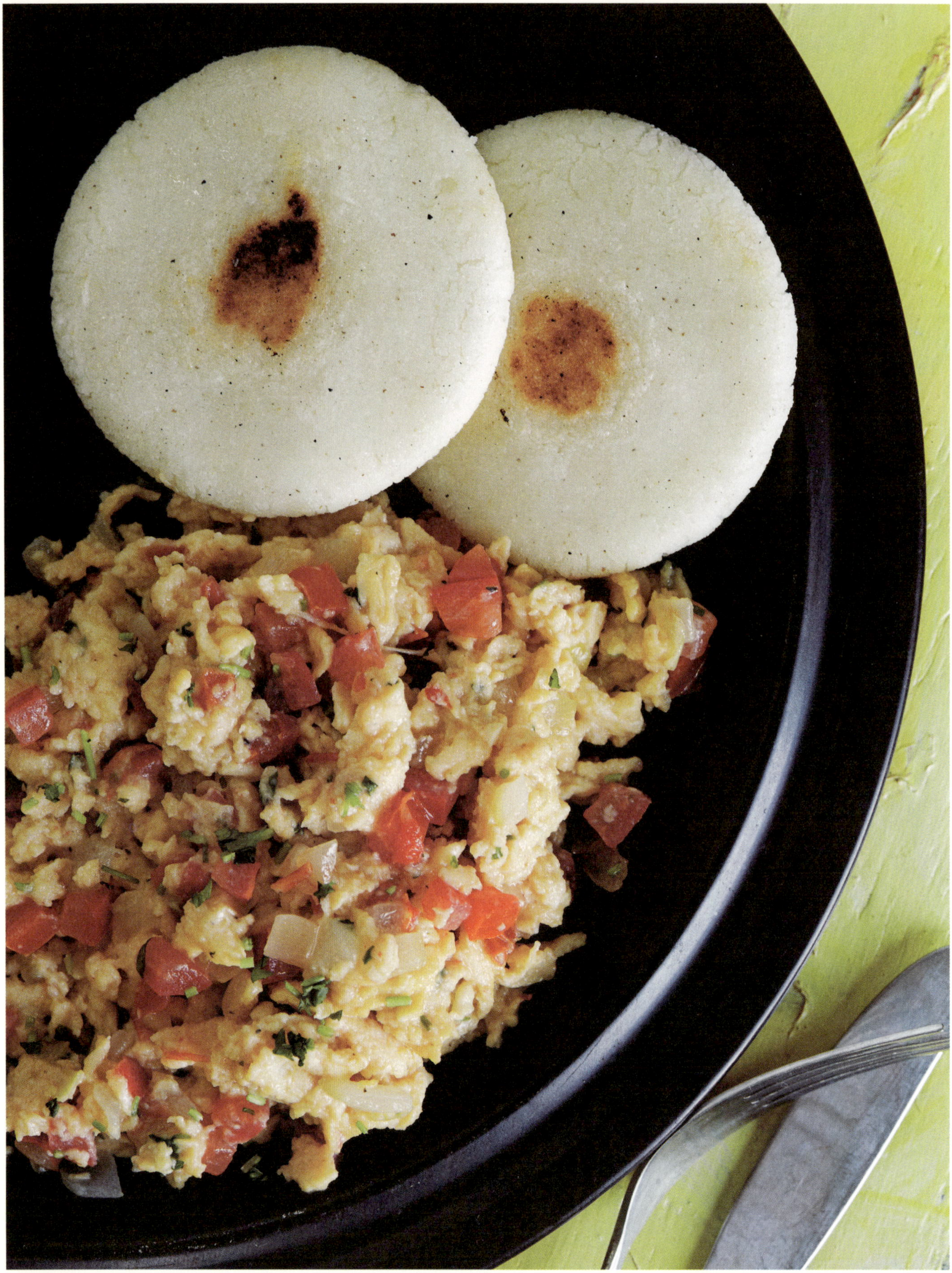

Venezuela

PERICO

Colourful Scrambled Eggs

GF

8 eggs
2 tbsp olive oil
½ cup diced onions, red or brown
½ cup de-seeded and diced tomatoes
1 tbsp chopped coriander or parsley, to garnish

At home in Venezuela, Sunday is the day when all the family gets together for a full day of feasting, first in the morning with the immediate family (10+) and then in the late afternoon with the extended family (50+) — cousins, aunts and uncles all get together for another 'celebratory' meal. Because there is always a reason to celebrate! These colourful eggs are nicknamed 'parakeet' eggs and are always in the centre of the table, alongside black beans, queso fresco (see page 208) and arepas (see page 119). Just like the breakfast feast spread (see page 268–69) — that is what my grandmother's table looks like at Sunday brunch.

Prepare: 10 minutes; cook: 10 minutes
Serves: 4

Put eggs in a bowl and beat with a fork, adding salt and freshly ground pepper to taste.

Heat oil in a frying pan over a medium heat. Add onion and fry gently for 3–4 minutes, or until translucent. Add the tomatoes and cook for another 3 minutes.

Reduce to a low heat. Add eggs to the pan, and gently stir from time to time to scramble them — keep cooking just long enough to cook them through while keeping them soft. Finish with fresh herbs.

Serve with bread or arepas (see page 119).

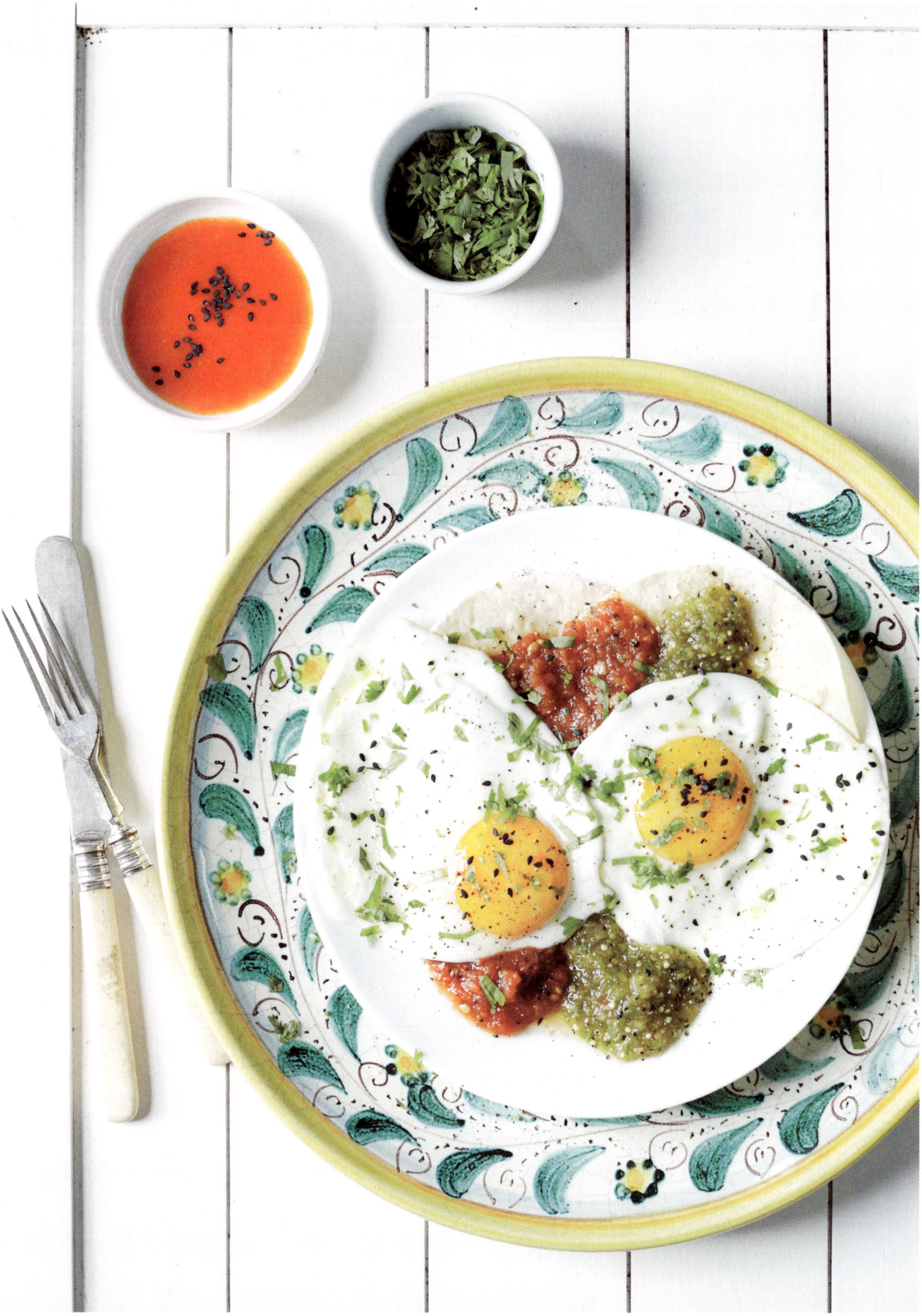

Mexico

HUEVOS DIVORCIADOS

Divorced Eggs

GF

8 corn tortillas (see page 115)
2 tbsp rice bran oil
8 eggs
salsa roja (see page 194)
salsa verde (see page 194)

Garnish
1 tsp black sesame seeds (optional)
handful of chopped coriander leaves
flaky sea salt

I was first served this bright and delightful treat in Mexico, and could only giggle with joy over the look, taste and name of these beauties. Ever since then, I have wanted a divorce every weekend! Divorced eggs give you the best of two worlds. You get one egg with tomatillo sauce (salsa verde), and another with a red tomato-chilli sauce (salsa roja). Who says divorces always end badly?

Prepare: 10 minutes; cook: 10 minutes
Serves: 4

Preheat oven to 100°C. Wrap tortillas well in foil and place in oven to warm.

In a large non-stick frying pan, heat ½ tablespoon of oil and fry 2–3 eggs the way you like them. Add more oil and continue with another batch, until all the eggs are fried. Keep warm in oven.

Put 2 tortillas on each plate. Add a heaped tablespoonful of salsa roja to one, and salsa verde to the other. Place an egg on top of each salsa, and garnish with black sesame seeds (if desired) and chopped coriander. Season to taste with flaky sea salt and freshly ground black pepper.

Chef's note: You could eat these eggs with a side of more warm corn tortillas, to dip into the sauce and egg yolk. You can also serve them with refried beans, queso fresco (see page 208) and crema agria (see page 211).

All countries

POLLO DESMENUZADO

Shredded Chicken

GF

1 kg boneless, skinless chicken breasts or thighs (or 1 whole chicken, portioned)
1 tbsp whole peppercorns
4 garlic cloves, smashed
2 bay leaves
1 onion, peeled and roughly chopped
1 tsp salt

I find that in many countries of Latin America, instead of chopping the chicken for stews, soups or fillings, they shred it finely. We start numerous chicken recipes by dumping a chicken in a pot full of water and aromatics. We take it out once cooked, shred it and we're ready for the day. The liquid is then used as stock or for Grandmother's chicken soup (page 30). Needless to say, I grew up eating a lot of chicken soup!

This shredded chicken is the base for chilaquiles (see page 50), tacos dorados (see page 46) and so much more.

Prepare: 10 minutes; cook: 20 minutes
Makes: approx. 2 cups

Place chicken, peppercorns, garlic, bay leaves, onion and salt in a large saucepan and cover with water. Bring to the boil over a high heat, then reduce to a simmer over a medium-low heat for 20 minutes or until chicken is cooked through. Skim the top as necessary.

Turn the heat off and remove chicken from liquid. Using two forks or clean hands, shred the chicken into a bowl, adding a bit of the stock so it doesn't dry out, and use for your desired dish. Strain and cool stock, and store in the refrigerator or freezer for later use.

Chef's note: You can use chicken with bones and skin intact, just make sure you discard both before shredding the chicken.

El Caribeño

Charbroiled Chicken Sinaloa Style

Venezuela

LA REINA PEPIADA

The Curvy Arepa Queen

GF

2 ripe avocados
pinch of lime zest
½ tsp lime juice
2 tbsp mayonnaise
1 cup shredded chicken
    (see page 42)
4 arepas (see page 119)
flaky sea salt

To talk about arepas is to talk about Venezuela. These cornmeal patties — which happen to be gluten free — are griddled and then baked, and used as a vessel for stuffing with anything from ham and cheese to shredded beef (also pictured), but the country's favourite is this zesty 'pimped out' chicken salad with avocado and mayonnaise. Most people only know one thing about Venezuela — we have won the Miss World or Miss Universe pageant many times. Yes, it's true; the country is obsessed with these contests, and we even have this arepa named in honour of a beauty queen. Venezuelan celebrity Susana Duijm won the first Miss World beauty pageant for Venezuela in 1955. People were enamoured with her, and the story goes that when she went to visit a local restaurant, the owner knew he had to make something special, and so this filling was born. At first, this arepa was only named 'la reina', the queen, but later 'pepiada' (pimped out/curvy) was added as Susana was known for her lovely curves.

Prepare: 10 minutes
Makes: 4 arepas

Cut open avocados, remove pits and scoop out flesh. Place in a medium-sized bowl. Add lime zest and juice, mayonnaise and cooked chicken, mix until just combined, and season to taste with flaky sea salt and freshly ground black pepper. Cut arepas open and stuff with chicken mixture.

    Chef's note: This recipe is like guacamole meets a chicken salad, minus the onions. Feel free to add coriander for extra flavour.

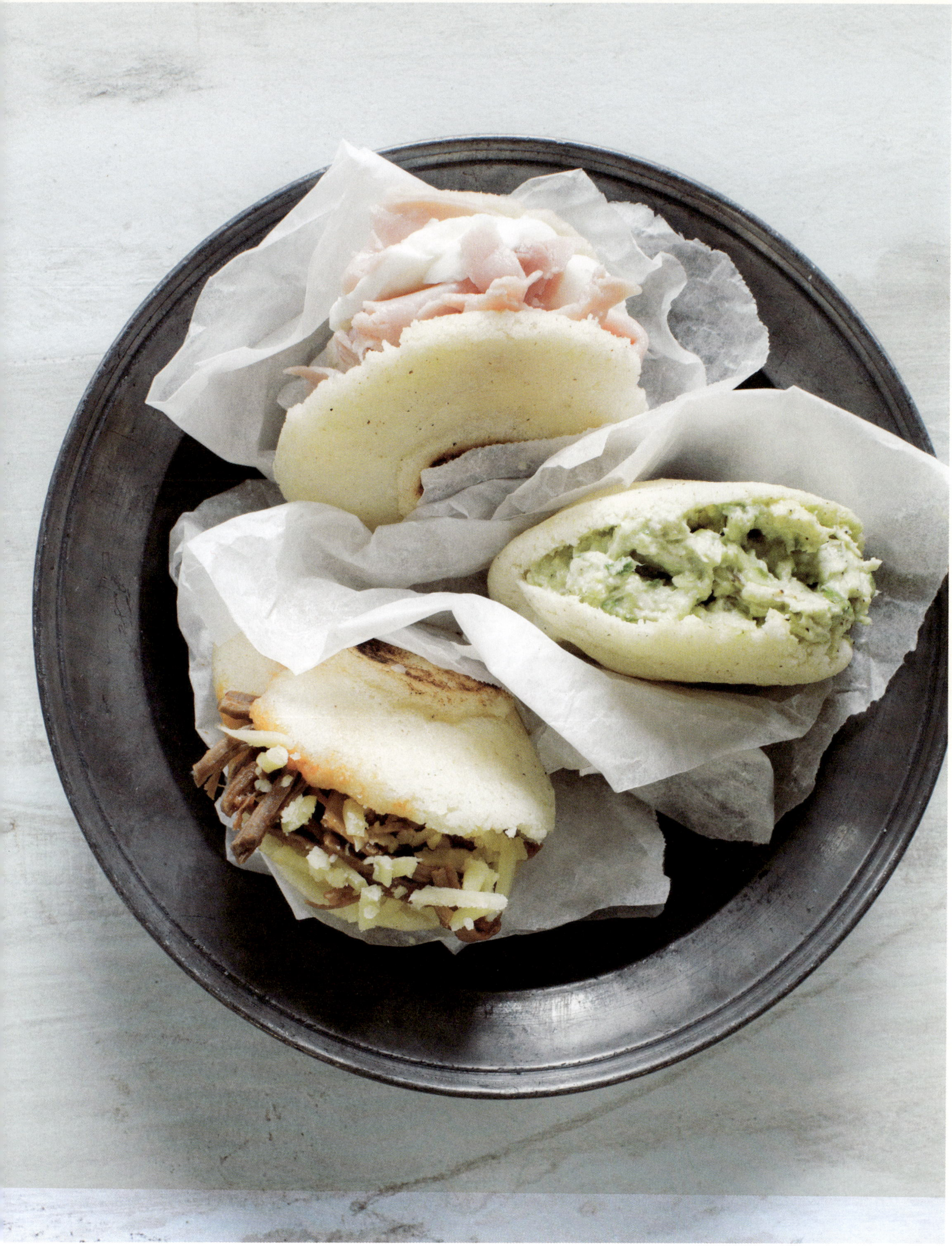

Mexico

TACOS DORADOS DE POLLO

Golden Tacos Filled with Chicken

GF

2 cups shredded chicken (see page 42)
1 tbsp unsalted butter or a little chicken stock
8 corn tortillas, slightly dampened with water
4 tbsp rice bran or avocado oil

Garnish
6 leaves iceberg lettuce, shredded
2 tbsp crema agria (see page 211) or sour cream
½ cup pico de gallo (see page 193) or chopped cherry tomatoes
¼ cup queso fresco (see page 208) or mild feta, crumbled
chopped coriander
hot sauce, to taste
lime wedges

Tortellini, spaghetti, pappardelle — all different shapes of pasta. It's the same with corn shells — sope, huarache and tortilla are all bases that are stuffed or topped with different types of Mexican speciality. Mexicans have taken their adoration of corn tortillas to the next level. If there is anything you can put inside or on top of a tortilla, they have perfected how to do it. In this case, the tortillas are filled with pre-cooked shredded chicken, beef or your favourite filling, then rolled into elongated cylinders and fried until golden and crisp. They are also called taquitos, and are a great appetiser adorned with your favourite garnishes.

Prepare: 20 minutes; cook: 20 minutes
Makes: 8 tacos

Reheat shredded chicken in a pan with butter or stock for a few minutes, until just warm.

Meanwhile, heat the corn tortillas one at a time in a small pan, about 20 seconds per side, to soften them (or heat them in the microwave on high for about 10 seconds). Keep them in an airtight container until ready to assemble the tacos (or wrap in foil and keep warm in the oven at 100°C). This will keep them flexible so they don't break when you fold them.

To assemble, place 2 tablespoons of chicken in the centre of a tortilla, roll up tightly and seal the overlap with a toothpick. Assemble all the tacos this way.

Heat oil in a shallow pan. Once hot, place one or two tacos in the oil, seam side up and cook until golden brown. Turn them gently, and continue to brown the other side. Transfer to a dish, and repeat until all the tacos are cooked. Remove the toothpicks prior to serving.

Garnish with shredded lettuce, crema agria, pico de gallo or chopped tomatoes, queso fresco or mild feta, coriander and hot sauce. Serve with lime wedges.

Chef's note: For an extra layer of flavour, you can fold some mozzarella into the chicken mixture and let it melt while frying the tacos.

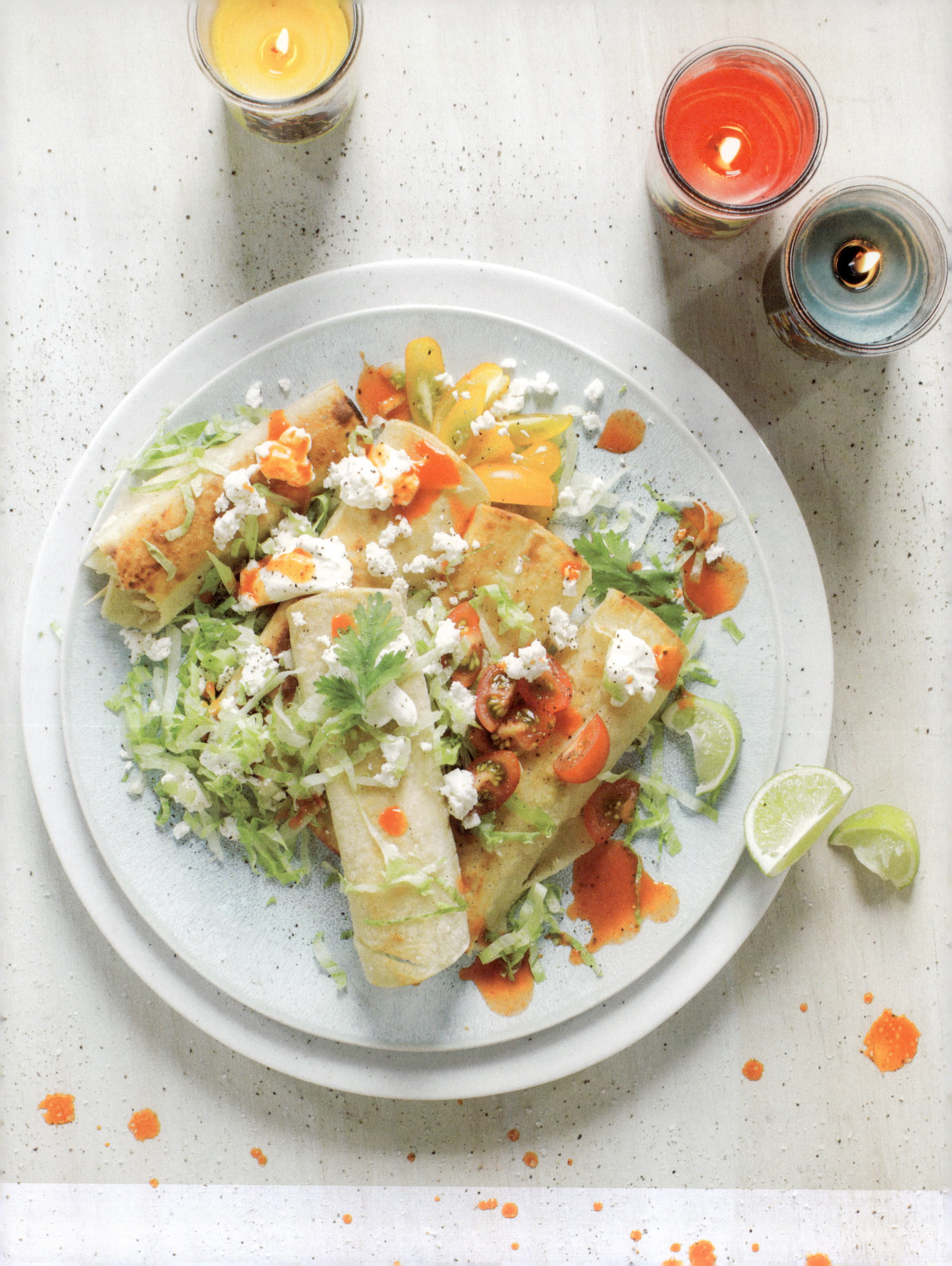

Mexico

POLLO EN ADOBO DE CHILE ANCHO

Ancho Adobo Chicken

GF

4 ancho chillies
2 tbsp vegetable oil
1 kg skinless chicken thighs
1 onion, peeled and julienned
2 cloves garlic, peeled and
    roughly chopped
2 cups chicken stock
2 tbsp shaved panela
    (unrefined cane sugar)
2 tbsp peanut butter
1 tsp ground cumin

Garnish
1 tsp toasted sesame seeds
1 tsp edible flowers
1 mango, peeled and
    julienned (optional)
handful of coriander leaves,
    chopped (optional)
lime wedges (optional)

Ancho chillies, known as 'poblano' in the non-dried form, look threatening — but the truth is that they're fruity and not very spicy; they taste like raisins with a kick. They're one of the most popular chillies in Mexico, used in moles, sauces, tamales, soups . . . anything where you'd like to add a mild amount of heat and tonnes of flavour.

The ancho, which literally means 'wide', is key in the 'holy trinity' of Mexican chillies, alongside pasilla negro and mulato. They can be found in specialist supermarkets or check online.

Prepare: 10 minutes; cook: 30 minutes
Serves: 4

Remove stems from chillies, then de-seed, devein and chop roughly.

Heat oil in a medium-sized heavy-bottomed saucepan. Pat chicken thighs dry. Season with salt and freshly ground black pepper. When the saucepan is nice and hot, place chicken thighs in and let them brown for 5–7 minutes. Turn them over and continue cooking for 5 minutes. Take them out and set aside.

In the same saucepan over a medium heat, cook onion until translucent, about 5 minutes. Add garlic and cook for 1 minute longer. Add chillies and cook until they release some of their aroma, about 1 minute. Add back the chicken, then stir in stock and panela and bring to the boil. Turn down to a simmer and continue cooking until chicken is cooked through, about 10–15 minutes. Don't cook for longer than 20 minutes, or the anchos will become bitter.

Take chicken out and set aside. Transfer sauce mixture to a blender and purée, then add peanut butter and cumin and purée again. Adjust seasoning with salt.

Return the chicken to the saucepan and pour ancho chilli sauce over, then reheat. Taste and if necessary add more panela for sweetness. Add more stock if the sauce is too thick, or if the sauce is too thin, reduce until the desired consistency. When ready to serve, garnish with toasted sesame seeds, edible flowers, mango slices, chopped coriander and lime wedges (if using).

Chef's note: You can make tacos with this chicken, or eat it as a platter accompanied by Mom's black beans (see page 15) and Mexican-style red rice (see page 148). I highly recommend using the mango and coriander for the tacos!

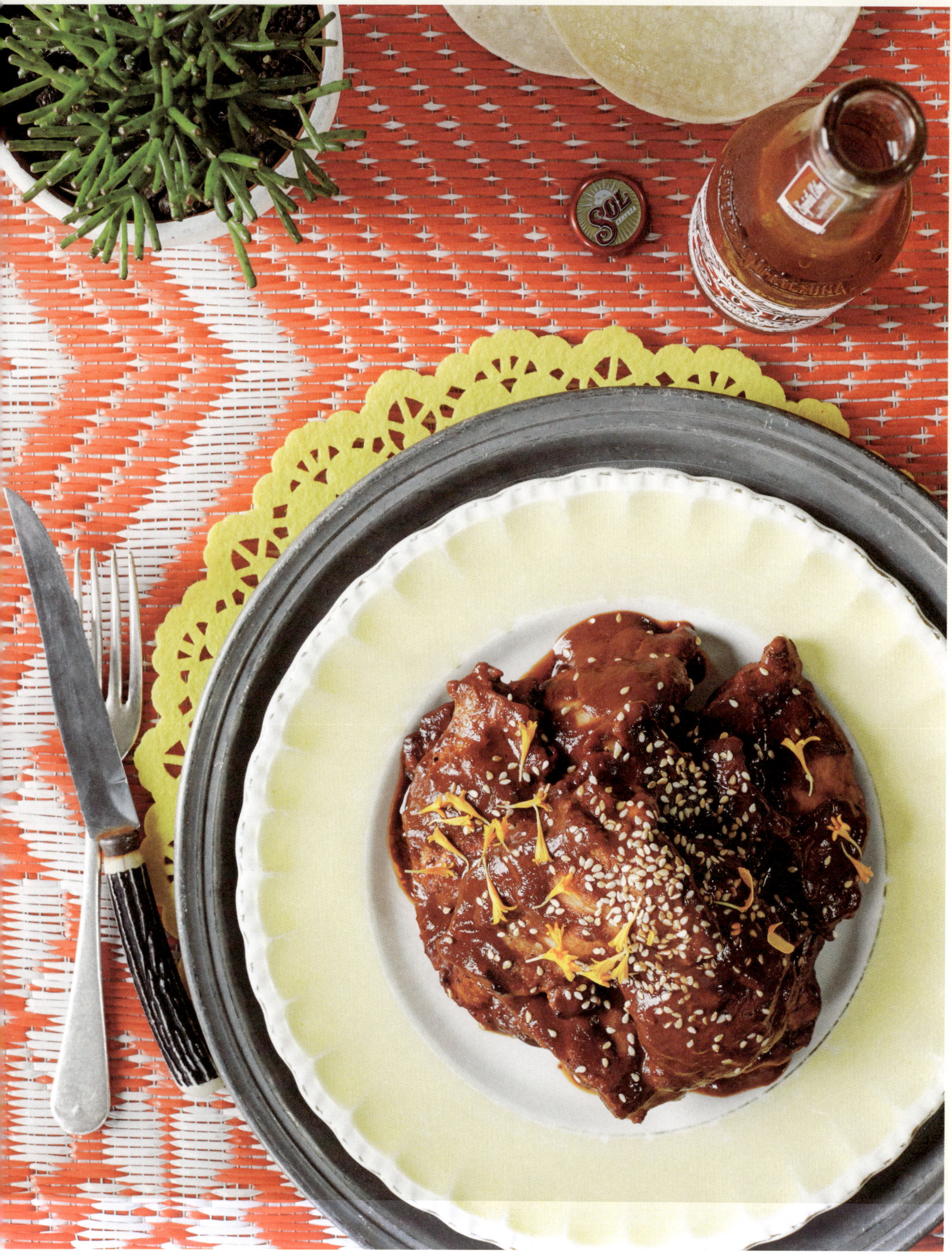
SOL

Mexico

CHILAQUILES CON POLLO

Chicken Chilaquiles in Green Sauce

GF

1 cup shredded chicken
(see page 42)
¼ cup chicken stock
½ cup salsa verde (see page 194)
300 g corn chips

Garnish
1 tbsp crema agria (see page 211)
or sour cream
Tabasco or other hot sauce, to taste
crumbled queso fresco (see
page 208), to taste
1 avocado, flesh diced
½ red onion, peeled and
finely chopped
handful of coriander leaves

Chilaquiles are one of those Mexican treats that once you have them, you wonder how you ever lived without eating them. They are the superior nachos, and a great use for left-over corn chips or salsas that you might have at hand. This tortilla 'stew' is a great combination of crunchy and soft corn chips, together with a bright green sauce that is garnished with crema agria or sour cream and other fixings. Try these today — you'll thank me.

Prepare: 20 minutes; cook: 10 minutes
Serves: 2

In a frying pan, warm shredded chicken and stock over a low heat. Add salsa verde and mix until heated through. Add a couple of handfuls of corn chips and let it simmer for about 2 minutes, until the corn chips get soft.

To serve, place some crispy corn chips on a plate and spoon the chicken/salsa verde mix on top. Garnish with more corn chips, crema agria or sour cream, Tabasco or hot sauce, queso fresco, avocado, red onion and a few coriander leaves. Put extra hot sauce in a little jug on the table.

Chef's note: You can make chilaquiles with anything. This recipe calls for chicken, but can easily be made with any other protein, including eggs for a great weekend breakfast or brunch. You can also make them with salsa roja (see page 194) instead of the salsa verde.

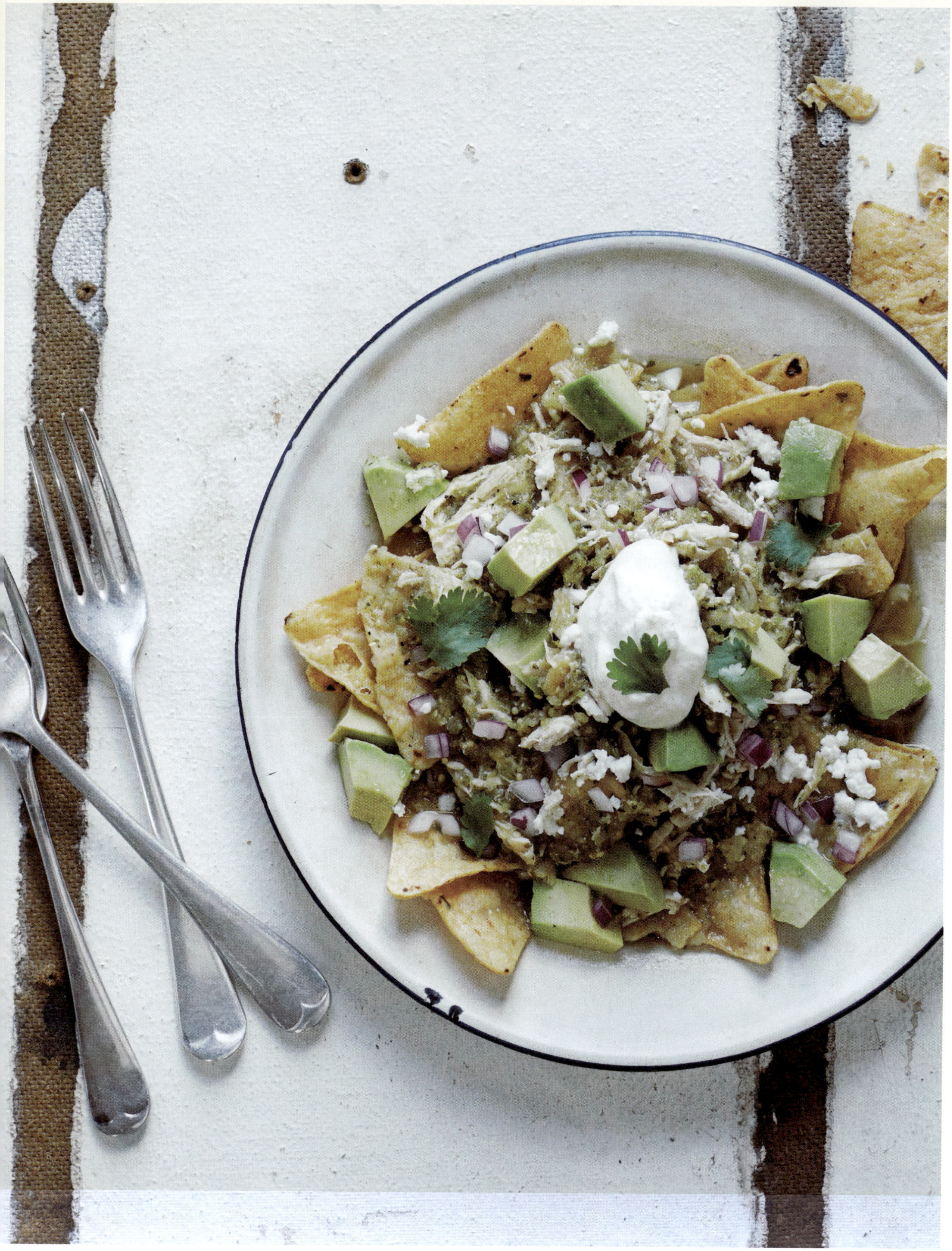

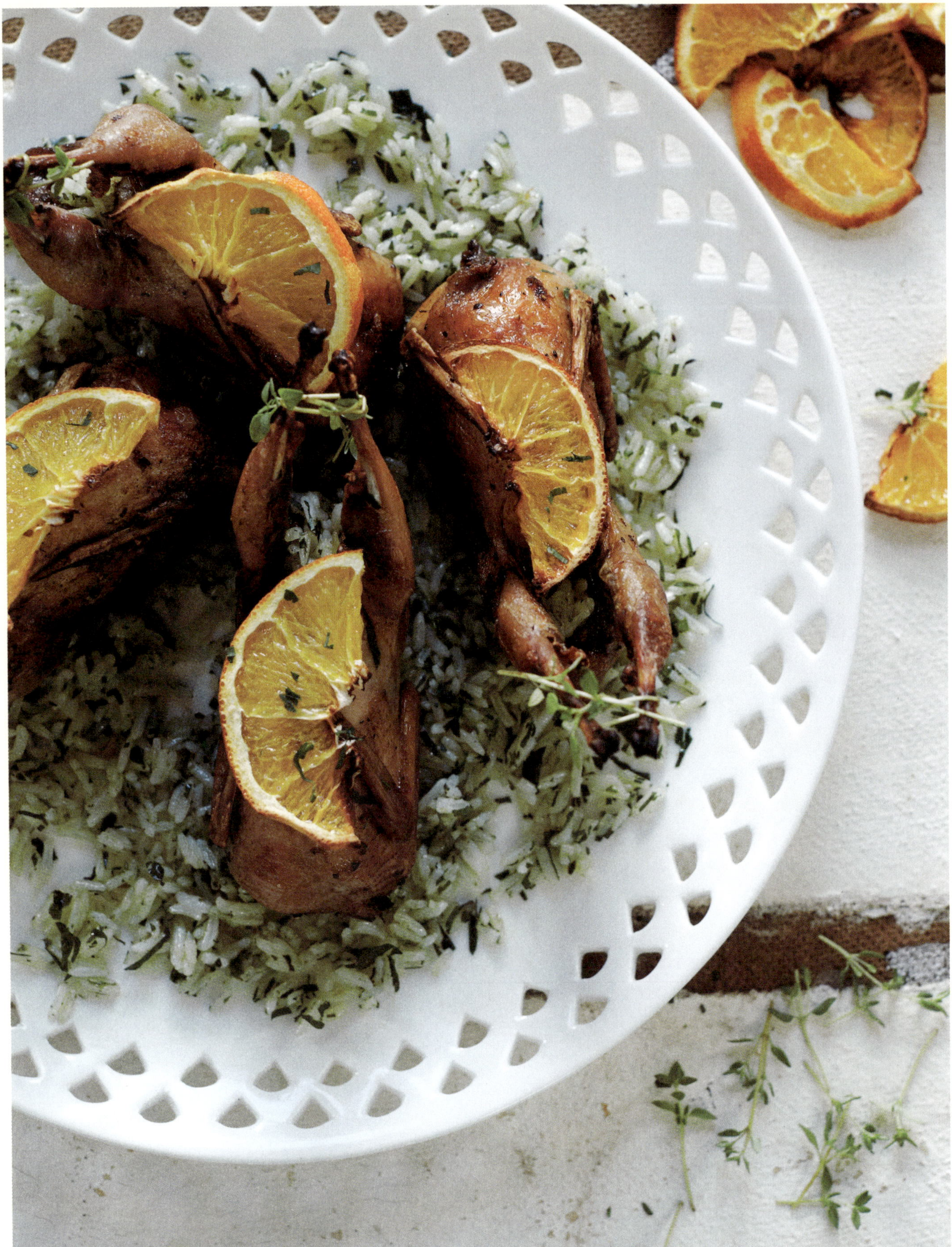

Venezuela

CODORNIZ CON NARANJA Y ARROZ VERDE

Stuffed Quail with Green Rice & Oranges

GF

1 orange, peel left on and thinly sliced
4 whole quail
4 cloves garlic, smashed
2 tbsp butter, at room temperature
1 tbsp olive oil
½ tsp orange zest
1 tbsp orange juice
½ tbsp honey or agave nectar
1 cup green pesto rice (see page 144)

Venezuelan parties, piñatas (children's parties), weddings and birthdays always have as appetisers quail eggs that you dip in a ketchup and mayo sauce. Both children and adults devour them. When I was a little girl, I wondered where these tiny eggs came from; now I love eating quail. Grandma took it upon herself to introduce me to quail — she likes it better than the eggs, and so do I. This quail dish is simple but memorable: the flavours of the pesto infuse wonderfully well with the honey and orange sauce. Guests are always pleasantly surprised by this tasty delicacy.

Prepare: 15 minutes; cook: 45 minutes
Serves: 4

Preheat oven to 120°C. Place orange slices in a single layer on a baking tray lined with a silicone mat or non-stick baking paper. Bake for about 25–30 minutes, until the orange slices are dry to the touch and a light golden brown. Set aside to cool.

Increase oven temperature to 180°C.

Season quail with salt and freshly ground black pepper. In a heavy-bottomed saucepan, sweat garlic cloves with 1 tablespoon of the butter and the olive oil. Wait until garlic is golden brown, then remove the garlic and set aside. Brown quail on all sides in the same pan, using the remaining butter. Add zest, orange juice and honey or agave nectar, and let it come to a simmer. Return garlic to pan. Remove quail, reserving the sauce, and stuff with green pesto rice.

Place quail and reserved sauce on a small baking tray or oven-safe pan lined with non-stick baking paper and finish cooking in the oven for about 10 minutes, basting them with the orange sauce halfway through to prevent them from drying out. Let them rest for about 5 minutes before serving with extra pesto rice, if desired, and garnished with orange slices on top.

Chef's note: If you're serving the quail for a special occasion, tie the ends of the drumsticks together with thyme.

Venezuela

PATO EN SALSA DE GUAYABA

Duck Breast with Guava & Wild Berry Sauce

GF

- 4 duck breasts
- 1 tbsp salt
- 1 tbsp olive oil
- 2 shallots, peeled and finely chopped
- 4 cloves garlic, peeled and finely chopped
- ½ cup red wine
- 1 cup chicken stock
- 30 g guava paste
- ½ cup blackberries, or mixed dark berries (thaw if frozen)
- zest of ½ lemon
- 1 tsp lemon juice

Garnish
- handful of microgreens
- handful of edible flowers

Guavas are cultivated in many tropical and subtropical countries. Venezuelans love them, and you'll find 'jugo de guayaba' (guava juices or smoothies) in bakeries, areperas or juice stands everywhere. We make many desserts with this fragrant fruit as well. Cubans make pastries filled with guava paste and cheese; they are to die for. Duck is not something you eat every day in Venezuela; it's rare to find it, but I created this dish because it's easy and has a combination of flavours I love — the tropical touch and the berries go so well together.

Prepare: 10 minutes; cook: 30 minutes
Serves: 4

Remove duck breasts from refrigerator, and let them come to room temperature — this helps them cook evenly. Pat skin dry with paper towel.

To sear duck breasts, evenly sprinkle salt on a heavy-bottomed frying pan and place over a low heat. Generously season duck with salt and freshly ground black pepper. Place duck skin side down in the salted pan, and cook for about 15 minutes on low. Fat will start to render from the skin; once a small pool of fat forms, pour it off into a container. Do this about 3-4 times. You don't want the fat to pool up higher than the skin, as it will start cooking the flesh, which you do not want yet. By slowly searing the skin over a low heat, the fat renders and gets crispy. You can strain the fat and reserve it for a later use, like for duck-fat potatoes or fries.

Meanwhile, heat olive oil in a separate pan. Gently fry shallots until translucent and garlic until lightly golden, seasoning with a pinch of salt and pepper. Add red wine, stirring and scraping the bottom of the pan, and reduce by half. Add stock, then guava paste, making sure you mix well to incorporate the paste. Reduce by half, and remove from heat.

Transfer liquid to a blender, add half the berries, lemon zest and juice, and blend until smooth. Season to taste. Set aside.

Once the duck skin is golden brown and crispy, flip the duck breasts over and cook for an additional minute, just to colour the bottom and sides. This will give you about medium rare; cook it a little longer if you prefer it more well done. Remove from heat and let it rest for about 8 minutes before slicing and serving.

To serve, pour a bit of guava sauce onto each plate, add some whole berries and fan the duck slices out on top. Garnish with microgreens and edible flowers.

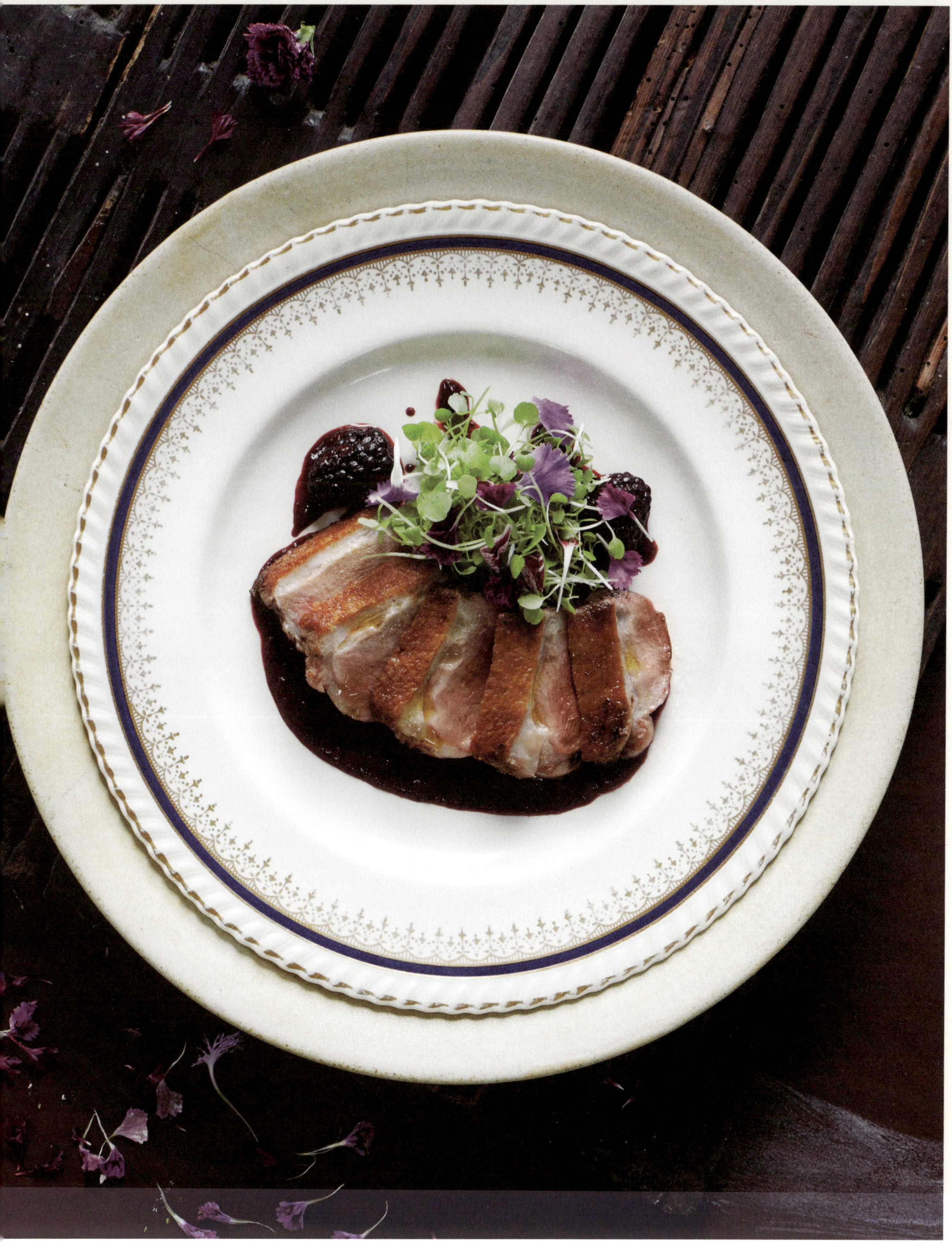

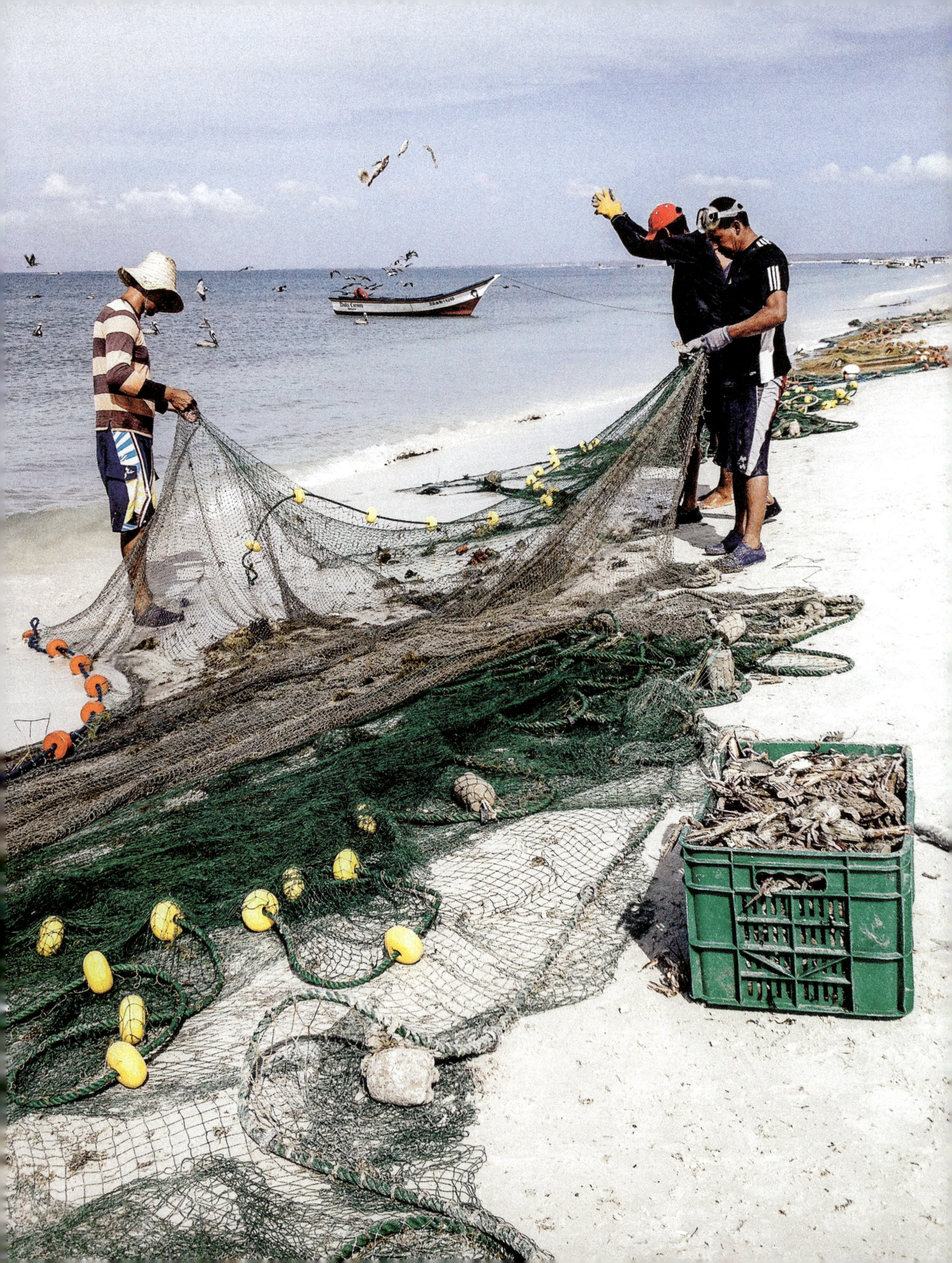

DEL MAR

FROM THE SEA

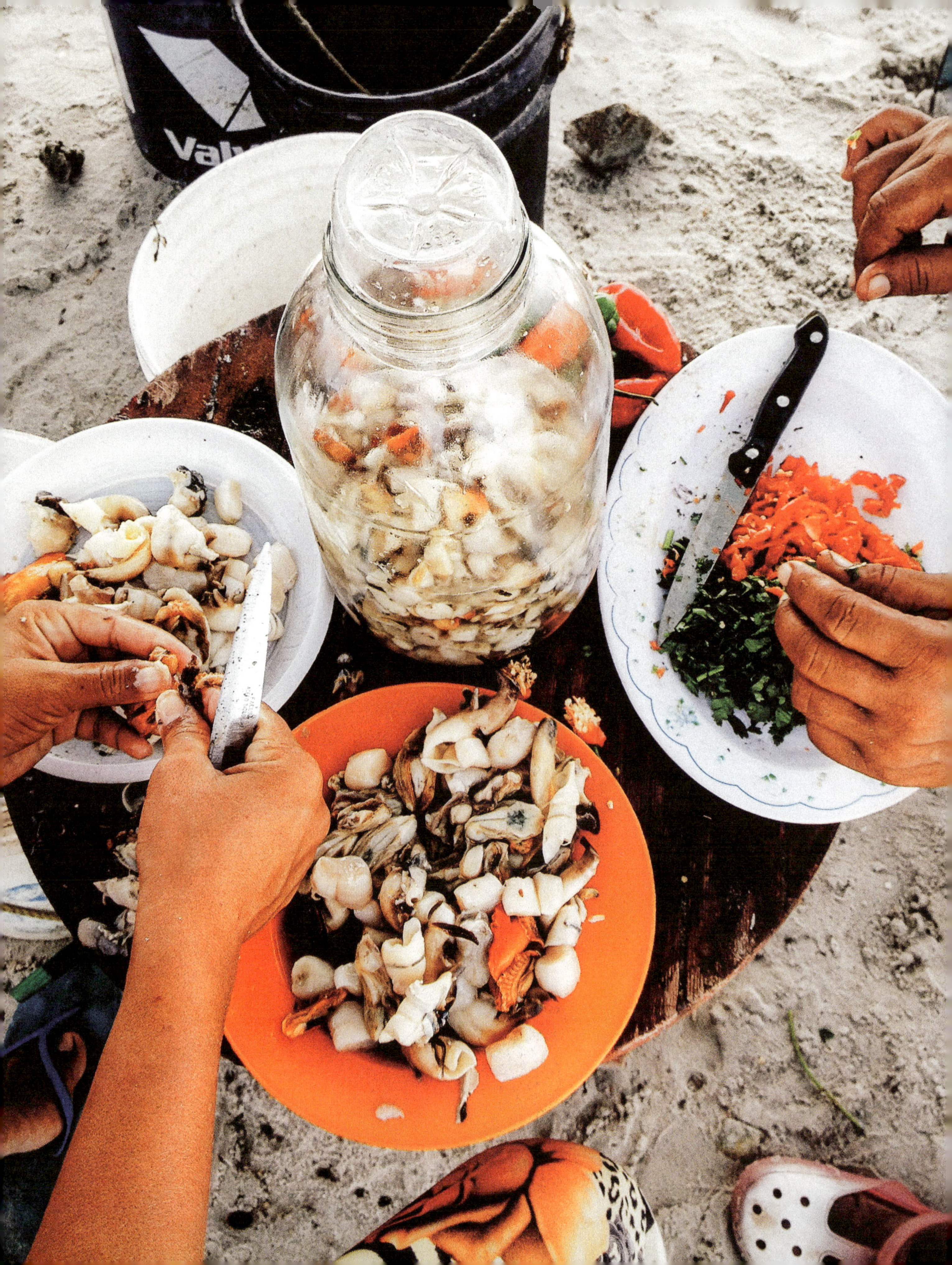

CEBICHE PERUANO
Peruvian Ceviche

CEBICHE DE CAMARONES Y VIERAS
Prawn & Scallop Ceviche

CHOROS A LA CHALACA
Open-faced Mussels Topped with Corn & Tomato Salsa

CAMARONES CON ADOBO DE GUAJILLO
Guajillo Adobo-marinated Prawns

TOSTADITAS DE PULPO
Octopus Tostaditas (Two Ways)

CASQUINHA DE SIRI
Stuffed Crab Shells

JALEA MIXTA
Crispy Seafood Salad

PESCADO EN HOJA DE PLÁTANO
Achiote-rubbed Grilled Fish Wrapped in Plantain Leaves

PESCADO EN SALSA VERDE
Fish Fillets in Green Sauce

CAMARÃO NA MORANGA
Creamy Prawn Stew in Pumpkin

KIKI'S MOQUECA
Seafood Stew in Coconut Milk

SALMÓN CON SALSA DE MANGO
Salmon with Caramelised Shallot & Mango Salsa

Peru

CEBICHE PERUANO

Peruvian Ceviche

GF

500 g fresh kingfish, gurnard or tarakihi fillets, deboned and skinned
1 red onion, peeled and thinly sliced (on a mandolin if you have one)
1 each red, yellow and green small capsicums, de-seeded and thinly sliced
1 fresh red or green chilli, de-seeded and finely diced
1 cup lime juice
2 ice cubes
pink Himalayan salt or flaky sea salt
1 bunch coriander, finely chopped, to garnish

Ceviche is a national obsession in Peru. My Peruvian friends who live outside of the country are eternally searching for the perfect ceviche. This dish is close to my heart, and I could eat it every day for the rest of my life. Mastering the art of ceviche-making is something for which I have to thank my stepfather; he is Peruvian and takes it very seriously. The most common ceviche is very simple: lime juice, ají limo which is a type of chilli (a cousin of the habanero), red onion and a touch of coriander. That is how I like it, especially if I make ceviche from a freshly caught fish. It's simplicity to perfection. I encourage you to drink the leche de tigre (tiger's milk), which is the liquid left after you eat your ceviche. It's not for the weak, but will definitely clear your sinuses and make you feel like a real tiger! I'm often asked how you know when the ceviche is done. Ceviche is like steak — it depends on your preference. I like to eat ceviche 5 minutes after it has been marinating in the lime juice because, just like steak, I like it medium rare. The lime juice will 'cook' the fish, so the longer you leave it the longer it will cook. You eat sushi and sashimi raw, so do not be afraid to eat your ceviche 5 minutes after starting to marinate. Just don't eat it right away, so that the fish can soak up a little lime juice and cook a little. Most people like it after 15 minutes of marinating. Serve with roasted kumara and steamed fresh corn, when in season.

Prepare: 20 minutes
Serves: 4–6 as an appetiser

Place a medium-sized bowl in the refrigerator or freezer to chill.

Dice fish fillets into 1 cm cubes and transfer to the cold bowl. Season the fish with salt and freshly ground black pepper to taste.

Add red onion, capsicums, chilli, lime juice and ice cubes. When the fish turns white, or is how you like it, remove the ice cubes.

When ready to serve season with salt and garnish with coriander.

Chef's note: The most important things to know about ceviche-making are: (1) use the freshest fish available, never frozen; (2) a semi-firm, white-fleshed fish that is not too fatty works best — try snapper, or trevally as well — and use a very sharp knife to cut the fish and the herbs to avoid bruising them; (3) be generous with the amount of salt, and even if you do not like chilli, I encourage you to add a touch of it — rub some of the chilli flesh inside the bowl, it will go a long way; (4) never use bottled lime juice, always fresh, and if you find it too strong you can use a combination of lime and lemon juice; (5) do not over-squeeze the fruit because the juice gets bitter; (6) the bowl in which you make your ceviche should be cold — remember to put the bowl in the refrigerator or freezer while you gather all the ingredients.

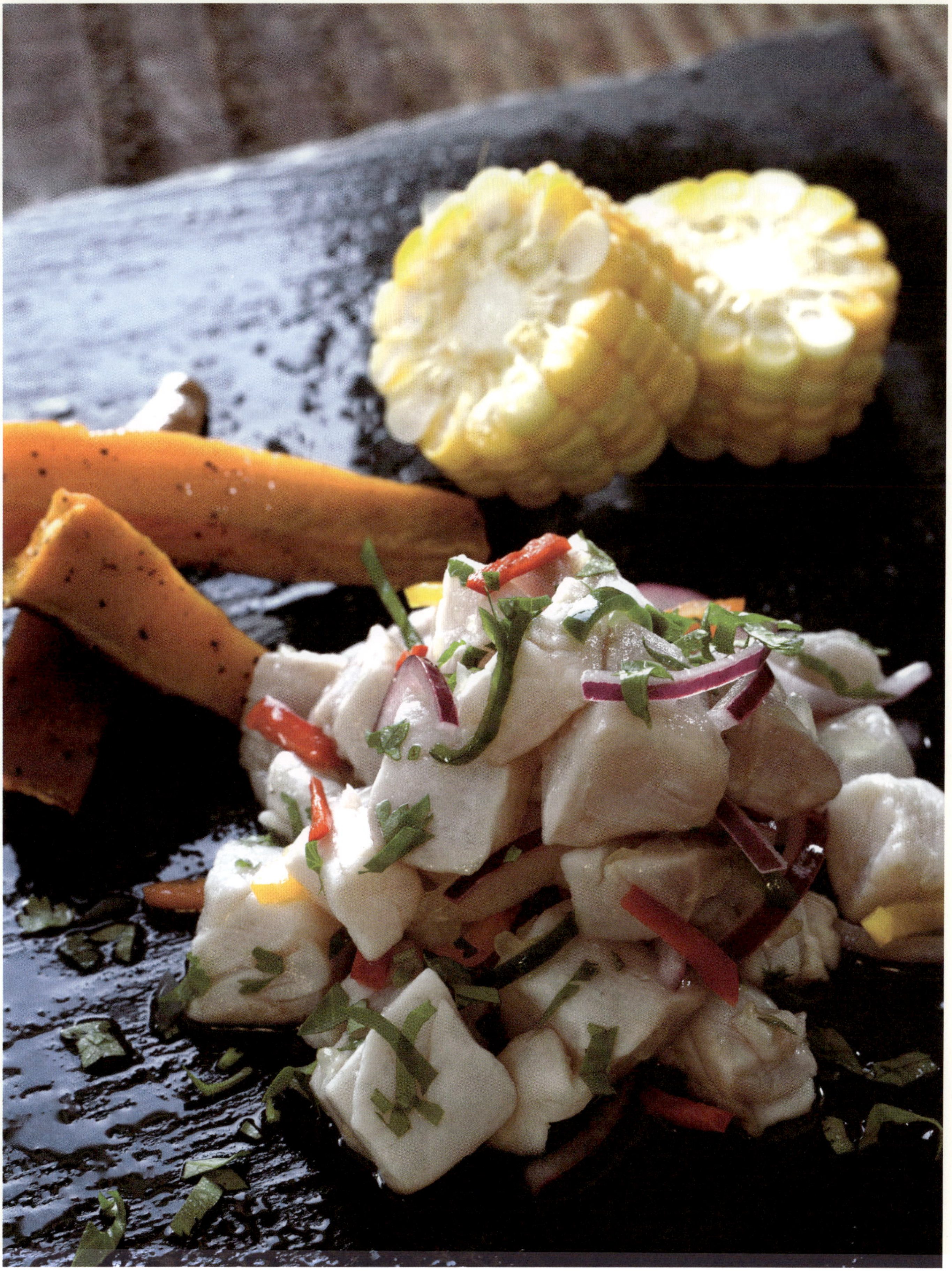

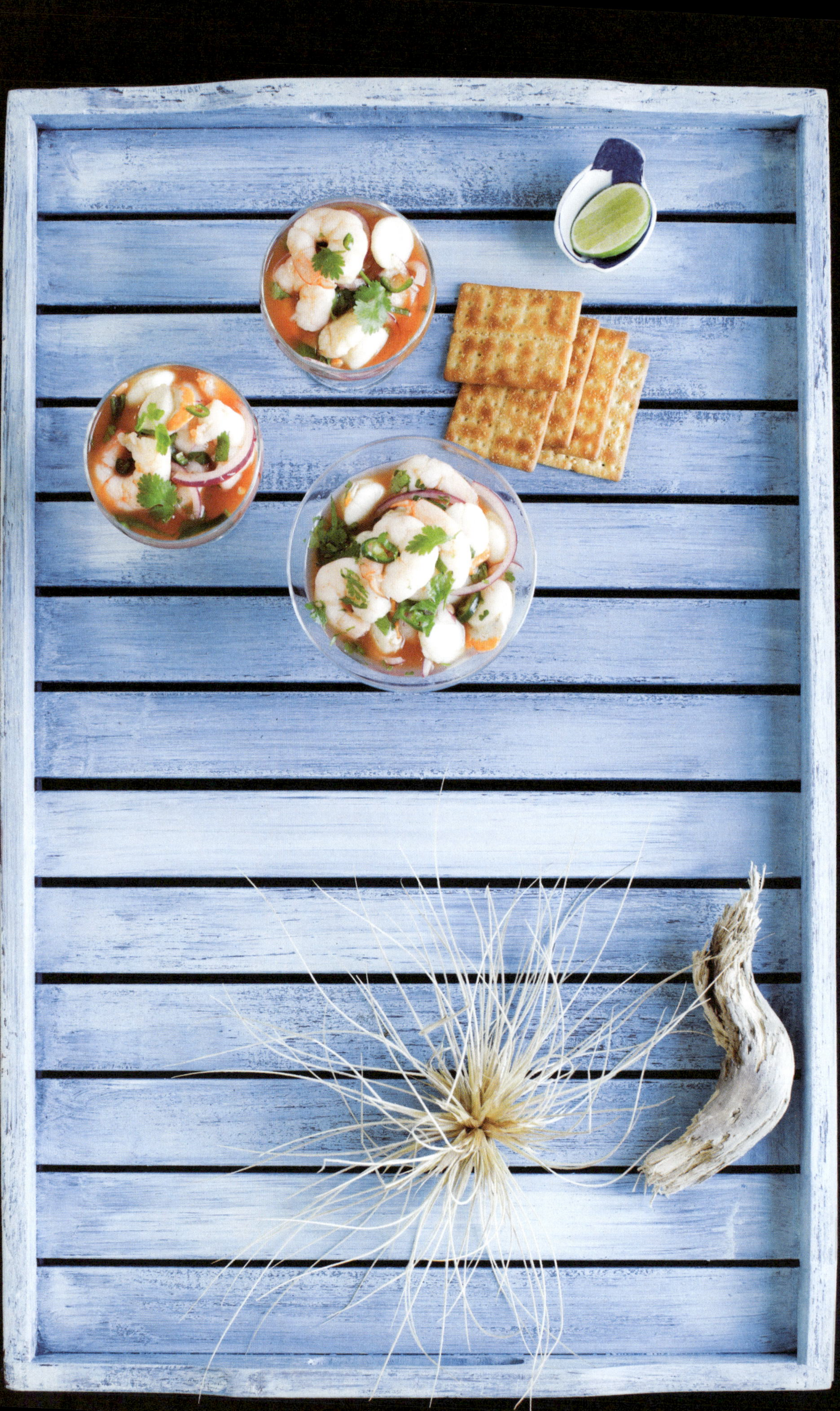

Ecuador

CEBICHE DE CAMARONES Y VIERAS

Prawn & Scallop Ceviche

GF

24 scallops
24 prawns, peeled and deveined
2 tbsp chopped parsley
½ medium red onion, cut into julienne strips
¼ cup fresh lime juice
1 tbsp tomato paste
2 tbsp tomato sauce
juice of 1 orange
1 tsp de-seeded and finely chopped serranos or fresh chillies (optional)
1 tsp Tabasco or hot sauce (optional)
pink Himalayan salt or flaky sea salt
3 tbsp chopped coriander, to garnish

Ecuadorian food is finally getting the recognition and attention it deserves, and it's very exciting to see. There is now a new generation of chefs who have been putting their gastronomy on the map, and for the first time Ecuador recently won several major cookbook awards. Ecuadorian food is incredibly diverse, and the clever use of their unique ingredients is inspiring. Because of their beautiful Pacific coastline, they also have marvelous seafood. A chef friend of mine who I worked with in New York taught me this recipe. It's a very traditional dish, and one of many kinds of Ecuadorian ceviche. We would constantly argue whether Ecuadorian or Peruvian ceviche was best. Well, he converted me . . . sort of, now I love both.

Prepare: 15 minutes; cook: 10 minutes
Serves: 6 as an appetiser or 4 as a main

Bring a large pan of salted water to the boil. Add scallops and poach gently until translucent, about 1 minute. If the scallops are small, poach for less time — always try one before getting all of them out of the water, remembering that they are going to continue cooking in the lime juice. Repeat with the prawns in the same poaching liquid, but poach for about 2 minutes. Save the poaching liquid for another use; strain it well and chill it.

Combine parsley, red onion, lime juice, tomato paste, tomato sauce, orange juice, chillies (if using) and hot sauce (if using) until well blended. Gently fold in prawns and scallops. Add a bit of cooled poaching liquid if necessary. Season with pink Himalayan salt or flaky sea salt and freshly ground black pepper to taste. Garnish with coriander.

The ceviche can be served with fried green plantains or saltine crackers (e.g. Arnott's Salada).

Chef's note: Scallops are not traditional, but they go very well with this recipe. Be careful not to overcook the prawns or scallops: they take very little time and will continue to cook in the lime juice. If you like Worcestershire sauce, you can add a teaspoon of it to the mixture. Also, if you are not a fan of tomato sauce you can substitute some de-seeded, chopped fresh tomatoes. If you use the poaching liquid to make a soup like chupe de camarones (see page 27) or for stock, just keep in mind that it will be a bit salty so taste before adding extra seasoning.

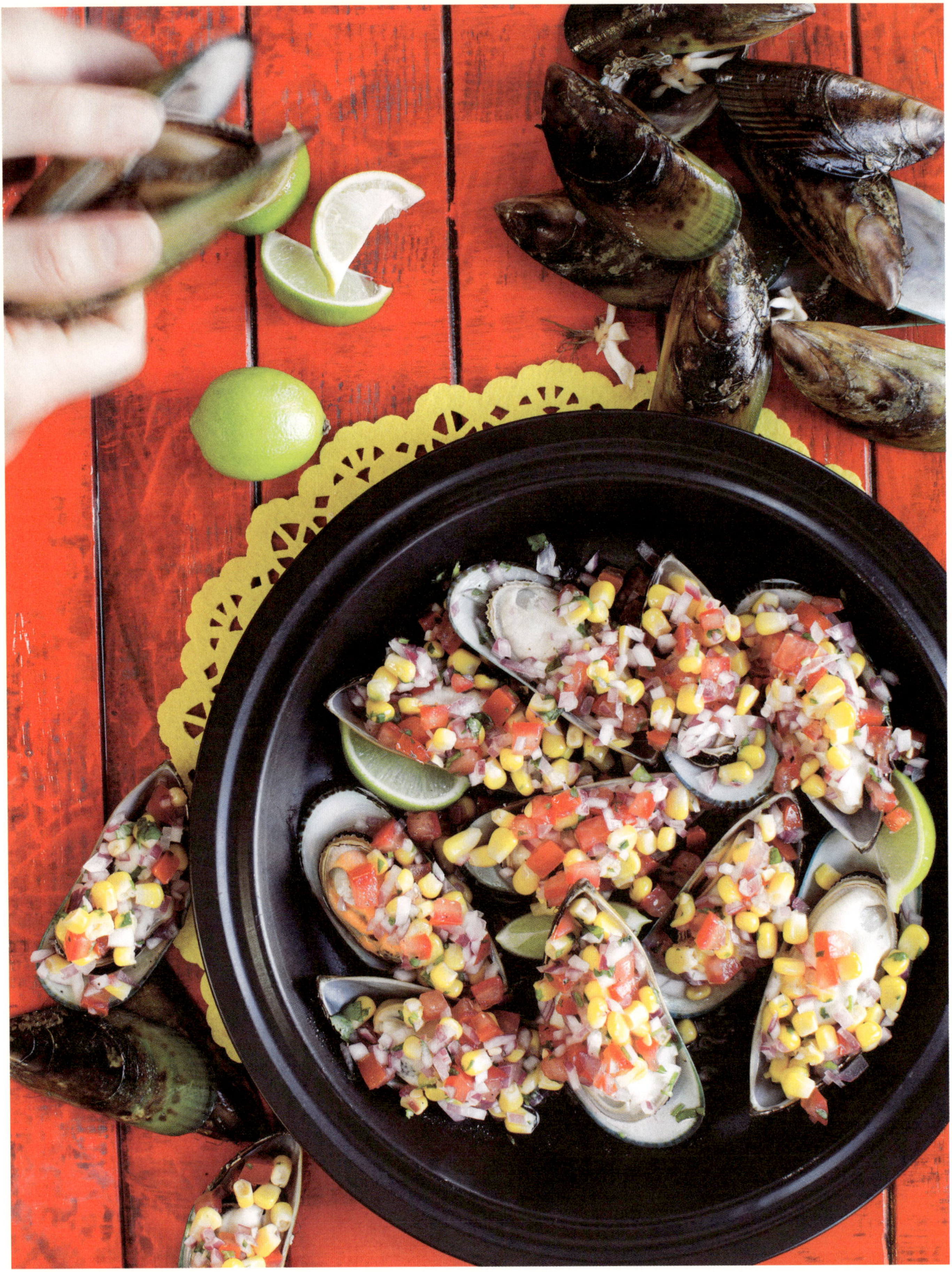

Peru

CHOROS A LA CHALACA

Open-faced Mussels Topped with Corn & Tomato Salsa

GF

36 green-lipped mussels
1 cup sweetcorn kernels (can be thawed from frozen or drained from a can) or 1 fresh sweetcorn with husk on
½ medium red onion, peeled and finely diced
2 tsp olive oil
¼ cup de-seeded and finely diced ripe tomato
8 sprigs fresh coriander, trimmed and chopped
juice of 2 limes
pink Himalayan salt or flaky sea salt

Garnish
lime wedges

These mussels are festive, colourful, delicious and the perfect healthy, summery appetiser. Using New Zealand green-lipped mussels is a real treat, and takes this dish to a whole new level. I tried this for the first time in Lima, the capital of Peru. Lima is considered one of the gastronomic capitals of the world, and because of its proximity to the South Pacific Ocean, there is abundant fresh seafood everywhere. Peruvians love mussels, and their shells were once used as fish hooks or pendants. The fresh chopped salad that goes on top of each mussel also goes well with barbecued fish; if in season, fresh corn is best.

Prepare: 30 minutes; cook: 10 minutes
Serves: 6 as an appetiser

Clean mussels and trim beards off. Place 1 cm of water in a large saucepan with a well-fitting lid. Add mussels, cover, and cook over a medium-low heat until mussels have opened. Remove all fully open mussels from pan, discarding any that have not opened. Remove one side of shell and leave mussels sitting on the half-shell.

If using fresh sweetcorn, microwave it with the husk on for 3–5 minutes on high. Let it cool, then peel off the husk and remove the kernels with a sharp knife.

Mix onion, corn kernels, olive oil, tomato, coriander and lime juice together in a bowl and season to taste with salt and freshly ground black pepper.

Place half-shelled mussels on a serving platter, pile on topping and serve with lime wedges on the side.

Chef's note: If you find the taste of the red onion a bit strong, peel it and cut it in half, then soak it in water with 1 tablespoon salt for about 30 minutes; then chop. Or you can dice the onion and soak it in vinegar for at least 30 minutes; this will pickle the onion and bring out its sweetness.

Mexico

CAMARONES CON ADOBO DE GUAJILLO

Guajillo Adobo-marinated Prawns

GF

For the adobo sauce
8 dried guajillo chillies, cut lengthwise and de-seeded
2 cloves garlic, peeled
¼ cup rice bran (or other neutral-tasting) oil
¼ cup orange juice
1 tbsp lemon juice
2 tbsp brown sugar or shaved panela (unrefined cane sugar)
½ tsp salt
½ tsp ground cumin
pink Himalayan salt

500 g large prawns, peeled, deveined

Garnish (optional)
1 tbsp chopped coriander
lime or lemon wedges

I love, love, love guajillo chillies. People are often intimidated by them because of their large size and colour, but they barely have any heat! Instead, they add layers of surprising flavours. This is a total crowd-pleaser — make sure you always make extra because people will go back for seconds. You can also use this sauce as a marinade for fish, pork or chicken, or use in tamales (see page 135) These prawns make great prawn tacos!

Prepare: 20 minutes; marinate: 30 minutes; cook: 10 minutes
Serves: 4–6

Put guajillo chillies in a saucepan and cover with water. Bring to the boil, then simmer for 20 minutes until soft. Drain, reserving about ¼ cup of the liquid.

Put ½ cup fresh water and the chillies into a blender. Add the rest of the adobo sauce ingredients and blend until smooth. Add a bit of the chilli water if desired (this will add more heat). Strain through a sieve and set aside.

Place prawns in a non-metallic bowl, pour marinade on top and refrigerate for about 30 minutes.

Preheat barbecue to a high heat. Remove prawns from marinade (keeping this for later, if desired), pat dry and season with pink Himalayan salt and freshly ground black pepper.

If you want extra sauce, put reserved marinade in a small saucepan with remaining chilli water. Bring to the boil, then simmer for a couple of minutes, until reduced by half, and set aside.

Grill prawns for about 3 minutes on each side. Garnish with coriander. Serve immediately, with lime wedges and the extra sauce (if using) on the side or on top.

Chef's note: You can also cook the prawns on the stovetop or under an oven grill. If cooking on the stovetop, use a cast-iron or heavy-bottomed frying pan and make sure it's really hot before you add the prawns. You want them to caramelise and char a little. If cooking them in the oven, preheat oven grill to high. Lightly oil a large baking tray and arrange the seasoned prawns on it in a single layer. Grill, watching closely and turning halfway through, until prawns are just cooked through and are starting to brown (4–5 minutes). You can also use coconut oil for cooking the prawns; it will add another layer of flavour.

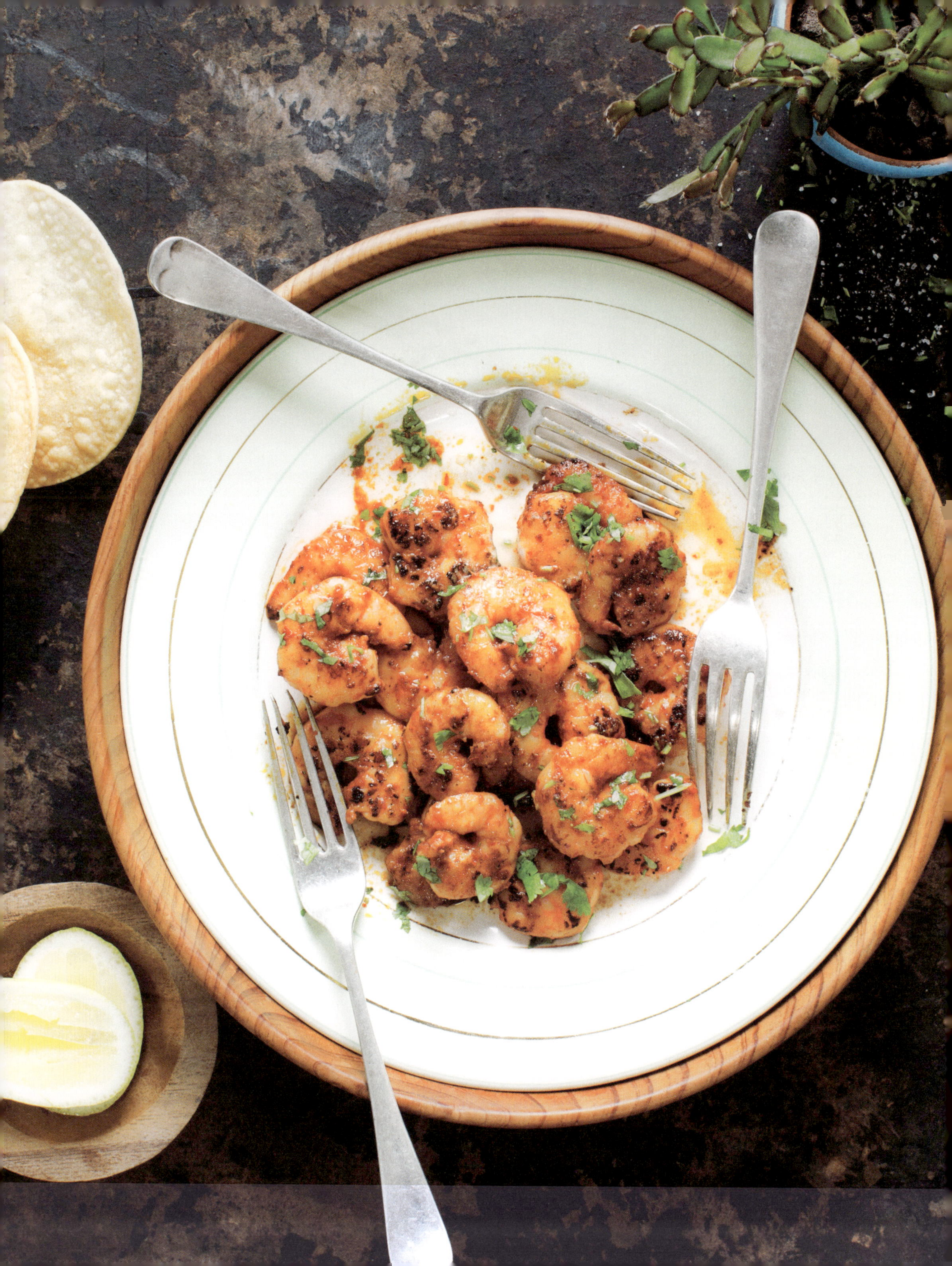

Mexico

TOSTADITAS DE PULPO

Octopus Tostaditas (Two Ways)

GF

For the poached octopus
1 kg octopus
2 tbsp salt
1 medium-sized potato, any kind (optional)

For the seared octopus
¼ cup olive oil
3 cloves garlic, smashed
pinch of guajillo chilli or chilli flakes
1 kg octopus
pink Himalayan salt

To serve
bite-sized round corn chips
¼ iceberg lettuce, shredded
¼ red cabbage, shredded
chilli salt (see page 193), chilli flakes or habanero chilli oil (see page 188) (optional)

Most are intimidated by pulpos (octopus): they immediately think 'hard and rubbery'. I love octopus! My husband's family lives in Spain and we eat pulpo a la Gallega almost every day when we are there. Here are two different methods of preparing octopus. I personally prefer poaching it for tostaditas, but I encourage you to try both ways and choose your own favourite. To tenderise fresh octopus, my mother-in-law says to massage and beat it for at least 10 minutes: 'Dale duro pero con amor,' she says — 'Beat it but do it with love.' In most fish markets, however, it is more common to find it frozen; if that is the case, defrost the octopus and then put it into the boiling water as the freezing will have helped tenderise it. When poaching octopus, my mother-in-law likes to use the potato as a reference — when your potato is done, your octopus should also be done.

Prepare: 10 minutes; cook: 45 minutes
Serves: 6–8

To massage octopus, place in a large sealable plastic storage bag, and beat with a mallet or rolling pin for at least 10 minutes. Remove from the bag and prick with a fork a few times in the body and each tentacle.

For poached octopus, bring a large stockpot of water to the boil with the salt. With a pair of tongs, submerge the octopus for 15 seconds then take it out for 15 seconds; repeat two more times. This process plumps the tentacle suction cups and shocks the octopus flesh. The tentacles will curl up and look all fancy and chef-y as they cook; my mother-in-law swears this also helps tenderise it. Then leave octopus fully submerged in the water, add the potato (if using), and lower the heat. Simmer for about 30–45 minutes, until potato and octopus are fork-tender. Discard potato (unless reserving — see chef's note). To keep the meat tender and soaking up flavour, let it cool completely while still in the liquid. Once cool, chop into bite-sized pieces. You can serve it straight away — or if you want to go the extra mile, add flavour and heat by searing and charring the tentacles whole with a little habanero chilli oil.

For seared octopus, heat olive oil in a medium-sized Dutch oven or stove-safe casserole over a medium-high heat. Add garlic and chilli flakes and fry for about 1 minute. Season octopus with pink Himalayan salt to taste and sear until golden brown on all sides. Cover, lower heat and cook gently for 45 minutes. Uncover and remove from heat. Let octopus rest for 10 minutes before slicing and serving.

To serve, place octopus slices on top of corn chips, and top with lettuce, cabbage and chilli salt or flakes or habanero oil if desired.

Chef's note: If you decide to use the potato, save it together with the strained poaching liquid to make chupe de camarones (see page 27). The poaching liquid will keep for 3–4 days in the refrigerator and for one month in the freezer.

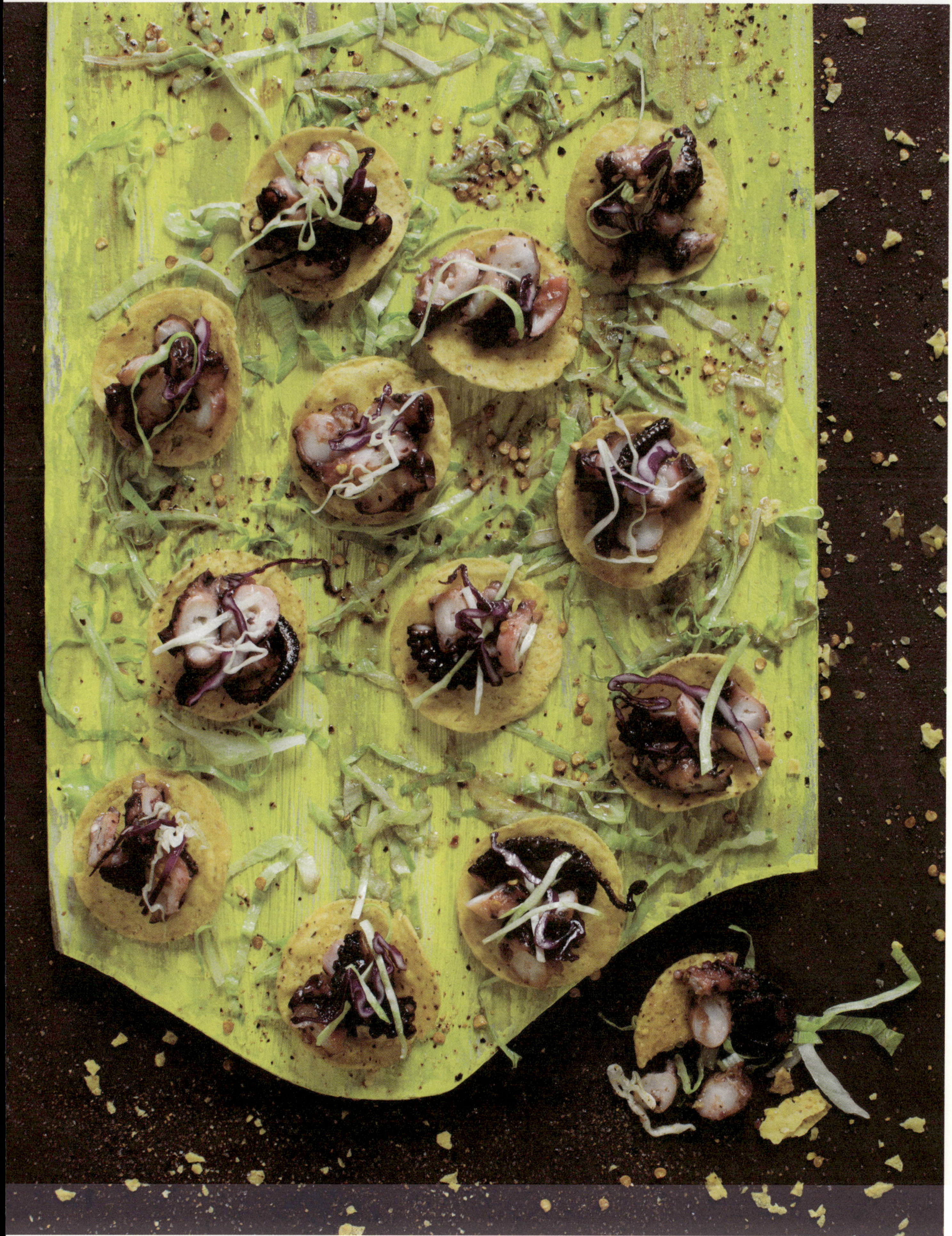

Brazil

CASQUINHA DE SIRI

Stuffed Crab Shells

GF

2 tbsp olive oil
½ cup chopped onion
4 tbsp chopped de-seeded red capsicum
4 tbsp chopped de-seeded green capsicum
3 cloves garlic, peeled and minced
1 tbsp lemon juice
2 cups de-seeded and diced tomato (approx. 4 tomatoes)
1 cup coconut milk
pinch chilli flakes (optional)
500 g cooked crab meat
flaky sea salt

Garnish
4 tbsp fresh gluten-free breadcrumbs
8 tbsp grated Parmesan
2 tbsp chopped parsley

If I had a tagline for Brazil, it would be 'Brasil, se mueve a otro ritmo' — 'Brazil, you move to your own rhythm'. Brazil is very different from the rest of the South American countries. First, they speak Portuguese. Second, while most Latinos love to dance, Brazilians are always, always dancing — even their walk is a dance! Their food is the same: it is unique, a beautiful dance of flavours, with a smooth balance between sweet and sour. I particularly love food from Salvador in the state of Bahia, a coastal town by the Atlantic Ocean and the Bay of All Saints. Salvador's love of carnival, New Year rituals, fresh seafood and coconut milk have a special place in my heart. Despite the name, this recipe is actually served in a dish. If you have shells feel free to use them!

Prepare: 15 minutes; cook: 20 minutes
Serves: 4

Preheat oven grill to 200°C.

In a medium-sized frying pan, heat olive oil over a medium heat, then add onion, capsicums and a pinch of salt. Cook for about 10 minutes, until soft. Add garlic and cook for 1 minute. Add lemon juice and tomato and stir until combined. Add coconut milk, simmering over a low heat until reduced by half (approximately 10 minutes), making sure that it doesn't boil or it will separate. Add chilli flakes, if using. Add crab meat and fold until coated with sauce. Season to taste with flaky sea salt and freshly ground black pepper.

Fill one large or four smaller ovenproof dishes three-quarters full of crab mixture. Sprinkle over breadcrumbs to cover each dish, then sprinkle Parmesan over the top. Grill for about 5 minutes, until golden brown. Sprinkle with chopped parsley just before serving.

Chef's note: You can serve this in crab shells in place of dishes, if you wish. Use regular breadcrumbs if gluten is not a concern.

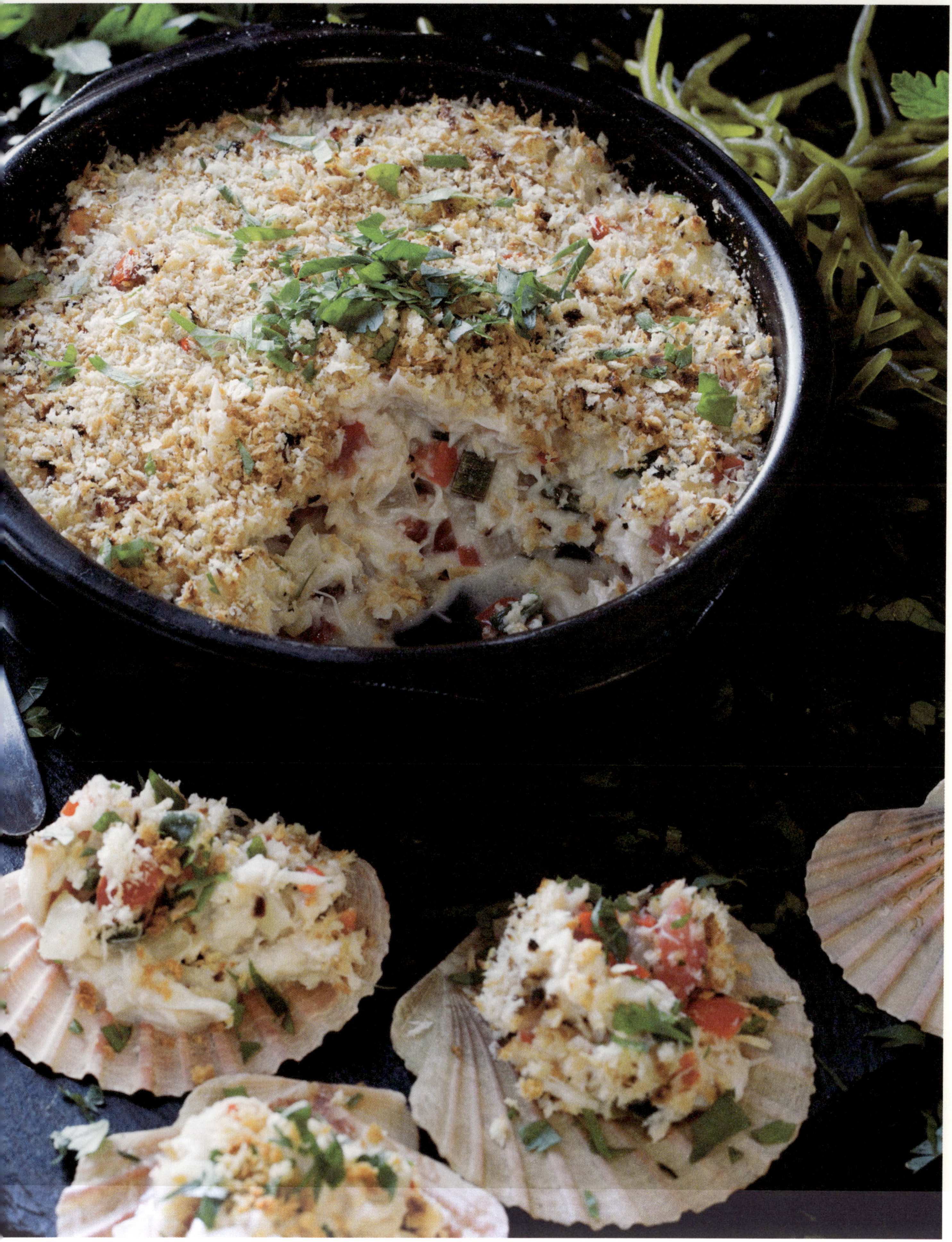

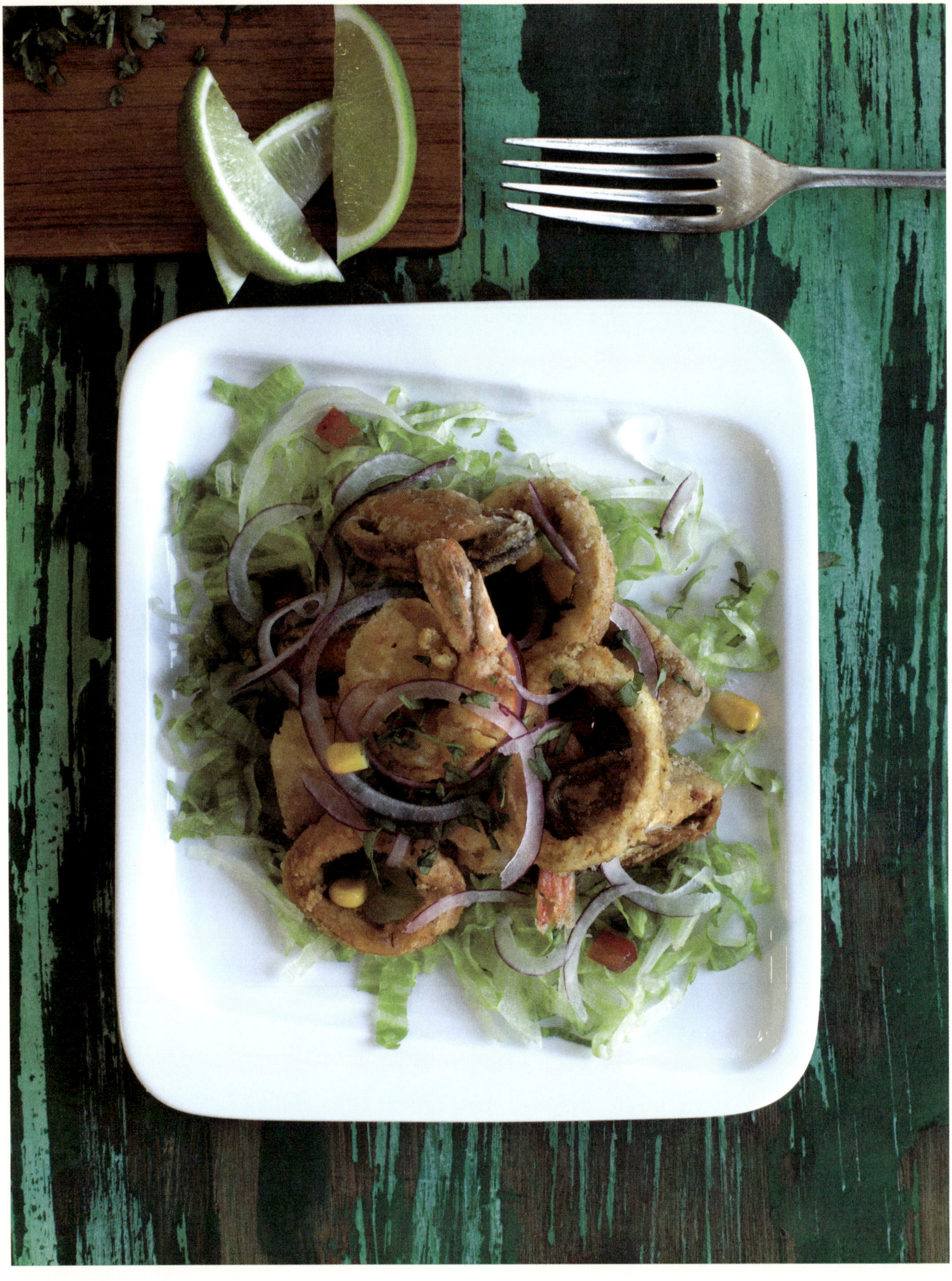

Peru

JALEA MIXTA

Crispy Seafood Salad

GF

12 green-lipped mussels
150 g squid, cleaned
200 g gurnard (or any semi-firm white-fleshed fish), skin removed
12 good-sized prawns, peeled and deveined
1 fresh sweetcorn with husk on, or ¼ cup sweetcorn kernels (either drained from a can or thawed from frozen)
1 cup fine cornmeal
¼ cup rice bran oil, or other neutral-tasting oil with a high smoke point

Garnish

½ iceberg or butterhead lettuce, shredded
¼ cup salsa criolla (see page 199)
1 tomato, de-seeded and diced, or chopped into quarters
chopped coriander or parsley
lime wedges

Jalea comes from the northern part of Peru, but is eaten along the whole Pacific coast. I love fried seafood; there is something so inviting and comforting about it, but I can't afford to eat all those calories all the time. However, this dish is so worth it, and I believe that one can have everything in moderation. In Spain, 'vamos de jaleo' means 'let's go partying', and that is exactly how your mouth feels after eating this succulent dish. All the different crispy textures and seafood flavours plus the citrus finish make your taste buds dance. It is traditionally served family style, placed in the centre of the table for everyone to share and enjoy.

Prepare: 15 minutes; cook: 20 minutes
Serves: 4 as an appetiser

To test whether mussels are alive, place in a saucepan with about ¼ cup water. Steam, covered, for about 3 minutes. The ones that open are good; the ones that do not should be discarded. Fully open the good mussels and remove from the shell.

Slice squid bodies into rounds, leaving the tentacles whole. Cut gurnard into 2 cm cubes. Combine mussels, squid, gurnard and prawns in a large bowl.

If using fresh sweetcorn, microwave it in the husk on high for 3-5 minutes while mussels are steaming. Let sweetcorn cool slightly before peeling husks off. Carefully cut kernels off with a sharp knife and set aside.

Season all the pieces of seafood with salt and freshly ground black pepper. Toss in cornmeal until evenly coated. Heat oil in a heavy-bottomed frying pan over high heat until ripples appear in the oil. Carefully add the coated seafood, frying in batches so that the pan is not too crowded. Fry for about 2 minutes on each side, until golden brown. You can also use a deep-fryer heated to 180°C, cooking the seafood for about 4 minutes. Transfer cooked seafood to a plate lined with paper towels, and season with a pinch of salt. Continue to fry until all the seafood is done.

To serve, top the lettuce with the fried seafood, and spoon salsa criolla on top. Garnish with corn kernels, tomatoes and chopped coriander or parsley, and lime wedges on the side.

Chef's note: There are no rules about what types of seafood to use in your jalea. You can just use fish, or fish and calamari; some people like to add scallops. It's up to you. Also, you can use rice flour or plain flour instead of the cornmeal if you wish. Yuca con mojo (see page 177) goes really well with this dish.

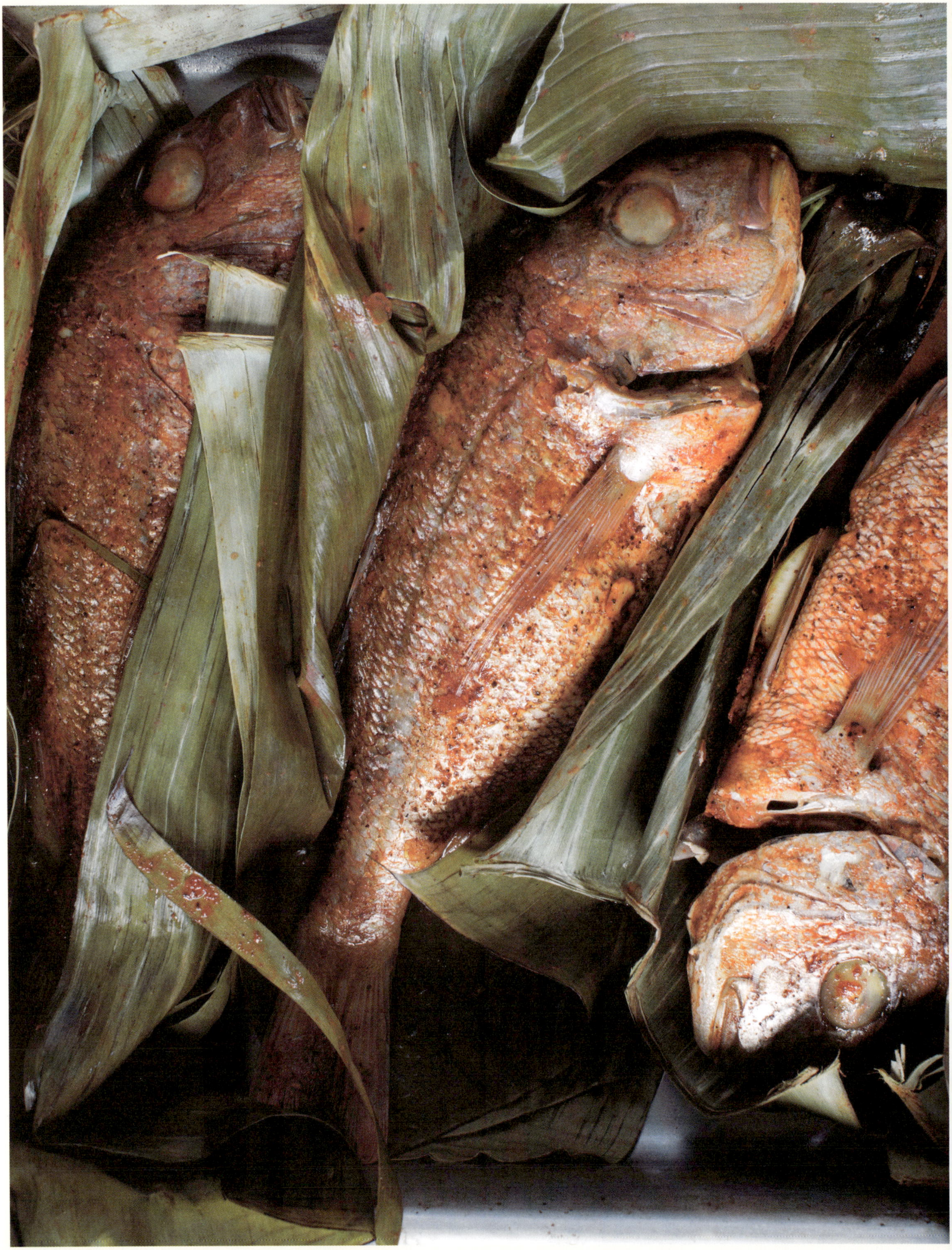

Mexico/Caribbean

PESCADO EN HOJA DE PLÁTANO

Achiote-rubbed Grilled Fish Wrapped in Plantain Leaves

1 packet plantain leaves
40 g achiote paste
¼ cup orange juice
1 tbsp lime juice
2 cloves garlic, peeled and roughly chopped
½ tsp chopped fresh or ¼ tsp dried oregano (preferably Mexican)
1 tsp white vinegar
½ cup white wine
4 whole snapper
1 lemon, sliced (optional)
pink Himalayan salt

Different variations of this dish can be found throughout Mexico's Yucután peninsula, Panama and Ecuador. It is popular among the Q'eqchi', a central American Mayan group located largely in Guatemala. For me, it is fascinating what a scent can do. The smell of plantain leaves passing through fire instantly takes me back to Venezuela, where plantain leaves are used to wrap Christmas tamales called hallacas, and often other foods or sweets. We often use achiote seeds, while the achiote paste is more likely to be used in Mexican cooking. Place these beauties in the centre of your table, accompanied by Mexican-style red rice (see page 148) and mango and passionfruit salad (see page 170), or have a fish taco party. The lemon slices for stuffing are optional.

Prepare: 1 hour; cook: 15 minutes
Serves: 10–12

If the plantain leaves are frozen, place them on a dish and defrost in the refrigerator overnight. If you are in a hurry, place them in cold water for about 20 minutes or microwave on high for 3–5 minutes.

In a blender, process achiote paste, citrus juices, garlic, oregano, vinegar and wine until smooth. Place fish on a non-metallic tray, score across the fish skin with a sharp knife and pour the marinade over. Cover and refrigerate for up to 1 hour.

Meanwhile, prepare plantain leaves by carefully cutting them to the desired length. For a 30 cm snapper, cut 40 cm squares. To release the natural oils in the leaves and make them more flexible, blanch the leaves in boiling water for a couple of minutes, or run each side over a gas flame for a few seconds until they become shinier. You can prepare all the leaves at once, saving them in a stack covered with a damp kitchen towel in the refrigerator. They will keep for up to 3 weeks.

Preheat barbecue to medium-low or oven to 200°C.

Place a fish in the centre of a square plantain leaf, tuck lemon slices inside (if using) and season with Himalayan salt and freshly ground black pepper. Fold two sides of the leaf over the fish to enclose it, then fold in the opposite sides to form a packet or tamale pouch. Tie the packet together with a strip of plantain-leaf rib, or just fold the ends like wrapping a gift.

If using the barbecue, grill fish pouches for about 8–10 minutes on each side — this will vary depending on the size of the fish. Alternatively, place fish pouches on a baking tray and bake for 15–20 minutes or until flesh is opaque and tender. Let them rest for 5 minutes before unwrapping and serving.

Chef's note: You can easily turn this dish into tacos de pescado — warm some flour or corn tortillas and stuff them with some fish and lots of garnishes. I use spring onions that have been lightly brushed with oil and grilled, finely shredded red cabbage tossed with lemon juice and sea salt, sliced pasilla chillies that have been crisped up in hot oil, and of course lots of guacamole (see page 196).

Venezuela

PESCADO EN SALSA VERDE

Fish Fillets in Green Sauce

7 tbsp olive oil
6 cloves garlic
2 tbsp white wine
36 clams (approx.)
1 kg hake or other white fish,
    skin on (250 g each fillet)
juice of 1 lemon
pink Himalayan salt
½ cup chopped parsley
1 tbsp plain flour
½ cup frozen peas, thawed
    (or fresh shelled peas)
lemon wedges, to serve

This was the first dish my mother-in-law taught me how to make, after a lot of begging on my part. She is very protective of her recipes, so I had to sit down, take note of all the ingredients, run to the supermarket, get everything prepped and sorted, and then she came into the kitchen like an executive chef and whipped this dish up in no time. I had to film her because she was going so fast! This is traditionally made with merluza (hake), but you can use whatever white fish you like. It is considered a Basque specialty, from the Basque region in Spain, and because of the Spanish influence all over Latin America, you can find many variations to this dish everywhere. Some people blend the sauce, others finish it off with white asparagus; but all the principles are the same: buttery white fish fillets drenched in a parsley and garlic wine sauce. Serve with some good bread for dipping into the sauce.

Prepare: 10 minutes; cook: 20 minutes
Serves: 4

In a medium-sized saucepan, heat 1 tablespoon of olive oil with 2 peeled and crushed garlic cloves. After 1 minute, add white wine and let the alcohol burn off for another minute, then add clams. Cover and cook, shaking the pan occasionally, until all the clams have just opened up — check every few minutes. There may be a few clams that don't open; discard these and set the good ones aside. Strain cooking liquid and set aside.

Meanwhile, season the fish with lemon juice and pink Himalayan salt and set aside. Mince remaining garlic.

In a shallow frying pan, heat remaining olive oil and minced garlic cloves with half the parsley over a very low heat, for 8–10 minutes. You do not want the garlic to get any colour, so you have to watch it closely. Sprinkle flour over and mix thoroughly for 1–2 minutes.

Pat dry your fish. Add fish skin side up with 2 tablespoons of water and clam cooking liquid and cook for 5 minutes. Flip fish over and add remaining parsley, peas and clams. Cover and cook for an additional 5 minutes, until fish is cooked through. Season to taste and serve immediately with lemon wedges.

Chef's note: You can add more cold water or wine to loosen up the sauce if necessary. While this is technically a simple dish, the tricky part is carefully watching the heat so that the parsley and garlic don't burn, as they will change colour and get bitter. Some cooks also lightly flour the fish with plain flour or rice flour. If doing this, lightly fry it in the olive oil before adding the clam cooking liquid.

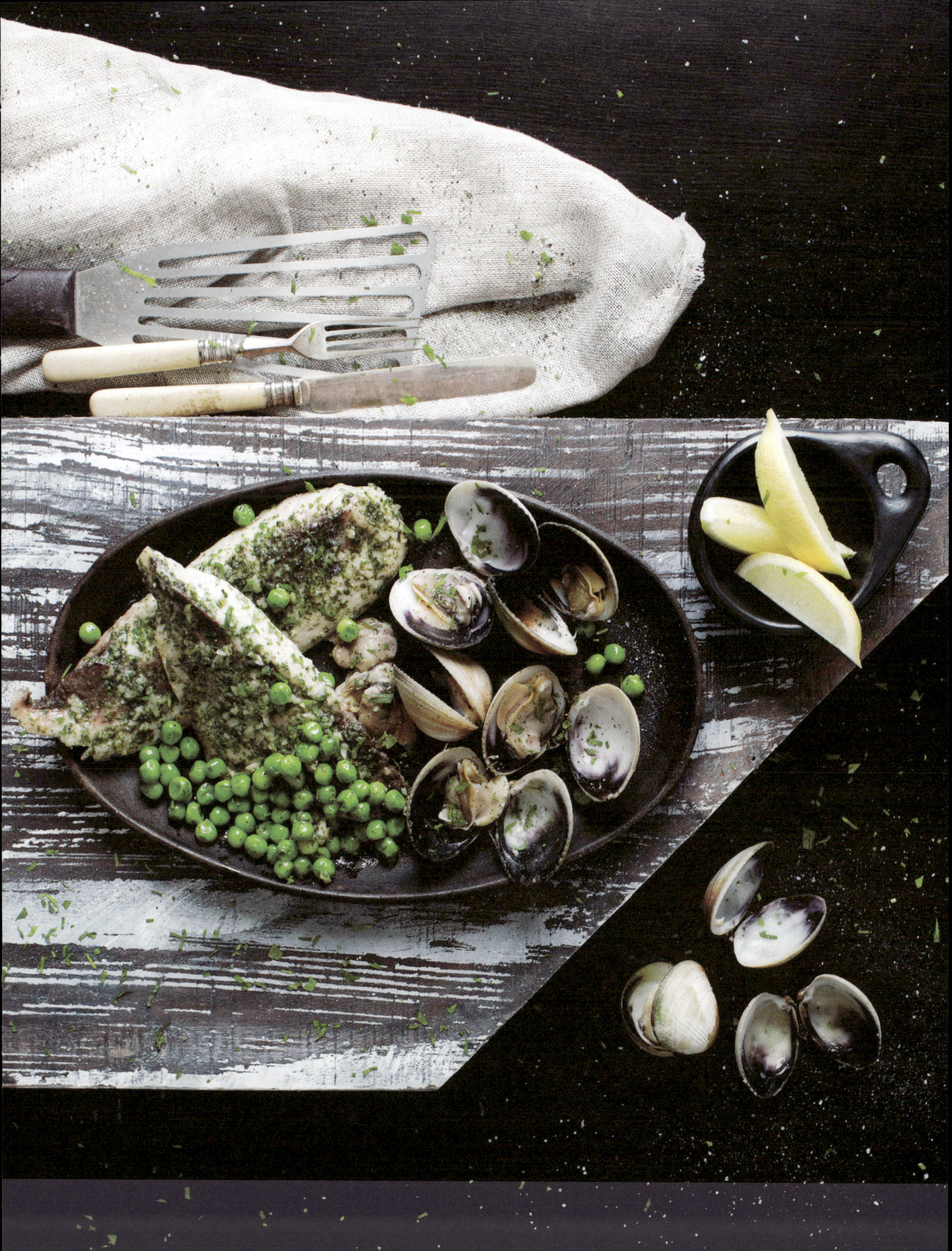

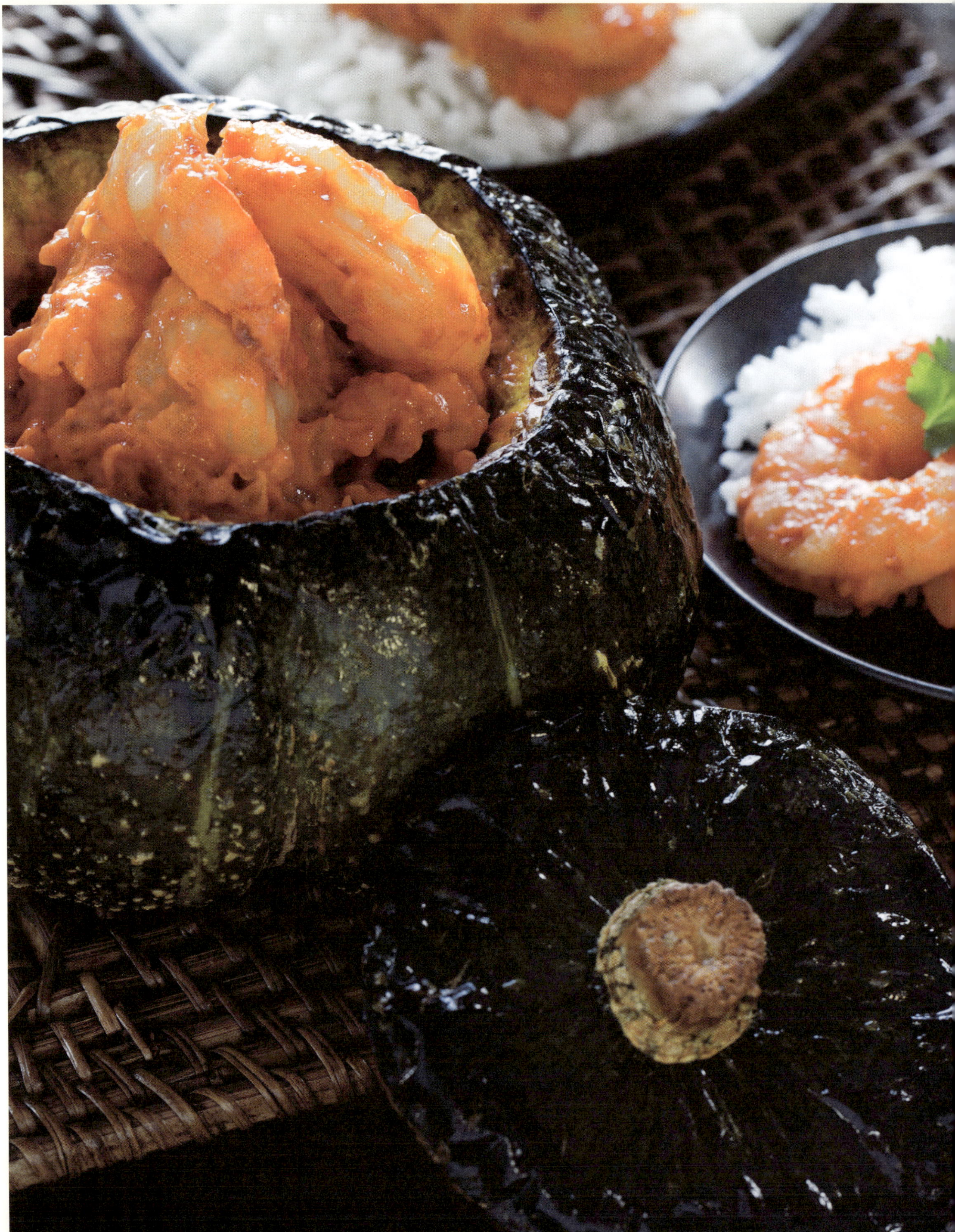

Brazil

CAMARÃO NA MORANGA

Creamy Prawn Stew in Pumpkin

GF

For the pumpkin
1 large pumpkin (about 2 kg)
    or 6 acorn squash
1 tbsp vegetable oil

To marinate prawns
1 kg prawns, peeled and deveined
1 tbsp lime or lemon juice
2 cloves garlic, peeled and crushed
½ tsp salt
¼ tsp freshly ground black pepper

For the sauce
2 tbsp olive oil
1 onion, diced
2 cloves garlic, peeled and
    finely chopped
1 red chilli, finely chopped
    (optional)
400 g can whole tomatoes, blended
1 bay leaf
1 cup cream

This is a total crowd-pleaser — from the city of Salvador — and one of the most delicious ways to eat prawns. I clearly remember the first time I ate this dish. There was this gorgeous large black woman dressed all in white with a huge turban, and the fresh smell of seafood, coconut, lime and coriander — all the delightful smells I often crave. She was using a mortar and pestle to crush the garlic, and did so with such strength, grace and ease in combining all the ingredients together. I was sold just on seeing how the dish was made. Then I tried it, and I was in love. This dish, with its impressive and unique presentation, is often a showpiece at Brazilian dinner parties, Christmas feasts and special occasions.

Prepare: 30 minutes; cook: 1 hour
Serves: 6

Preheat oven to 180°C.

Cut a hole in the top of the pumpkin or squashes and remove seeds with a spoon. Rub the entire outside with vegetable oil. Cover with foil. Roast in the oven until the flesh inside is semi-soft, about 30 minutes for a pumpkin and less for the smaller squashes, then remove foil and continue to cook for the same length of time. The pumpkin or squash is done when the inside flesh is fork-tender. Remove from oven and set aside.

Meanwhile, mix prawns with the marinade ingredients in a non-metallic bowl and set aside.

For the sauce, add olive oil to a large stockpot and sweat onion over a medium heat until translucent. Add garlic and chilli (if using), and sweat for 1 more minute. Add tomato, bay leaf and cream. Simmer on low for 5 minutes, stirring occasionally.

Add prawns to the stockpot, and continue to simmer until prawns begin to just turn pink, about 3 minutes. Remove from the heat.

Scrape out some of the soft flesh of the pumpkin and mix it into the sauce. When ready to serve, season to taste, reheat the prawns and sauce over a low heat and fill the inside cavity of the pumpkin.

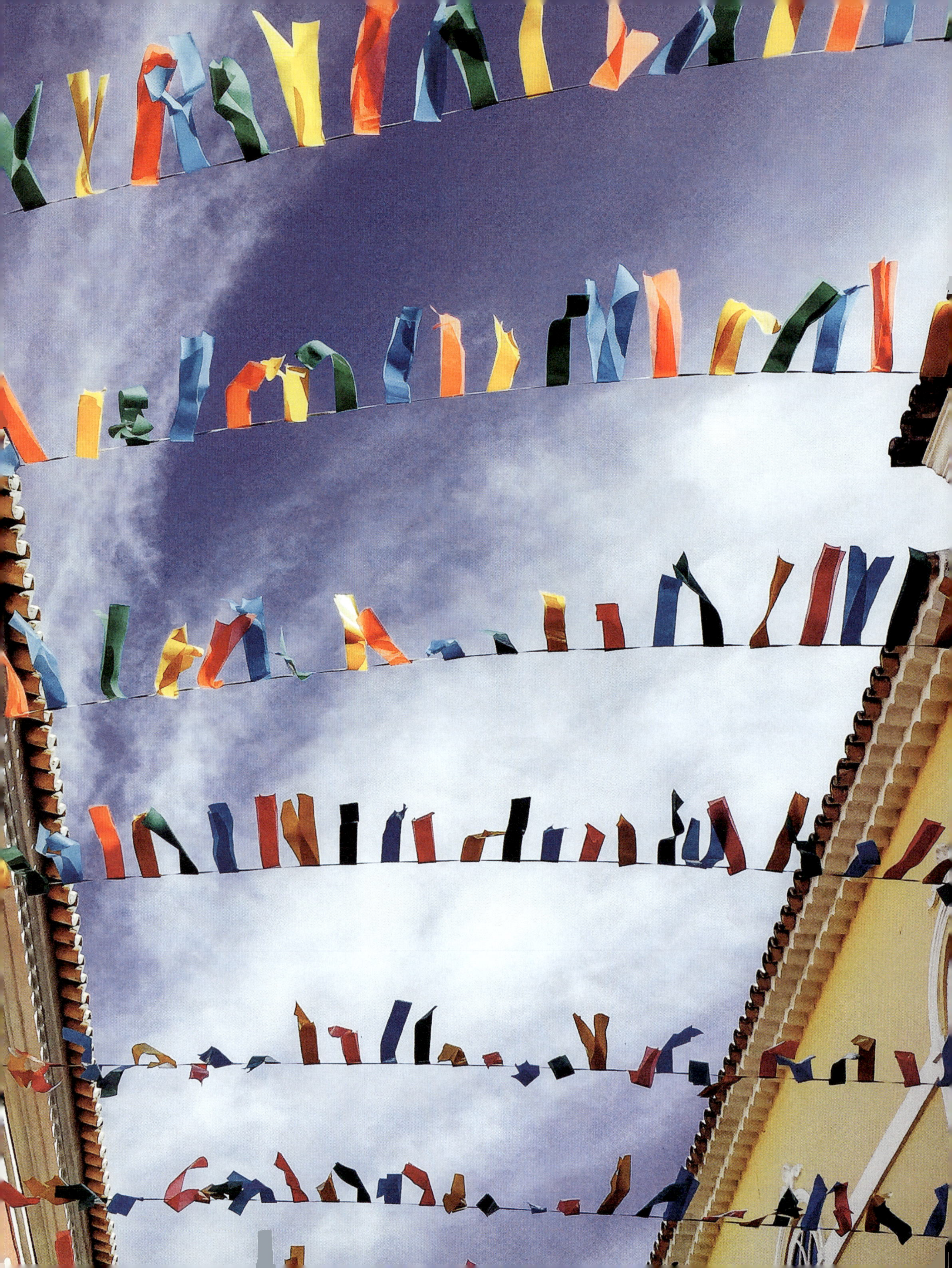

Brazil

KIKI'S MOQUECA

Seafood Stew in Coconut Milk

2 tbsp olive oil
2 onions, thinly sliced
2 red capsicums, de-seeded and sliced
2 green capsicums, de-seeded and sliced
3 red chillies, de-seeded and sliced
2 cloves garlic, peeled and chopped
3 tomatoes, chopped
400 ml can coconut milk
425g can Wattie's tomato and onion pasta sauce
1 tbsp tomato paste
1 kg white fish, such as monk fish or lemon fish
1 kg prawns
3 handfuls coriander leaves, chopped

Moqueca is a Brazilian seafood stew, traditionally from Bahia, and it's typically made with fish and prawns. It's commonly made in beautiful clay pots called moquequeiras, and the onions and capsicums are cut into rounds. It looks beautiful and effortless. This recipe is from my charming friend Kiki. After I tried this in many Brazilian restaurants, she taught me how to make it — in New Zealand, ironically, because she is originally from the dish's home of Brazil.

Prepare: 15 minutes; cook: 30 minutes
Serves: 4–6

Heat the olive oil in a deep frying pan over a medium heat and sweat the onions until transparent. Add capsicum and chilli and cook until fairly soft (but do not overcook). Add garlic and cook for 1 minute.

Add the chopped tomatoes and cook for 5 minutes until juice is running. Add the coconut milk, pasta sauce and tomato paste and simmer for approximately 15 minutes.

Turn off the heat and leave until it is time to serve. The sauce needs to be thick because when you cook the fish it releases water.

Add the fish and simmer for 5 to 8 minutes. Add the prawns and simmer until they are cooked, approximately 5 minutes. Season with salt and pepper to taste. Garnish with coriander to serve.

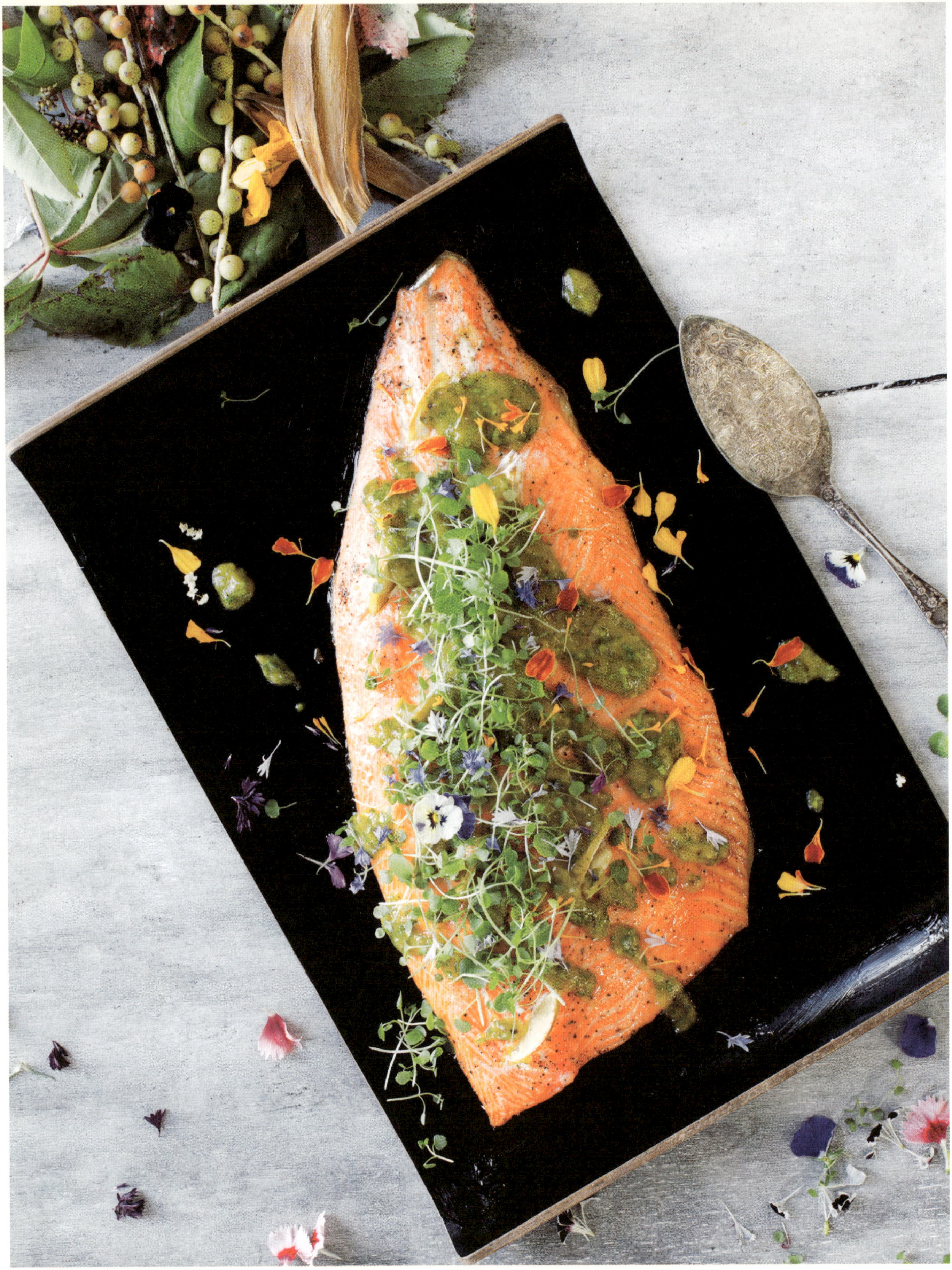

Venezuela

SALMÓN CON SALSA DE MANGO

Salmon with Caramelised Shallot & Mango Salsa

GF

1 kg salmon fillet, skin on
4 bay leaves
4 cloves garlic, peeled and halved
½ lemon, sliced into half-rounds
1 tbsp liquid honey
1 tbsp extra virgin coconut oil
flaky sea salt or pink Himalayan salt

For the salsa
½ tbsp extra virgin coconut oil
½ cup finely chopped shallots
1 ripe mango, flesh puréed in a blender
juice of 1 lemon
zest and juice of ½ lime
2 tbsp chopped parsley
2 tbsp chopped coriander

Garnish
edible flowers and/or micro watercress

This recipe was inspired by my aunt Morela, who is my grandmother's sister and the family's head chef. My grandmother has nine siblings and they are all great cooks, but Morela is considered the star. Her magic hands make anything taste delicious. Anytime we get together for Sunday lunch at her house, at least 50 people show up. That is because she has seven children, and everyone brings their significant other or an extra friend whose eyes light up when they hear that Tía Morela is there. She has inspired me so much, and has had a huge impact in my life and on my cooking. I mostly remember her creative salmon recipes. Dear Tía, I hope you like my Kiwi–Latino salmon.

Prepare: 10 minutes; cook: 20 minutes
Serves: 4–6

Preheat oven to 180°C.

Place salmon on a baking dish lined with non-stick baking paper. Make several cuts along the fillet, being careful not to cut too deeply. Tuck bay leaves, garlic halves and lemon slices into the cuts. Brush honey and coconut oil over the fillet. Season with salt and pepper. Bake for 15–20 minutes to give a pink centre, or cook longer if preferred.

Meanwhile, prepare the salsa. To a medium-sized frying pan over a medium-high heat, add coconut oil and shallots. Caramelise shallots until lightly browned, about 8 minutes, then remove from the heat. Stir in mango purée, lemon juice and lime zest and juice, and season to taste with sea salt and pepper. Add chopped parsley and coriander.

To serve, spread mango salsa on top of the fillets and garnish with edible flowers and/or micro watercress.

Chef's note: The flaky salt in the salsa is key to giving this dish the right texture and an unexpected burst of flavour.

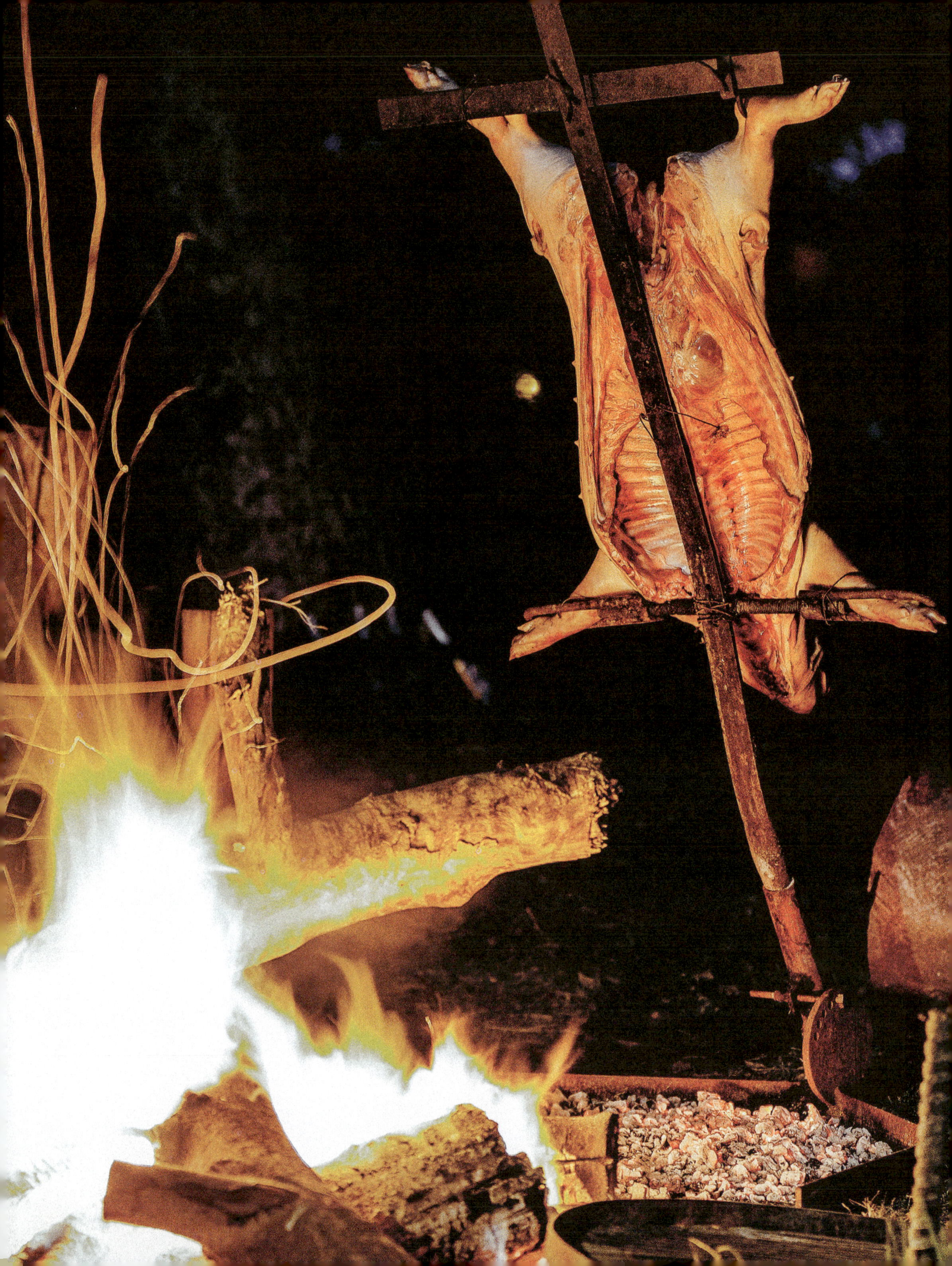

CARNES

MEATS

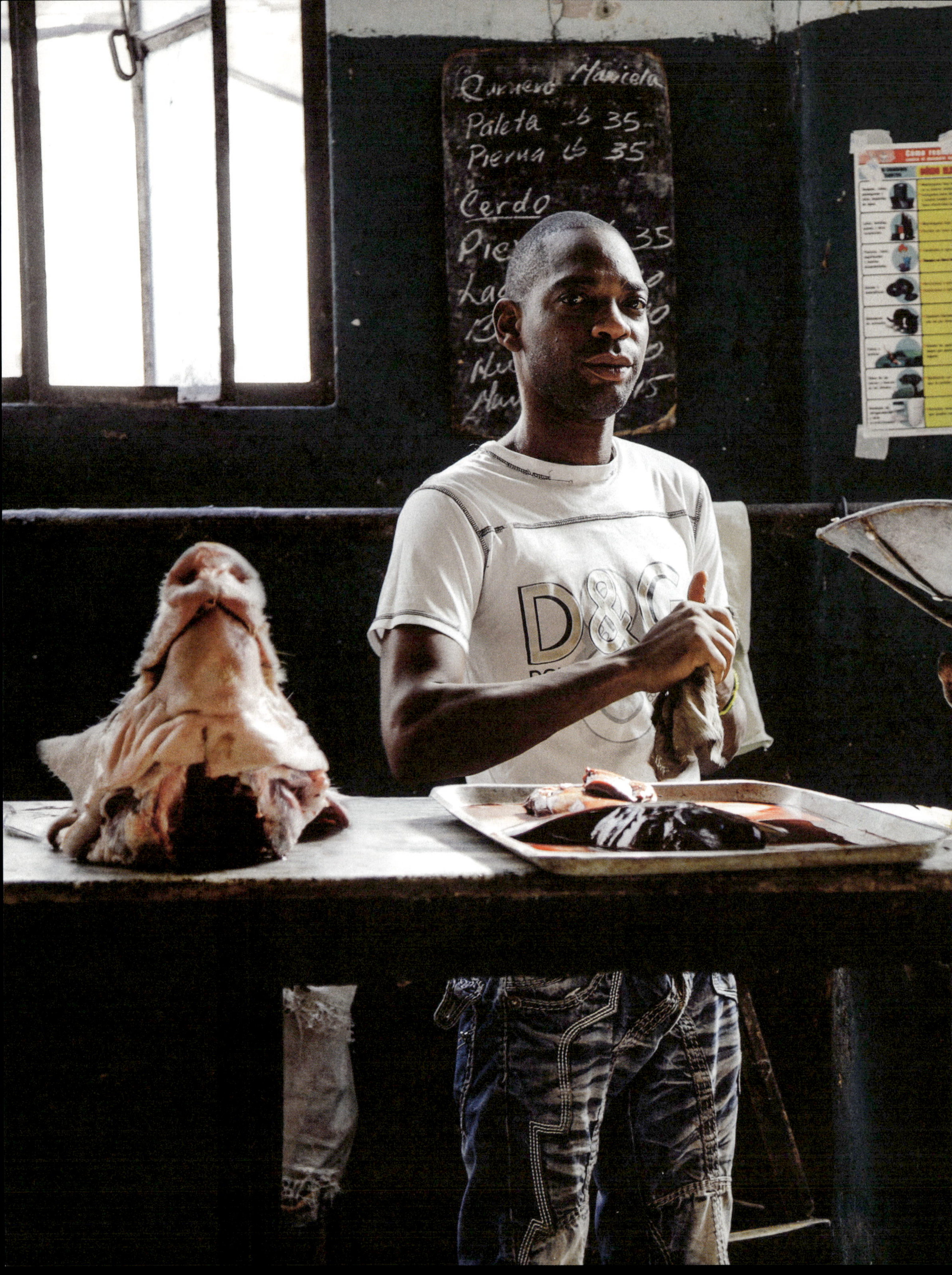
Paleta
Pierna
Cerdo
D&G

CARNITAS
Braised & Fried Pork

CHORIPÁN
Latin Sausage Rolls

LECHÓN CON MOJO
Pork Roast with Garlic

CORDERO CON CHIMICHURRI DE MENTA
Barbecued Lamb Chops with Mint Chimichurri

PASTEL DE CHOCLO CON PEBRE
Corn Pie with Pebre Salsa

BOLLOS PELONES
Beef-stuffed Corn Buns

ARRACHERA
Beer-marinated Skirt Steak

LOMO SALTADO
Beef Stir-fry Peruvian-style

CARNE MECHADA
Shredded Beef in Tomato Sofrito

ASADO NEGRO
Panela-braised Beef Eye of Round

Mexico

CARNITAS

Braised & Fried Pork

GF

1 tbsp sea salt
1½ kg boneless pork shoulder
375 ml can (1½ cups) evaporated milk
1 orange, cut in half
2 sticks cinnamon
10 cloves
2 bay leaves

When I think of carnitas (little meats), an image of a Mexican food market comes to mind. The overwhelming amount of people, the fruits, vegetables and flowers, the vivid colours, are all mesmerising. There are meat and poultry butchers, fish and seafood on display, live music and godly aromas coming from food stalls. It's truly a feast for all your senses. In these markets you will find rustic carnitas stands with a whole butchered pig in a huge copper caldron, simmering away until all the liquid is gone and then fried in its own succulent fat. Trying to recreate this at home is not an easy task — I tested about five different recipes — but the resulting dish is exquisite and leaves you feeling joyful and fulfilled. You can serve carnitas as a platter with Mexican rice and beans or make tacos — serve in warmed tortillas with other fillings of your choice.

Prepare: 10 minutes; cook: 4½ hours
Serves: 4–6 (makes approximately 20 tacos)

Preheat oven to 125°C.

Rub sea salt over pork shoulder. Place pork in a 5-litre Dutch oven or casserole. Pour in evaporated milk and add the juice from the orange, the juiced orange halves, cinnamon, cloves and bay leaves. Cover and place in oven for 3½–4 hours. Halfway through the cooking time, gently turn pork over and continue to cook. The pork is done when the meat pulls away easily and it is very tender.

Once pork is done, remove from oven and let it rest for 10 minutes.

Meanwhile, strain the braising liquid through a fine strainer (lined with cheesecloth or paper towel to remove the milk solids) into a small saucepan. Use a ladle to remove the oil that floats to the top, and place oil in a large frying pan. This will be used to fry the pulled meat later. Simmer the braising liquid until reduced to about ¼ cup. Remove from the heat and set aside.

Pull the pork meat apart with two forks, or use a knife to chop it into smaller pieces — 'little meats'. Heat reserved oil in the large frying pan over a medium-high heat. Add pulled meat, and stir occasionally until meat is crisp and golden brown. Fry in two batches if necessary. Transfer meat to a medium-sized bowl.

Pour the reduced braising liquid over the crisp meat, and serve immediately. Carnitas can be served inside a corn tortilla (see page 115) or a flour tortilla (see page 113), along with your favourite salsa or pico de gallo (see page 193), chopped onions and coriander.

Chef's note: If you can find a pork shoulder with the fat still on, this is ideal. Braise it with the fat side up. When fully done, cut fat away and crisp it in the oven at 200°C. Let it rest for a few minutes, then cut it into pieces and garnish your taco with this 'chicharrón'.

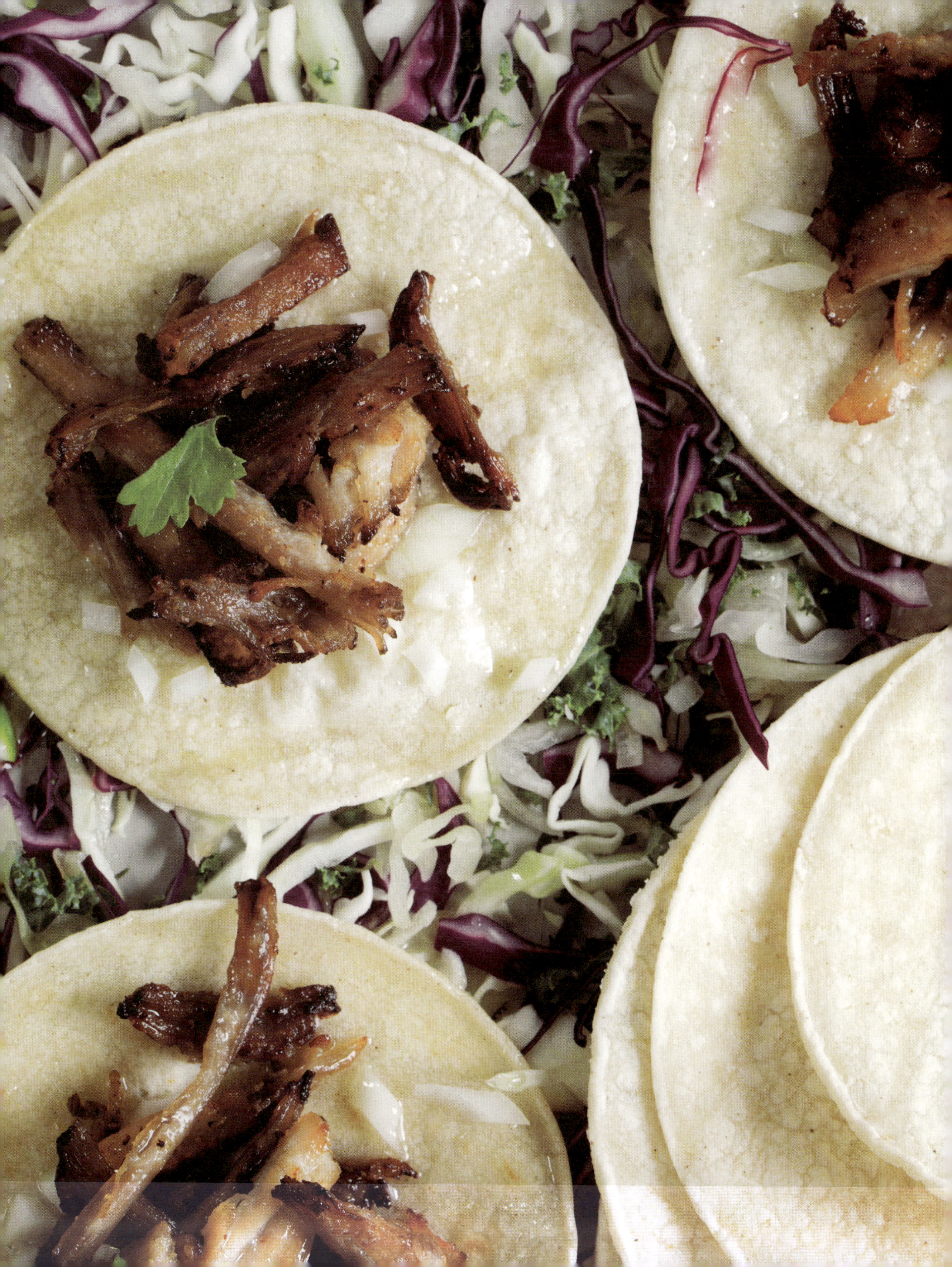

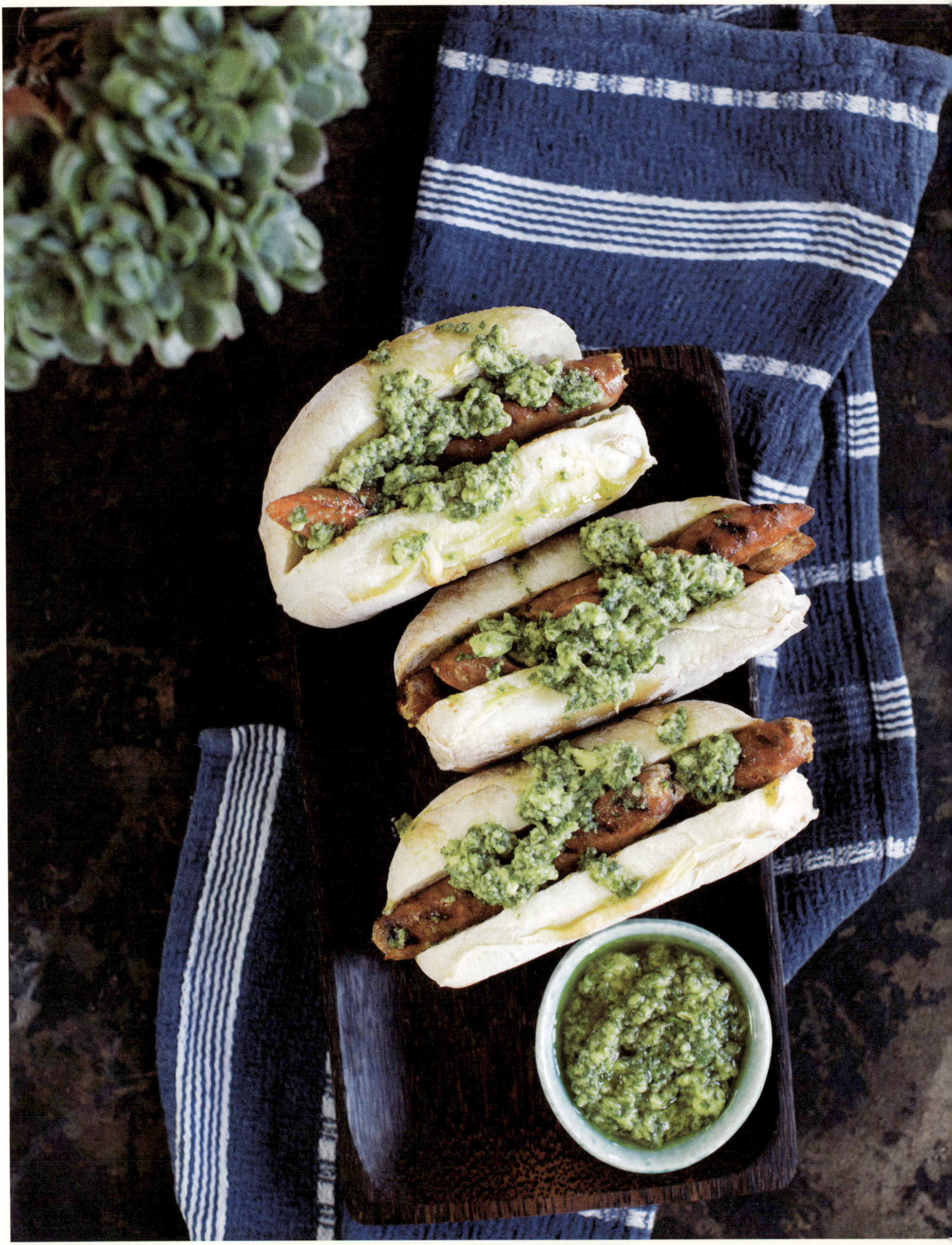

Venezuela

CHORIPÁN

Latin Sausage Rolls

4 chorizos or sausages of choice
4 ciabatta pockets
1 tbsp butter
1 cup guasacaca (see page 200)

In Latin America we are so obsessed with food and eating well that even a simple sausage roll or hot dog is layered with flavours. We never just add ketchup or tomato sauce to a sausage roll, or eat a hot dog with just mustard. In places like Colombia and Venezuela, hot dogs are total extravaganzas with garlic aïoli, mini french fries, Parmesan, onions and even slaw on top — and you crave them after a big party night! Choripanes are very popular in Argentina, Bolivia, Brazil, Chile, Peru, Puerto Rico, Uruguay and Venezuela. Everyone has their own version. This is the Venezuelan one; we mainly eat them at weekend barbecues.

Prepare: 10 minutes; cook: 10 minutes
Serves: 4

Preheat a grill pan or cast-iron skillet to a medium-high heat. Grill chorizos or sausages on all sides until fully cooked, about 5–7 minutes depending on size.

Slice open ciabatta pockets, spread with butter and lay on grill to lightly toast for about 1 minute.

To assemble, tuck chorizo or sausage in and top with guasacaca.

Cuba

LECHÓN CON MOJO

Pork Roast with Garlic

GF

For the marinade
8 large garlic cloves, peeled and lightly crushed
1 cup orange juice
¾ cup lemon juice
¼ cup apple cider vinegar
2 onions, peeled and grated
1 tsp dried oregano
½ tbsp ground cumin

3 kg pork shoulder, bone-in and skin-on

Traditionally this dish is cooked for Nochebuena (Christmas Eve) and served alongside the festive Moros con Cristianos (rice and beans) and yuca con mojo (see page 177). My Cuban friend Grettel taught me how to make lechón, but we used this marinade instead of using naranja agria (bitter oranges), which are sometimes hard to get hold of, and we roasted a small pork shoulder instead of doing the traditional thing, which entails digging a hole in your backyard and spit-roasting a 15 kg pig. Another good thing about making lechón is having left-overs to make Cuban sandwiches (see page 130) the next day.

Prepare: 45 minutes; marinate: overnight; cook: 6½ hours
Serves: 4–6

Combine all marinade ingredients and set aside. Place pork in a large roasting pan and stab it with a knife everywhere except the skin. Toss the marinade on top and put some of the garlic inside the incisions. Cover with plastic wrap and marinate in the fridge overnight, turning or basting the meat several times.

Preheat oven to 150°C.

Remove meat from marinade, keeping marinade aside. Pat meat dry and season generously with salt and freshly ground black pepper. Let it rest for at least 30 minutes at room temperature.

Return marinade to the roasting pan and place pork skin side up inside the pan. Cover pork with foil and cook for approximately 6 hours, basting with the liquid every 30 minutes. Your meat is ready when it is falling apart and tender (internal temperature of approx. 75°C).

Once done, remove pork from the oven and uncover the meat. Turn the oven up to 200°C and place pork back in the oven for 20–30 minutes. Keep an eye on it, removing it when it has crisped nicely. Let the meat rest for 15 minutes before carving.

Chef's note: I like to put the lechón into the oven as soon as I wake up on Christmas Eve, so that I have time to make a sauce from the braising liquid. Strain the liquid, keeping both parts; the solids are just garlic and onions. Put the liquid in the freezer to cool, then skim the fat off the top. Fry the solids in a little olive oil, stir in a ¼ cup of white wine, then add the skimmed braising liquid. Reduce, taste and season. Pour the sauce on top of the crispy pork meat.

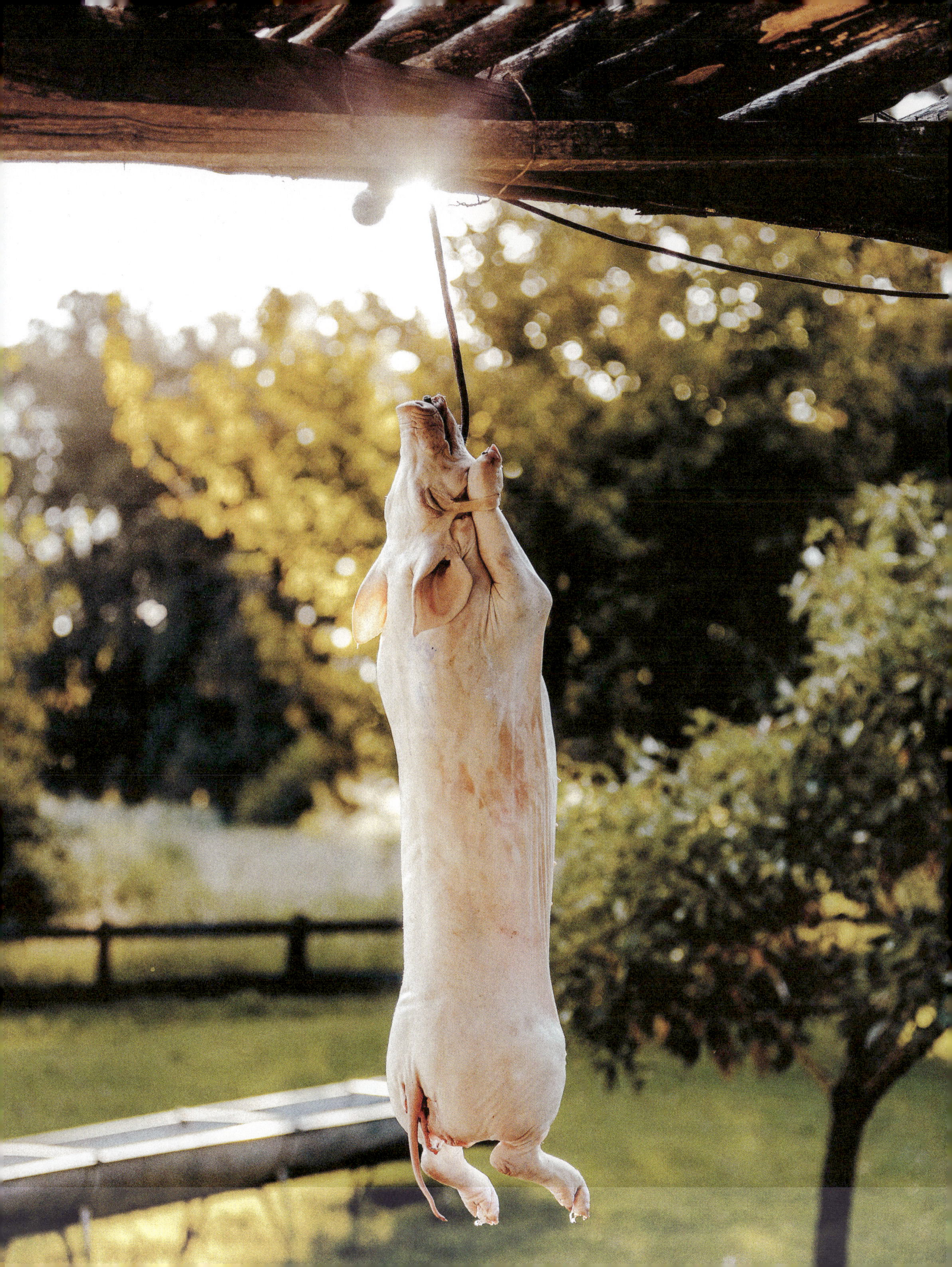

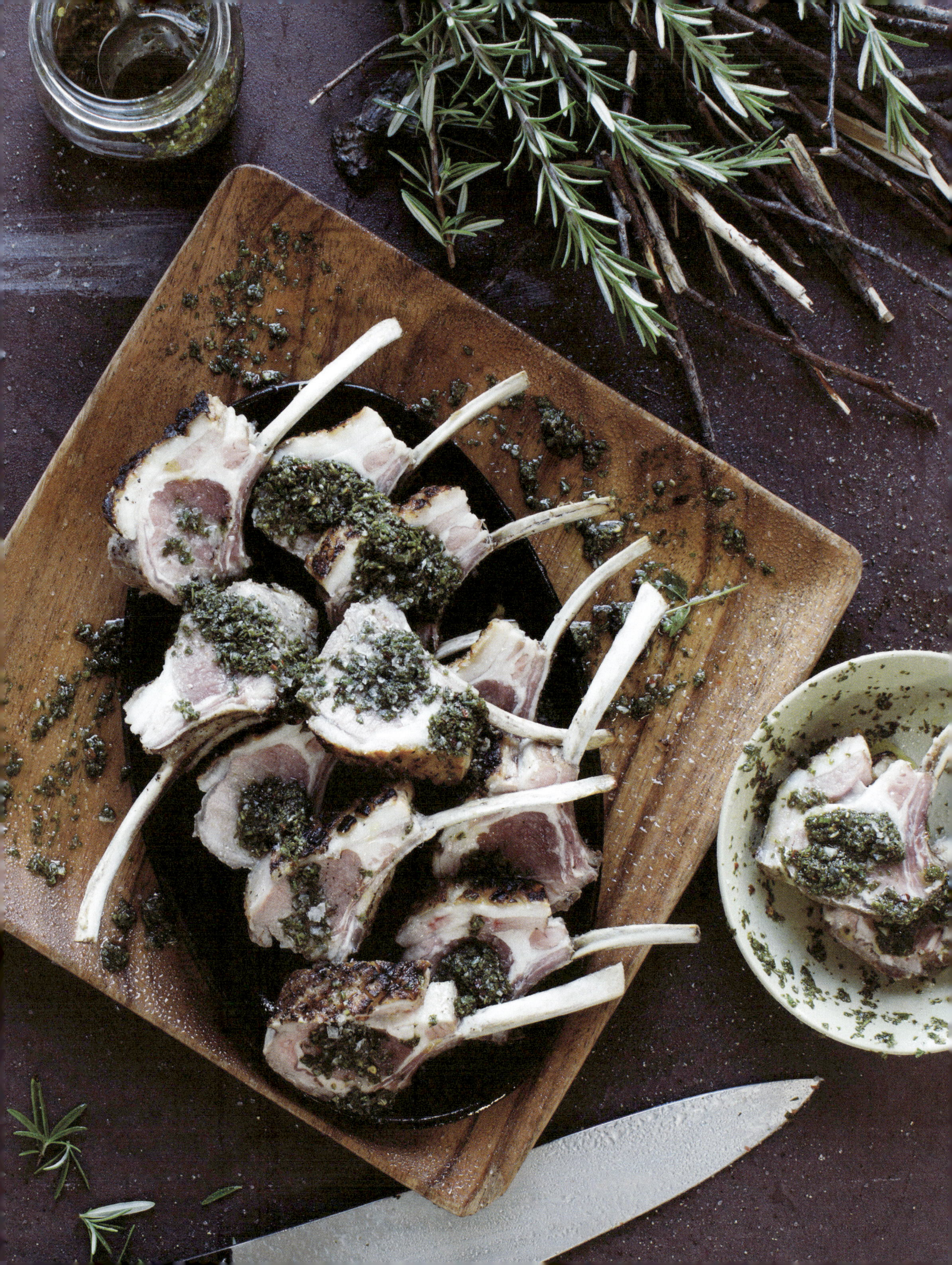

Argentina

CORDERO CON CHIMICHURRI DE MENTA

Barbecued Lamb Chops with Mint Chimichurri

GF

2 racks of lamb, Frenched and cut into chops
1 tbsp olive oil
1 cup mint chimichurri (see page 202)

New Zealand lamb is my favourite lamb, but maybe I'm a bit biased because of my love for this New Zealand icon — even my local New York butcher knows about my passion. He always saves me some fresh chops and calls me when they come in. There is a part of me that only likes to use local meats, but when it comes to lamb, hmmm, that does not apply. When the quality of the meat is good you don't need much, and some mint chimichurri goes perfectly with the chops, taking them to the next level of 'sabor' (savour)!

Prepare: 10 minutes; cook: 15 minutes
Serves: 4–6

Preheat grill or barbecue to high or heat a heavy-bottomed grill pan over a high heat. Generously season lamb with salt and freshly ground black pepper and brush with olive oil. Grill chops on one side until golden brown and slightly charred, 3–4 minutes. Brush with a little mint chimichurri, then turn the chops, brush with more chimichurri and continue grilling to medium done-ness, 2–3 minutes more.

Remove chops to a serving platter, brush with more chimichurri and let them rest for 5 minutes. Serve with remaining mint chimichurri.

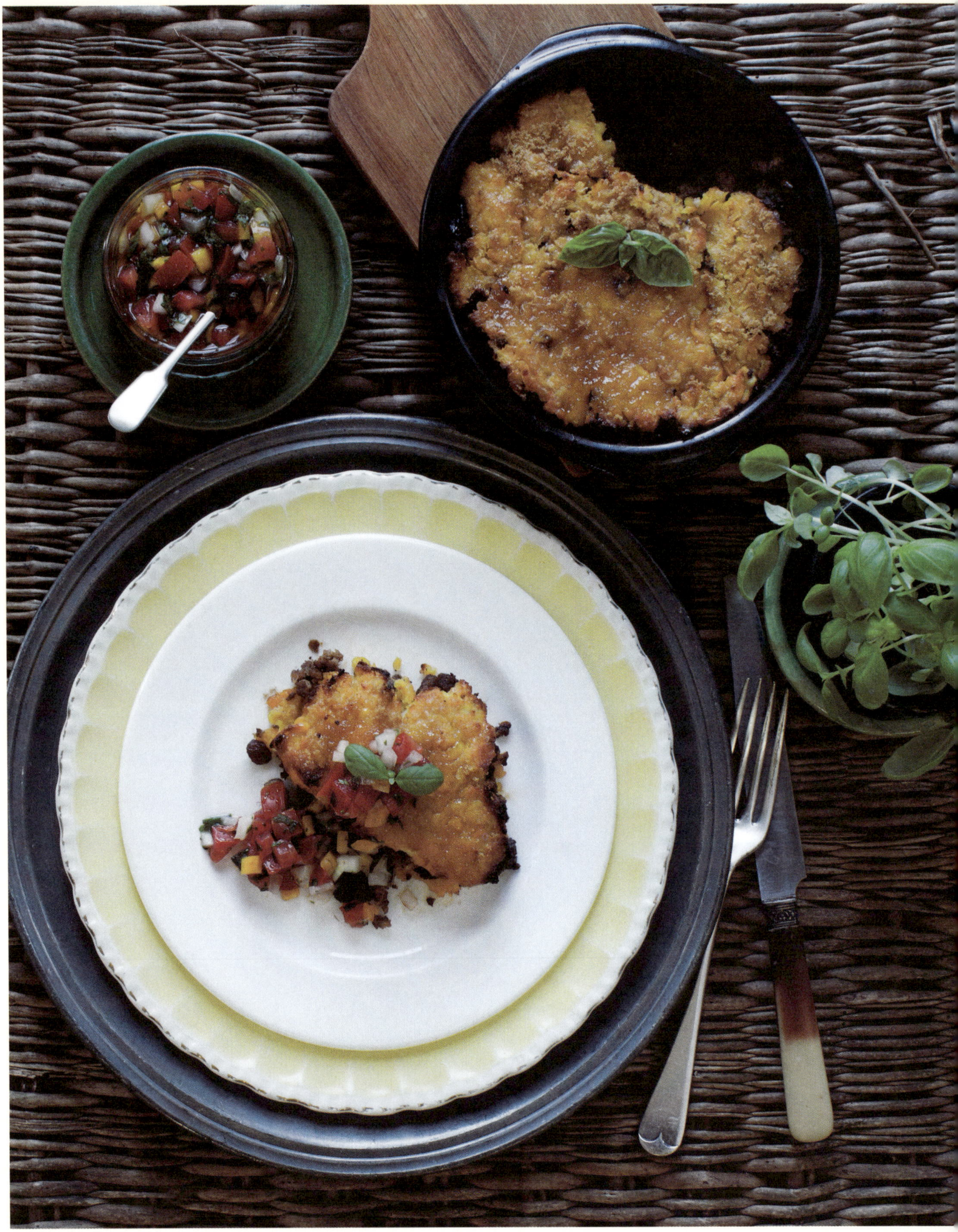

Chile

PASTEL DE CHOCLO CON PEBRE

Corn Pie with Pebre Salsa

a little butter
3 eggs

For the beef
1 tbsp olive oil
1 cup diced onion
2 cloves garlic, peeled and finely chopped
500 g minced beef
1½ tsp paprika
1 tsp cumin
½ tsp dried oregano
3 tbsp raisins
½ cup sliced and pitted Kalamata olives

For the corn
4 cups freshly cut corn kernels (or drained canned corn)
1 cup whole milk
6 basil leaves, roughly chopped
1 tbsp butter
¼ tsp salt
1 tsp raw sugar

For the pebre salsa
1 cup de-seeded and medium-diced tomato
¼ cup finely diced onion
1 tbsp finely diced de-seeded yellow capsicum
¼ cup olive oil
1 tbsp lemon juice
1 tbsp chopped coriander

Variations of this dish are served in the north of Argentina, Bolivia and Peru, while in Mexico they have their own pastel de elote, which is more like a cake and not stuffed. This Chilean version is served in individual portions in a paila (earthenware bowl). My mother, who has now lived in Santiago, the capital, for 10 years, said that what truly made her feel like she belonged was the day she learned to make pastel de choclo con pebre. Pebre is an amazingly versatile sauce, used as a marinade as well as the perfect complement for pastel de choclo, or put on top of bread, stews or grilled meats.

Prepare: 30 minutes; cook: 30 minutes
Serves: 6 as a main course

Preheat the oven to 180°C. Lightly butter six small ovenproof dishes and place them in a baking dish. Set aside.

Fill a small saucepan with enough water to cover the eggs (added later). Bring water to the boil, then lower the temperature to a simmer. Gently place eggs in the water, and let them simmer for 9 minutes. Remove from the heat and cool in a bowl filled with iced water. Peel off the shells and slice into ½ cm rounds. Set aside.

While the eggs are simmering, gently sweat onion in olive oil over a medium heat, until soft and translucent. Add a pinch of salt to release some of the moisture. Reduce the heat to low and add garlic, continuing to cook for 1 minute.

Return the temperature to medium-high, then add beef, paprika, cumin, oregano and salt to taste. Cook until beef is just browned, stirring occasionally. Do not overcook, as it will continue to bake in the oven. Remove from the heat and set aside.

For the corn mixture, place corn, milk and basil in a blender. Pulse until puréed but not completely smooth. In a medium saucepan, combine puréed corn with butter, salt and raw sugar over a medium-low heat. Cook for about 5 minutes, until the corn mixture has thickened slightly. Set aside.

Combine all salsa ingredients in a medium bowl and season to taste with salt and freshly ground black pepper.

To assemble, place 3 tablespoons of corn mixture over the bottom of each dish. Add ¾ cup beef. Sprinkle some raisins and olives over, add 3 slices of hard-boiled egg and top with 4 tablespoons of corn mixture. Sprinkle the tops with raw sugar and transfer to the oven. Bake for 25 minutes, then change the oven to grill setting for 3-4 minutes until the tops are golden brown. Let the dishes sit for 5 minutes before serving with the pebre salsa.

Venezuela

BOLLOS PELONES

Beef-stuffed Corn Buns

GF

500 g minced beef
2 tbsp Worcestershire sauce
2 tbsp olive oil
1 cup diced onion
1 cup diced de-seeded red capsicum
4 cloves garlic, minced
½ tsp ground cumin
2 tbsp tomato paste
1 cup red wine
3 cups canned whole tomato, pulsed in blender
2 sprigs oregano
small bunch parsley stems, tied together with butcher's twine (optional)
¼ cup olives
2 tbsp capers, plus 1 tbsp caper liquid
¼ cup raisins
grated Parmesan, to serve (optional)

For the dough
¼ cup achiote oil (see page 188)
2 cups warm chicken stock or warm water
1 tsp salt
1½ cups pre-cooked white cornmeal (I use Harina P.A.N. brand)

For wrapping
large squares of cheese-cloth or foil

I call bollos pelones the quick fix when you are craving hallacas! Hallacas are the traditional Venezuelan tamales that we only make at Christmas. I think the real reason we only make them once a year is because they are a true labour of love that requires lots of hands, lots of different palates to help you get to the perfect consistency, and hours and hours of work. Here is the recipe for bollos pelones: they are divine, and their smell and taste transports me back to my grandma's kitchen. They still take a bit of time, but you could ask a neighbour, friend or sister to come over and make them together; you won't regret it.

Prepare: 1 hour; cook: 1 hour
Makes: 8–10

Season beef with salt, pepper and half of the Worcestershire sauce. In a heavy-bottomed pan (big enough to brown the meat rather than boiling it), heat olive oil over a medium-high heat. Sweat onions and capsicum until softened then add garlic and cook for 1 minute. Add beef and brown. Use a fork if necessary to break the meat apart. Stir in cumin and tomato paste. Add wine, stirring to scrape up the flavour on the bottom of the pan, and reduce by half, uncovered; about 5 minutes. Add tomato, oregano and parsley stems (if using), and stir in. Add olives, capers and liquid, raisins and the rest of the Worcestershire sauce, and simmer, uncovered, for about 25–30 minutes until reduced by three-quarters. (This can also be made the day before.) Season to taste with salt and freshly ground black pepper, and set aside. While the meat mixture is resting, get ready to assemble (remove the parsley stems before assembling).

Meanwhile, make the dough. In a large mixing bowl, combine achiote oil, warm stock or water and salt. Add in cornmeal while mixing by hand, little by little so it does not form clumps. The dough will form quickly. Set aside to rest for 5 minutes.

To assemble, divide the dough into 8–10 equal portions. Use your hands to make a flat circle of one piece of dough, about 1 cm thick. Using one hand to gently hold the dough in a cup shape, use a slotted spoon to place about 2–3 tablespoons of beef mix in the centre of the dough circle. Then use both hands to bring the dough edges towards the centre, pressing together to fully enclose the beef.

Place each bollo in the centre of a piece of cheese-cloth or foil. Bring all the edges together, twist and tie at the top with butcher's twine.

To cook, fill a large stockpot with water and bring to the boil. Drop in the wrapped bollos and simmer for about 20–30 minutes, until they float. Remove with tongs and set aside to cool for 5 minutes before serving. To serve, unwrap bollos and serve with extra beef mixture on the side and on top, plus Parmesan if wished.

Chef's note: Cubans call this meat mixture a picadillo — they use green capsicum instead of red and they leave out the capers. This is a very versatile recipe that can be eaten with white rice and a side of fried ripe plantains, or used as a filling for empanadas, arepas, pastries, tamales, fritters or stuffed potatoes. Bollos can be frozen: simply thaw to room temperature and then heat in boiling water for 15–20 minutes.

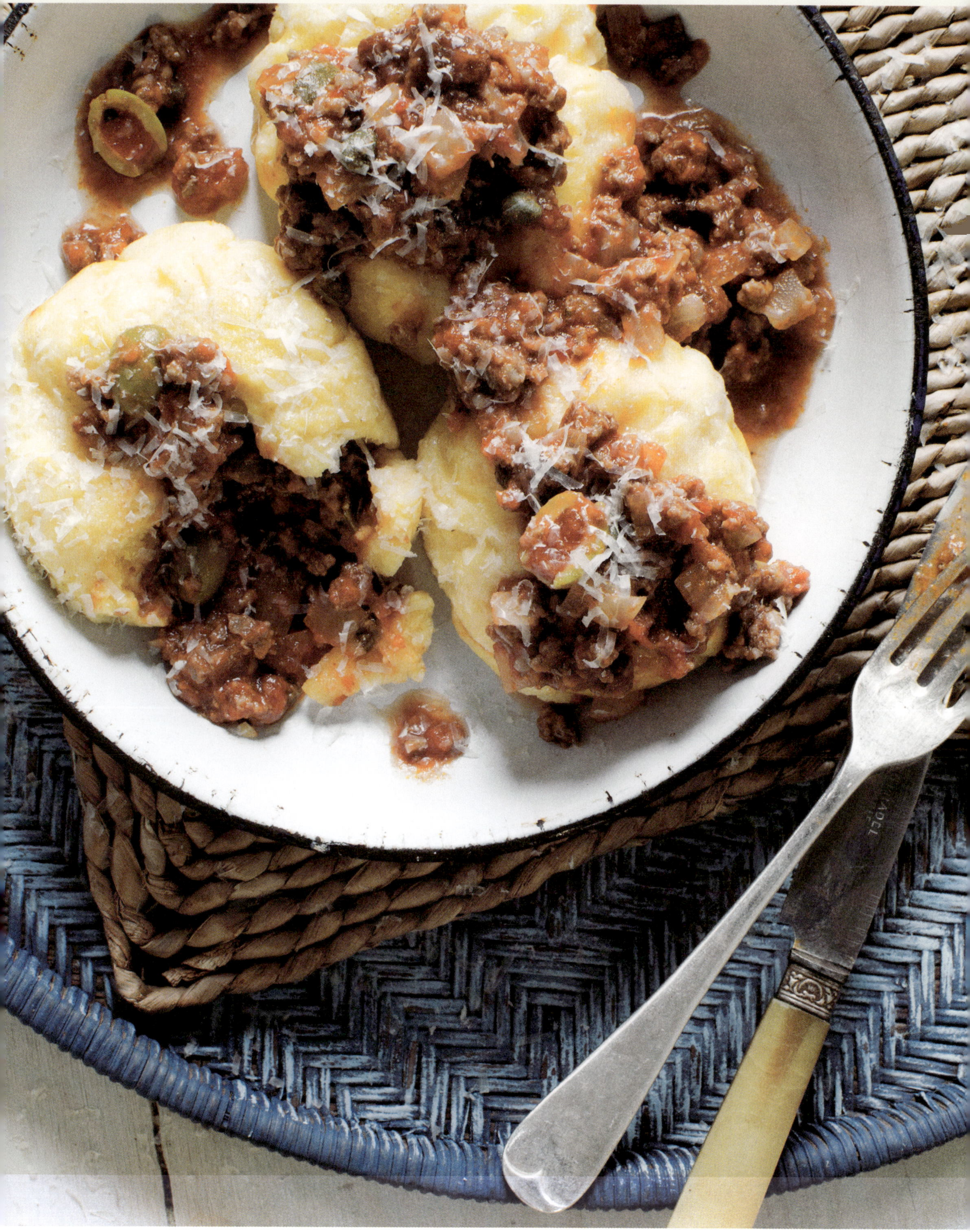

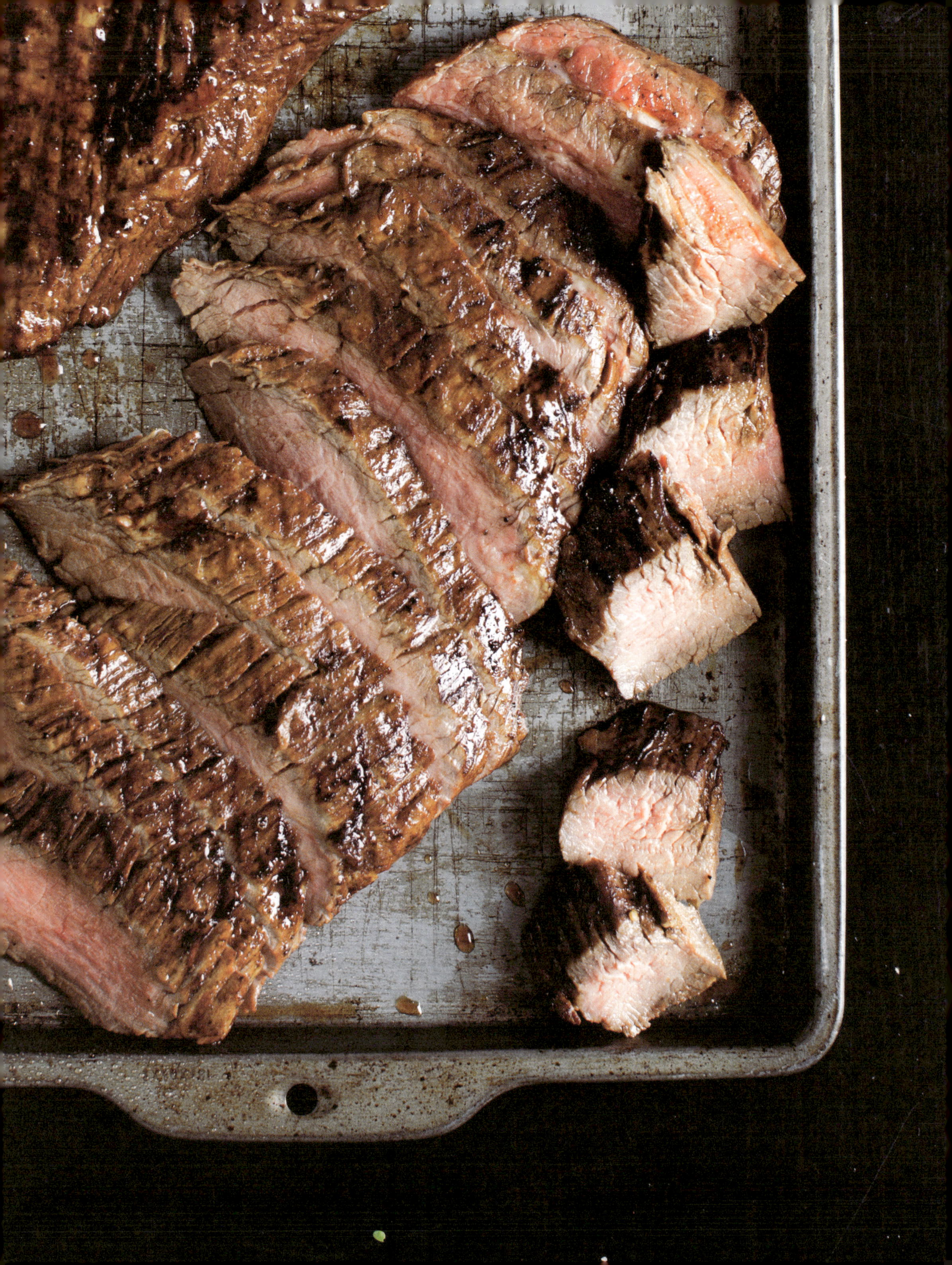

Mexico

ARRACHERA

Beer-marinated Skirt Steak

GF

For the marinade
¼ cup soy sauce
¼ cup vegetable oil, plus more for searing
1 Sol beer (Mexican beer)
2 tbsp Worcestershire sauce
1 onion, roughly chopped
2 cloves garlic, smashed
1 tsp freshly ground black pepper
¼ tsp ground cumin
¼ tsp dried oregano
¼ tsp cayenne pepper
juice of 1 lime

1 kg skirt steak

Arrachera is the name given in Mexico to this cut of beef — skirt steak. It's not to be confused with flank, which is the cut of meat used for the shredded beef on page 105, although in many recipes they can be used interchangeably. Skirt is a long, thin cut of meat with well-defined, open fibres which comes from the diaphragm muscle of the cow, and it's covered with a tough membrane that needs to be removed before cooking. Latinos love skirt and flank steak — they are such inexpensive but flavourful cuts of meat. I think a good marinade helps to tenderise the meat, and this one is bang on perfection! Marinade some skirt steak and then flash the meat on the barbecue; never cook it more than medium rare, it's a crime. You can also use this beef in a quesadilla (see page 139).

Prepare: 15 minutes; marinate: 1 hour to overnight; cook: 15 minutes; rest: 15 minutes
Serves: 4–6

Combine all the marinade ingredients, and pour the marinade over the meat. Cover with plastic wrap and place in the refrigerator for a minimum of 1 hour or a maximum of 12 hours.

Remove steak from marinade. Preheat a heavy-bottomed grill pan or barbecue to medium-high. Brush grill with oil and cook steak for approximately 3 minutes on each side (or to your liking). Remove from heat and let rest for 15 minutes before slicing steak into strips 2 cm thick, against the grain.

Peru

LOMO SALTADO

Beef Stir-fry Peruvian-style

GF

For the marinade
½ cup red wine
¼ cup soy sauce
½ tsp ground cumin
4 cloves garlic, smashed
pinch of freshly ground
    black pepper
2 tbsp water

1 kg skirt or flank steak
3 medium Agria potatoes, peeled
¼ cup duck fat, warmed through
    until just liquefied
2 tbsp rice bran oil
1 large red onion, sliced 1 cm thick
4 tomatoes, de-seeded and
    cut into 8 wedges
perfect white rice (page 144)
    to serve
chopped coriander, to
    garnish (optional)

Along with ceviche, this dish is an ultimate favourite of Peruvians. It is a clear example of the fusion of cultures. Chinese immigrants came to Peru in search of work, and brought with them an abundance of techniques that have since become infused with traditional Peruvian ingredients. Lomo saltado involves stir-fried beef, onions and tomatoes, served over white rice with fries on top. For the fries I use the duck fat I save from cooking the duck breast on page 54. This is a hearty, feel-good dish. If you feel it has too many carbs, just leave some of them out. The marinade is bang on, and the balance and combination of flavours go perfectly together: the crunch of the red onion, the acidity of the tomato and the tasty and tender meat.

Prepare: 20 minutes; marinate: 2 hours; cook: 30 minutes
Serves: 4

Combine marinade ingredients in a non-metallic bowl or re-sealable plastic bag. Cut steak into strips, about 5 cm by 2 cm, and add to marinade. Let sit in the refrigerator for up to 2 hours. Drain excess marinade from steak, reserving for later use.

Preheat oven to 190°C. Cut potatoes into 6–8 pieces lengthwise, to make steak fries. Toss in duck fat and season with salt and freshly ground black pepper. Place potato on a baking tray lined with non-stick baking paper, and roast in oven for about 25 minutes until golden brown and crispy.

Meanwhile, in a large frying pan, heat oil over a high heat and sear steak strips in three or four small batches so that the meat does not steam. Set aside.

To the same pan, add the reserved marinade and gently cook the onion until soft; about 3 minutes. Add the tomato for 1 minute, just until combined, then remove from the heat.

Serve steak over perfect white rice, garnish with onion and tomato and top with potato fries. Sprinkle with coriander, if using.

Chef's note: If using eye fillet or another cut of meat that has less tough meat fibres than skirt or flank, marinate for less time; about ½ hour. The meat is traditionally cooked in a wok, but for this home-made version a cast-iron or heavy-bottomed pan works well. Make sure that the pan is very hot before adding the meat and remember to sear it in small batches.

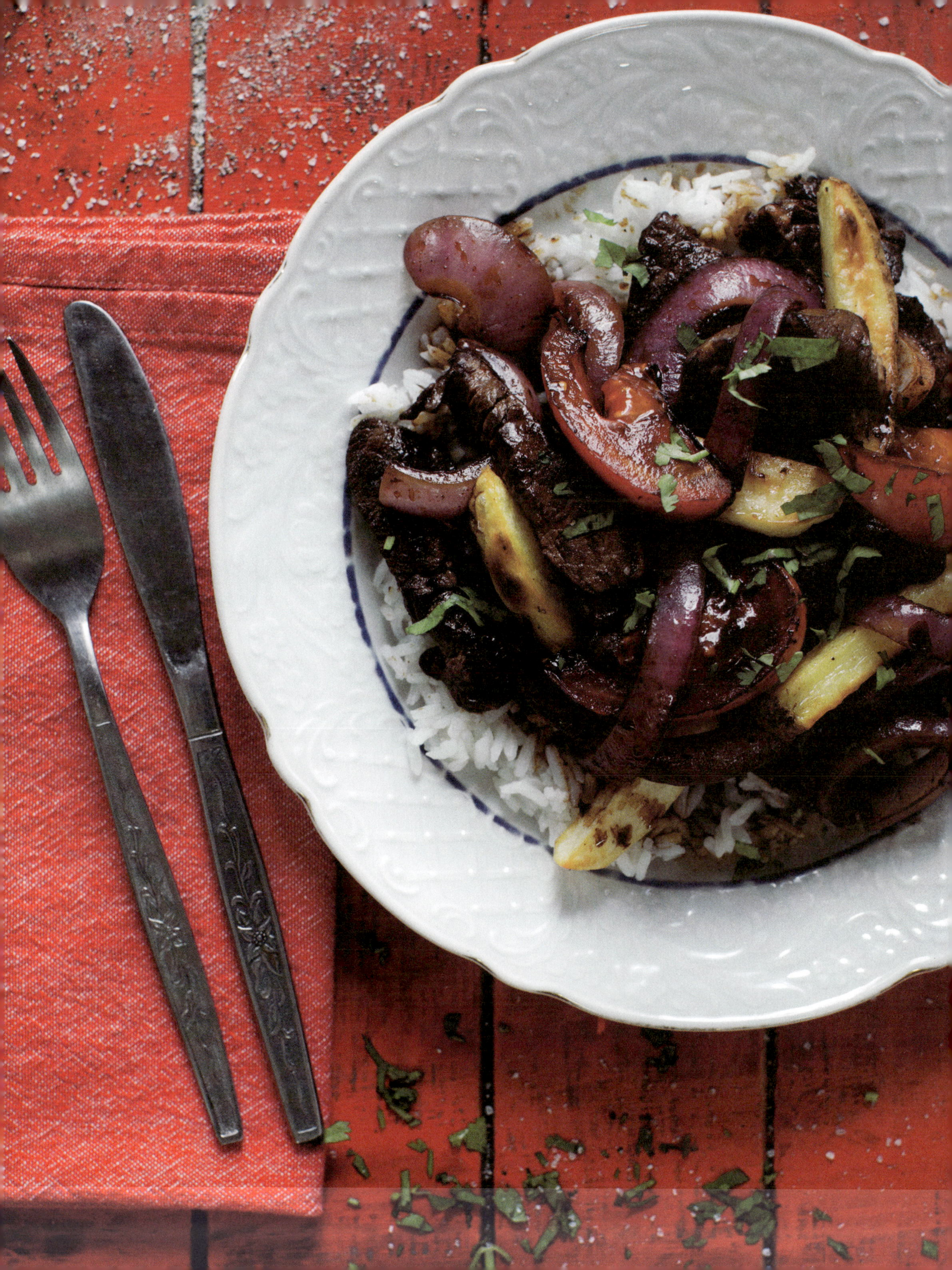

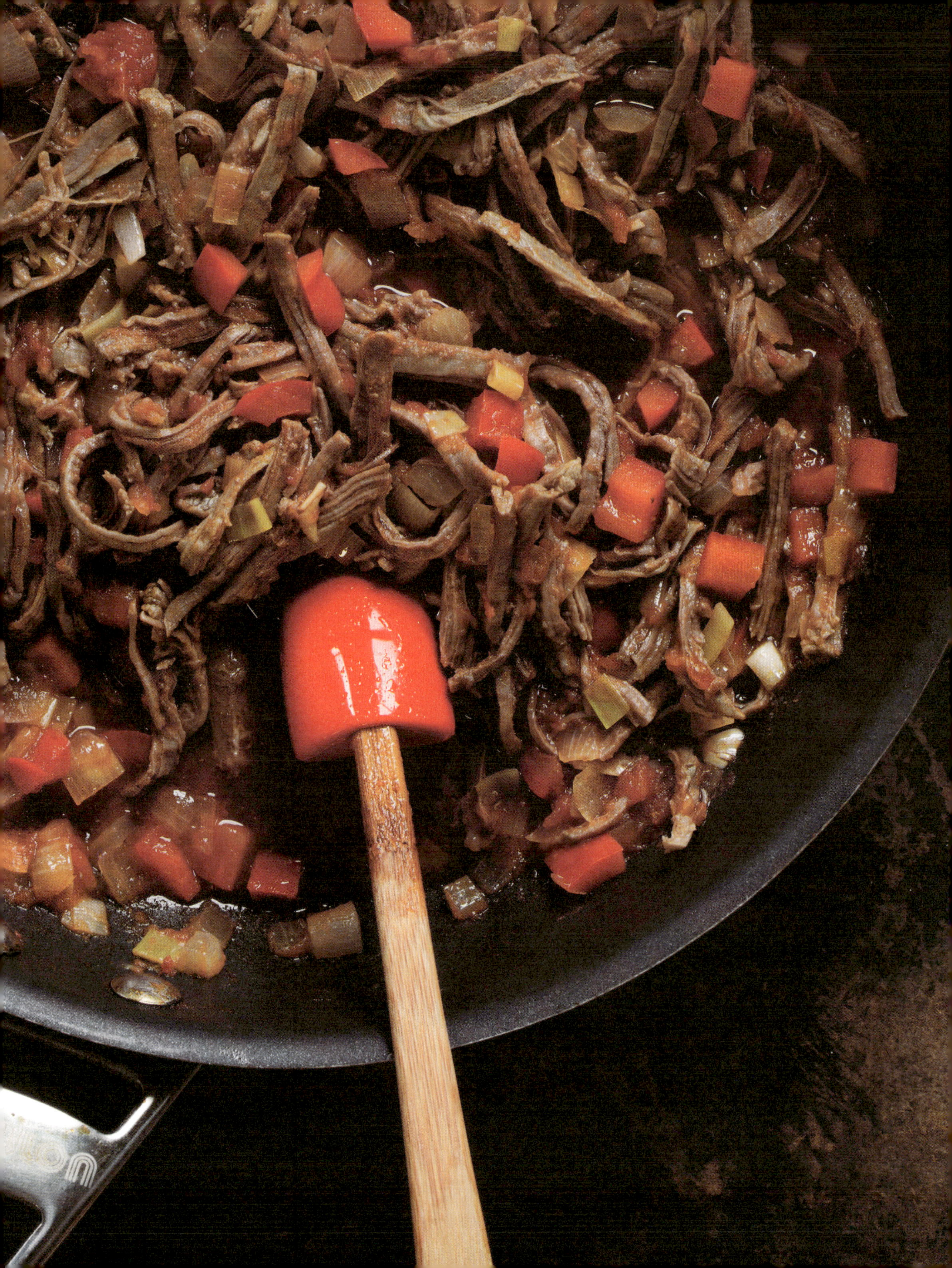

Venezuela

CARNE MECHADA

Shredded Beef in Tomato Sofrito

GF

1 kg flank steak

For poaching
1 onion, peeled and quartered
2 cloves garlic, smashed
5 black peppercorns
2 bay leaves

For the sofrito
2 cups diced onion
1 leek, white part only, chopped
1 cup diced de-seeded red capsicum
¼ cup olive oil
2 cloves garlic, peeled and minced
2 cups peeled and chopped tomatoes, pulsed in the blender (you can use canned Italian plum tomatoes)
approx. 1 cup poaching liquid (see above)
2 tbsp tomato sauce or shaved panela (unrefined cane sugar)
ground cumin to taste
1 tbsp Worcestershire sauce

La carne mechada is part of Venezuela's national dish, pabellón, which consists of this shredded beef plus white rice, black beans and fried ripe plantains. In my family home, pabellón was eaten at least once a week, and this is one of my abuelito's (grandpa's) classics. I remember getting up to go to school and he would be at the kitchen table shredding the meat at 7 a.m. He would say 'Mientras mas repose mejor' — 'The longer it rests, the better' — and it's true. It's best to leave it resting in the sauce for a couple of hours before serving, that way you allow all the flavours to get to know each other, bond and sing.

Prepare: 30 minutes; cook: 2½ hours; rest: ½–2 hours
Serves: 6

Cut flank steak once lengthways and once across. In a large stockpot, combine steak with onion, garlic, peppercorns and bay leaves. Add enough cold water to cover the ingredients by 10 cm, and bring to the boil. Simmer over a moderate heat for at least 2 hours, or until meat is easy to pull apart. Remove meat from liquid and set aside to cool. Strain liquid and reserve it to make soups, sauces or black beans (see page 15).

While your beef is cooking, heat a large frying pan over a medium heat. Sweat onion, leek and capsicum in oil until soft, add garlic and sweat for about 2 more minutes. Add tomato and bring to a simmer for about 15 minutes, adding ¼ cup of the beef poaching liquid if the sauce is getting too dry.

Pull or shred beef into long thin pieces and transfer to a bowl. Fold shredded meat into sofrito along with ½ cup of poaching liquid. If you feel the sauce is too dry, add more poaching liquid until you get the desired consistency. Add tomato sauce or panela, cumin, Worcestershire sauce, and salt and freshly ground black pepper to taste. Allow the stew to rest for at least 30 minutes, then reheat and serve.

Chef's note: This dish freezes very well, so I encourage making a large batch and freezing what you don't eat on the day. Or save it for the next day to stuff arepas (see page 119) or for stuffing a tortilla to make a taco — just add some shredded lettuce, crema agria (see page 211), coriander and hot sauce.

Venezuela

ASADO NEGRO

Panela-braised Beef Eye of Round

GF

To marinate
1 kg beef eye of round, completely trimmed of outer fat
2 tbsp dark soy sauce
1 tbsp Worcestershire sauce
4 cloves garlic, smashed

To braise
2 tbsp neutral-tasting oil, e.g. rice bran oil
120 g shaved panela (unrefined cane sugar)
1 cup red wine
1 leek, white parts only, chopped (about 1 cup)
3 stalks celery, roughly chopped
1 medium onion, peeled and roughly chopped
1 tbsp tomato paste
½ cup orange juice
½ cup water
1 tbsp soy sauce
1–2 sprigs oregano
½ tsp ground cumin

Yes, this dish takes a bit of time, but I guarantee it is worth it! It is the perfect dish to make during the winter — even though in Venezuela it could be 40-plus outside we'll still eat asado negro! It's also one you can prep the day before a dinner party, because it will taste better the next day, and it also freezes well. I went to a lot of trouble to try to get this recipe right. My family in Caracas all agree that my auntie Gladys makes it the best. So I tried going after the secret recipe, but no luck! I also tried my auntie Solange's version (she lives in Miami), but because her measurements were a bit vague I wasn't happy with it. Then, in Spain visiting my in-laws, I went to this adorable Venezuelan restaurant called La Cuchara. I loved their asado negro, so I asked chef Leo to teach me how to make it. He is a real sweetheart and took the time to teach me; here is a blend of his version and mine.

Prepare: 30 minutes; cook: 4 hours
Serves: 6–8

Marinate beef with soy, Worcestershire sauce, garlic, salt and freshly ground black pepper, while preparing the other ingredients. For this dish, it is particularly important to have all the ingredients measured and ready, so that the caramel you make later does not burn.

In a heavy-bottomed saucepan or Dutch oven, heat oil until very hot, just below smoking point. Carefully sear all sides of the beef, including the ends; about 1 minute on each side. Then add half the shaved panela and continue to sear the meat, turning and coating the meat with caramel, for about 5 minutes. Be careful not to let the caramel burn, or it will turn bitter and separate. If you think it is about to burn, or is ready, add wine and deglaze the pan (stir to bring in all the caramel off the pan). Reduce liquid by half. Add vegetables and gently cook for about 5 minutes, then add tomato paste and liquids, oregano, cumin and the rest of the panela. Add reserved beef marinade, bring to a boil and simmer, covered, for 4 hours.

Remove beef and set aside to rest and cool. Blend braising liquid in a food processor until smooth. Adjust seasoning, if desired, then return sauce to pan.

Don't attempt to cut your asado until it's completely cooled because it will fall apart (unless you want that type of shredded beef consistency). Using a serrated knife also helps, but my suggestion is to slice the beef into 1.5 cm rounds, then put them back in the sauce and reheat gently before serving.

Chef's note: After searing the meat on the stovetop, you can also braise it in the oven at 150°C for 4 hours.

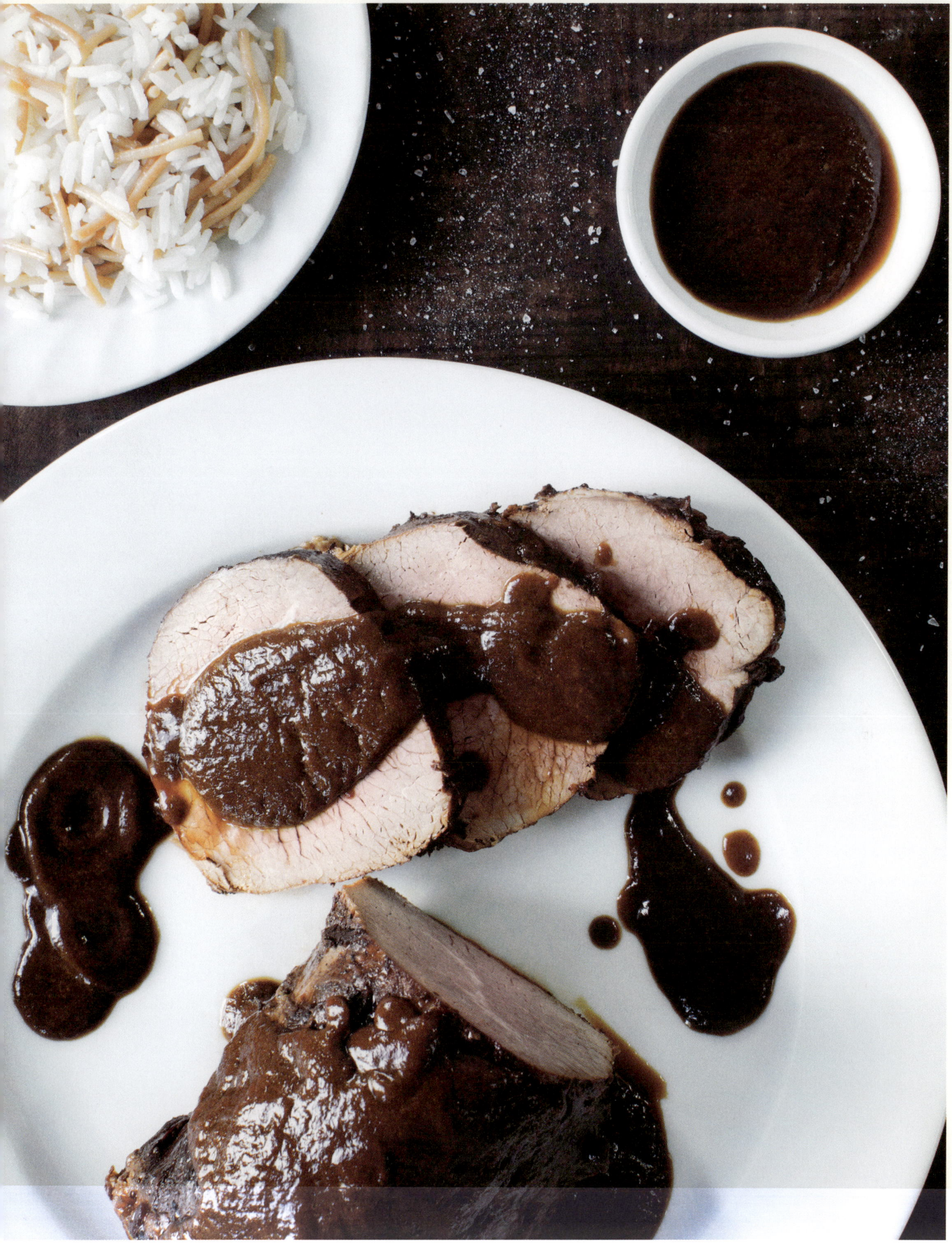

LA PREFERIDA

POLLERIA TOÑO
PIERNA Y MUSLO
$19.01/kg
Fresco

Sandwich | Burrito | Torta Cubana | Taquitos y Canapés | Hamburguesa

PARA RELLENAR

DISHES WITH FILLINGS

Por amor a Guanajuato
Mariscos
Coca-Cola
mariscos
MARY
MARY

TORTILLAS DE HARINA
Flour Tortillas

TORTILLAS DE MAÍZ
Corn Tortillas

AREPAS

CHIPAS

CACHAPAS
Corn Pancakes Stuffed with Buffalo Mozzarella

EMPANADAS

PUPUSAS CON CURTIDO
Cheese-filled Corn Pupusas with Curtido Slaw

LLAPINGACHOS
Kumara & Cheese Patties with Peanut Sauce

SANDWICH CUBANO
Cuban Sandwich

MANDOCAS
Anise, Panela & Cheese Fritters

TAMALES
Steamed Corn Parcels

QUESADILLAS DE ARRACHERA
Skirt Steak Quesadillas

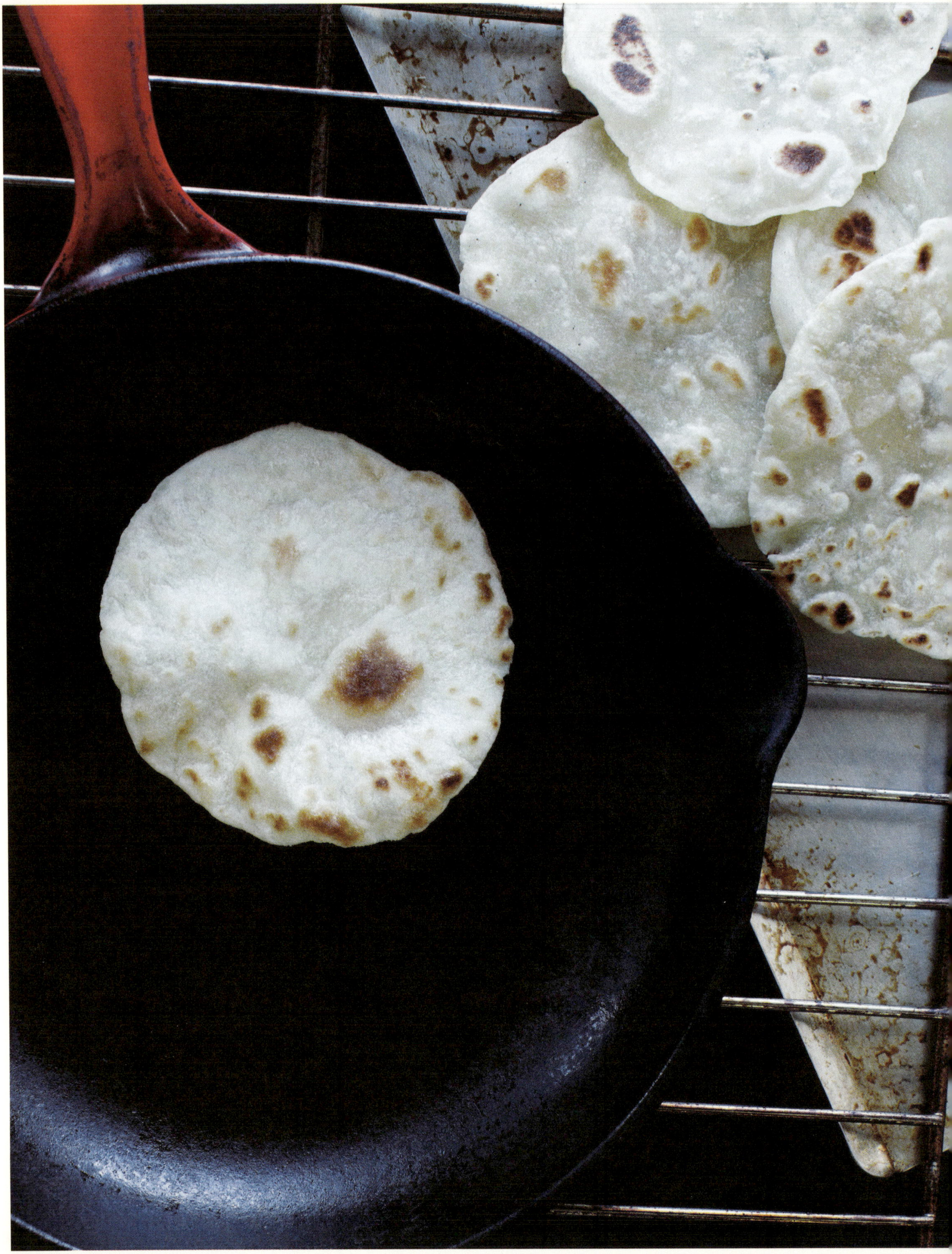

Mexico

TORTILLAS DE HARINA

Flour Tortillas

225 g plain flour, plus more for dusting
1 tsp salt
⅓ cup soft lard, cut into small chunks
½ cup cool water

After making these, I usually get a belly-ache from eating too many! I can't stop myself: home-made tortillas are always, always better than bought. Get your hands dirty, make an event out of it, get the children involved and try these beauties — they're totally worth it! With these tortillas, lard is the way to go. The tortillas are more elastic, way tastier and more traditional. And if you divide the amount of lard used by the amount you get, it's hardly anything. For those of you who can't tolerate gluten, corn tortillas (see page 115) are just perfect.

Prepare: 10 minutes; rest: 30 minutes; cook: 30 minutes
Makes: 16

Combine flour and salt in a large bowl. Add lard to flour mixture and combine with your fingertips until it looks like coarse crumbs. Add water in a steady stream, continuing to mix with your hands until a ball of dough begins to form; approximately 1 minute.

Dust a clean, flat work surface with flour. Knead dough for about 5 minutes, until well incorporated and less sticky. Wrap dough in plastic wrap and let it rest at room temperature for 30 minutes.

Divide dough into 16 even pieces and shape them into round balls. Cover with a damp tea towel. Using a rolling pin, roll each ball between two pieces of non-stick baking paper into 10 cm rounds. You can also use a tortilla press (see page 279). Keep the other dough balls covered with the damp tea towel while you work. Start by cooking the first ones you rolled or pressed, as that way you will let the gluten rest a bit before cooking.

In a large heavy-bottomed or cast-iron frying pan or a flat grill over a medium-high heat, cook two tortillas at a time (or as many as will fit) until light golden; about 2 minutes on each side. Repeat with the remaining tortillas. Store in an airtight container at room temperature for up to 2 hours. To reheat, microwave for 1 minute in a container with the lid on or wrap in foil and warm in the oven at 100°C for 10 minutes.

TISA
MAR
ESTRELLA

TISA
MAR
ESTRELLA

TISA
MAR
ESTRELLA

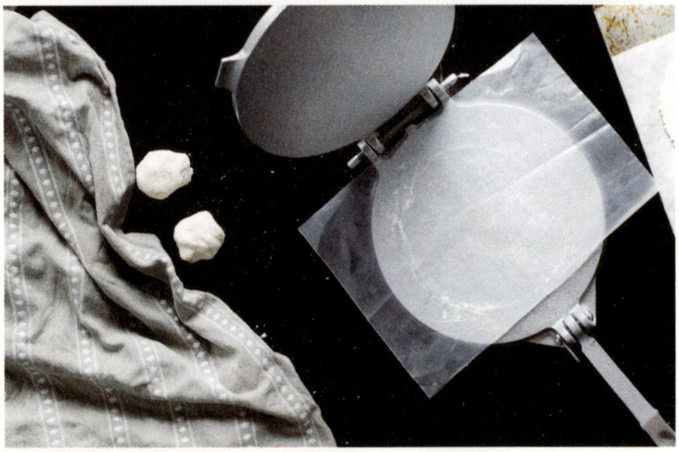

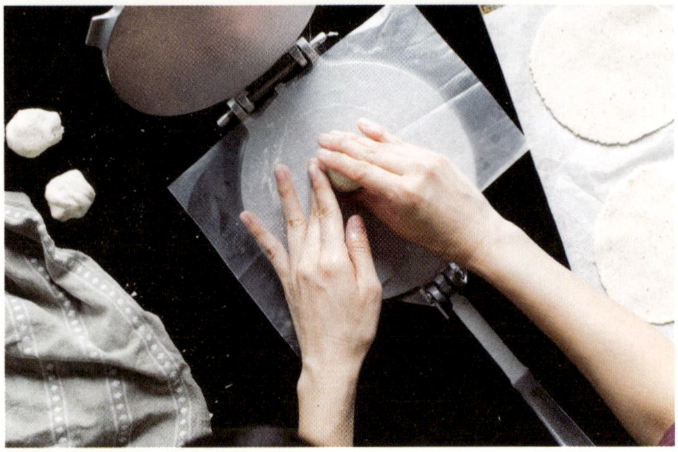

MATIC
TISA

Mexico

TORTILLAS DE MAÍZ

Corn Tortillas

GF

1¼ cups warm water
¼ tbsp salt
2 cups instant corn masa flour
(Maseca or Tío Pablo brand)

People often ask what's more traditional — flour or corn tortillas? It's obviously corn, because this is a native ingredient to Mexico and they were making corn tortillas well before flour came into play. But there is nothing wrong with loving flour tortillas (see page 113) and using them to make your favourite tacos. Note that the corn ones are gluten free. Even though you can now find great corn tortillas in the supermarket, I invite you to make your own, just for the fun of it. Just three ingredients create magic: corn flour, water and salt. Hardly any kneading or resting is required. It is important, though, to use the right kind of corn flour (see page 278), and it's best to have a tortilla press (see page 279).

Prepare: 15 minutes; cook: 20 minutes
Makes: 16

Place the warm water and salt in a large bowl, and slowly start mixing in and kneading the masa flour until it is all incorporated and a smooth dough is formed which doesn't stick to your hands. If the dough feels dry, add some teaspoons of water, one by one. Once dough is ready, cover with a damp tea towel so it does not dry out.

Divide dough into 16 equal portions and form into little balls. Leave them in the bowl with the damp tea towel over as you work with each one. Line the tortilla press top and bottom with non-stick baking paper (or a heavy-duty sealable bag), cut into two equal pieces that are slightly larger than the diameter of the press plates. If you don't have a tortilla press, use two small chopping boards, lined similarly.

Preheat a heavy-bottomed frying pan or griddle to medium-high. Flatten each ball of dough into a tortilla. Cook on the hot griddle for 1–2 minutes on each side, or until the tortilla fills with air and gets golden brown spots; don't burn it. Put each cooked tortilla into an airtight container in which you can keep them warm; the steam helps them stay soft and elastic.

If making the tortillas in advance, let them cool and store in the fridge in an airtight container. When ready to serve, microwave for 1 minute in a container with the lid on or wrap in foil and warm in the oven at 100°C for 10–20 minutes.

Chef's note: Tortillas can be filled with anything, but as a little girl my mom used to stuff them with the simplest things: cheese, or just a bit of salted butter on a warm tortilla. They were the best!

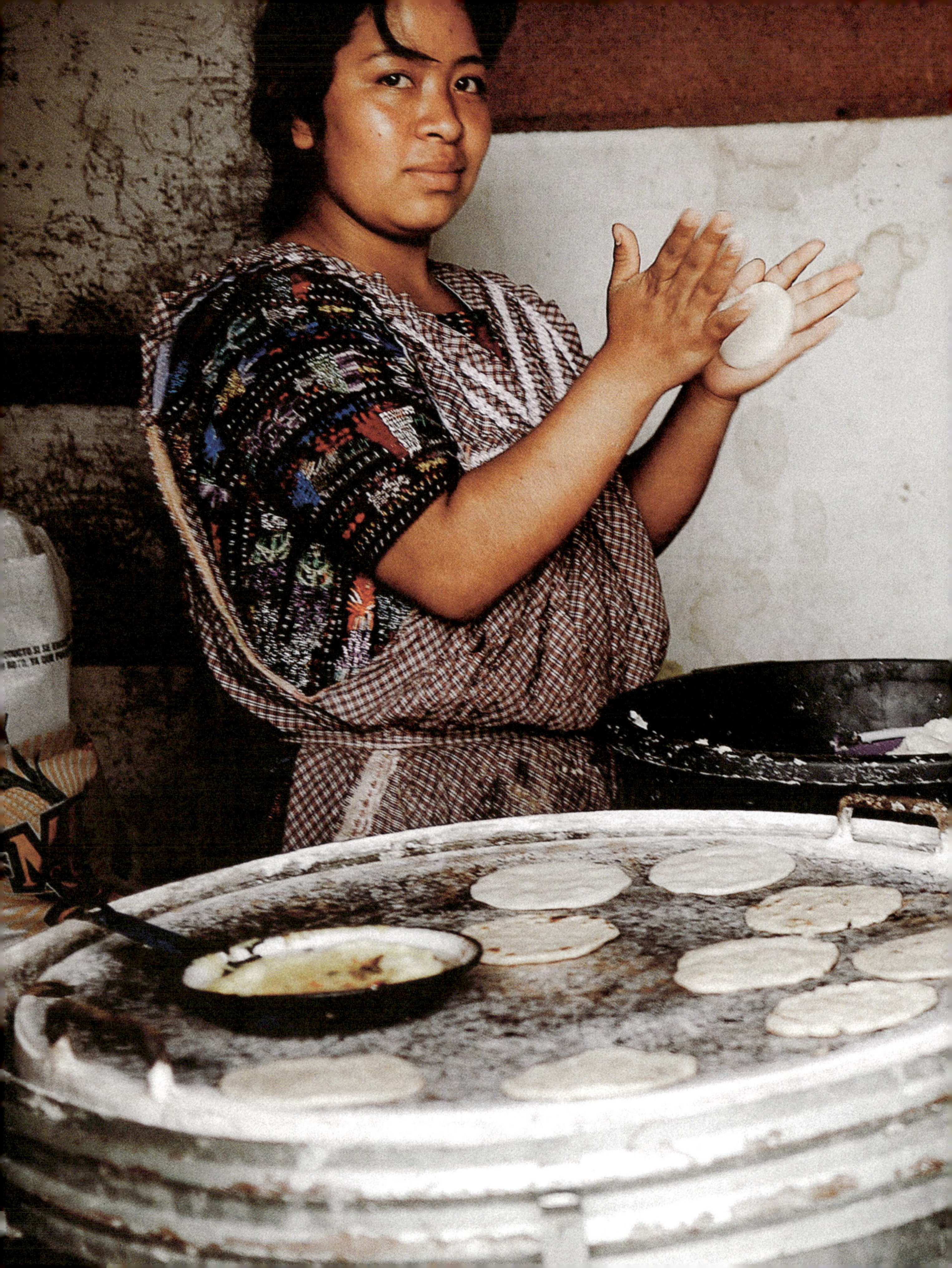

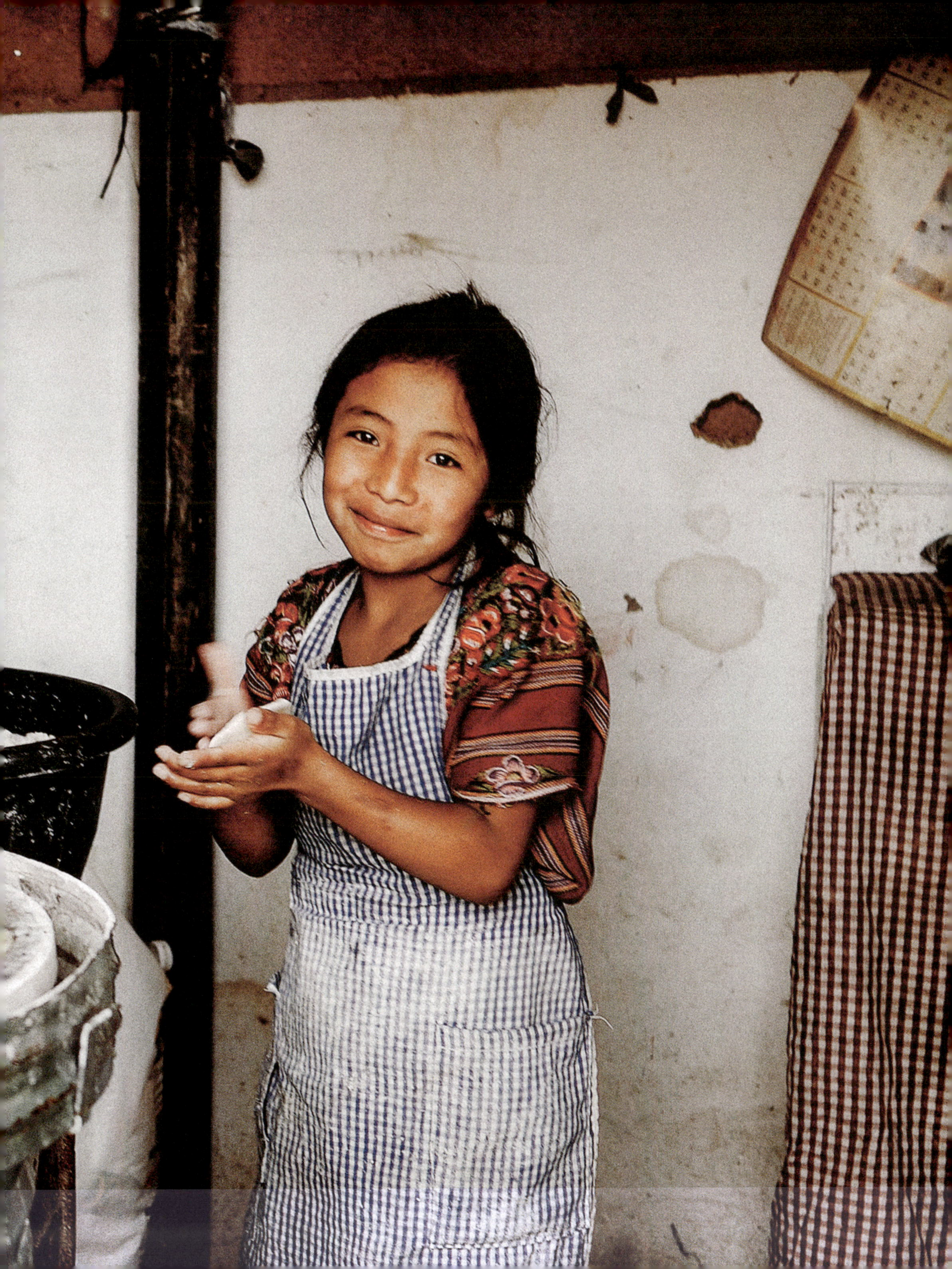

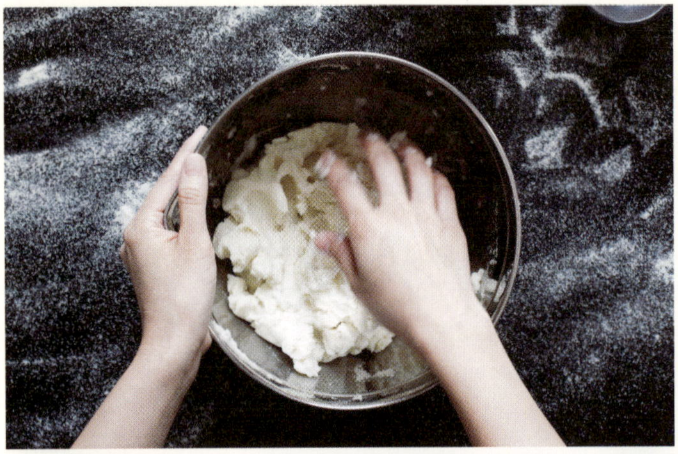
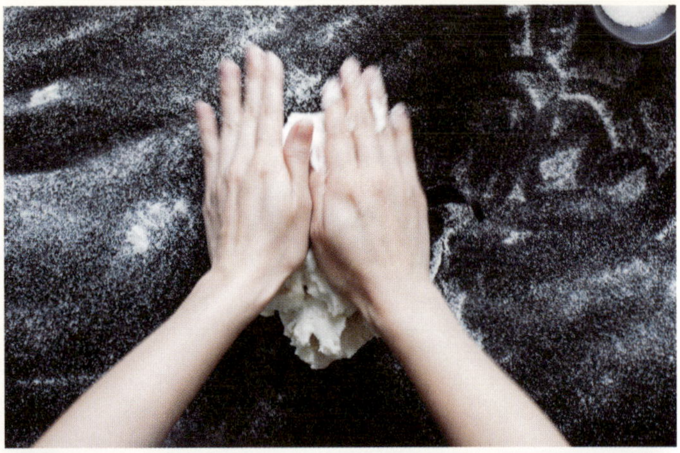
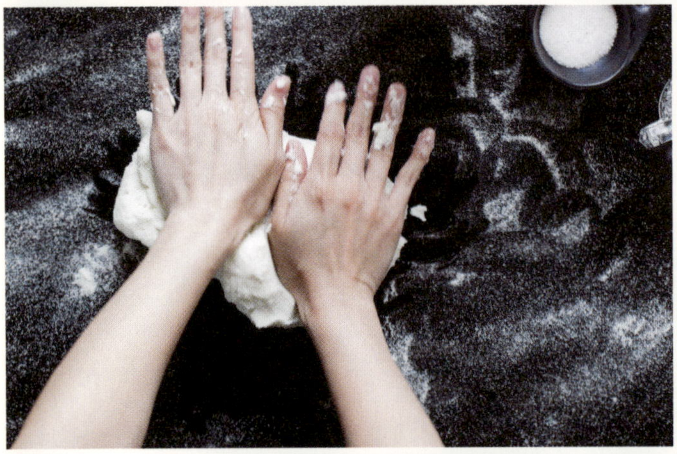
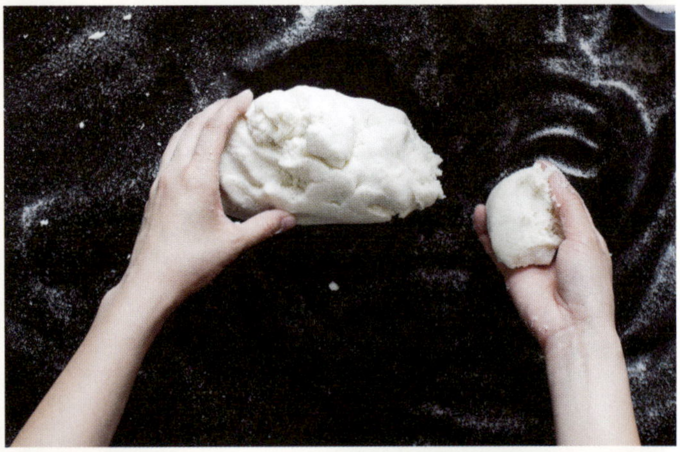
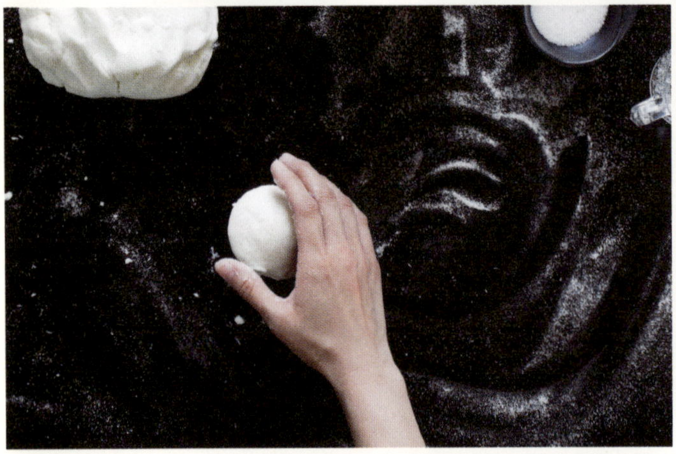
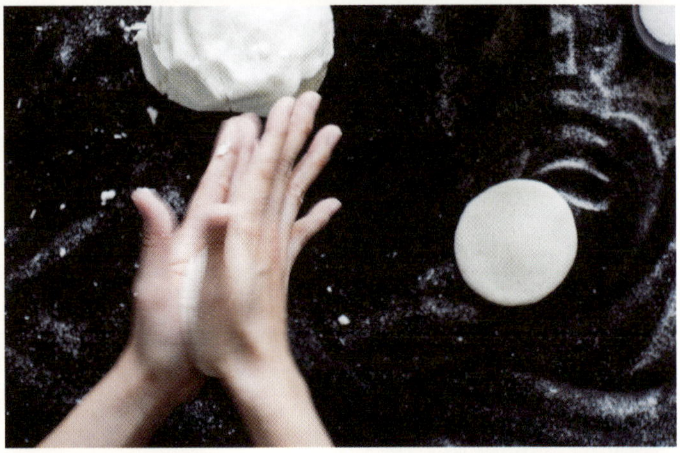
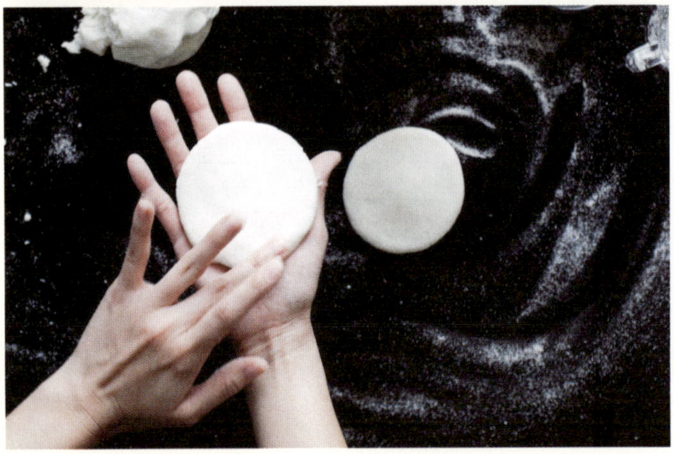
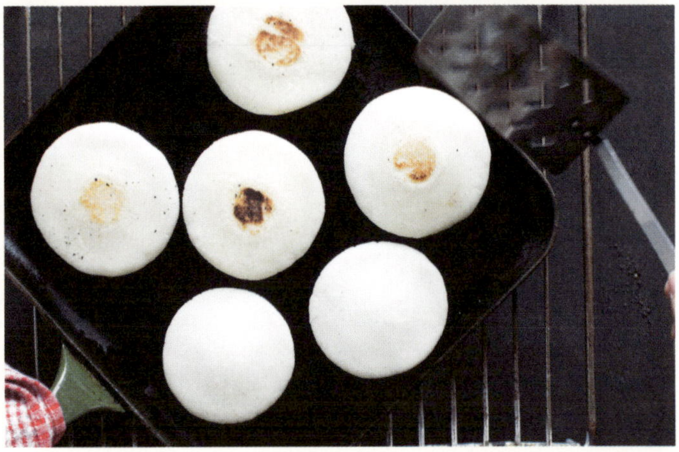

Venezuela

AREPAS

GF

2½ cups lukewarm water
1 tsp salt
2 cups pre-cooked white cornmeal
(I use Harina P.A.N brand)
1 tbsp vegetable, canola or rice bran oil for brushing the pan

Venezuelans and Colombians eat arepas as their everyday bread, much as Mexicans and Central Americans eat tortillas and Salvadorians eat pupusas. Arepas are magical little pockets of deliciousness, made from a special white cornmeal, and are slightly crispy on the outside and soft and hollow-y on the inside. They are often grilled, but can also be baked, boiled or fried. You can stuff them with whatever you like. Among the more popular arepa stuffings in Venezuela are la peluda (shredded beef and shredded yellow cheese), la reina pepiada (chicken avocado salad; see page 44) and jamón y queso (ham and cheese).

Prepare: 10 minutes; cook: 20 minutes
Makes: 8 medium-sized arepas

Preheat oven to 180°C.
    Pour warm water into a large bowl, add salt and mix.
    Slowly start adding and mixing the cornmeal with your hands, until the mixture comes together and is smooth and without lumps. Once combined, let the dough rest for about 5 minutes (no need to cover it).
    Meanwhile, heat a heavy-bottomed frying pan or flat grill plate over a medium-high heat and brush with oil.
    Knead dough again until smooth, about 3 minutes, until it doesn't stick to the bowl or your fingers. If it's too dry, add ½ tablespoon of water at a time as you knead. Divide dough into eight even-sized balls and form each ball into a flat, round disc of even thickness. They should be about 10 cm in diameter and 2 cm thick.
    On the stovetop, grill batches of arepas, as many as will fit into your pan, for about 3 minutes on each side or until they form a golden-brown crust. Place arepas on a baking tray lined with non-stick baking paper, and place in oven for about 7–10 minutes, or until arepas sound hollow when lightly tapped. You can also put the arepas directly onto the oven shelf.
    To stuff arepas, split them open like a pita bread, not all the way through but just enough to get some of the hot, soft insides out. True arepa eaters put the insides on the side of the plate, mix them with butter and/or cheese and eat them separately.

Paraguay

CHIPAS

GF

250 g tapioca flour, plus extra for dusting
2 tsp salt
2 tsp anise seeds, crushed
2 eggs
75 g lard, softened
1 tbsp grated Parmesan
150 g shredded mozzarella or Italian fontina
¼ cup milk

'Chipas... chipas... chipas' — that's what you'll hear throughout the streets of Paraguay or at sporting events. Vendors carry large baskets containing bags of these treats. There are different types — they vary in size and shape and some may have added spices like anise or fillings like chicharrón (crumbled crispy pork skin). But in my opinion, the best chipas are home-made and baked in tatakuas, igloo-shaped wood-fired clay ovens similar to pizza ovens. Because of the tapioca flour, lard and cheese, the texture is slightly dense and cheesy on the inside but a bit crispy on the outside. The cheese Paraguayans use is their 'queso Paraguay', which can only be found there. It's similar to an Italian fontina, but I find that a combination of mozzarella and Parmesan works nicely.

Prepare: 25 minutes; rest: 30 minutes; cook: 15 minutes
Makes: 20

Preheat oven to 200°C.

Combine flour, salt and anise seeds. Set aside. Beat together eggs, lard, cheeses and milk. Add in flour mixture. Mix until a rough dough begins to form. Turn dough out onto a lightly floured surface and knead for about 5 minutes, pushing the dough down and over on itself. Transfer back to the bowl and cover with plastic wrap. Let it rest for 30 minutes in the refrigerator.

Line a baking tray with non-stick baking paper or a silicone mat. Measure out 35 g dough balls, or make rounds from a heaped tablespoonful. Make a small hole in the centre of each dough ball, and place 5 cm apart on the baking tray. Bake for 12-15 minutes, until golden brown.

Chipas can be stored in an airtight container for up to 3 days. To reheat, use a toaster or the oven at 120°C, heating until warm to the touch.

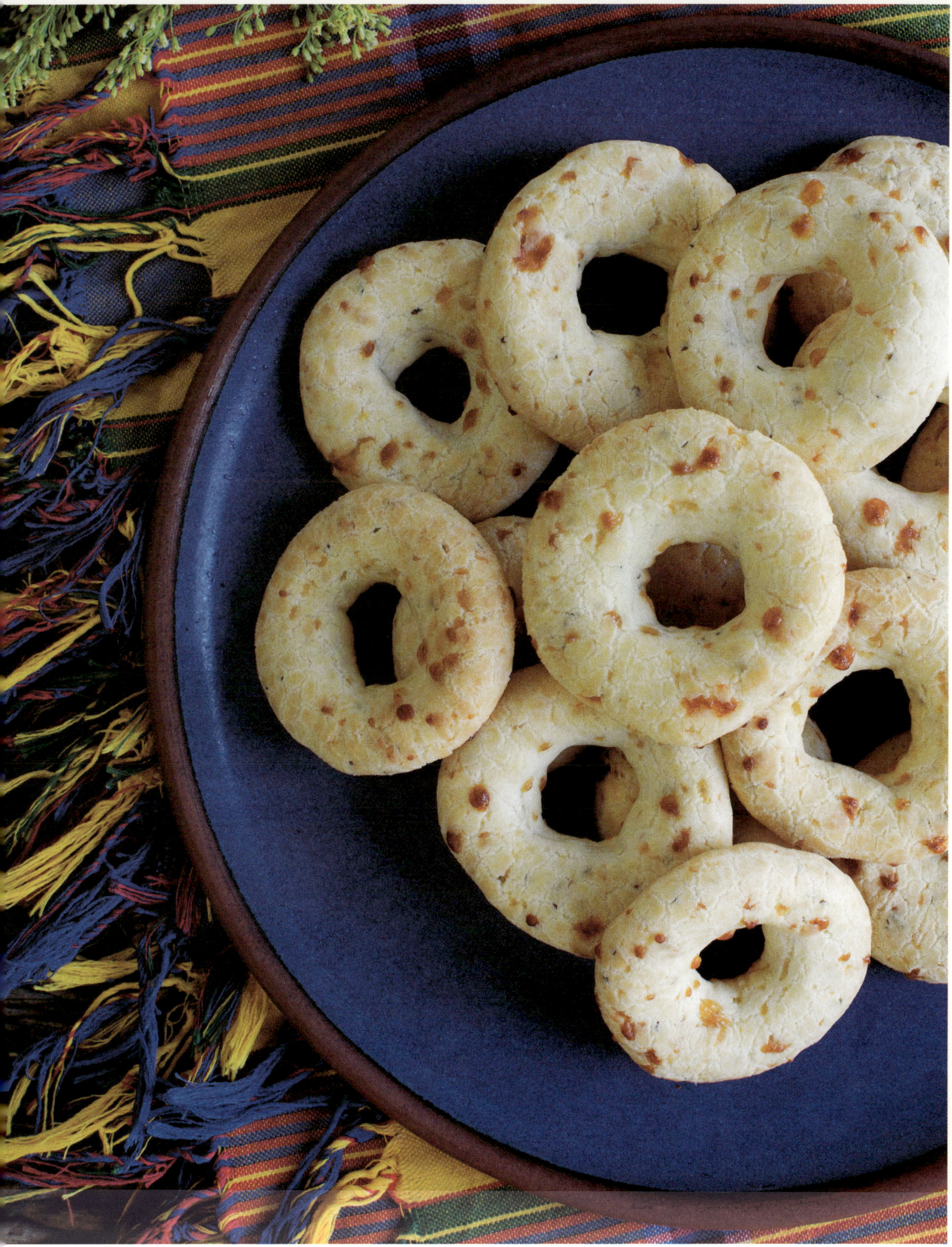

Venezuela

CACHAPAS

Corn Pancakes Stuffed with Buffalo Mozzarella

GF

3 cups sweetcorn kernels
 (cut raw off fresh cobs,
 or thawed frozen, or
 canned and drained)
1 tbsp sugar
1½ tsp salt
⅔ cup milk
1 egg
5 tbsp pre-cooked white cornmeal
 (I use Harina P.A.N. brand)
oil for frying
4 balls fresh buffalo
 mozzarella, sliced

In Venezuela, cachapas are mostly eaten during the weekends, and you will go to the best place that makes them no matter how far it is from your house, just to satisfy that craving. I also have strong memories of eating cachapas during Easter, when entire families pack up their cars and head for the beach — which for us was 6 hours away, including a ferry ride, to Margarita Island. The one thing that kept me and my cousins happy was that we got to stop along the road to eat cachapas, plus the thought of eating this treat at the local wooden shack every day while on the island. We were not allowed to eat meat during Easter, but could have plenty of these soulful sweet and savoury corn pancakes for breakfast, lunch and dinner.

Prepare: 20 minutes; cook: 20 minutes
Makes: 8

In a blender, place corn kernels, sugar, salt, milk, egg and cornmeal. Pulse until just combined, but don't purée.

Lightly oil a griddle or heavy-bottomed frying pan and place over a medium-high heat. Use a ladle to add cachapas mixture to the pan, shaping them like a pancake about 10 cm in diameter. When bubbles start to form on top, lower the heat and continue to cook for about 2 minutes. Flip over and cook for another 2–3 minutes or until cooked through. Place slices of mozzarella on one half of each cachapa and fold the other half over. Serve immediately.

Chef's note: You can stuff a cachapa with whatever you like, but they are traditionally served with some crema agria (see page 211) or butter inside and on top, and Venezuelan cheese or a ham and cheese combo inside. Some grilled haloumi with sliced ham would also do the trick.

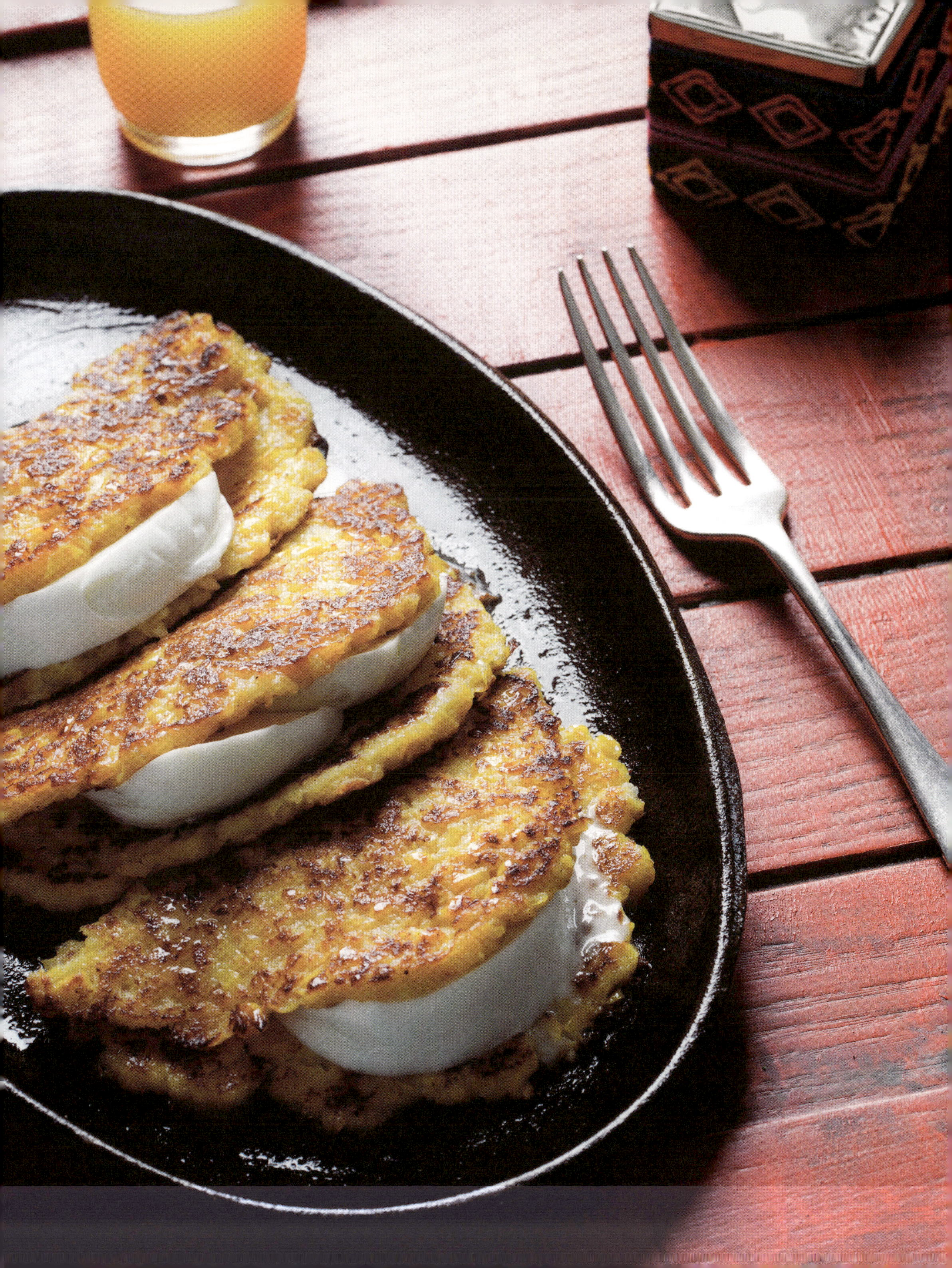

Argentina

EMPANADAS

For the dough
3¼ cups plain flour (you can also use 00 or self-raising flour)
250 g unsalted butter, cold and cubed
1 tbsp salt
1 tbsp sugar
½ cup water
1 egg, beaten

For the filling
1 tbsp olive oil
1 medium onion, finely diced
2 cloves garlic, peeled and minced
¼ cup red wine
1 tsp sugar
500 g minced beef (top sirloin or chuck)
1 tsp salt
1 tsp paprika
1 tbsp chopped fresh rosemary
1 tbsp chopped fresh basil
18 green olives, pitted and halved
2 tbsp olive liquid
¼ cup sliced spring onion, white and light-green parts only

A lot of countries have their own version of empanadas, but the Argentinians take it to a new level. They are traditionally made by rendering beef suet, to keep the meat really moist, and often the beef is hand-chopped. The repulge, the decorative border, is a true art. I went through at least three dozen empanadas before they looked anything like what I had seen my friends doing. If you feel put off by the repulge, don't worry; just press them together with a fork. If you do want to try it, there are plenty of videos online to watch. It's great to make these with family or friends. One person can roll and stamp out the dough, while the others fill and fold. They are crispy and just a bit flaky on the outside, and moist and packed with meat and flavour in the inside.

Prepare: 1 hour; cook: 45 minutes
Makes: 36

Using a stand mixer fitted with the dough hook, combine all dough ingredients except egg and mix on low speed until a dough forms; about 2–3 minutes. Remove dough from bowl and divide it into four equal parts. Flatten each part into a round disc, and wrap with plastic wrap. Let them rest in the refrigerator for 30 minutes — about the time it will take to make the filling.

In a large frying pan, heat olive oil over a low heat, and sweat onion and garlic for about 2 minutes. Add wine and sugar and stir to incorporate well. Let reduce by half, about 2 minutes. Add beef, salt, paprika, rosemary and basil, and stir with a wooden spoon to break up the beef. Continue to cook on low for about 5 minutes. Add olives, olive liquid and spring onion, and cook until all liquid has evaporated; another 1–2 minutes. Remove from the heat and set aside to cool. You don't want to overcook the beef, since it will cook further in the oven.

Preheat oven to 180°C.

Line two baking trays with non-stick baking paper. Set aside.

Remove one portion of dough from the refrigerator. Unwrap it and place it between two large pieces of baking paper, or use a little flour to dust a flat surface and a rolling pin. Roll dough out to about 3 mm thick. Using a 10 cm ring cutter, cut out rounds and place them on one of the prepared baking trays. Save all the dough trim; you can lightly knead it back into a ball and re-roll it until you have used it all.

Place 1 tablespoon of filling, including an olive half, in each dough circle. Pinch dough together to form a half circle, and use the tines of a fork to press the edges together. Line empanadas up on the other baking tray. Keep the tray in the refrigerator, and continue adding empanadas until it is full, returning it to the refrigerator between additions.

Brush empanadas with beaten egg. Bake for 20–25 minutes, until tops and edges are golden brown. Remove from oven and place on a rack to cool. Store in an airtight container for up to 3 days.

Chef's note: Empanadas take time and are rather labour-intensive, so I suggest making a large batch — they keep in the refrigerator for up to 3 days or in the freezer for up to a month. To reheat, simply put them back in a 180°C oven for about 20 minutes.

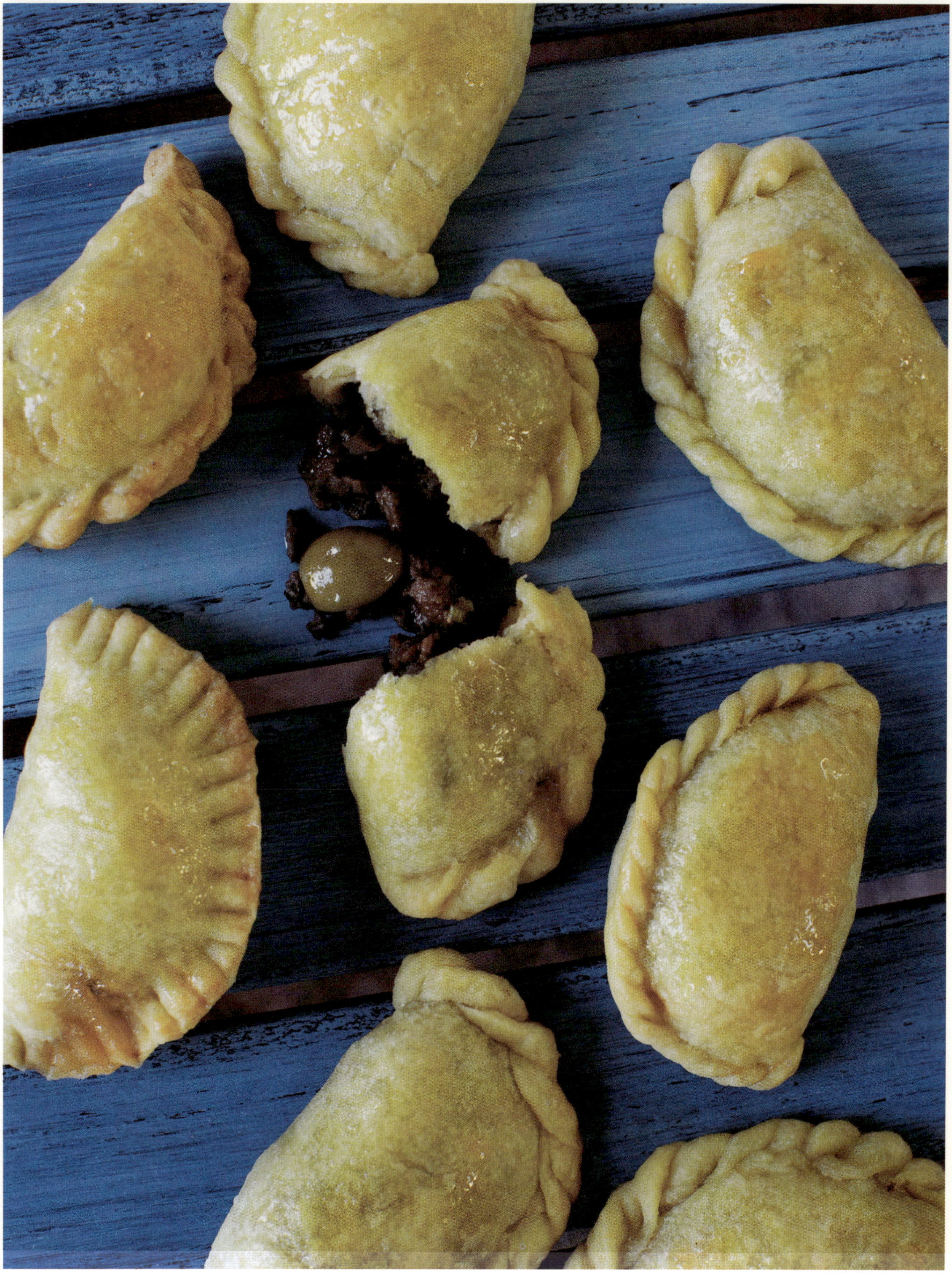

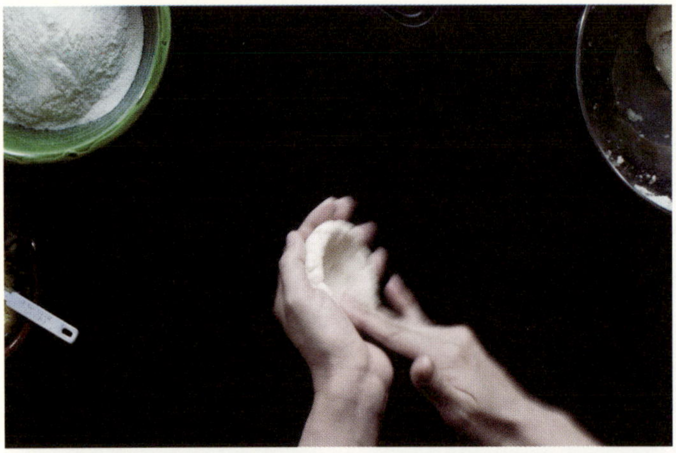
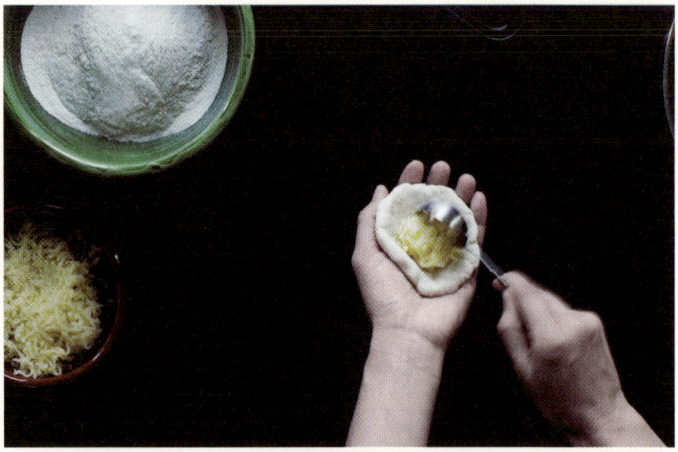
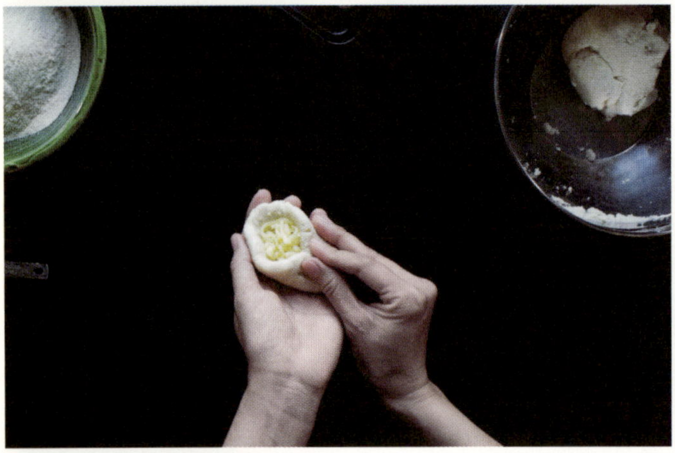
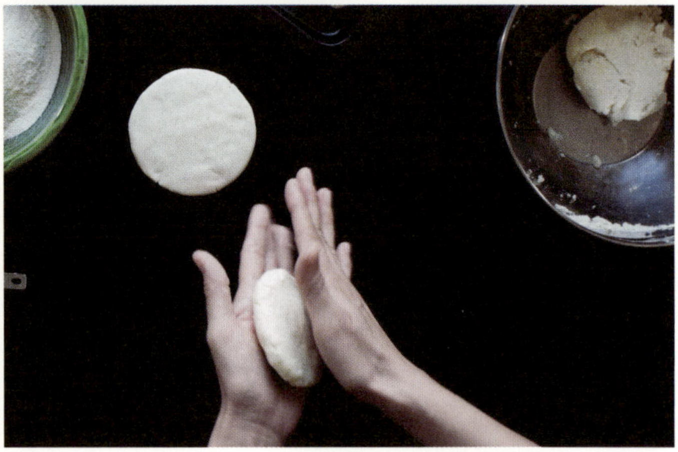
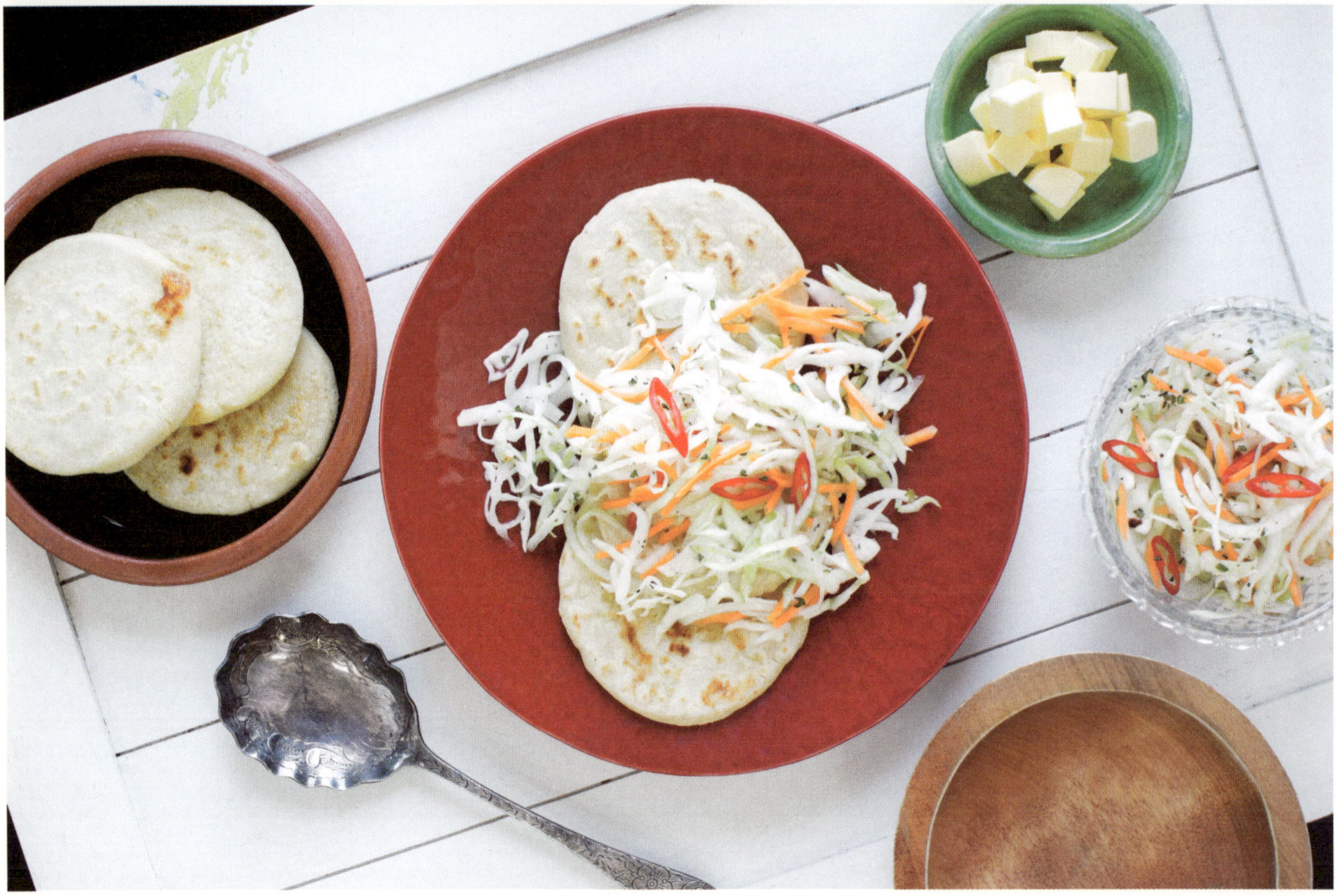

El Salvador

PUPUSAS CON CURTIDO

Cheese-filled Corn Pupusas with Curtido Slaw

For the curtido slaw (makes approx. 4 cups)
½ cup apple cider vinegar
¼ cup water
2 tsp salt
2 tsp granulated sugar
1 tsp chopped fresh oregano
1 chile de árbol, crushed, or
    ½ tsp chilli flakes (optional)
¼ head green cabbage, shredded
    (2 cups, packed)
1 large carrot, grated (1 cup)
½ white onion, peeled
    and thinly sliced
2 tbsp olive oil
flaky sea salt
juice of ½ lime

For the pupusas
1¼ cups lukewarm water
1½ cups instant corn masa
    flour for tortillas (Maseca
    or Tío Pablo brand)
1 tsp salt
1 cup shredded mozzarella
rice bran oil, as needed

To serve
butter
Gouda cheese, grated (optional)

Imagine a small stuffed pita which tastes like a cheese-filled corn tortilla. Salvadorian pupusas are similar to the traditional Venezuelan arepas but they are filled before cooking with wild greens, squash blossoms, beans with tiny pork pieces (ground to a paste) and/or cheese, and served with condiments on top. Just like arepas and tortillas, people are passionate about them and eat them at all hours of the day.

Prepare: 30 minutes; cook: 10 minutes
Serves: 6

To make the slaw, combine the vinegar, water, salt, sugar, oregano and chilli (if using) in a bowl and whisk until combined. Pour over cabbage, carrot and onion, and mix well. Cover and refrigerate while making pupusas.

Place the warm water, instant corn masa flour and salt in a bowl and slowly start mixing and kneading the flour until it is all incorporated and a smooth dough is formed, which doesn't stick to your hands. If the mixture is too dry, add a little more water. If the mixture is too sticky, add a little more flour. Let dough stand for 5 minutes.

Form dough into 6 balls. Flatten each ball with your hands, and make an indentation in the centre, forming a small cup. Fill the cup with 1½ tablespoons of mozzarella and wrap the dough around the filling to seal it. To ensure that the filling does not leak, pat the dough back and forth between your hands to form a round disc about 5 mm thick. Repeat with remaining balls and set aside.

Lightly grease a heavy-bottomed frying pan or griddle with oil. Sear both sides of the pupusas, about 3 minutes each side over medium heat until golden brown.

Dress slaw with olive oil, flaky sea salt, freshly ground black pepper and lime juice. Serve with butter and shredded Gouda (if desired) alongside the curtido slaw.

Chef's note: While the curtido slaw is traditional, the extra cheese on top is not — but the Gouda gives it an extra-nice cheesy touch.

Ecuador

LLAPINGACHOS

Kumara & Cheese Patties with Peanut Sauce

GF

500 g orange kumara or sweet potato peeled and cut into chunks
1 tbsp salt
1 cup finely chopped white onion (about 2 medium onions)
2 tbsp achiote oil (see page 188) or avocado oil
2 tbsp unsalted butter
½ tsp paprika
1½ cups shredded mozzarella
1 egg, beaten

For the peanut sauce (makes approx. 1½ cups)
½ cup peanut butter
1 cup coconut milk
½ cup agave nectar, liquid honey or melted panela (unrefined cane sugar)
juice of 1 lime
2 tbsp soy sauce
½ tsp chilli flakes (optional), or Tabasco or sriracha sauce

Garnish
pickled red onions (see page 199; optional)
lime wedges
chopped coriander

Traditionally, llapingachos are the golden potato and cheese cakes or patties that form part of Ecuador's culture. I have made them with sweet potato/kumara for a more nutritious version; and after many unsuccessful attempts at flips, I added egg as a binding agent. I also made my own version of the traditional creamy/milky peanut sauce. Llapingachos are usually found in markets, served with the peanut sauce, a fried egg, diced tomato, shredded lettuce, julienned red onion curtido (relish) and avocado slices, and often you'll pick up some kind of pork side (ribs or sausages). They make a good breakfast or lunch dish at home; pan-fried chorizo goes really well with them.

Prepare: 30 minutes; cool: 30 minutes–1 hour; cook: 30 minutes
Makes: 20 medium-sized llapingachos

Place kumara or sweet potato in a medium-sized saucepan. Cover with cold water and add salt. Simmer over a medium heat until soft, about 15–20 minutes.

Gently pan-fry onion with 1 tablespoon achiote or avocado oil and a pinch of salt until soft; about 10 minutes. Set aside to cool.

Once kumara or sweet potato is soft, strain and transfer to a bowl. Mash with butter, onion mixture and paprika. Season to taste with salt. Mix in mozzarella and beaten egg. Place mash in the refrigerator to cool for at least 30 minutes, as it will be easier to handle once cooled.

Meanwhile, make the peanut sauce. In a blender or food processor, mix all ingredients with a little salt until the texture is smooth and loose. You can vary the quantities of agave nectar (or other sweetener), chilli flakes (or hot sauce) and salt to suit your taste.

Remove the bowl of kumara or sweet potato from the refrigerator. Divide into 20 patties and place on a baking dish or plate.

In a non-stick pan over a high heat, use 1 teaspoon achiote or avocado oil at a time to sear patties. Let them set over the high heat until they form a smooth crust (if not, they tend to fall apart); then lower the heat to medium so that they will start cooking inside. Cook for about 3 minutes each side, until golden brown. Be careful when turning them, as they are very delicate.

You could also cook them in the oven at 180°C on a baking tray lined with baking paper for 25 minutes, then 5 minutes on oven grill. Watch them carefully so that they do not burn!

Serve with peanut sauce, pickled red onion, lime wedges and coriander.

Chef's note: This makes a large batch, because you can keep them (and the sauce) in the refrigerator for about a week — just reheat in the oven when you crave them. The achiote oil gives them a more authentic flavour, but avocado oil works fine too. If you have a grinder and want to add ¼ teaspoon of achiote powder to the mash, that's okay too.

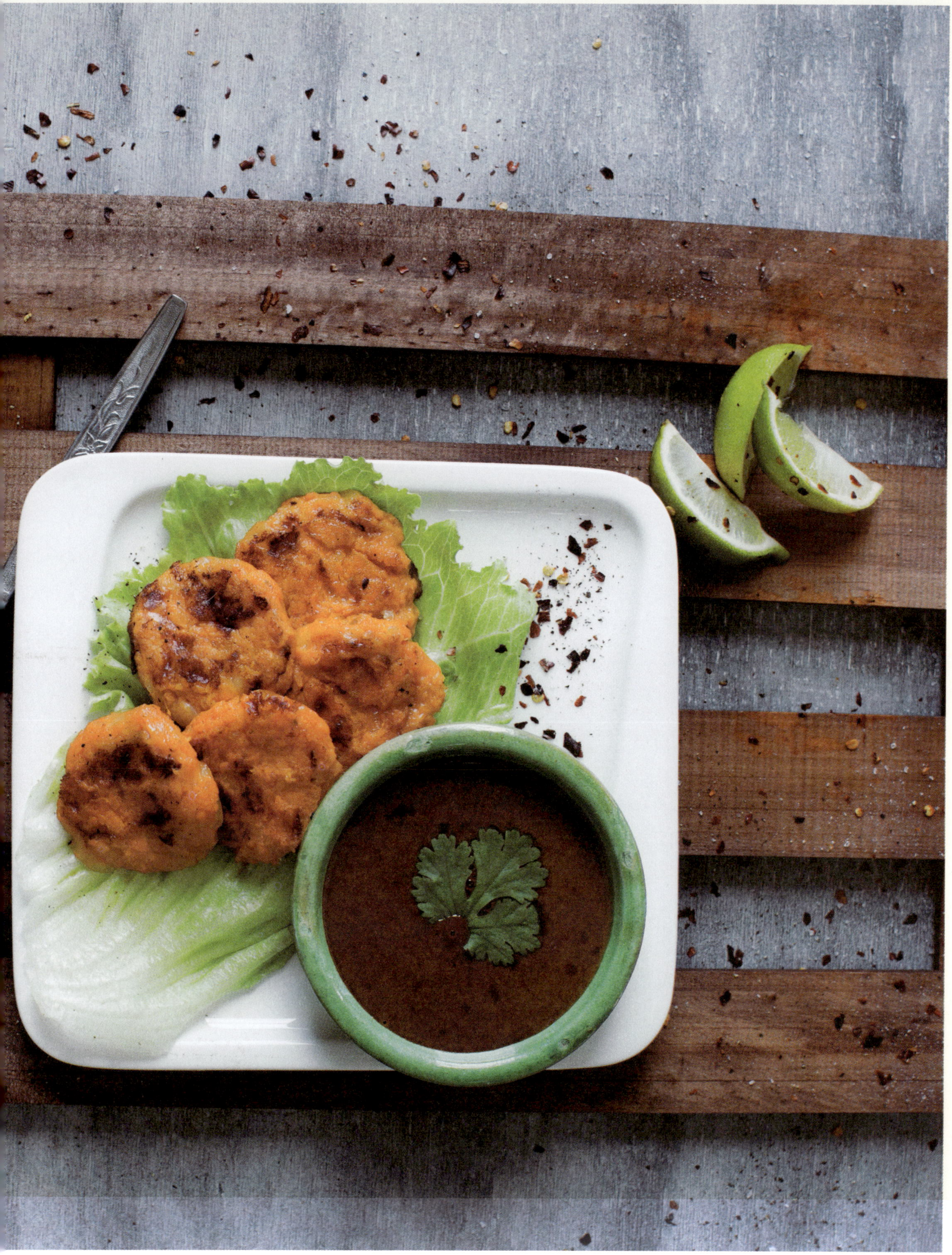

Cuba

SANDWICH CUBANO

Cuban Sandwich

12 slider buns
50 g butter, melted
4 tbsp yellow hot dog mustard
150 g sweet-cured shaved ham
100 g lechón con mojo (see page 92) or roast pork
50 g Swiss cheese, sliced
6 large dill pickles, thinly sliced

A recent movie, called *Chef*, dedicated half of its running time to showing us just how the cubano is made! It's a true art form. Everything needs to be perfect: just enough lechón but not too much, the right ham, the correct temperature of the plancha (grill), and a flawless press that allows the cheese to melt and the bread to turn the exact shade of golden brown. These flavours go so well together and that is what makes this classic sandwich so loved by everyone.

I have taken it upon myself to give you these Cuban sliders. My Cuban friends are probably rolling their eyes right now, but these are cute, fun and the perfect nibbles for a party.

Prepare: 10 minutes; cook: 20 minutes
Makes: 12

While assembling the sandwich, heat up a large flat griddle or sandwich press over a medium-high heat.

Spread both sides of the sliders with butter and mustard, reserving some butter for the outside of the sliders and the press or griddle. Layer up the bottom half with ham, pork and cheese. Top with a slice of pickle. Brush the outsides of the sliders, top and bottom, with butter. Lightly brush butter onto the press or griddle, too. Cook the sandwich until cheese is melted and meats are warm, about 2-3 minutes per side or 4-5 minutes in the sandwich press.

Chef's note: In some households, cubanos are pressed with a brick wrapped in foil.

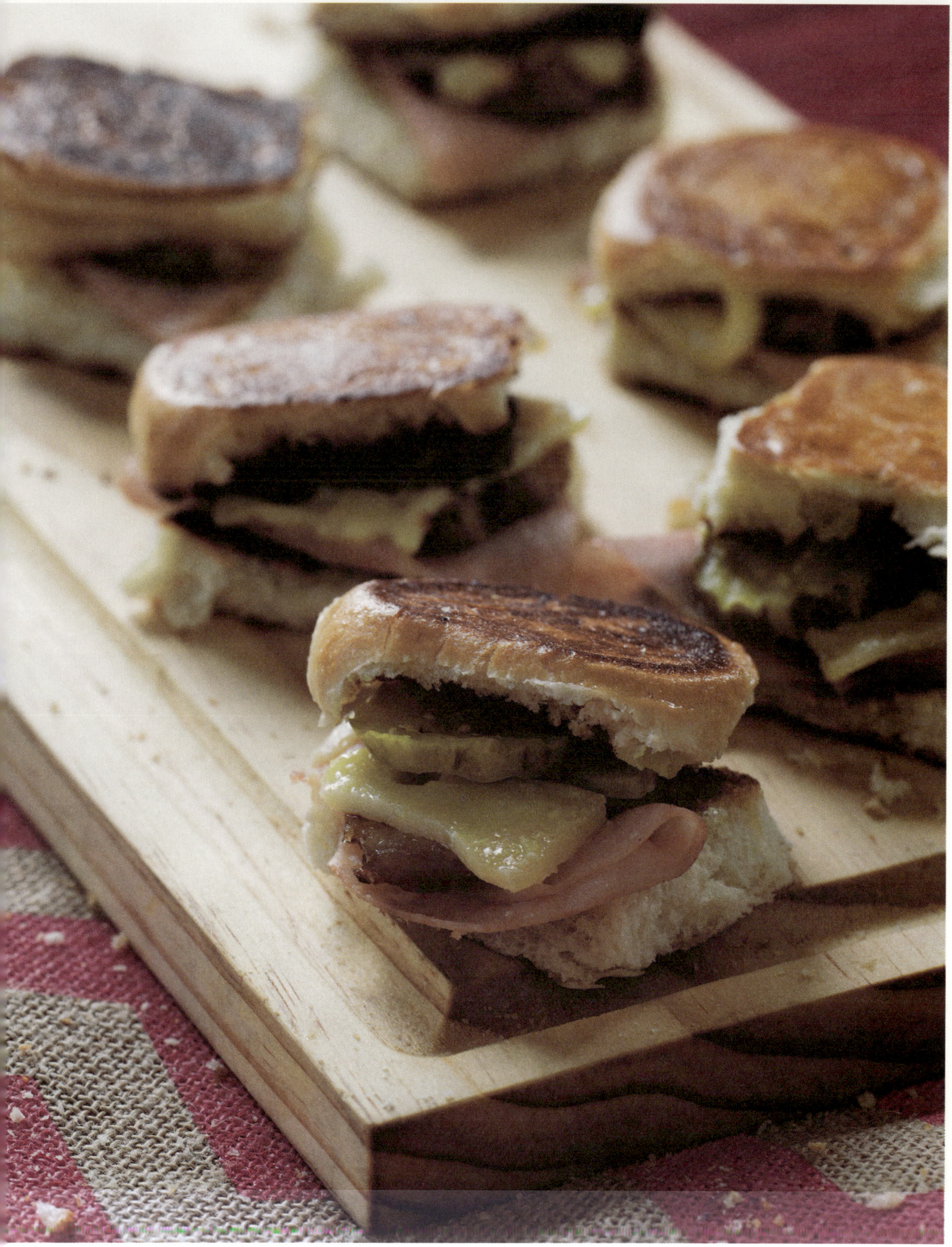

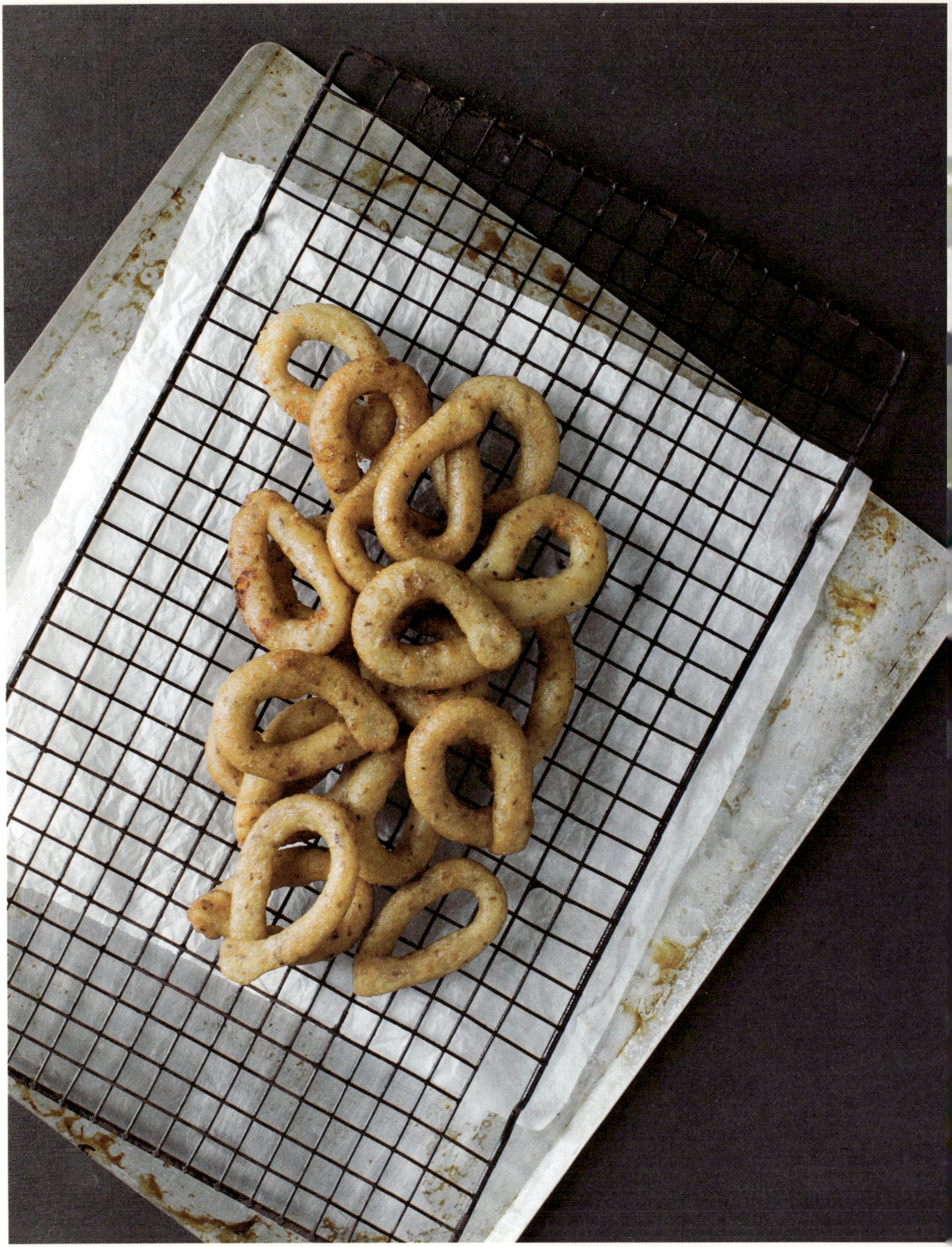

Venezuela

MANDOCAS

Anise, Panela & Cheese Fritters

GF

¾ cup shaved panela (unrefined cane sugar), melted carefully in the microwave with 1 tbsp water
1 tsp salt
2 tsp anise seeds, toasted
2 cups warm water
2 cups pre-cooked white cornmeal (I use Harina P.A.N brand)
225 g shredded mozzarella
½ cup rice bran oil for frying

My grandfather (abuelito) Hernan is from the state of Zulia, which is known for its oil, heat and food. Mandocas come from there, so Abuelito makes them the best. He would spoil me with this glorious breakfast treat on weekends. They are like a doughnut with cane sugar (panela), spices and cheese infused inside the masa (cornmeal dough); truly decadent. The smell of the anise and the melted panela would literally get me out of bed. He knew he had to make a dozen just for me. Dip them in crema agria (see page 211) and eat with finely shredded cheese and butter, and a cafecito (coffee) on the side — they'll become a brunch habit!

Prepare: 25 minutes; cook: 15 minutes
Makes: 20

Mix panela, salt, anise seeds and water together with a wooden spoon in a large bowl. Slowly add and start kneading the cornmeal, a couple of tablespoons at a time, until the mixture comes together into a dough. Lastly, knead mozzarella into the dough. The dough should be soft and kneadable, but not sticky. If dough is too wet and sticky, add a little more cornmeal. If it's too dry, add a little more water. Let it rest for 5 minutes on the work surface (no need to cover).

Heat oil to 180°C in a large frying pan, or use a deep-fryer. Divide dough into 20 pieces, and roll each one into a smooth ball. Using the palms of your hands on a flat surface, roll each ball into a log shape about 12 cm long. Bring ends together and overlap them to form a tear-shaped loop. Press ends together.

Fry loops of dough in batches until dark golden brown, turning once. Let them drain on a wire rack lined with paper towel.

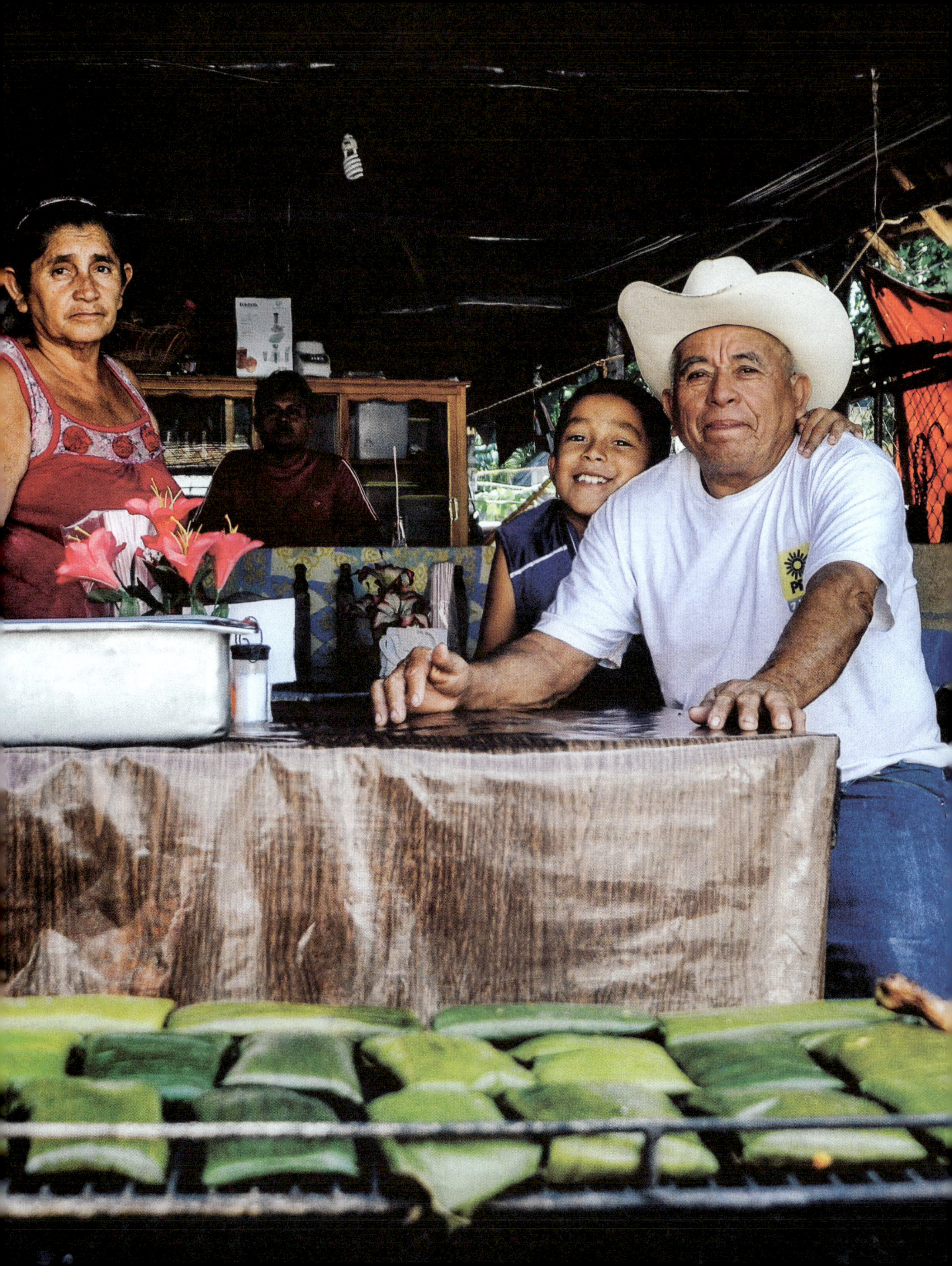

Mexico

TAMALES

Steamed Corn Parcels

GF

1 packet corn husks
2 cups shredded chicken (see page 42) or shredded pork (see page 25), or a mixture
butcher's twine (optional)

For the dough
2 cups chicken stock, warmed
1 tsp baking powder
1 tsp salt
¼ cup milk
2 cups white corn flour for tortillas (Maseca or Tío Pablo brand)
100 g softened lard, cut into small pieces

Optional sauces
1½ cups mole (see page 205) or
1½ cups adobo sauce (see page 66)

Garnish
1 cup crema agria (see page 211)
1 cup salsa verde (see page 194)
habanero chilli oil (see page 188)
1 cup pickled vegetables (see page 162)
1 cup pico de gallo (see page 193)

Just about every country in Latin America has a version of tamales. They were an easy way to carry food in the early days, since each was wrapped in its own package. Aztec, Mayan, Olmeca and Tolteca civilisations used tamales as portable food to support their armies, or to feed hunters and travellers. Tamales are made of masa (a corn-based dough), filled with meats, cheeses, fruits, vegetables, chillies — you name it — and steamed or boiled inside a leaf wrapper. In Mexico the most common fillings are pork and chicken, in either red/green salsa or mole. If using pork, follow the instructions for cooking the pork shoulder for pozole rojo (see page 25). Tamales are cooked in large batches and usually eaten during festivities, such as Las Posadas, Christmas, the Day of the Dead and Mexican Independence Day. You need a steamer for this recipe.

Prepare: 2 hours; cook: 1 hour
Makes: 30

Separate corn husks and soak in warm water for about 15–20 minutes, so they can bend without breaking.

In a large bowl, mix warm chicken stock, baking powder, salt and milk. Slowly start adding and mixing the corn flour with your hands until the mixture comes together and is smooth and without lumps. Add lard, kneading with your hands until it is fully incorporated. If the dough is too wet add a bit more corn flour, 1 tablespoon at a time — don't make it too dry. Let dough rest for about 5 minutes.

Mix shredded meat with the sauce of your choice. Place two softened corn husks together with the smaller pointy ends facing away from each other, like a canoe. Use a large spoon to spread a portion of dough into a rectangle in the centre of the corn husks, leaving a 4 cm border at the tapered ends of the husks and a 2 cm border on the other sides. Add a generous amount of meat filling in the middle, about 1 heaped tablespoon.

Pull the long edges of husk towards each other and overlap them so that the dough is now wrapped around the filling. Fold the two tapered edges over to fully wrap the tamale and tie with a strip of husk or butcher's twine. Repeat with the rest of the dough and filling.

Fill bottom of a steamer with water and line steamer rack with some of the extra corn husks. Without crowding, arrange tamales upright in the steamer; fill any spaces with crinkled-up foil. Cover tamales with more husks and then the steamer lid. Bring water to a boil, and steam tamales over a medium heat for about 1 hour. They are ready when the filling pulls away from the husks.

Place garnishes in dishes in the centre of the table with the tamales alongside.

(See next page for instructional photos.)

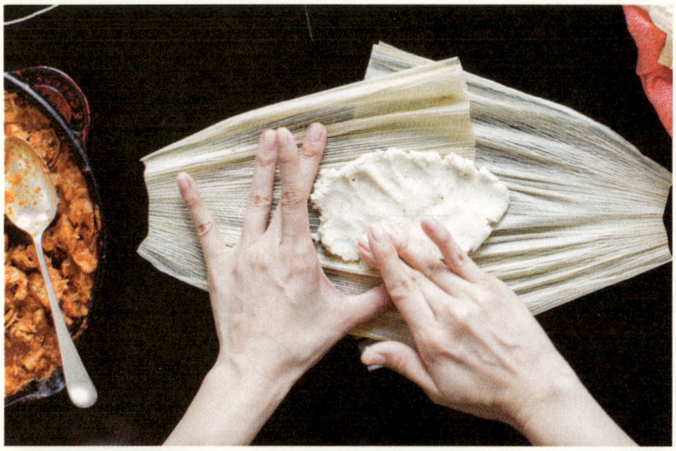
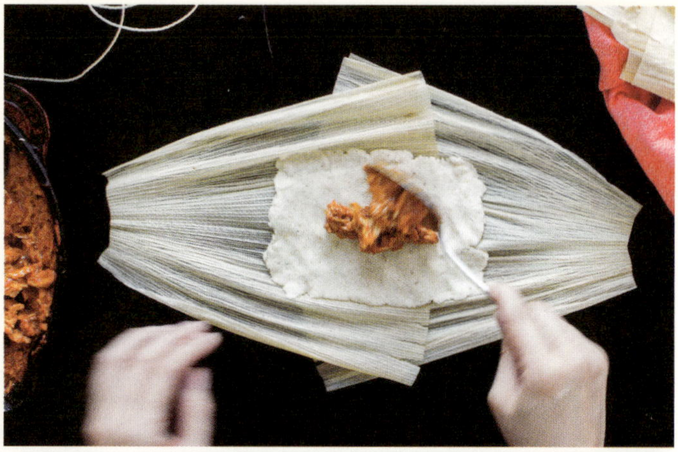
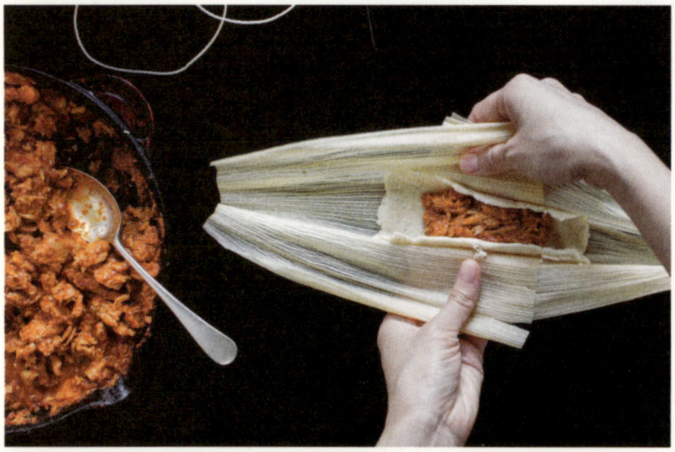
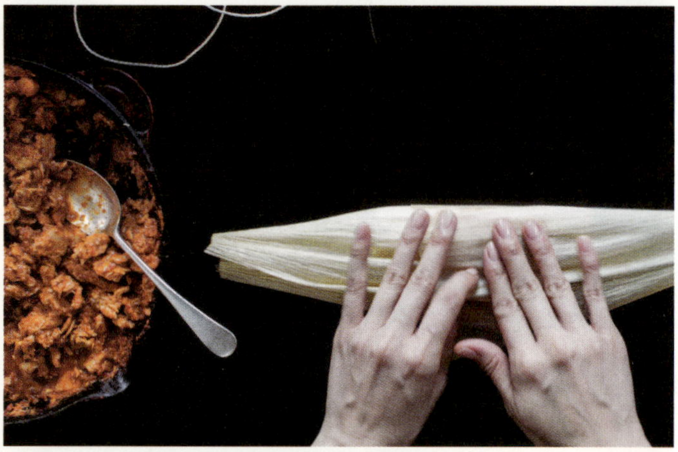
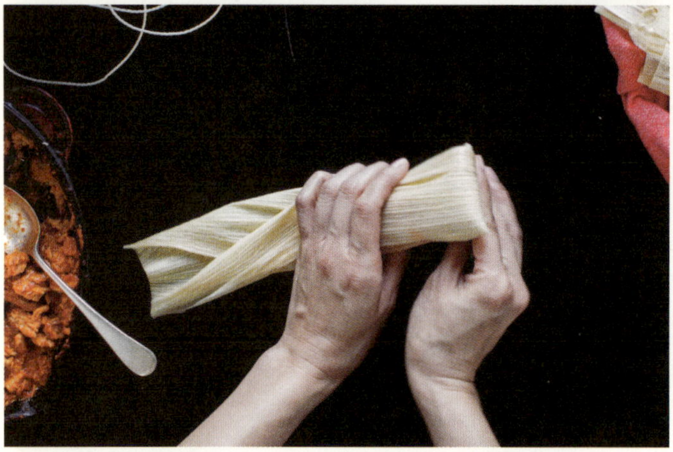
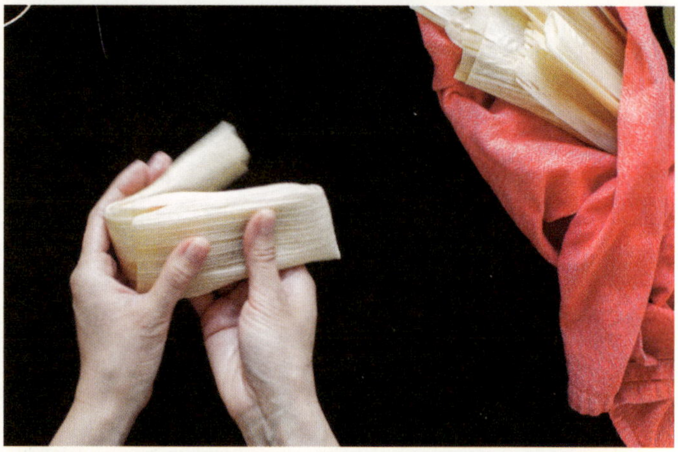
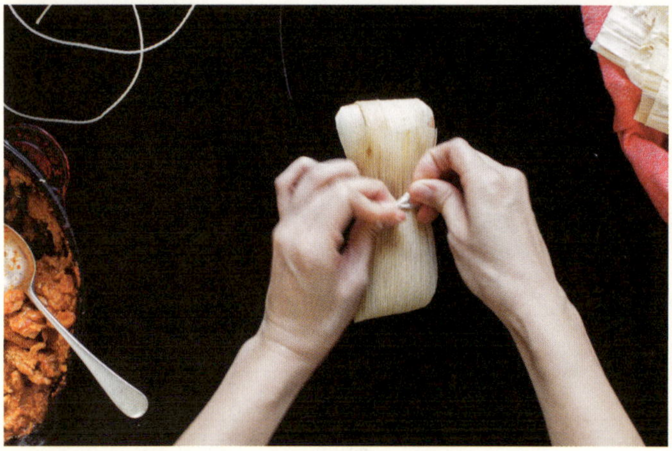
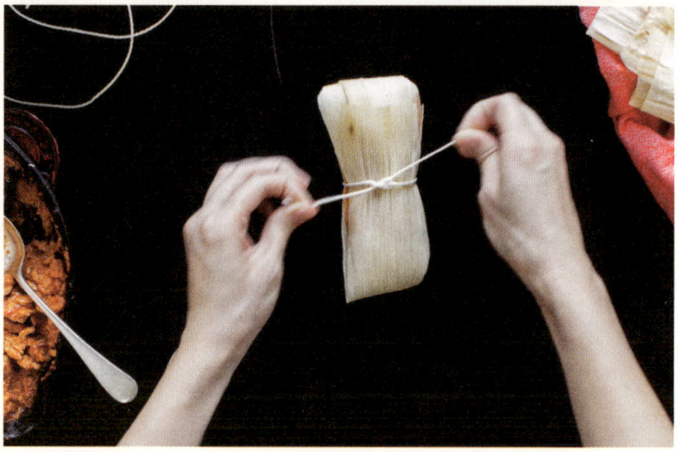

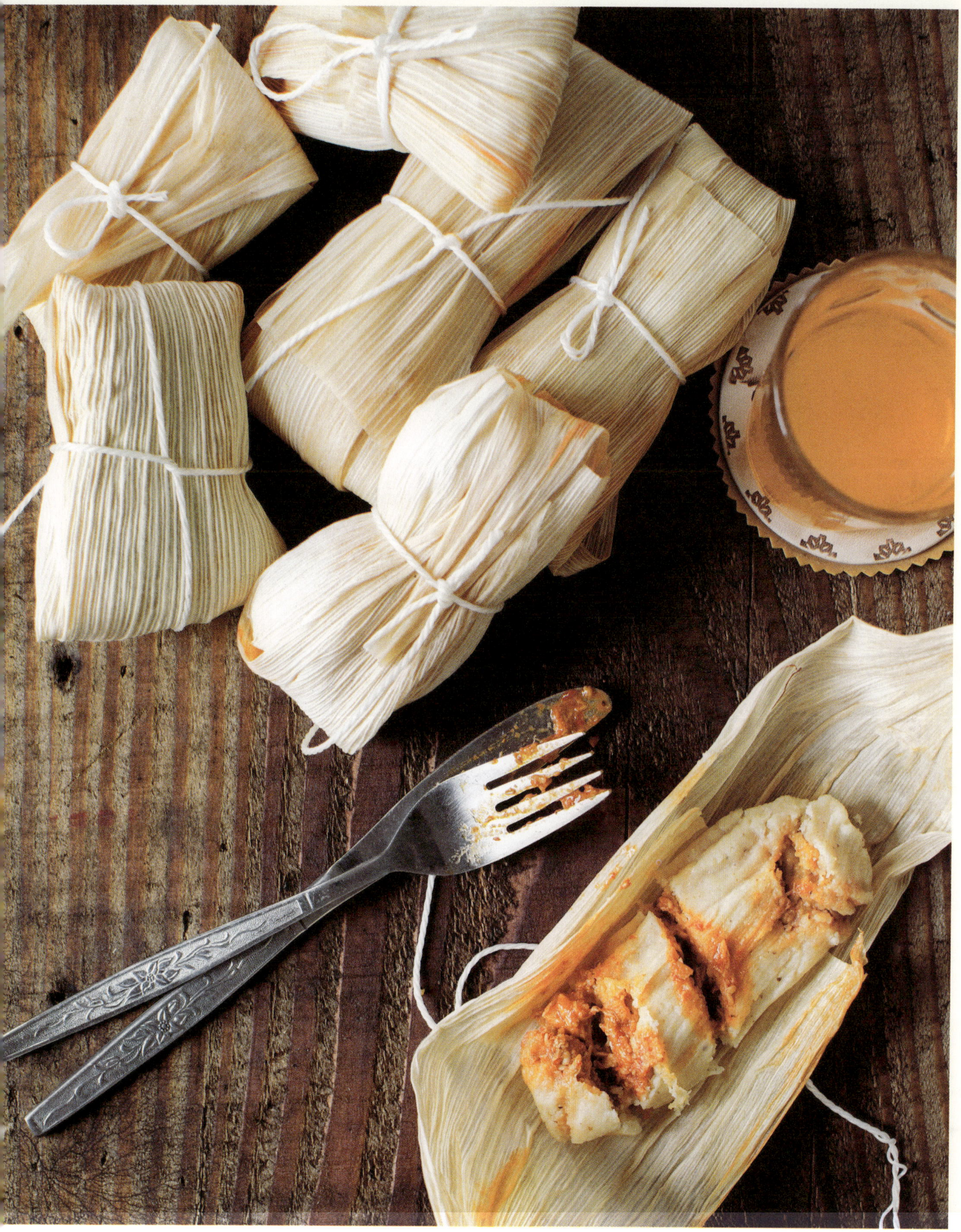

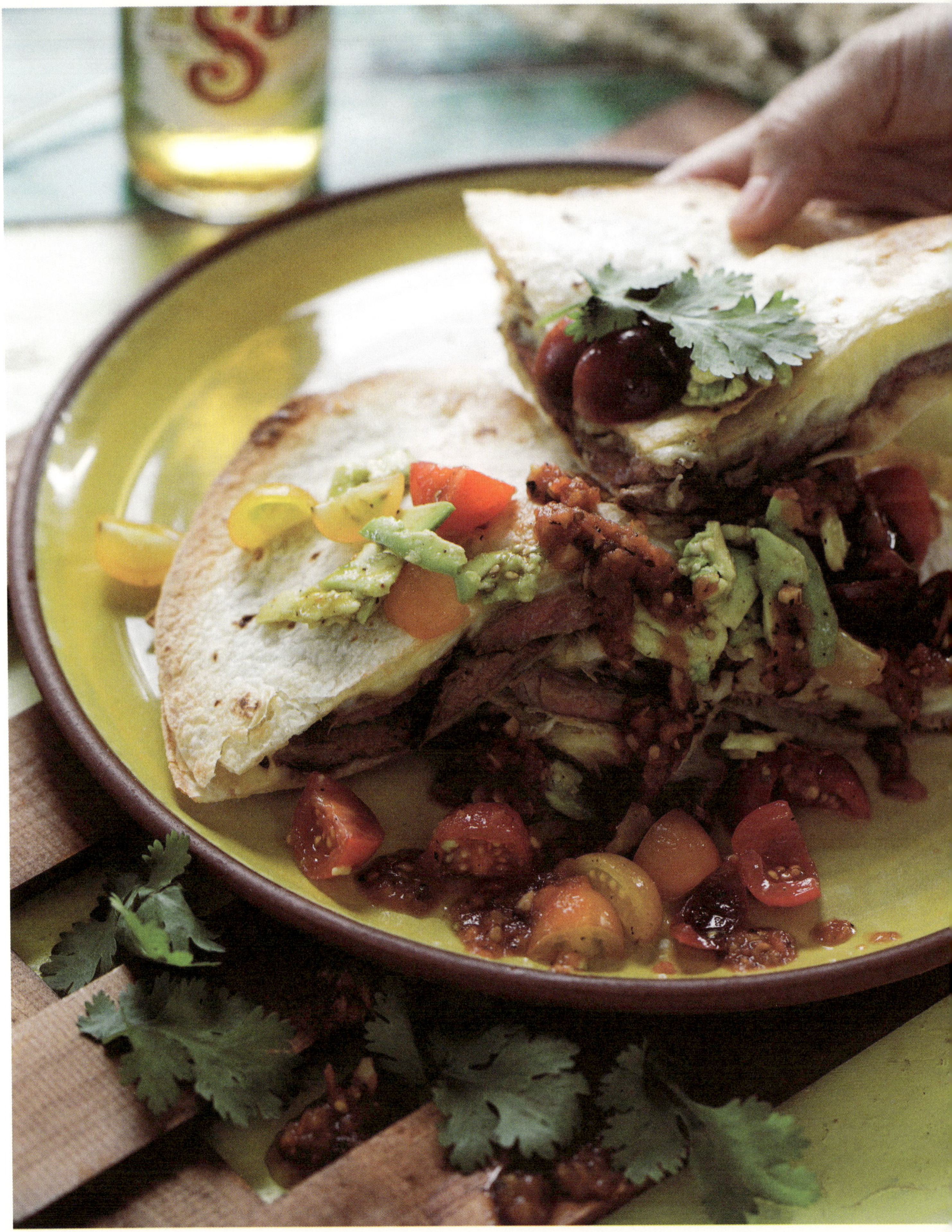

Mexico

QUESADILLAS DE ARRACHERA

Skirt Steak Quesadillas

8 large (20 cm) flour tortillas (see page 113, or use good-quality storebought))
2 cups shredded mozzarella
450 g sliced arrachera beef (see page 101)

Garnish suggestions
chopped pickled jalapeños
guacamole (see page 196) or sliced avocado
salsa roja (see page 194)
chopped tomatoes or pico de gallo (see page 193)
crema agria (see page 211)

When most people think of a quesadilla they think of the Tex Mex version, with lots of fillings and toppings plus sour cream. 'Queso' in Spanish just means cheese, and in central and southern regions of Mexico when you order a quesadilla you will most likely be served just a corn tortilla filled with stringy white Oaxaca cheese, cooked with no additional oil on a comal (a smooth, flat griddle) until the cheese has completely melted. Often the quesadillas will be served with a side of salsa roja or salsa verde and guacamole. The first time I had this in Mexico, I was a bit disappointed by the look of it and asked for a side of chicken and beans. The waiter laughed, asking if I was touring from the USA. He encouraged me to try their version, and I was sold! That cheese with the perfect home-made buttery tortilla was simplicity to perfection. I've combined both versions in this recipe, because I do love a good Tex Mex quesadilla as well.

Prepare: 15 minutes; cook: 15 minutes
Serves: 4

Preheat oven to low, about 80°C.

Place one tortilla in a large heavy-bottomed frying pan over a medium heat. Place ½ cup cheese on top, together with a quarter of the sliced meat, and top with another tortilla. Cook until cheese starts to melt, about 2 minutes. Flip over and cook on other side until golden and cheese is melted, another 2 minutes. Repeat with the rest of the tortillas, cheese and meat, keeping quesadillas warm on a plate in the oven until ready to serve.

Top as desired with chopped jalapeños, guacamole or sliced avocado, salsa roja, chopped tomatoes or pico de gallo and crema agria.

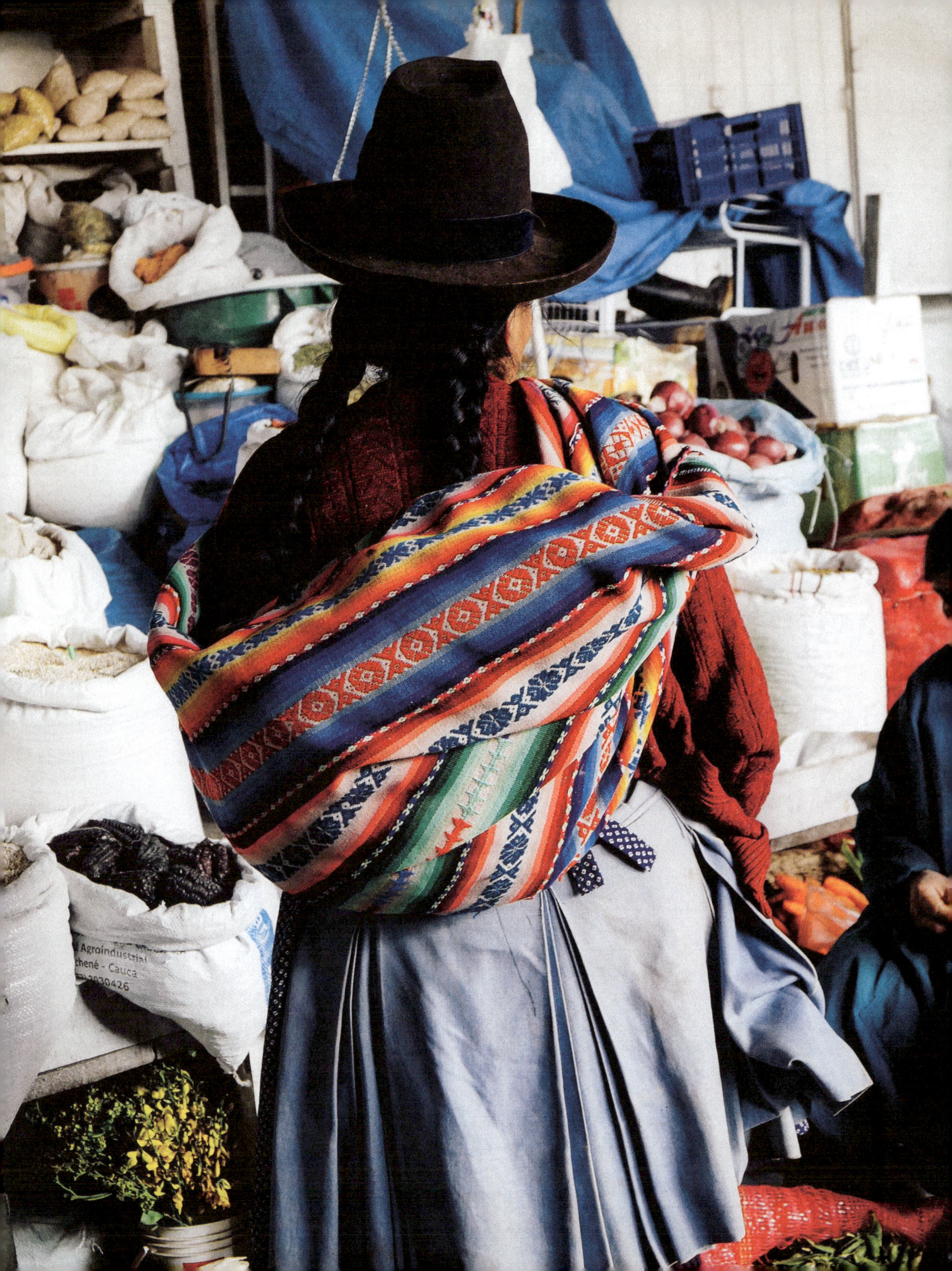
Agroindustrial
Cauca

ARROCES

RICE

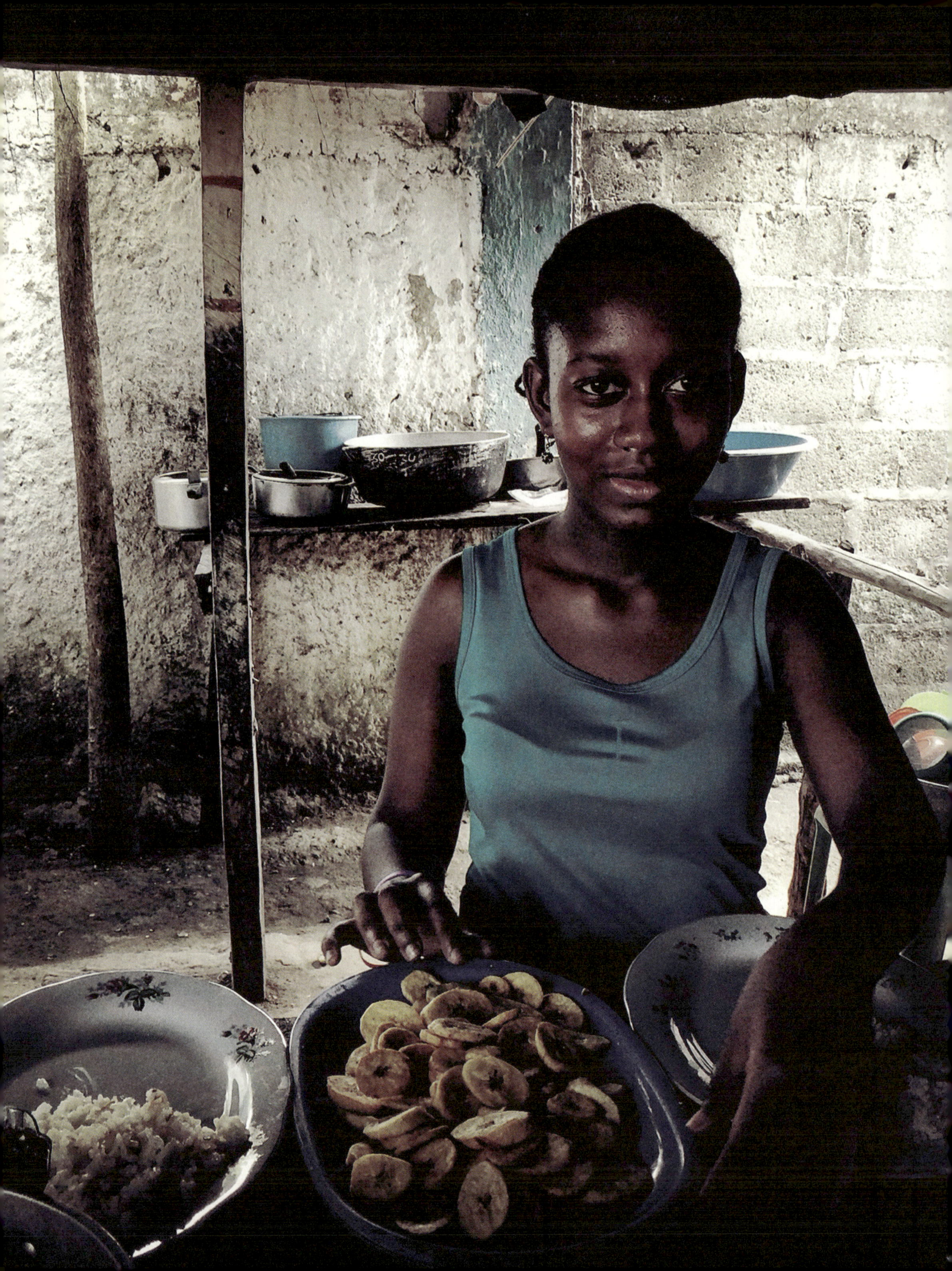

ARROZ BLANCO
Perfect White Rice

ARROZ VERDE
Green Pesto Rice

ARROZ con COCO
Coconut Rice

ARROZ ROJO
Mexican-style Red Rice

ARROZ con FIDEOS
Rice and Noodles

GALLO PINTO
Ticos' Rice & Beans

ARROZ NEGRO
Black Ink Rice

ARROZ con POLLO
Chicken & Rice

Venezuela

ARROZ BLANCO

Perfect White Rice

GF

2 cups water
1 tsp salt
1 tbsp rice bran oil, or any neutral-flavoured oil
1 cup white long-grain rice, preferably jasmine or a Thai long-grain

My grandmother makes rice every day — no matter whether she made pasta, potatoes or any other type of starch, there is always white rice at the table. She even has a special pot in which she has been making it for over 30 years. She jokes that I will inherit this family treasure because it is the secret to perfect white rice . . . but I've nailed it my own way.

Prepare: 5 minutes; cook: 20 minutes
Serves: 4

Combine water, salt and oil in a medium-sized saucepan over a high heat. Bring to the boil and straight away add the rice. Only stir the rice when you first put it in the pan, then just let it come back to the boil. Lower the heat to a simmer and cover the pan. Leave it alone, and let it cook until done. It will take about 15 minutes — set a timer and check it at this time; some rices need an extra 5 minutes of cooking, but no longer. Leave the rice off the heat, covered, for an extra 5 minutes before fluffing with a fork — no need to drain it.

Chef's note: The trick to perfect rice (and perfect pasta) is salty water, and using good-quality ingredients always helps. Your water must taste salty — I always check my water, especially when changing salt brands. When the water comes to a boil, add the rice quickly; don't let water evaporate off for too long before adding the rice, or your measurements will be out.

Venezuela

ARROZ VERDE

Green Pesto Rice

GF

For the pesto
(makes ½ cup)
1 cup lightly packed basil leaves
½ cup lightly packed parsley leaves
½ cup olive oil
1 garlic clove, peeled and crushed
½ tsp salt
1 pinch freshly ground black pepper

2 cups perfect white rice (see opposite)

Different countries have different versions of this rice. My aunt Maritza taught me how to make it over the phone, and it's now become a favourite among my friends. The combination of basil, parsley, olive oil and garlic make this dish fresh and aromatic, and the sharp, bright green looks festive and appetising. Only add one clove of garlic, because the rice should be the perfect complement to your main, rather than overpowering it. Arroz verde is ideal for stuffing quail (see page 53), or as a side to duck or beef eye of round (see page 106).

Prepare: 10 minutes
Serves: 4

Using a hand blender, combine all pesto ingredients until fully incorporated and a paste consistency.
 Ensure that the rice is completely cool before mixing with the pesto, otherwise the pesto will turn brown. Add the bright green pesto to the rice, little by little, and fluff with a fork until well incorporated.

Chef's note: If you love coriander, you can add some coriander leaves to the pesto; also mint. Be careful not to drown the rice in pesto; some rices absorb the oil faster than others which is why you only add a bit at a time.

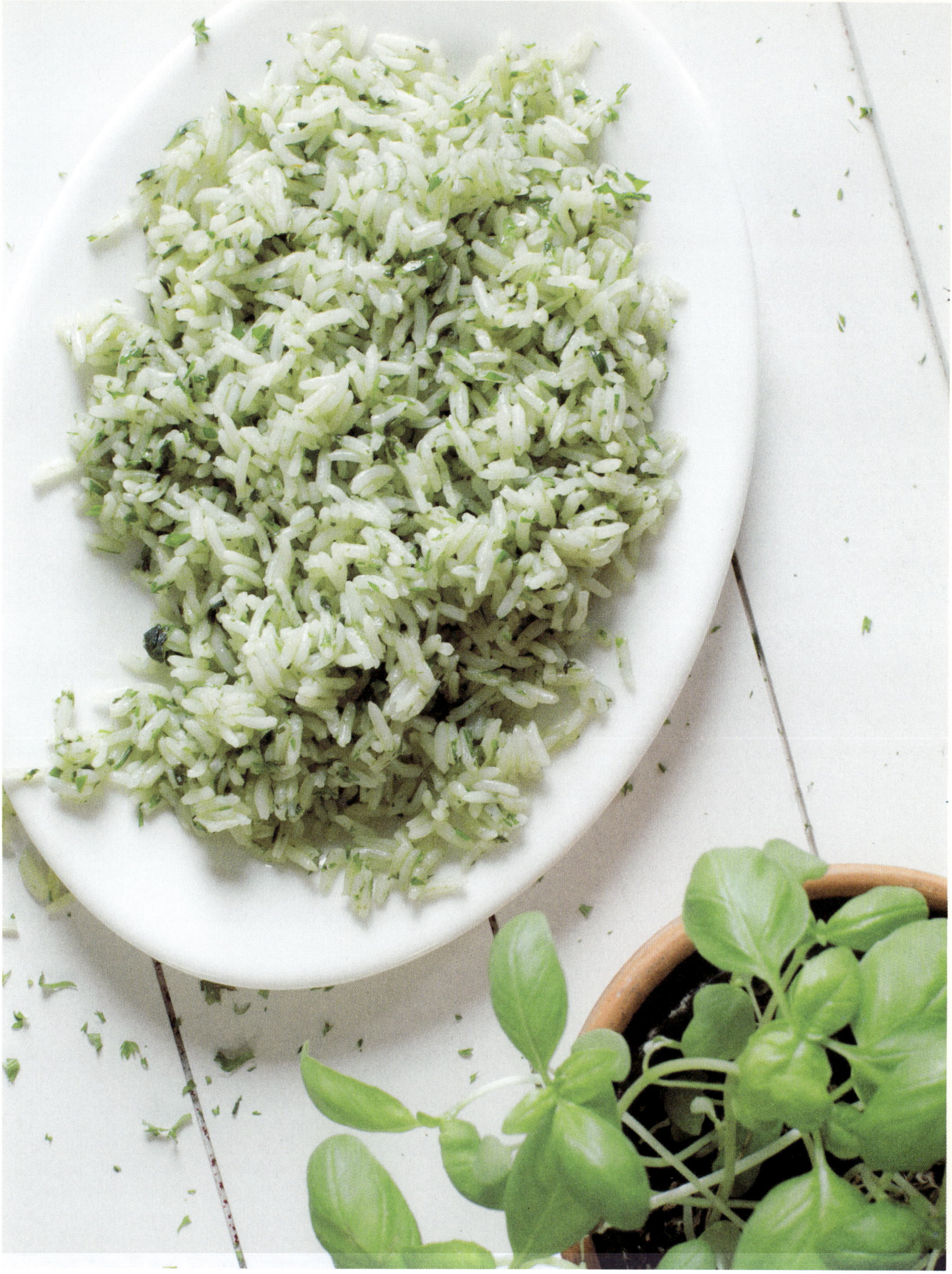

Colombia

ARROZ CON COCO

Coconut Rice

GF

1 tbsp coconut oil
1 cup white long-grain rice
1 cup Coca-Cola
1 cup coconut milk
1 tsp salt
1 tbsp sugar
¼ cup raisins
¼ cup toasted coconut flakes (optional)

Be adventurous and try this, but beware — it's addictive! It goes very well with fish; on the Colombian coast, they serve arroz con coco alongside a whole fried fish and fried green plantains. The combination of the fragrant sweetness of the coconut infused in the rice and the crispy-salty-limey fish is simply divine.

Prepare: 5 minutes; cook: 30 minutes
Serves: 4

Heat oil in a saucepan over a medium-high heat. Add rice to hot oil and stir until rice is lightly toasted.

Add Coca-Cola, coconut milk, salt and sugar, bring to the boil and stir. Reduce the heat to low and simmer, covered, stirring every 5 minutes (set a timer) so that the rice doesn't stick to the bottom of the pan. After 10 minutes, add raisins and fluff rice with a fork. Continue to cook until rice is tender, 5-10 minutes more. The liquid will have evaporated to just below the level of the rice and little holes will start to form on the surface.

Remove pan from the heat and rest for 5 minutes. Fluff rice with a fork, sprinkle with toasted coconut flakes (if using) and serve.

Chef's note: The coconut flakes are not traditional, but I feel they add extra flavour and texture. This dish goes well with achiote-rubbed grilled fish (see page 75) or fish fillets in green sauce (see page 76). The trick for stopping the rice getting lumpy is to toast it well; then, once the rice comes to the boil, stir it once then lower the heat and set a timer. Stir about every 5 minutes; because of the sugar content, it will readily stick to the bottom of the pan.

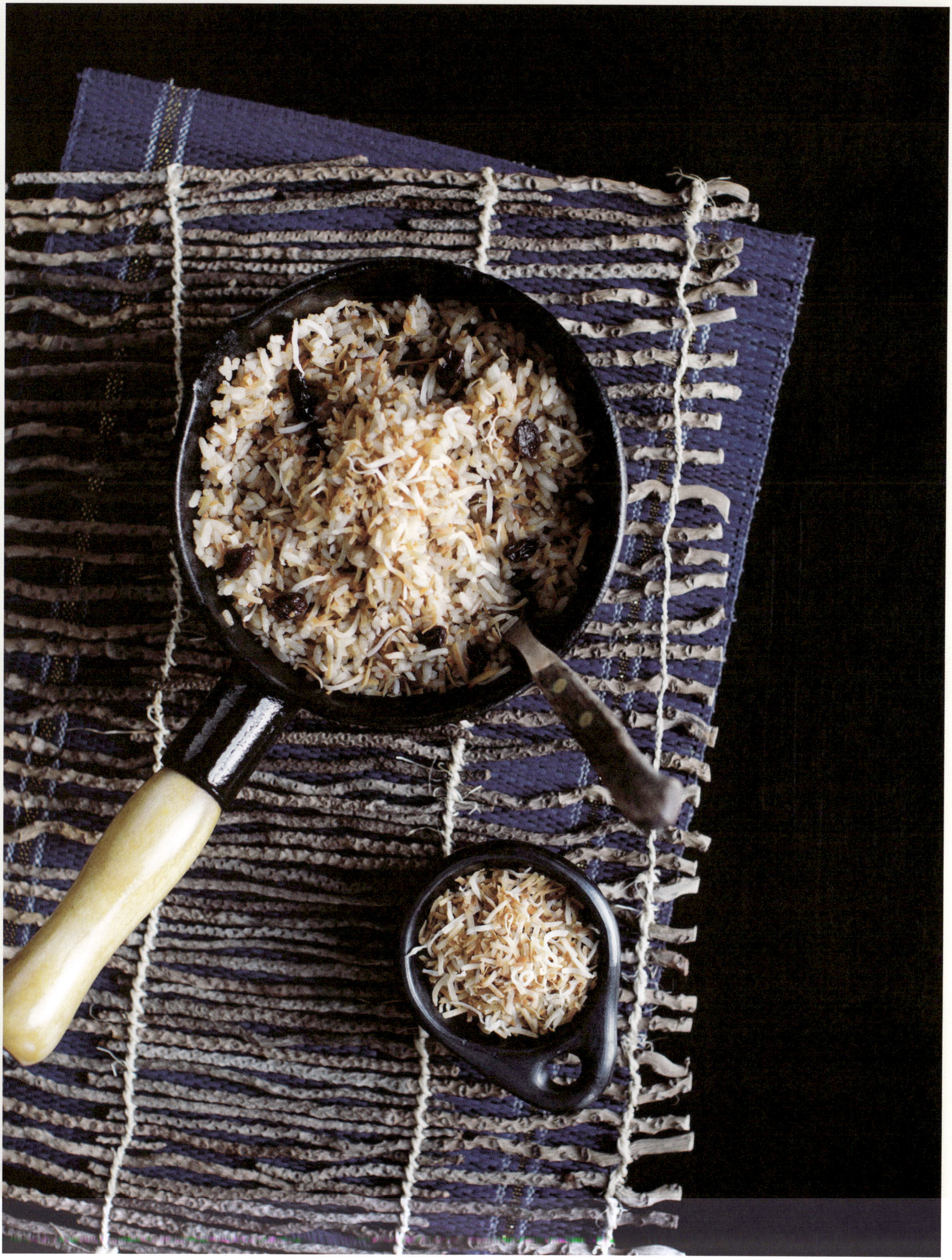

Mexico

ARROZ ROJO

Mexican-style Red Rice

GF

- 1 tbsp rice bran oil
- 1 onion, diced
- 1 clove garlic, smashed
- 1 cup white long-grain rice
- 1 cup canned tomato purée (or plum tomatoes pulsed in a blender)
- 1 cup vegetable stock, chicken stock or water
- ¼ cup finely diced carrot
- ¼ cup defrosted frozen or fresh peas

This delicious rice is a classic. Every time you order a main course in Mexico, a version of this rice will most likely be served as the perfect accompaniment. Many people are turned off by rice because they are used to eating Thai, Indian or sushi rice which has very little seasoning or flavour. But in Latin America we love rice and eat it every day, adding creative combinations of flavours and herbs, seasoning or stock. This particular rice absorbs all the gusto from the tomatoes, carrots and onions, so looks gorgeous and tastes beautiful. It will add love to any mundane dish.

Prepare: 10 minutes; cook: 20 minutes
Serves: 4–6

In a medium-sized saucepan, heat oil over a medium heat and gently fry onion and garlic until light golden brown. Add rice, toss with a wooden spoon until coated with oil, and stir for a few minutes until lightly toasted. Add tomato, stock or water and salt to taste, and bring to the boil. Lower the heat to a simmer and continue to cook, covered, for about 10 minutes. Add carrots and peas, and mix until just incorporated. Continue to cook for 5 minutes, until peas are warmed and carrots are cooked through. Leave to rest for 5 minutes, then fluff with a fork.

Chef's note: The amount of salt you add will depend on whether you use stock or water and on how salty your stock is.

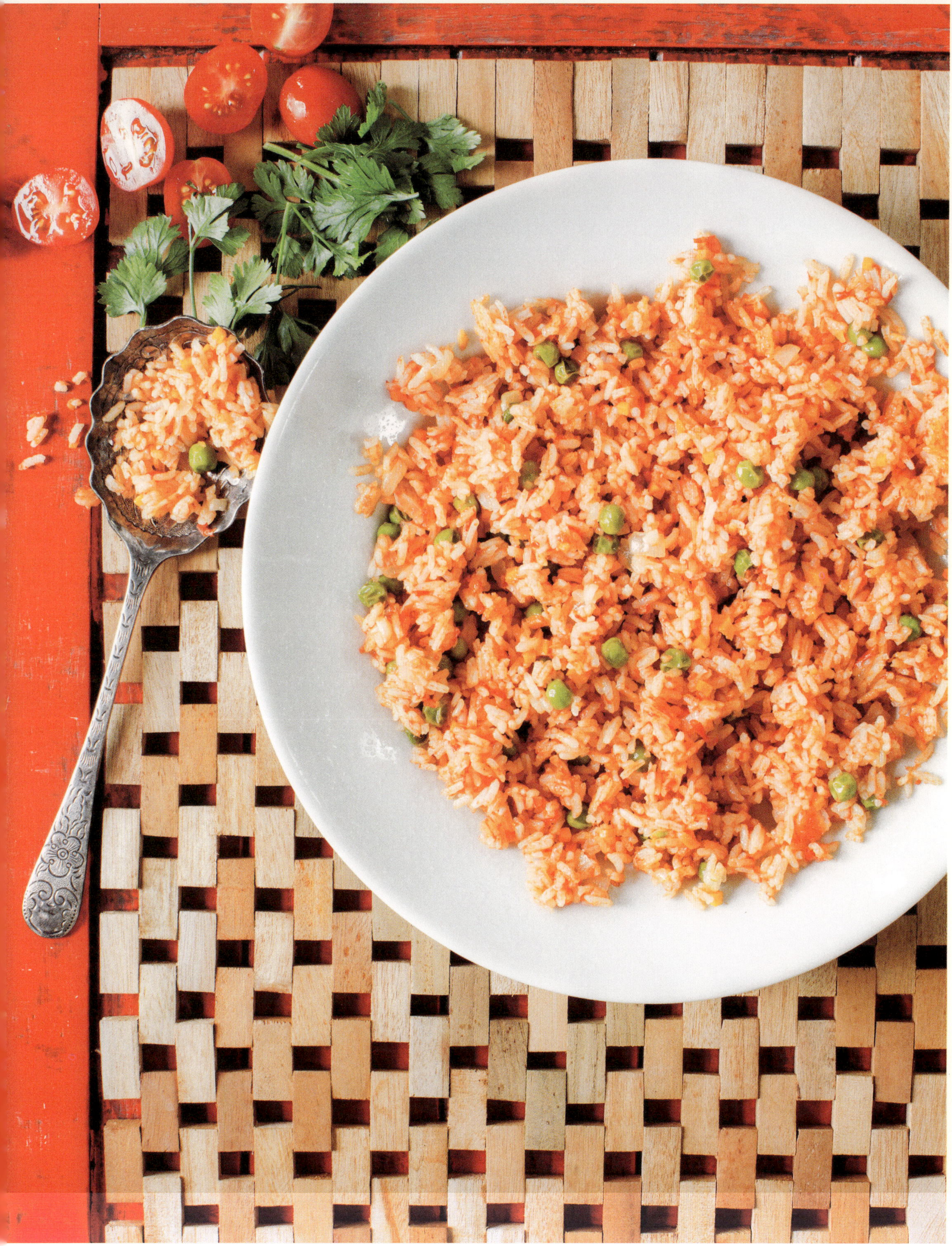

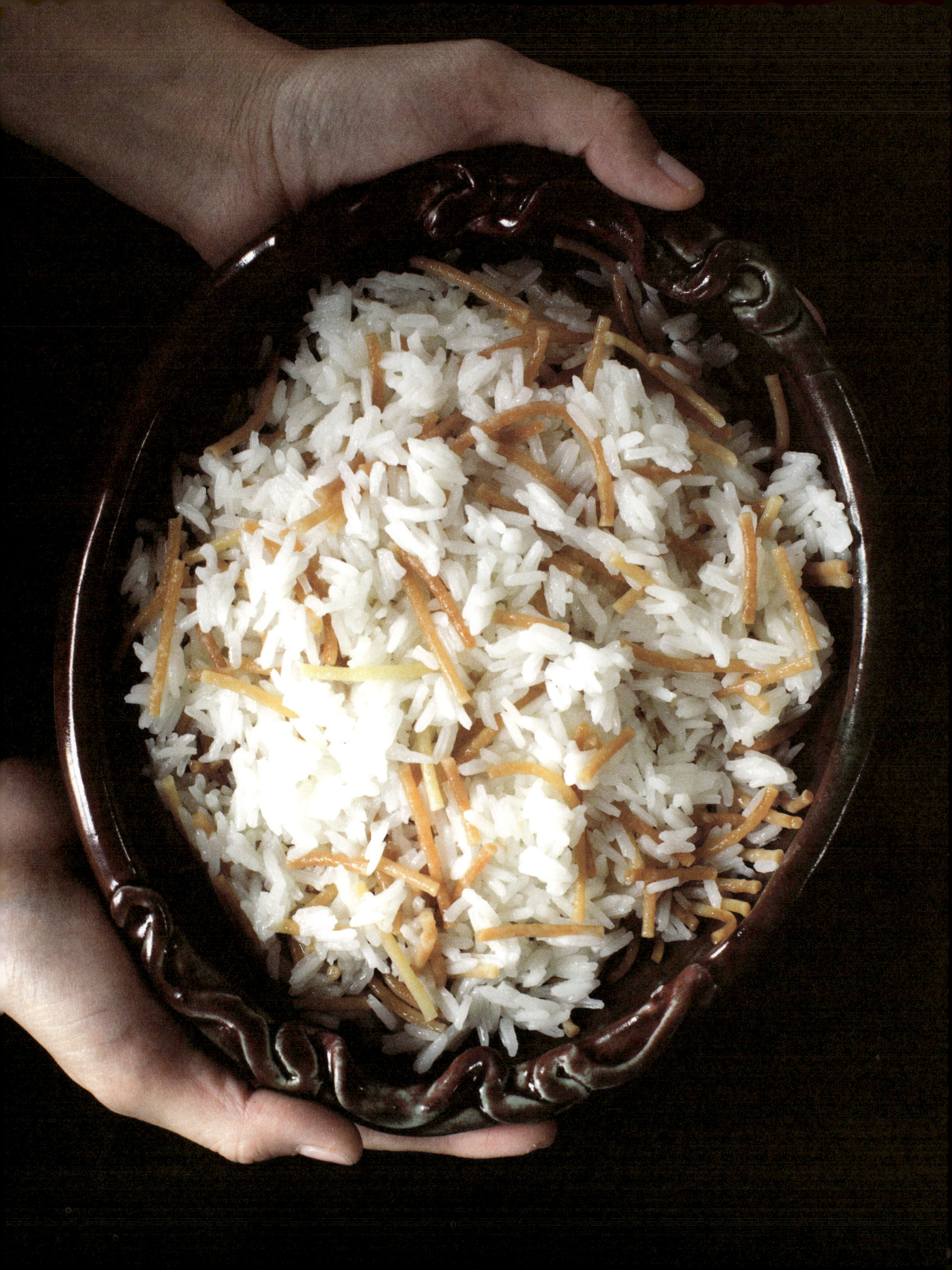

Peru

ARROZ CON FIDEOS

Rice & Noodles

GF

1 tbsp rice bran or other neutral-tasting oil
150 g dried spaghetti, broken into pieces about 2 cm long
1 tsp soy sauce
4 cups water
2 cups white long-grain rice

This is comfort food at its best. The Chinese influence on Peruvian cuisine is so obviously present in this dish. I used to eat this straight from the pot. My grandmother would make it for me all the time, but then I tried it in Peru as well. It is a children's favourite and just smells and tastes like home.

Prepare: 5 minutes; cook: 25 minutes
Serves: 6–8

In a medium-sized saucepan, heat oil and gently cook spaghetti until very golden brown; about 5 minutes. Add soy sauce and stir. Add water and salt to taste (see perfect white rice chef's note on page 144), bring to the boil, stir in the rice and then cover. Simmer for 15–20 minutes, without stirring. Turn off heat and leave covered for 5 minutes. Fluff rice with a fork, and serve.

Costa Rica

GALLO PINTO

Ticos' Rice & Beans

GF

1 tbsp rice bran oil
1 small onion, diced
¼ cup diced de-seeded red capsicum
¼ cup diced de-seeded yellow capsicum
2 cups cooked perfect white rice (see page 144)
2 tsp Worcestershire sauce
2 tsp soy sauce
425 g can black beans, liquid retained, or Mom's black beans (see page 15)
½ cup chopped coriander

Many Hispanic countries in Latin America have a rice and bean dish they adore and call their own. Cubans have congri or Moros y Cristianos, Venezuelans have their national dish pabellón of rice, beans, shredded beef (see page 105) and plantains, Brazil worships the feijoada (see page 17) and Dominicans love pinto beans as part of the dish la bandera Dominicana (meaning the Dominican flag), which is their traditional lunch available in every café or made in most homes. For Costa Rica, gallo pinto is the national dish. The capsicums and onions are gently fried before the rice and beans get mixed together, they add extra flavour and some crunch. 'Ticos', as Costa Ricans are called, eat it morning, noon or night — my favourite is at breakfast, with eggs, sweet plantains, crema agria and tortillas. This is a fast yet super-tasty version. Get ready to eat it straight from the bowl!

Prepare: 10 minutes; cook: 15 minutes
Serves: 4–6

In a large frying pan, heat oil over a medium heat, then add onion and capsicums. Gently fry for about 5 minutes, until lightly seared. Add rice, Worcestershire sauce and soy sauce. Continue to cook for 2–3 minutes to warm the rice. Lower the heat to medium-low, and add beans with some of their liquid. Mix together until combined evenly. Season to taste with salt and freshly ground black pepper and add the coriander at the end. Serve straight away.

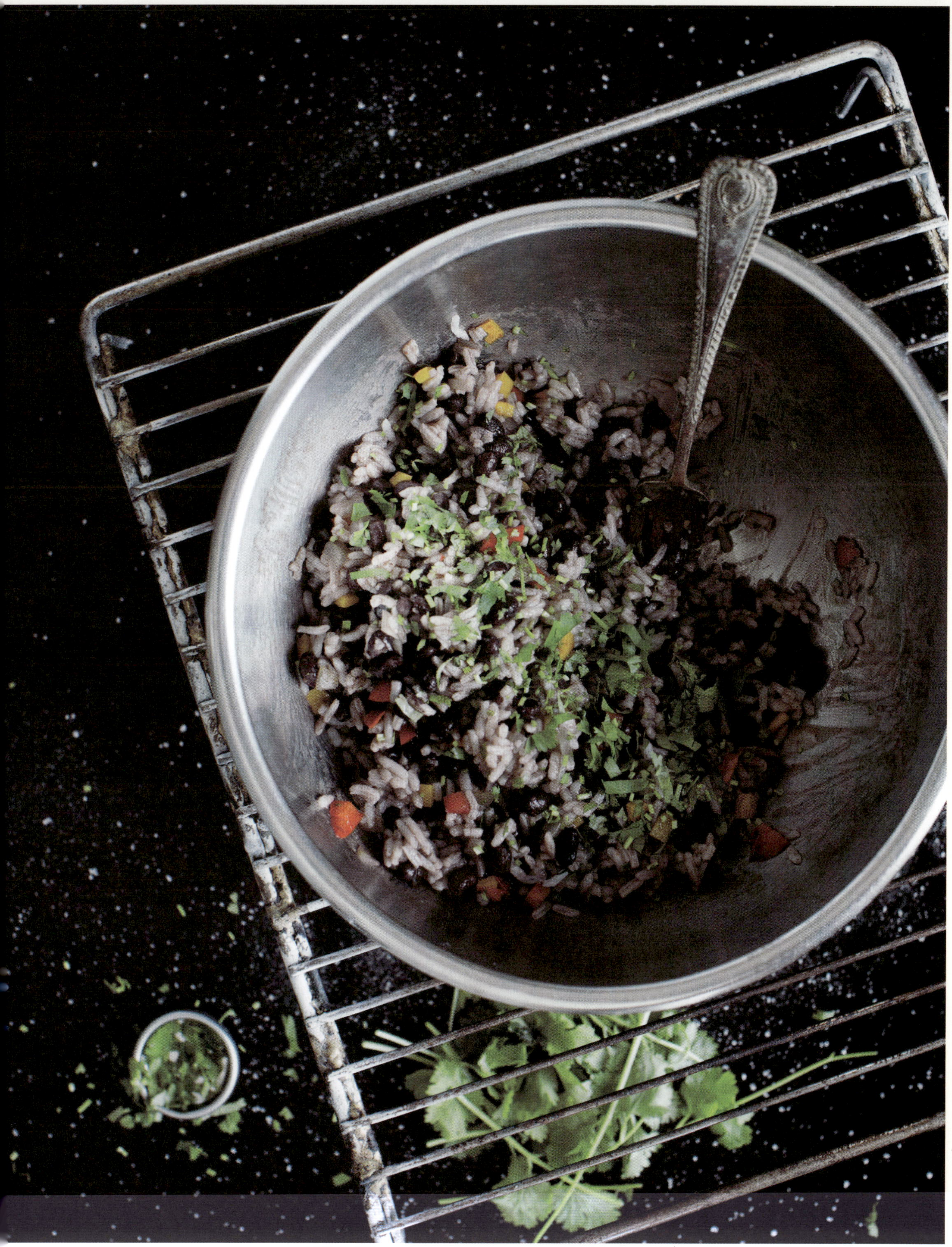

Peru

ARROZ NEGRO

Black Ink Rice

GF

300 g squid, including tentacles
4 tbsp olive oil
3 cloves garlic
½ cup packed parsley leaves
2 cups fish stock
1 small onion, finely diced
½ cup finely chopped de-seeded red capsicum or 'little sweetie' peppers
1 tbsp squid ink
1 cup canned Italian plum tomatoes, blended
1 cup white long-grain rice
2 tbsp white wine

Garnish (optional)
chopped coriander
2 piquillo chillies, thinly sliced
1 capsicum, deseeded, roasted and thinly sliced
1 tbsp queso fresco (see page 208)

Some dishes are like a first kiss — memorable, and it will never be the same again. Once, in Spain, I tried arroz negro — and, just like that first kiss, it changed me forever; I was in love. Then I tried it in a Peruvian restaurant, and it was like being kissed for the very first time all over again; but was this time even better? Peruvian cuisine is a combination of Spanish cuisine with local ingredients, but also has influences from China, West Africa, Italy and Japan through people immigrating from these countries. The result is superb. Here is my version of this amazing dish.

Prepare: 30 minutes; cook: 45 minutes
Serves: 4–6

Clean squid, remove cartilage, and slice bodies into rings and tentacles in half. Season with ½ teaspoon salt and 1 tablespoon olive oil. Set aside.

With a mortar and pestle, mash garlic, parsley, 1 teaspoon salt and 1 tablespoon olive oil into a paste. Set aside. Prepare the rest of your ingredients.

To a paella pan or large, deep frying pan add 2 tablespoons olive oil over a low heat. Add garlic and parsley paste and sweat carefully over a low heat; don't burn the garlic or parsley or they will turn bitter (and they will continue to cook later). Add 1 tablespoon of stock and turn the heat to medium-low, then add onion and capsicum and sweat until onion is translucent. Add ½ tablespoon squid ink and mix until fully incorporated.

Meanwhile, in a small saucepan bring remaining stock, 1 teaspoon salt and remaining squid ink to the boil. Turn off the heat and set aside. Make sure your stock is sufficiently salty because you want all that flavour to be absorbed by the rice.

Turn the heat under the paella pan to medium and add squid. Cook for about 1 minute, then add tomato. Let it simmer for about 5 minutes. Add rice, stir to incorporate and spread into an even layer. Once it begins to bubble, add stock mixture, bring back to a boil then simmer, uncovered, until almost completely absorbed. Rotate pan occasionally to ensure that it cooks evenly. After 20 minutes, check the rice; it should be almost done. If not, add ¼ cup stock or water, cover with foil and cook for an extra 5-10 minutes. Pour in wine. Turn heat off, cover with foil and leave for 5-10 minutes until ready to serve.

Garnish with chopped parsley, piquillo chillies or capsicum and queso fresco if desired.

Chef's note: The stock you use will affect how much salt you add. The water must taste salty — almost like the ocean — to ensure that all that flavour goes into your rice. Otherwise, your rice will be bland.

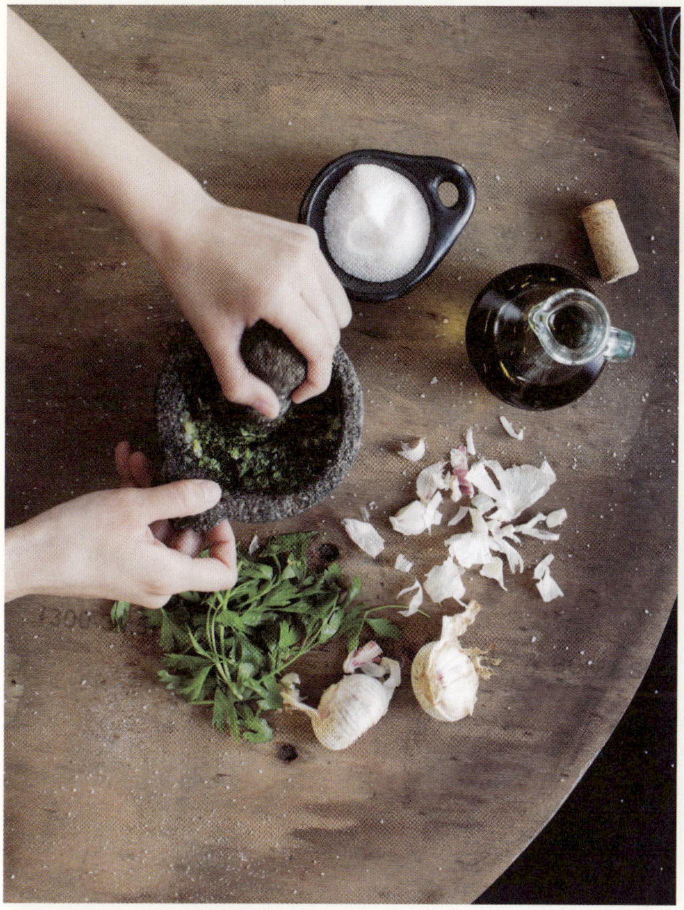
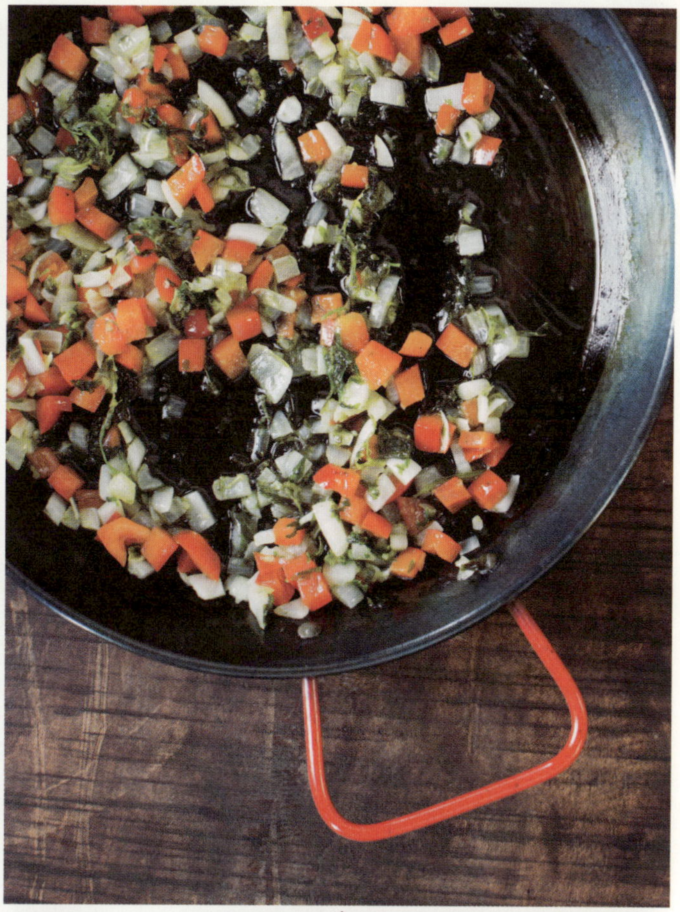
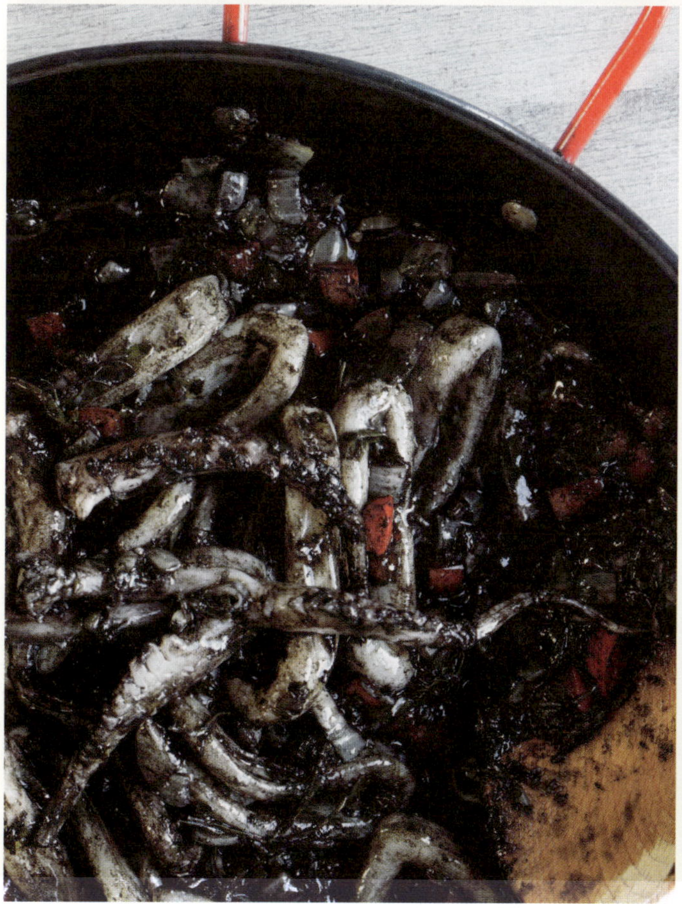
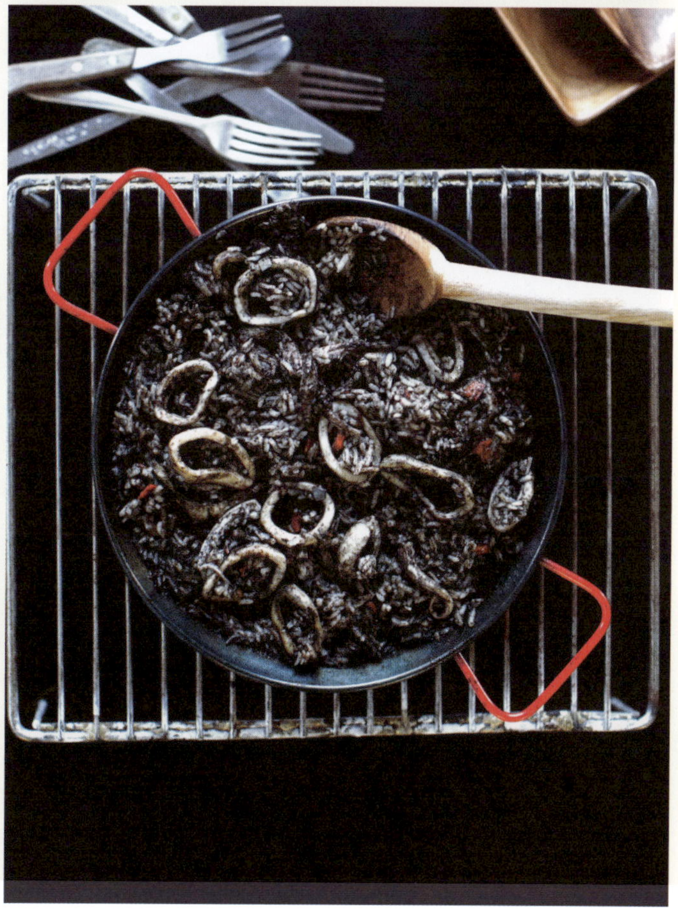

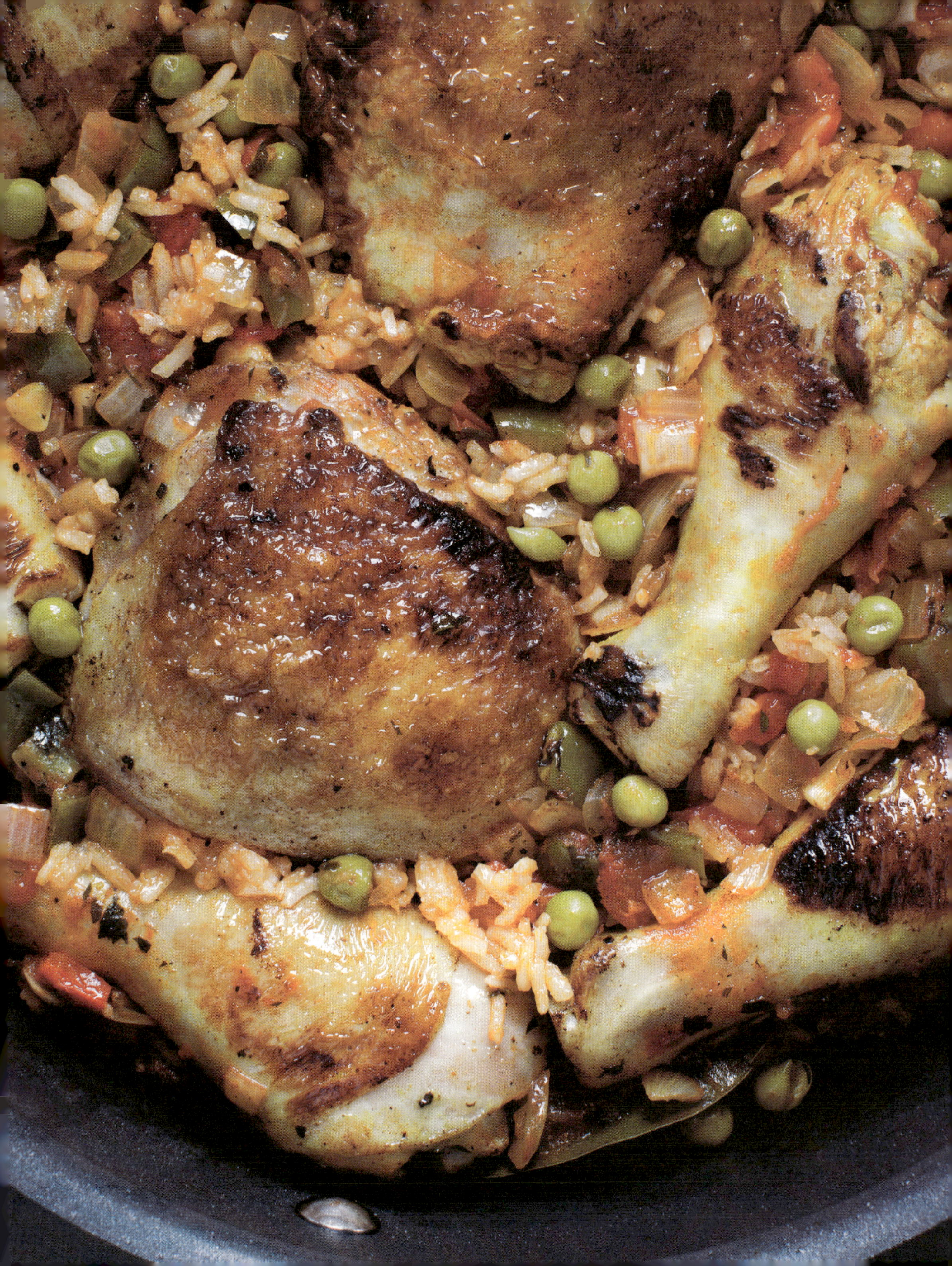

Cuba

ARROZ CON POLLO

Chicken & Rice

GF

3 chicken legs (thighs and drumsticks)
olive oil for browning

For the marinade
¼ cup orange juice
2 tbsp lemon juice
2 tsp apple cider vinegar
4 cloves garlic, crushed
¼ tsp ground cumin
¼ tsp turmeric
¼ tsp oregano (fresh or dried)
1 tbsp salt
1 tsp freshly ground black pepper, or to taste

For the rice
1 small onion, diced
1 small green capsicum, de-seeded and diced
3 tbsp de-seeded and diced piquillo chillies
1 tbsp tomato paste
½ cup liquid from the piquillo chilli jar
½ cup tomato sauce
¼ tsp ground cumin
1 tbsp chopped parsley
1 bay leaf
¼ tsp saffron threads or 1 tbsp achiote oil (see page 188)
2 cups jasmine rice
1 cup lager-style beer
2 cups chicken stock
1½ cups canned or frozen peas, thawed

Garnish
sliced piquillo chillies
chopped parsley and/or coriander

Arroz con pollo is a sensitive and serious subject of discussion between friends and families in different countries. When trying to decide which arroz con pollo recipe to include, I decided to have a dinner party to see which version was best. Invited were another Venezuelan, two Cubans, a Costa Rican, a Puerto Rican and a Chinese friend (don't they make great fried rice?). This was not a good idea. Dinner became a heated debate about what ingredients and procedures to follow, which spices and herbs were traditional to what country, the type of rice, shredded chicken versus bone-in thighs, risotto or paella consistency . . . Oh! — and let's not leave out achiote or saffron! Much drama. There was rolling of eyes and very spirited conversation. Everyone likes it the way their mom or grandma makes it, usually in big batches for the family on Sunday or special occasions. Here is the version I decided was best!

**Prepare: 20 minutes; marinate: 2 hours; cook: 1 hour
Serves: 6**

Separate the chicken drumsticks from the thighs. Combine all marinade ingredients with chicken in a large bowl or sealable plastic bag, and let marinate for 2 hours in the refrigerator. Flip the bag or stir the bowl after 1 hour to allow both sides of the chicken to marinate well. Remove chicken from marinade and pat skin dry with paper towel. Season with salt and pepper. Reserve remaining marinade except for crushed garlic.

In a large Dutch oven or heavy-bottomed saucepan, heat olive oil over a medium-high heat. In two batches, brown chicken until golden brown; 2–3 minutes per side. Remove from the heat and set aside.

In the same pan, fry onion, green capsicum and piquillo chilli until onion is transparent, adding a little extra oil if needed. Add tomato paste, stirring and cooking for about 30 seconds, then add piquillo liquid, tomato sauce, cumin, parsley, bay leaf, saffron or achiote oil and reserved marinade. Bring to the boil, then lower the heat and simmer, uncovered, until the liquid has mostly reduced; about 10 minutes.

Add rice, beer, chicken stock and ½ tablespoon salt, then nestle chicken back into the pan, cover, and bring to the boil. Lower the heat and simmer until the rice is done, 20 minutes. Add peas and cook for 5 minutes. Let it sit for about 5 minutes before serving, garnishing with sliced piquillo chillies and chopped parsley and/or coriander.

Chef's note: The type of rice is 'essential', according to the 'experts'. My grandmother makes this with a long-grain rice and Cubans make it with arroz de Valencia, a short-grain rice. Obviously the type of rice will change the flavour and texture of the dish, but it's delicious either way. The short-grain rice will release more starch so will have more of a risotto-like consistency, while the jasmine rice will be more separated and drier. Depending on what rice you use, the cooking time will vary. Also, depending on the stock you use you might need to add more or less salt.

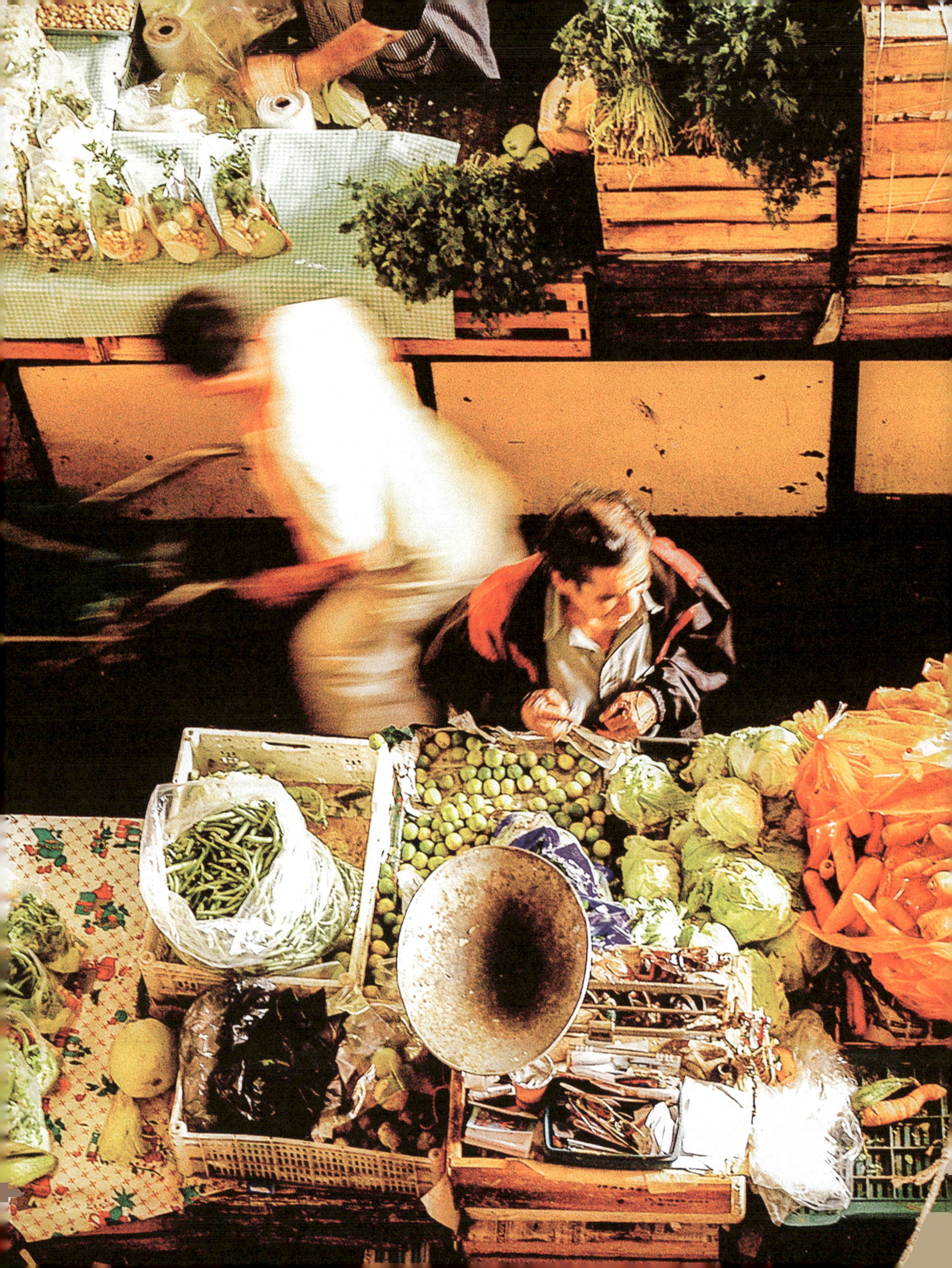

ENSALADAS Y VEGETALES

SALADS & VEGETABLES

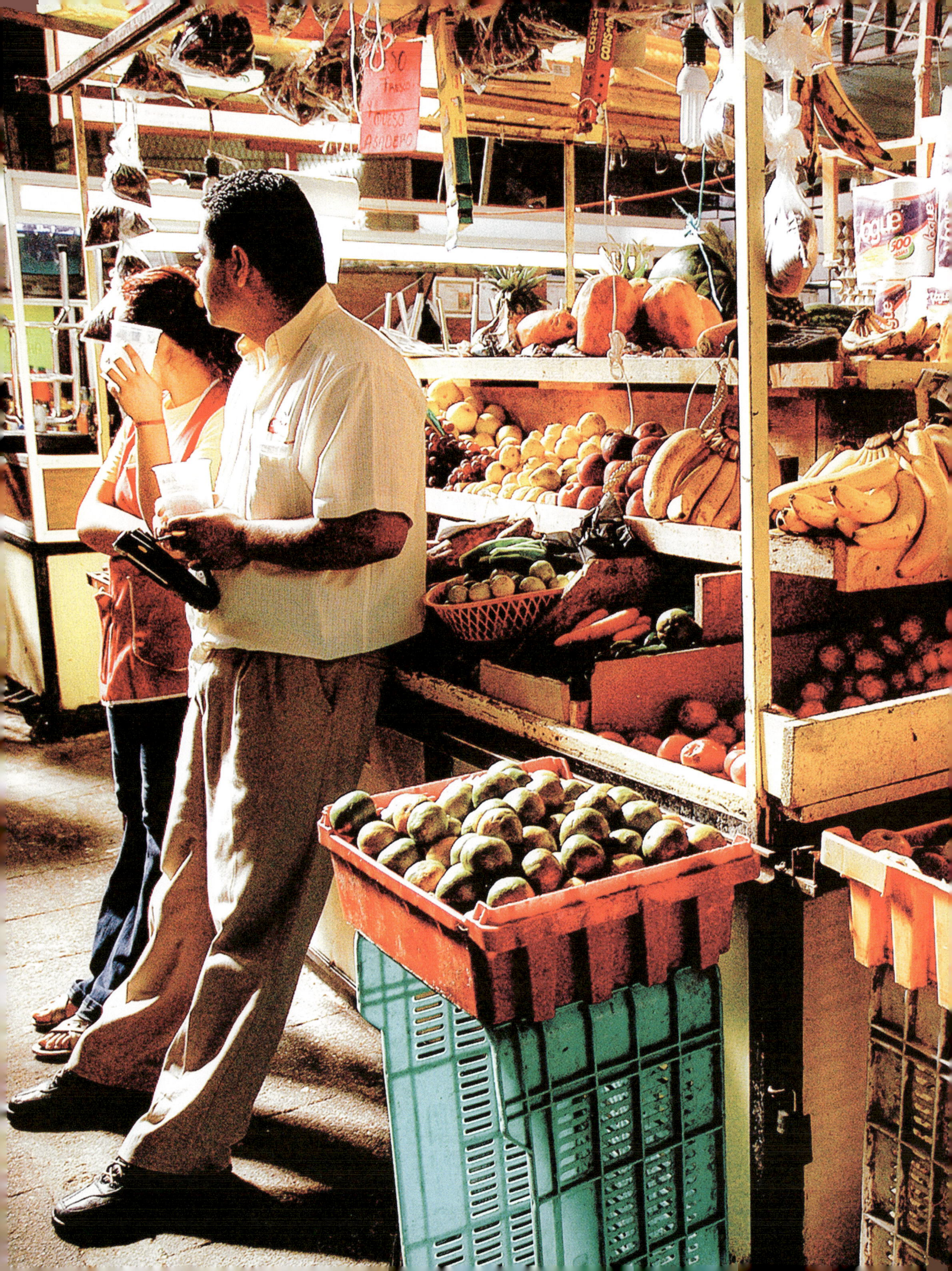
Vogue

ENCURTIDO HONDUREÑO
Pickled Vegetables

ENSALADA CON CILANTRO
Wedge Salad with Coriander Dressing

CARPACCIO DE VENADO CON ENSALADA
Venison Carpaccio with Watercress, Palm Hearts & Avocado

ENSALADA CON SANDÍA Y MEZCAL
Mezcal Watermelon Salad

ENSALADA CON MANGO Y MARACUYÁ
Mango & Passionfruit Salad

ELOTE DEL MERCADO
Street Corn

TOMATES RELLENOS
Tomatoes Stuffed with Quinoa

YUCA CON MOJO
Cassava with Garlic & Citrus Sauce

HONGOS CON CHIPOTLE
Chipotle & Beer Mushrooms

PAPAS A LA HUANCAINA
Potatoes in Huancaina Sauce

Honduras

ENCURTIDO HONDUREÑO

Pickled Vegetables

GF

1 onion, peeled and sliced
1 carrot, peeled and sliced
1 red capsicum, de-seeded and sliced
4 red radishes, halved lengthwise
¼ head cauliflower, cut into florets (optional)
1 jalapeño, sliced (optional)
1 beetroot, peeled and cut into wedges
1½ cups apple cider vinegar
1½ cups water
4 cloves
2 tbsp salt
½ cup sugar
½ tbsp black peppercorns
2 tsp ground cumin
2 tsp dried oregano

To serve
olive oil for drizzling
chopped parsley or chives (optional)

In Latin America, pickled vegetables are called 'encurtido', or 'chilera' if it includes chillies and is spicy. We use or serve some sort of pickled vegetable with tacos, tamales, soups, rices — the list is endless. They add an extra layer of flavour and crunch to even the most boring of meals. Encurtidos can also be served as an appetiser to start off a meal, and it's a great way to preserve extra veggies from the garden or when you have too many. Many Honduran encurtidos include beets, which give a pretty pink colour. Encurtidos need to be refrigerated for at least three days before serving.

Prepare: 15 minutes; cook: 10 minutes; stand: 3 days
Makes: 2 large mason jars full

Combine all vegetables except beetroot in a bowl. Set aside.
    To a saucepan, add beetroot, vinegar, water, cloves, salt, sugar, peppercorns, cumin and oregano. Bring to the boil and stir until sugar and salt dissolve, then pour over sliced vegetables. Let the mixture cool completely at room temperature.
    When cool, transfer to sterilised mason jars with tight-fitting lids. Ensure that the liquid completely covers the vegetables in the jar. Refrigerate for at least 3 days before serving, to allow the flavours to develop. Keep refrigerated after opening jars. Serve drizzled with olive oil and, if desired, parsley or chives.
    Chef's note: Use any vegetable combination you like, and feel free to add different types of chilli to add more heat and flavour.

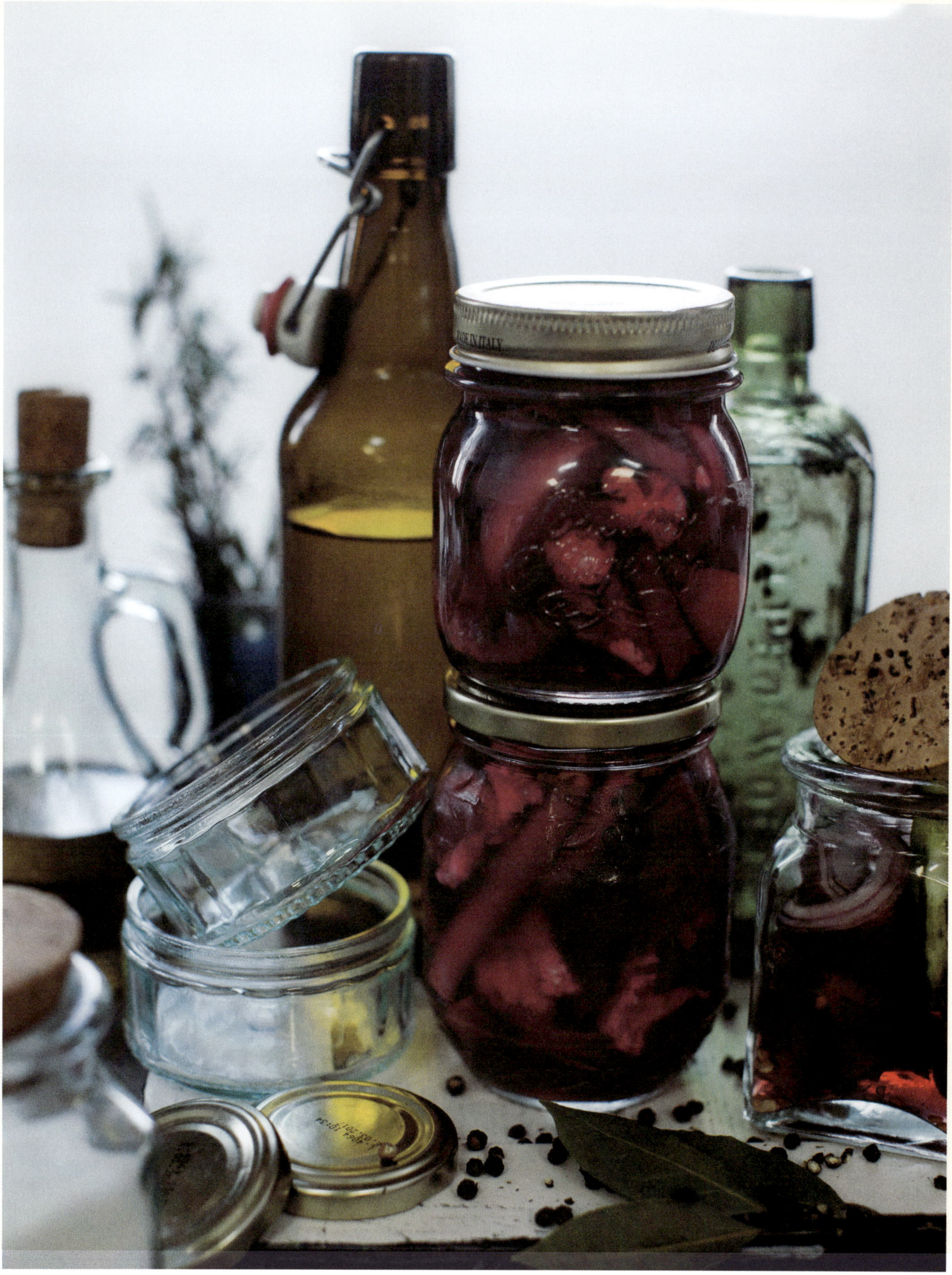
MADE IN ITALY

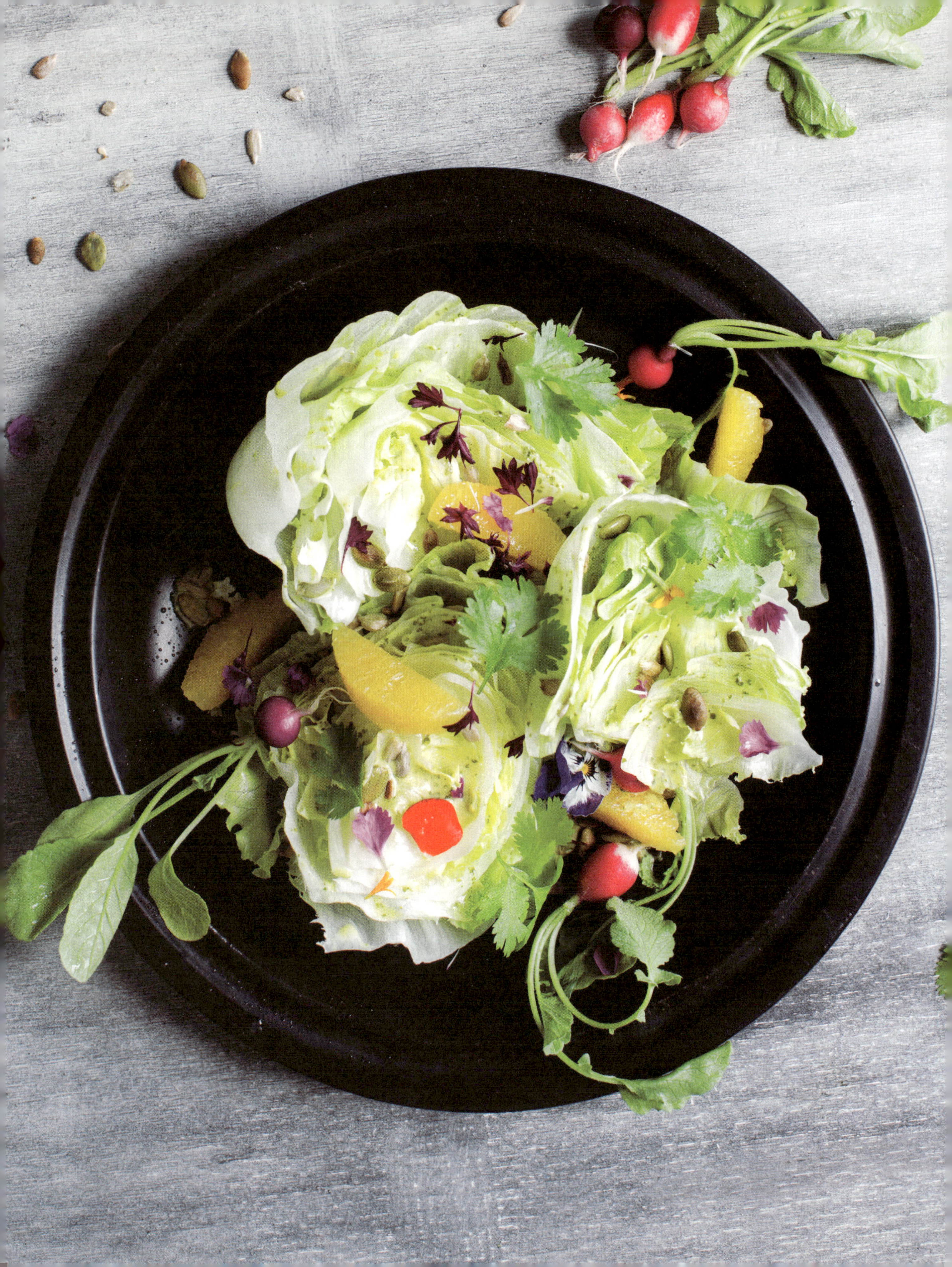

Mexico

ENSALADA CON CILANTRO

Wedge Salad with Coriander Dressing

GF

For the dressing (makes 1¼ cups)
1 egg
¼ cup lemon juice
½ cup tightly packed coriander leaves
1 clove garlic
¾ cup avocado or rice bran oil
flaky sea salt

For the salad
2 iceberg lettuce heads, cut into wedges
1 orange, peeled and segmented
1 small bunch radishes, thinly sliced
1 tsp toasted pumpkin seeds
1 tsp toasted sesame seeds
1 tsp sunflower seeds
edible flowers, to garnish (optional)

As a Hispanic, I'm constantly trying to find ways to include the flavours from home in any dish I make. It's not because the originals are lacking in flavour, but because it reminds me of home and the special ingredients turn it into a comfort food for me. This salad is my Hispanic version of a wedge salad. It's full of creamy avocado, sweet orange, spicy radish and seeds that take me back to my beloved roots.

Prepare: 5 minutes
Serves: 4 as a side

Combine egg, lemon juice, coriander (reserving some to garnish) and garlic in a food processor. Blend until coriander is just starting to break up; about 30 seconds. Slowly pour in avocado oil while the motor is running, until emulsified. Season to taste with flaky sea salt and freshly ground black pepper.

On each plate, arrange two wedges of iceberg lettuce and top with the orange, radish and seeds. Drizzle the salad dressing over, garnish with coriander and edible flowers (if using) and serve. Extra dressing can be stored in the refrigerator for up to 3 days. If dressing separates, whisk together until emulsified.

Chef's note: I like to toast the seeds in large batches, and save them in an airtight container for other salads, or have them as a snack.

Venezuela

CARPACCIO DE VENADO CON ENSALADA

Venison Carpaccio with Watercress, Palm Hearts & Avocado

GF

1 kg boned venison loin, fat and sinew removed
1 tbsp olive oil
3 palm hearts
1 bunch watercress
1 avocado
juice of 1 lemon
flaky sea salt to taste
½ cup shaved Parmesan
edible flowers for garnish (optional)

For the dressing
2 cloves garlic
pinch of salt
2 tsp Dijon mustard
1 tbsp lemon juice
3 tbsp olive oil

I fell in love with venison in New Zealand. Before this I'd been a bit scared of it; even though I love game meat, what I had tried before was too gamey. After going hunting with the boys in New Zealand I realised that the freshness and the deer's age contributes to the meat's tenderness and taste. Also, how you cook the meat is very important. Because the loin is so lean, it's best to just sear it and serve it rare to medium rare. Venison is low in fat and cholesterol, and packed with protein, vitamins and minerals. Better yet, it will most likely be free of antibiotics and synthetic hormones, especially wild venison. The salad that goes with this is very simple but traditional. At most barbecues or barbecue restaurants in Venezuela you will usually be served a big bowl of salad with the oil, vinegar, salt and pepper put on the table for you to dress it yourself.

Prepare: 10 minutes; cook: 30 minutes; rest: approx. 30 minutes
Serves: 4 to 6 as an appetiser

Preheat a heavy griddle pan that's large enough to hold the venison comfortably. If your pan is too small, cut the venison into two and grill in two batches. Season venison well with fine salt and freshly ground black pepper and brush with ½ tablespoon of olive oil. Place on the hot pan and sear/brown all over, about 3–5 minutes. Remove from the pan and place on a plate to rest for 30 minutes or until cooled.

Meanwhile, make the dressing. Mash garlic with salt in a mortar and pestle, until it forms a paste. Mix in mustard, lemon juice and olive oil. Season to taste with salt and freshly ground black pepper.

Slice palm hearts into rounds about ½ cm thick. When ready to serve, chop watercress and peel and slice avocados, adding some lemon juice to prevent oxidation. Keep avocado aside. Dress watercress with olive oil, lemon juice and flaky sea salt.

Slice venison loin with a sharp knife. If you want your pieces extra thin, place the slices between two pieces of plastic wrap and pound with a mallet or rolling pin. Place venison slices, slightly overlapping one another, over the whole of a large platter. Drizzle remaining olive oil over the venison. Add the dressed watercress, palm hearts, avocado slices, shaved Parmesan and edible flowers (if using). Drizzle over dressing. Adjust seasoning with a little extra flaky sea salt and freshly ground black pepper.

Chef's note: If you make the salad on its own you can simply dress it with olive oil, vinegar, salt and pepper, but if you are making the carpaccio as well then use this dressing, which is my 'go to' vinaigrette for most salads. You can also make a beef carpaccio instead of a venison one — the best cut is eye fillet or beef tenderloin, which you cook for the same length of time.

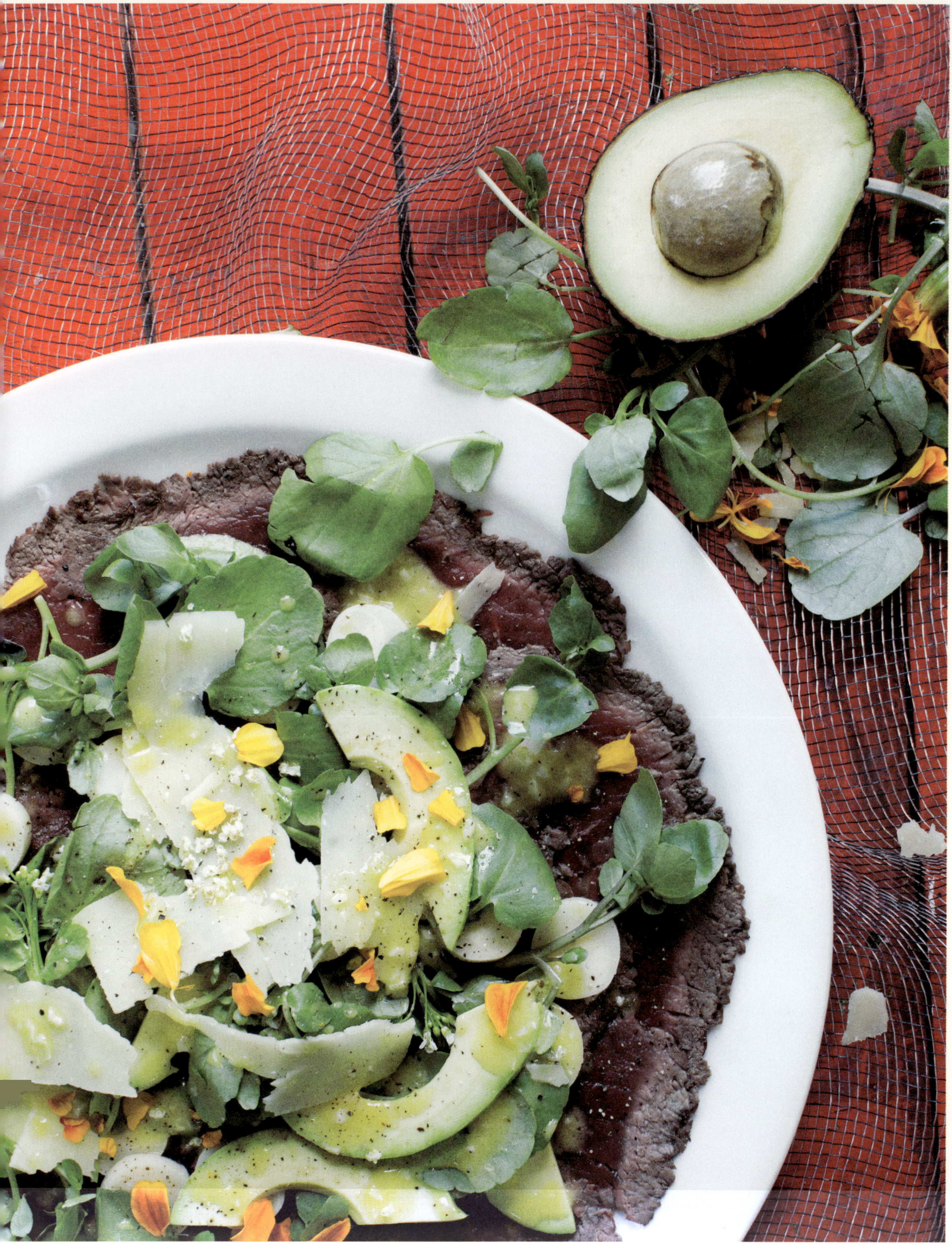

Mexico

ENSALADA CON SANDÍA Y MEZCAL

Mezcal Watermelon Salad

GF

**For the dressing
(makes approx. ¾ cup)**
1 tsp Dijon mustard
2 tbsp lime juice
2 tbsp orange juice
½ cup olive oil
flaky sea salt

For the salad
¼ cup mezcal or tequila
400 g seedless watermelon, diced
2 heads baby gem lettuce
¼ cup queso fresco (see page 208) or feta cheese
1 green chilli, sliced (optional)
1 red chilli, sliced (optional)
1 sprig mint, leaves picked and torn

This is the perfect summer salad for me. It has all the flavours that make my mouth water. Watermelons are light and refreshing, and go so well with mint, queso fresco and chillies. If you can't find mezcal (mescal) in your local liquor store, use tequila.

**Prepare: 10 minutes
Serves: 4 as an appetiser**

For the dressing, whisk together mustard, lime juice, orange juice and olive oil. Season to taste with flaky sea salt and freshly ground black pepper.

For the salad, drizzle mezcal or tequila over watermelon. Let it sit for 5 minutes to absorb the mezcal.

Separate and wash baby gem lettuce leaves, then toss with dressing and top with watermelon. Crumble queso fresco or feta over the watermelon. Garnish with chillies (if using), mint and flaky sea salt.

Chef's note: I used mezcal here to get a smokier, outdoorsy barbecue feel. If you wish, you can also char slices of the watermelon before dicing on a very hot grill, 1–2 minutes each side, to complement this flavour and get some beautiful-looking grill marks. The dressing will keep in the fridge for up to 3 days.

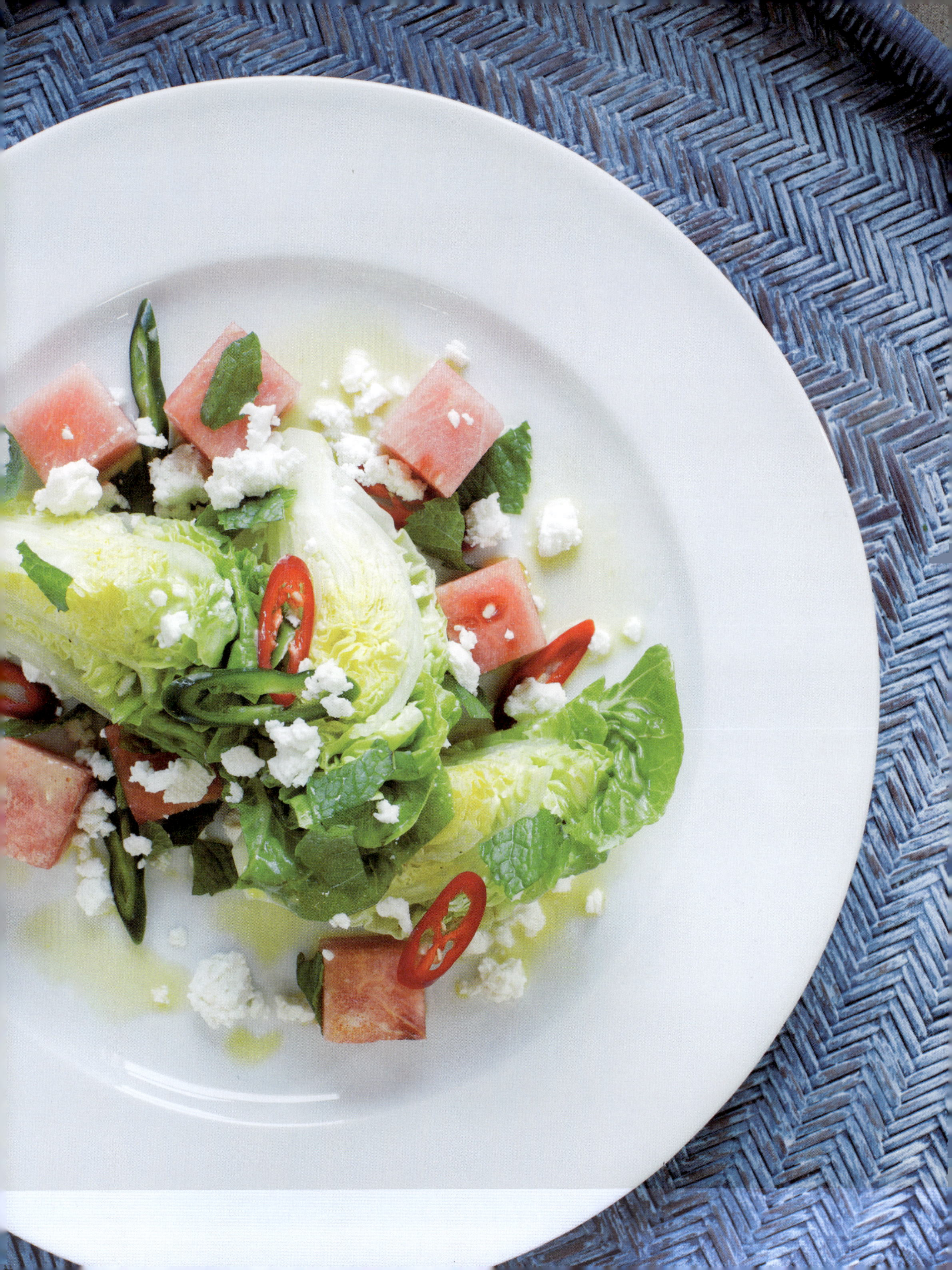

Caribbean

ENSALADA CON MANGO Y MARACUYÁ

Mango & Passionfruit Salad

GF

For the dressing
(makes ¼ cup)

1 clove garlic, peeled
3 tbsp passionfruit juice, or pulp of 1 fresh passionfruit
1 tbsp lemon juice
2 spring onions, sliced, white and green parts separated
¼ tsp Dijon mustard
2 tbsp olive oil
1 tsp liquid honey (optional)
flaky sea salt

For the salad

300 g mixed greens (1 large bag)
1 mango, peeled and sliced into matchsticks
1 spring onion, green parts only, sliced
½ radicchio, shredded

What's not to love about the passionfruit/mango flavour combination and the contrast of colours and textures in this beautiful salad? In Venezuela passionfruit is called 'parchita', in Puerto Rico 'parcha', in the Dominican Republic 'chinola' and in most other places 'maracuyá', though spelt 'maracujá' in Brazil! The common denominator in all these countries is that this gorgeous fruit is adored and frequently used in juices, desserts, yoghurts, drinks and ice creams wherever it's available.

Prepare: 10 minutes
Serves: 6

For the dressing, mash garlic with a pinch of salt in a mortar and pestle, until you form a paste. Mix in passionfruit juice or pulp, lemon juice, spring onion and mustard, and whisk in olive oil and honey (if using). Season to taste with flaky sea salt and freshly ground black pepper.

Add mixed greens, mango, spring onion and radicchio to a large bowl. Drizzle passionfruit dressing along the sides of the bowl and mix carefully with two large folks. Season to taste and serve immediately.

Chef's note: Make sure your salad leaves are washed and then dried so that the dressing sticks to them and does not get watered down. Don't drown your salad in the dressing. Start by adding a couple of tablespoons at a time to the side of the bowl and use your hands or two forks to mix until the leaves are lightly coated.

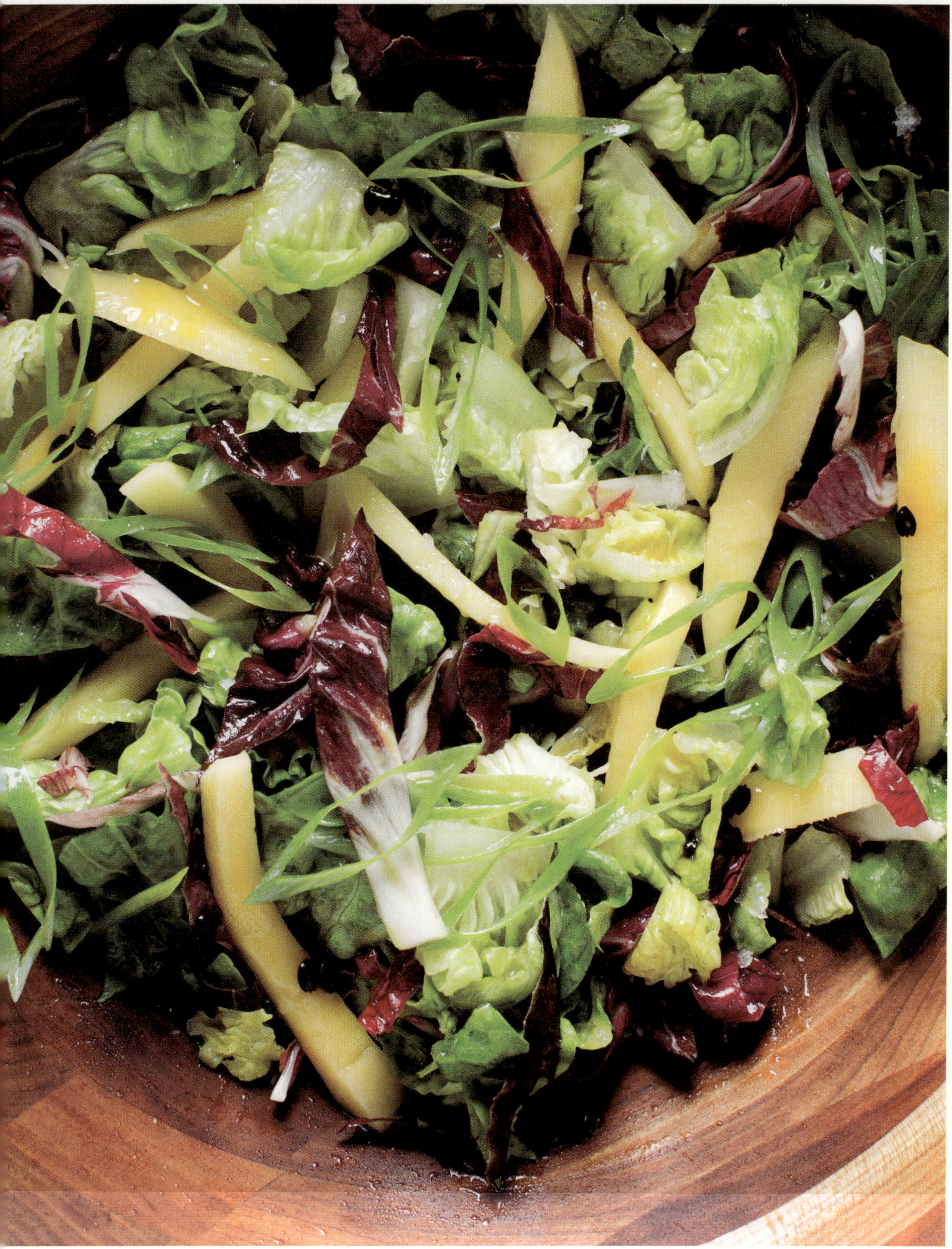

Mexico

ELOTE DEL MERCADO

Street Corn

GF

4 fresh sweetcorn, husks on
1 tbsp salt
2 tbsp butter, melted
¼ cup chipotle mayonnaise (see page 190)
100 g finely grated Parmesan or other hard cheese
chilli salt (see page 193), to taste
2 limes, cut into wedges

These appetising treats are extremely popular nowadays. I first tried these beauties about 15 years ago in Mexico City at the Mercado (Market) de San Ángel, in the San Jacinto Plaza — if you visit Mexico City, this is a 'must go' place on a Saturday afternoon. Ever since then, when sweetcorn is in season I make these by the dozen on the barbecue. Later I had them in a lovely area of Mexico City called Xochimilco. The place reminded me of the floating markets in Thailand, expect that families come here on weekends for a picnic. The canals of Xochimilco are filled with canoes selling tostadas and doraditas, and the corn sellers paddle along offering this corn straight from their small charcoal grills. Together with mariachi bands adding a festive spirit, it's like a scene out of a movie.

Prepare: 10 minutes; cook: 15 minutes
Serves: 4

If using a charcoal or wood-fired grill, get it going early so that it's nice and hot when you want to char the corn. Alternatively, set the burners on a gas grill to the highest heat setting, cover and preheat for 10 minutes. Clean and oil the grilling grate.

Place corn cobs in a large stockpot, cover with water and add salt. Boil for 10 minutes, then drain and leave to cool in the husk. When cool enough to handle, peel, brush with butter and grill on barbecue until slightly charred.

Brush liberally with chipotle aïoli, then roll in finely grated cheese to coat. Sprinkle with chilli salt. Serve with a fresh lime wedge on top.

Chef's note: You can make these in several different ways. For example, you could also microwave the corn, husks on, for 3–5 minutes on high, then peel, brush with butter and finish under a hot oven grill. Or you can remove the husks and grill them on the barbecue — up to you!

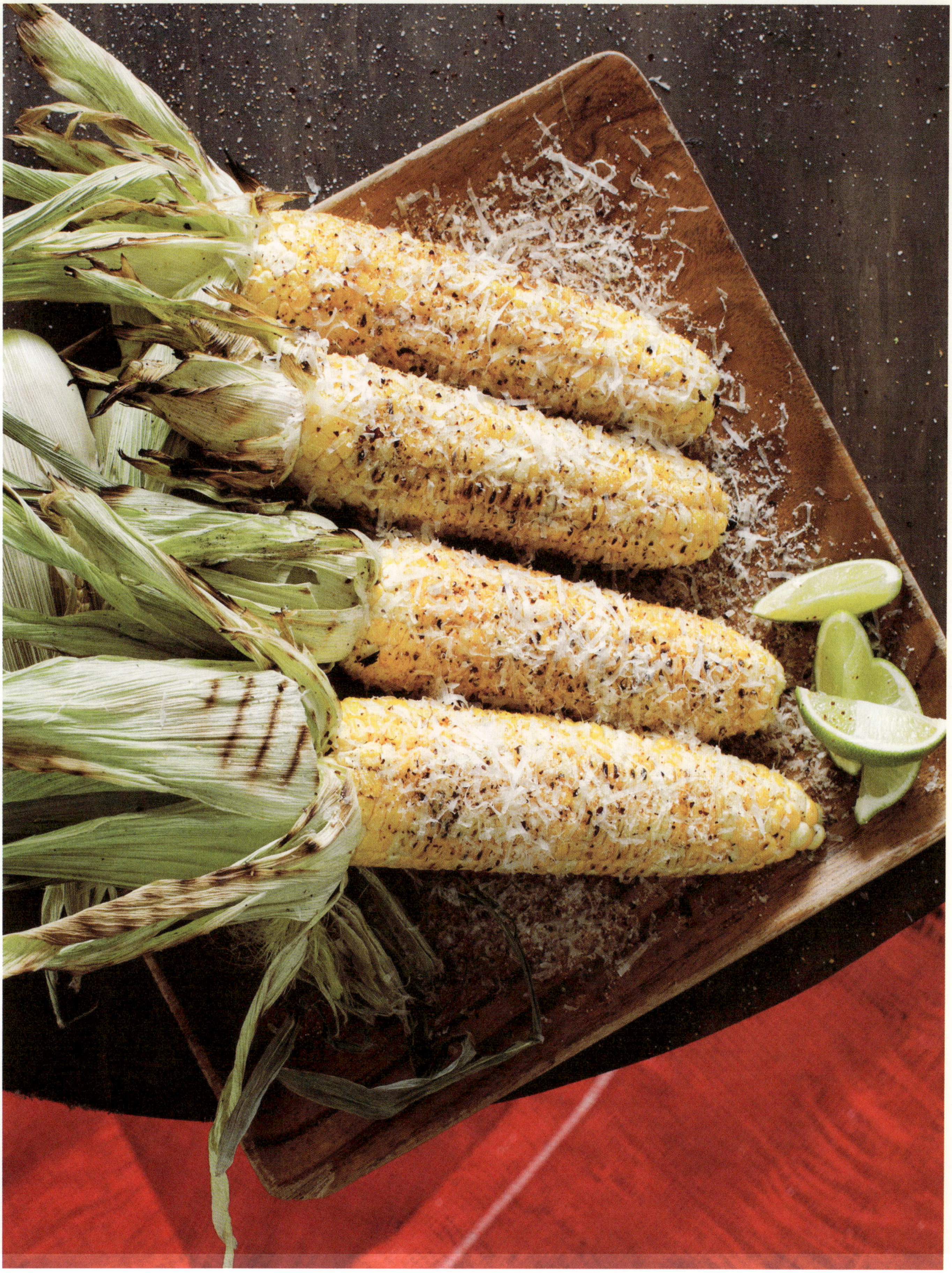

Bolivia

TOMATES RELLENOS

Tomatoes Stuffed with Quinoa

GF

1 cup quinoa
1 tbsp olive oil
¼ cup finely chopped onion
1 green capsicum,
 de-seeded and diced
2 cloves garlic, peeled and minced
2 cups vegetable stock or water
1 tsp salt, plus more to taste
8 heirloom tomatoes (or
 on the vine)
1 stalk celery, diced
1 jalapeño chilli, diced (optional)
1 spring onion, finely chopped
3 tsp chopped fresh oregano
2 tbsp chopped fresh parsley
1 tbsp lemon juice
2 tbsp soy sauce

If you love quinoa, you will be delighted by this recipe. All the different aromas and textures from the quinoa, peppers and celery plus all the fresh herbs, and a bit of spiciness, make for a fiesta in your mouth — a simple but delish dish. Quinoa is an important crop, grown mainly on the high plains of the Andes from Colombia to Chile. Not so long ago, quinoa wasn't loved and craved like it is now, but recently 'la quinua' has experienced a renaissance. This recipe is an homage to Bolivia and to this beloved Andean crop.

Prepare: 30 minutes; cook: 35 minutes
Makes: 8

If quinoa isn't pre-rinsed, then rinse it in a sieve under cold running water for about 2 minutes, stirring it with your hand. Leave in the sieve to drain.

In a medium-sized saucepan, heat olive oil. Add onion and capsicum and gently fry over a medium heat until soft; about 5 minutes. Add garlic and fry for an extra minute. Add drained quinoa and stir to incorporate. Add vegetable stock or water and 1 teaspoon salt. Cover and simmer for 15 minutes, then remove from the heat and let it stand, still covered, for 5 more minutes. Don't peek!

While quinoa is cooking, prepare tomatoes. Cut a small slice from the bottom so that the tomatoes can stand on a flat surface. Cut the tops off and scoop out the tomato flesh, discarding the seeds and ribs inside the tomato. Set aside until quinoa is ready.

When quinoa is done, remove lid and fluff quinoa with a fork. Mix in celery, jalapeño (if using), spring onion, 2 teaspoons oregano, parsley, lemon juice and soy sauce. Season to taste with salt and freshly ground black pepper.

Fill tomatoes with quinoa mixture. Garnish with remaining chopped oregano.

Chef's note: Since tomatoes range in size, there might be some quinoa left over at the end — refrigerate and eat the next day as a salad with some greens. I also tend to peel the thin membrane off the outside of the celery, but you can just dice it if you prefer.

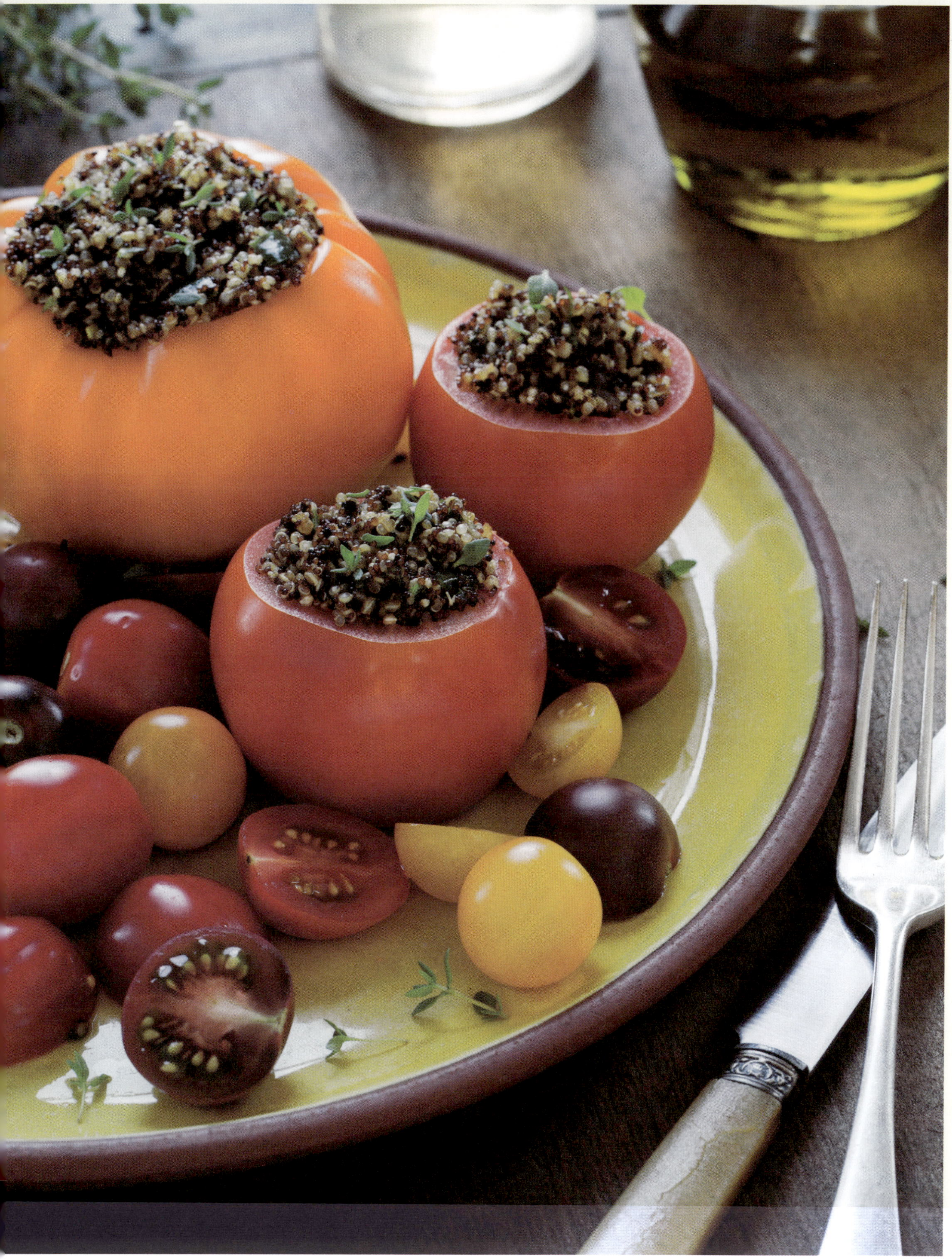

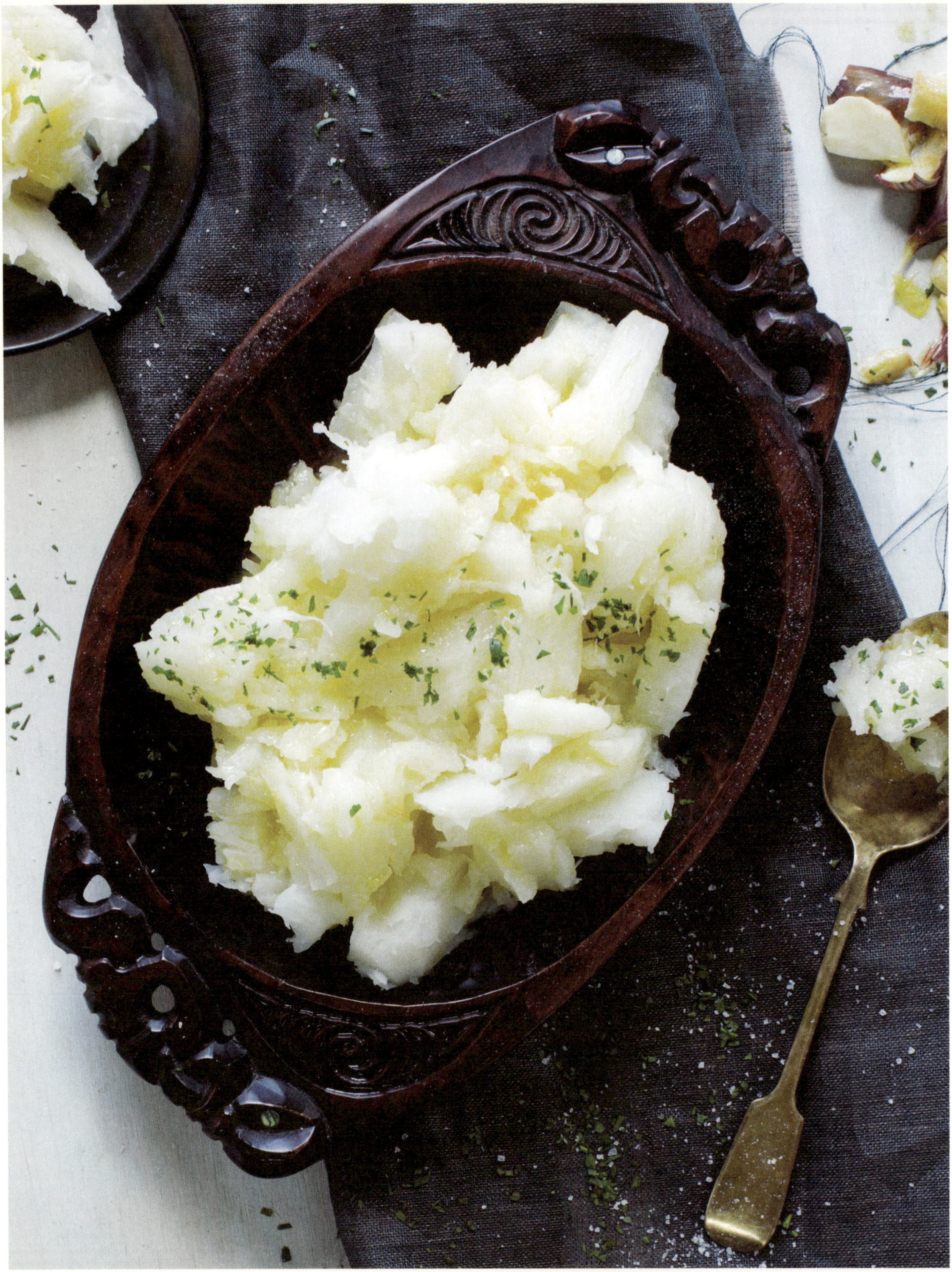

Cuba

YUCA CON MOJO

Cassava with Garlic & Citrus Sauce

GF

1¼ kg fresh yuca (cassava) or 1 kg frozen
4 tbsp orange juice
2 tbsp lemon juice
2 tsp apple cider vinegar
4 tbsp olive oil
6 cloves garlic, smashed, with skin on

Mojo is believed to have migrated to Latin America from Spain and Portugal, via the Canary Islands. Starting around 1492 with Columbus's trip to the Americas, Canary Islanders — or 'Isleños' as they're called — were brought by Spain and Portugal to help colonise the Americas, being sent mostly to Cuba, Puerto Rico, the Dominican Republic and Venezuela. It was through these colonisations that the islands' cuisine came to influence Latin America. Cuba is known internationally for its mojo. I've included it here as it's very easy and packed with flavour. Traditionally, the dish is made using naranja agria, or bitter orange, but this version using orange juice is just as good. Yuca (cassava) is a cousin of taro and is widely used throughout Latin America because of its nutritional content, high fibre and being gluten free. If you can't find yuca, make the mojo with mashed potatoes.

Prepare: 10 minutes; cook: approx. 1 hour
Serves: 4–6 as a side

If using fresh yuca, remove the narrow ends and cut the main root crosswise into cylinders. Stand each cylinder on end and cut off the outer fibrous layer with a sharp knife. Cut each piece lengthwise into quarters (sticks), and cut off the bit of woody core in the inside corner. Frozen yuca usually comes already prepared. Chop yuca into 5 cm chunks.

In a medium-sized saucepan, cover yuca with cold water, add 1 tablespoon salt and bring to the boil. Simmer for about 20 minutes. Meanwhile, prepare a water/ice bath. Drain cooked yuca and shock it in the water/ice bath. Return yuca to saucepan, cover again with cold water and reboil with the new water until yuca loosens up and you can easily put a fork through the pieces.

Don't worry if the yuca breaks up but is still tough inside. Wait until it is completely soft throughout, about 45 minutes total cooking time. Leave in the water until ready to serve, then drain.

Combine orange and lemon juice with vinegar. Set aside.

Meanwhile, in a large frying pan, heat olive oil over a medium-high heat. Just before the oil begins to smoke, remove the pan from the heat and add the garlic, tipping it away from you so it does not splatter you. Wait for 2 minutes. Pour the citrus/vinegar liquid over the garlic to stop it cooking. Season with 1 teaspoon of salt and immediately pour over the drained yuca.

Chef's note: Paraguayans cook yuca just until fork-tender, but Cubans cook it until very tender and almost falling apart — that's how I like it. Cooking times can vary a lot depending on the type of yuca; there's no rule for how long it will take to get fork-tender. Start testing with a fork 15 minutes after the water comes to the boil, and keep testing until it's soft enough. You can also fry the yuca after it's soft — it's delicious and very popular.

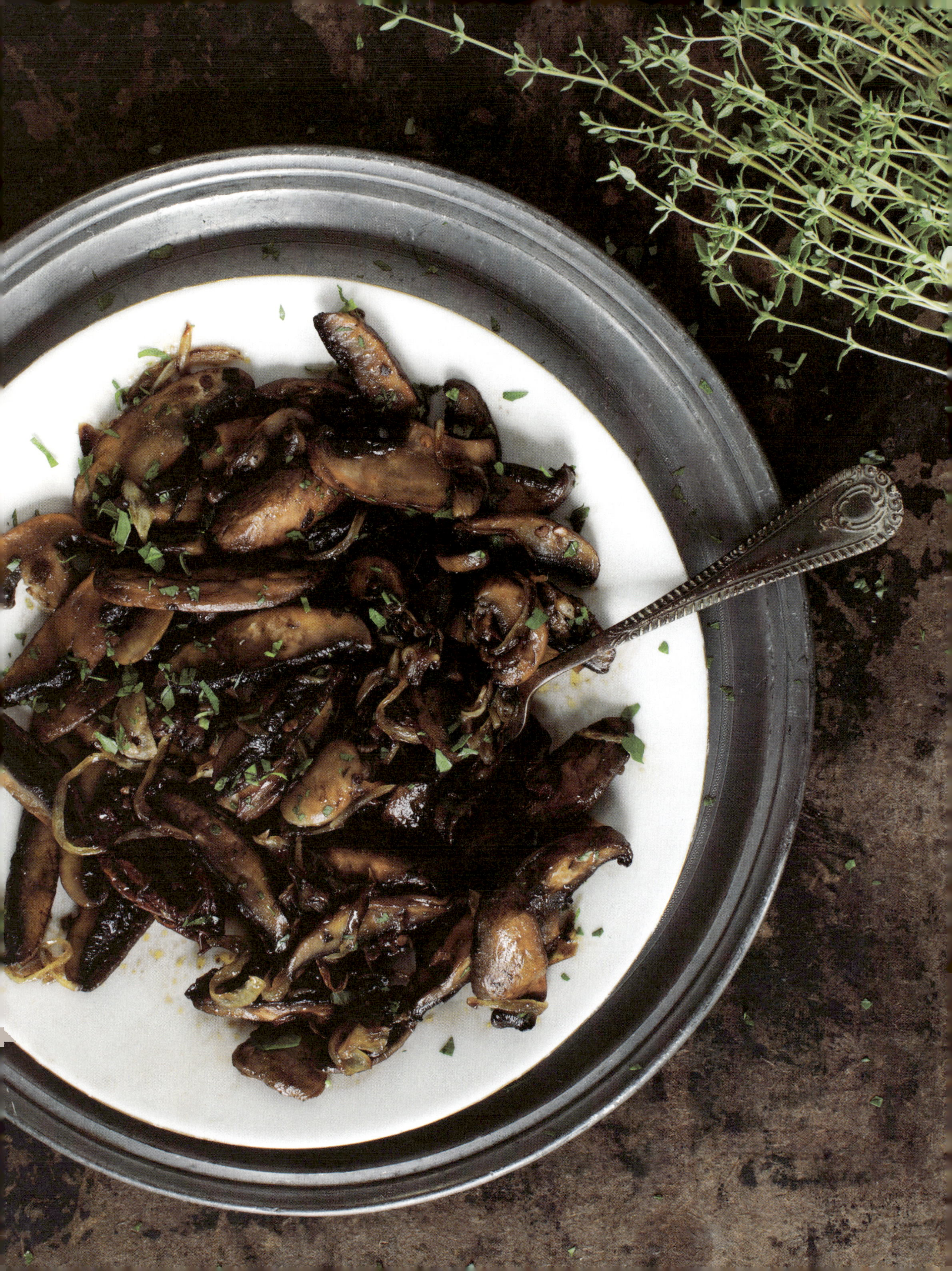

Mexico

HONGOS CON CHIPOTLE

Chipotle & Beer Mushrooms

1 onion, peeled and thinly sliced
3 tbsp avocado oil
1 clove garlic, smashed
2 tbsp chipotles in adobo sauce, roughly chopped
500 g shiitake or portobello mushrooms, sliced
2 tbsp Sol beer (Mexican beer; optional)
½ tbsp lemon juice
flaky sea salt
chopped herbs of choice, to garnish (optional)

Say mushrooms, and your mind usually goes to French or Italian cuisine; however, mushrooms are also used throughout Latin America. This recipe is perfect for vegetarians and you don't feel as though you're missing out on anything. The mushrooms get a kick from the chipotle pepper and are perfect for stuffing arepas, quesadillas, tacos or to include in your favourite meal as a side dish. Leave out the beer if you want it gluten free.

Prepare: 10 minutes; cook: 25 minutes
Serves: 6 as a side

In a large frying pan over a medium-high heat, gently fry onion with 2 tablespoons avocado oil for about 15 minutes, or until caramelised. Transfer to a dish and set aside. In the same pan, gently fry garlic in remaining avocado oil, then add chipotles in adobo sauce. Add mushrooms, fry gently for 3 minutes and season with salt. Add beer, if using, and simmer for 5 minutes. Finish with lemon juice, add back the caramelised onion and warm through. Season to taste with flaky sea salt and freshly ground black pepper, garnish with herbs, if using, and serve immediately.

Peru

PAPAS A LA HUANCAINA

Potatoes in Huancaina Sauce

500 g Agria potatoes (2–3 medium)
1 tbsp vegetable oil
½ cup diced onion
1 yellow capsicum, de-seeded and diced
1 clove garlic, smashed
100 g crumbled feta
2 water crackers
¼ cup evaporated milk or fresh cream
1 tsp turmeric
1 tsp lemon juice

Garnish
2 hard-boiled eggs, finely grated
habanero chilli oil (see page 188)
1 tbsp sliced black olives
1 tbsp chopped parsley

This is a Peruvian classic, and one to have as a staple. It originated in the town of Huancayo, which is known for its potatoes. The story goes that when a railway line was being built, street vendors set up shops to feed the workers, and a woman known as 'Huancaina' became famous for her potatoes covered with creamy cheese sauce. Traditionally this is made with ají amarillo paste from Peru, but since that's hard to find I used some other ingredients to bring you the closest version possible. It's the perfect side for simple lean proteins, barbecued meats and roast chicken.

Prepare: 10 minutes; cook: 60 minutes
Serves: 4–6 as a side

Preheat oven to 180°C. Peel potatoes and season with salt and freshly ground black pepper. Wrap in foil and place on a baking dish. Bake for about 45–60 minutes, until fork-tender. Set aside until cool enough to handle. (You can boil the potatoes instead if you wish.)

Meanwhile, in a frying pan over a low heat, warm vegetable oil and sweat onion and capsicum for about 10 minutes, until soft and translucent. Add garlic and cook for 1 minute until golden brown. Remove from the heat and transfer to a food processor. Add feta, crackers, evaporated milk or cream, turmeric and lemon juice, and process until smooth. Season to taste.

Slice potatoes into rounds 1 cm thick.

To serve, arrange the potato rounds on plates and pour over the cheese sauce. Garnish as wished with hard-boiled egg, a few drops of habanero oil, sliced black olives and chopped parsley.

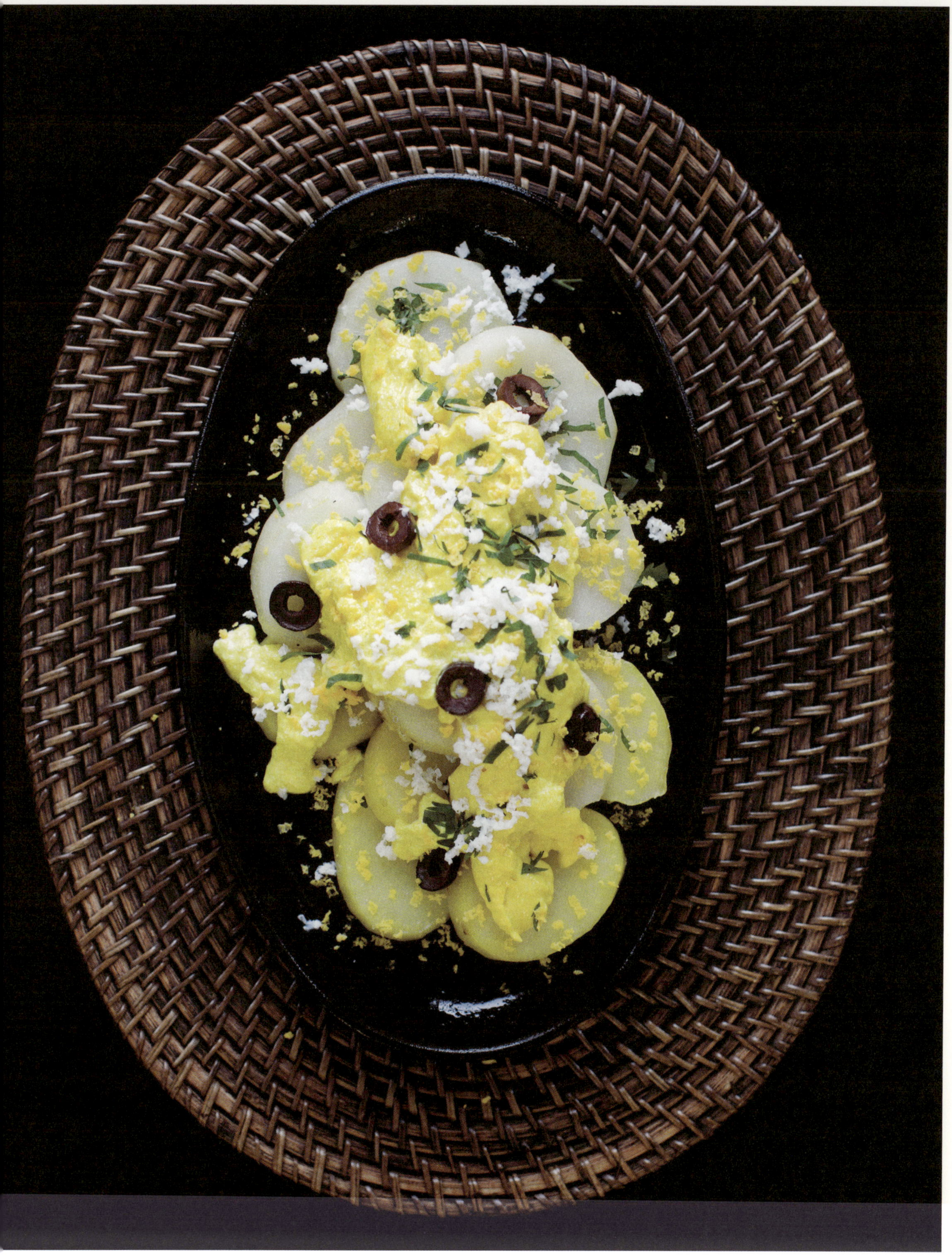

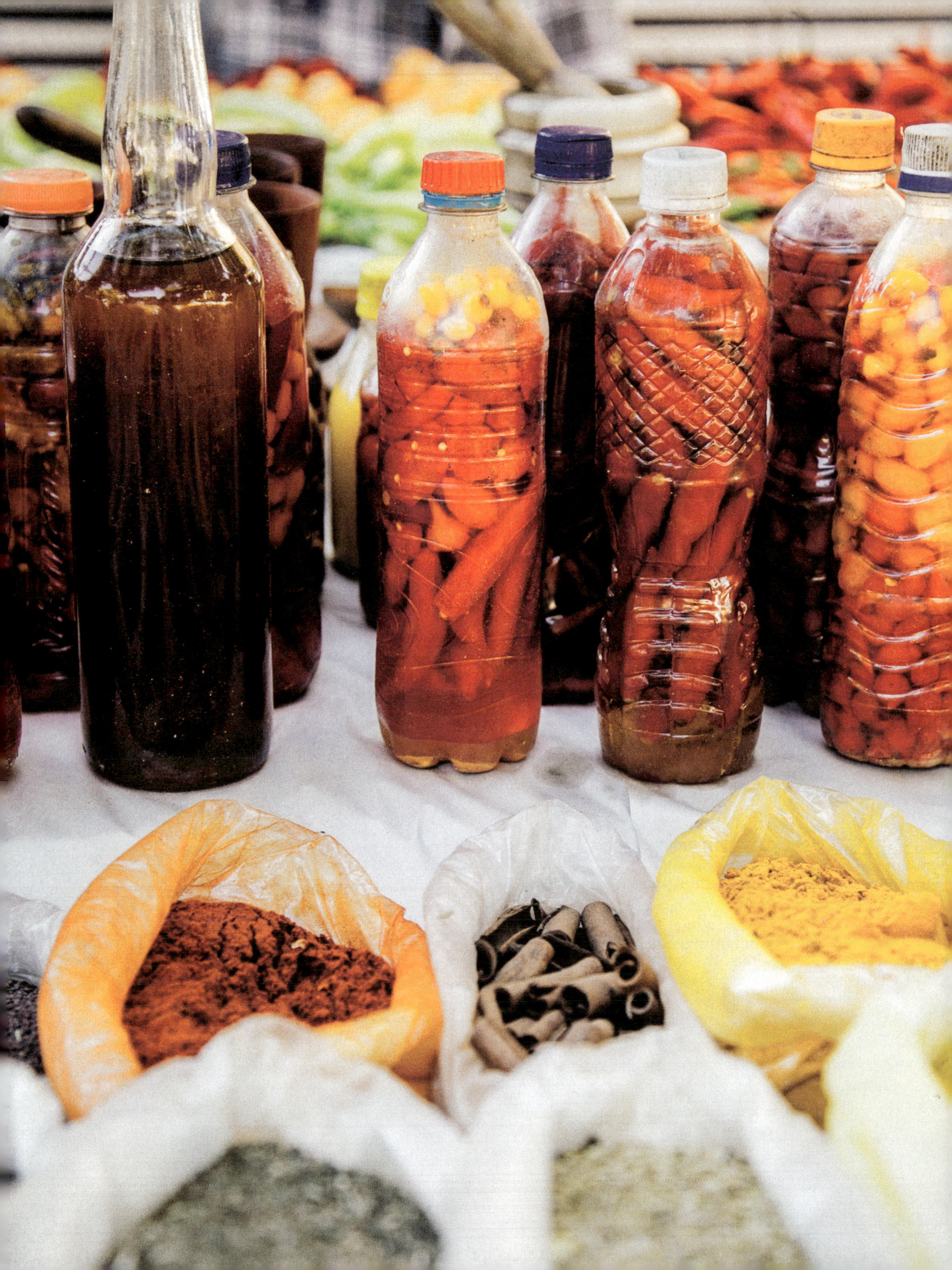

SALSAS, ADEREZOS Y MÁS

SAUCES, CONDIMENTS & MORE

MENU

Tostadas de Ceviche
Tostadas de Camarón
Tostadas de Pulpo

Cocktel de Camarón
Cocktel de Pulpo
Cocktel de Ostión
Cocktel de Campechano
Vuelve a la Vida

Sopas de Mariscos
Caldo de Camarón
Caldo de Pescado
Filete de Pescado Empanizado

MARISCOS EL AUSENTE
Restaurant - Bar

SUCURSA

* Carr. Juventino Rosas
  Tel. 73 31184
  (Servicio de Mariscos
  Cortes de Carne tipo A

* Alhóndiga # 18 Esq. 2
  Tel. 73 24847

* Interior del Mercado H

* Carrito frente al Ministe
  Público en la calle Alh

* Carrito en Boulevard E

Además contamos con salón de fiestas para sus eventos especiales: bodas, XV años, etc. Ubicado en carr. Gua

SOFRITO
Puerto Rican Cooking Base

ADOBO
Spice rub

ACIETE DE CHILE HABANERO
Habenero Chilli Oil

ACEITE DE ACHIOTE
Achiote Oil

MAYONESA
Basic Mayonnaise

MAYONESA CON CHILE CHIPOTLE
Chipotle Mayonnaise

PICO DE GALLO
Fresh Chopped Tomato Salad

SAL CON CHILE
Chilli Salt

SALSA VERDE
Charred Tomatillo Sauce

SALSA ROJA DE MOLCAJETE
Red 'Pestle & Mortar' Sauce

GUACAMOLE

SALSA CRIOLLA
Peruvian Salsa

CEBOLLA MORADA EN VINAGRE
Pickled Red Onions

GUASACACA
Creamy Avocado & Herb Salsa

CHIMICHURRI
Herby Salsa

MOLE

QUESO FRESCO
Fresh White Cheese

CREMA AGRIA
Salty Cream

Puerto Rico

SOFRITO

Puerto Rican Cooking Base

GF

2 tbsp olive oil
3 tbsp vegetable oil
4–6 cloves garlic, peeled
1 onion, roughly chopped
1 green capsicum, de-seeded and roughly chopped
approx. 12 mixed sweet mini capsicums, de-seeded and roughly chopped
1 bunch coriander, roughly chopped

Sofritos are the basis for many Hispanic dishes. The term was brought to the Caribbean by Spanish colonisers, who prepared it as a tomato base with paprika. Sofrito is also an Italian term meaning the same thing, though the Italian version has different ingredients. In most of Central and South America a form of sofrito is used as a base for most cooking. However, Puerto Ricans take the cake. It is a staple in their homes — you can't be Puerto Rican without an adoration for garlic and having your freezer filled with home-made sofrito ice cubes! Use it to give flavour to beans, grains, stews and rices. I have substituted the traditional cubanelle peppers and ají dulces with 'little sweetie' capsicums and large capsicum as well. You can find the Venezuelan variation used as the base for Mom's black beans (see page 15) and shredded beef (see page 105).

Prepare: 10 minutes
Makes: approx. 1 cup

Combine all ingredients in a blender: first the oils, garlic and onion, and pulse. Then add capsicums and coriander and process for 30 seconds until you get a herb-speckled purée with a pungent aroma.

At this point you can use the sofrito straight away, or pour the mixture into ice-cube trays, tightly seal them with plastic wrap and store in the freezer for up to 1 month. You can use them straight from frozen in many dishes.

Chef's note: You can also add olives and capers to your sofrito, but I find that this is too overpowering and not as versatile.

Venezuela

ADOBO

Spice Rub

GF

2 tbsp garlic powder
3 tbsp fine salt
1 tsp ground pepper
1 tsp ground coriander
2 tbsp onion powder
1 tsp ground achiote (annatto) seeds
1 tbsp ground cumin

Adobos are as essential a part of Latino cooking as sofritos, and can be 'secos' or 'mojado' (dry or wet). In Venezuela and some parts of Latin America, adobo is just a blend of spices; but in countries like Mexico and Peru, which are considered the capitals of adobo making, not only are spices used in the adobos but they tend to combine dry and wet ingredients, forming a paste used for marinading or seasoning. These days most people use store-bought adobos, but these contain sneaky bad ingredients and possibly MSG. Hence here is this very simple home-made adobo that can be made in large batches, stored in jars and used on steak, roast chicken, seared fish or even sprinkled on vegetables.

Prepare: 5 minutes
Makes: ½ cup

Mix all ingredients and store in a tightly closed jar.

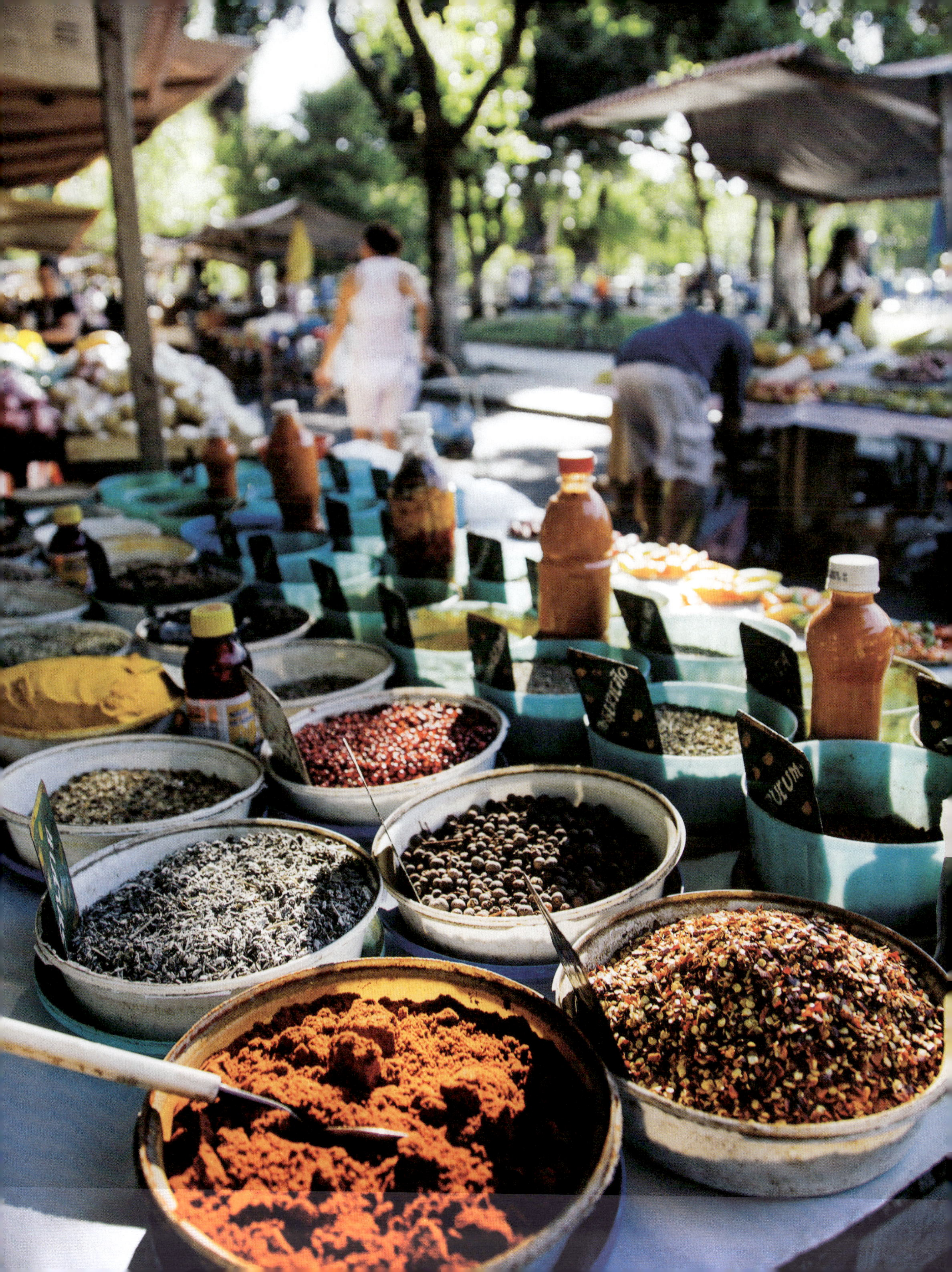

Mexico

ACEITE DE CHILE HABANERO

Habanero Chilli Oil

GF

½ cup oil (rice bran, refined avocado oil or peanut oil)
7 dried whole habanero chillies

This oil is for the valiant. I personally don't think it's too hot, but I can really take the heat and can taste all the different layers — like berries, tropical fruits and spices — of this gorgeous, fiery and potent pepper. This is an easy home-made picante (hot) sauce that will change your life. Be careful to only add a few drops at a time, though. I add this to almost everything, even to my lemon-ginger tea. Because it's an oil, it doesn't change the colour or consistency of my dishes — it just adds that extra kick.

Prepare: 5 minutes; cook: 5 minutes
Makes: ½ cup

Heat oil in a pan over a meduim heat with six of the habaneros until it just reaches smoking point; about 5 minutes. Let the oil cool for about 5 more minutes, then strain into a sealable jar. Thinly slice remaining habanero and add to the jar of oil before sealing. It will keep for about 3 months.

Chef's note: Make sure you use gloves while handling the habaneros, and be very careful when making the oil. Place the habaneros in the oil gently, or it might splash — and whatever you do, don't rub your eyes or nose. I've done this. It is very tingly and painful.

Venezuela

ACEITE DE ACHIOTE

Achiote Oil

GF

¼ cup rice bran oil
1 tbsp achiote (annatto) seeds

Latinos use achiote (annatto) seeds like Spaniards use saffron. These orange-red seeds from the achiote tree are used to give foods an orange or yellow colour, or for their flavour and aroma — it smells nutty and has an earthy, slightly sweet peppery taste. It can be found as a paste, powder or just the seeds, which get infused with hot oil to release the colour and flavour of achiote. The oil is used in bollos pelones (see page 98), the Venezuelan Christmas tamales called hallacas, or in llapingachos (see page 128).

Prepare: 5 minutes; cook: 5 minutes
Makes: approx. ¼ cup

Heat rice bran oil in a small saucepan until just before it starts to smoke; about 1 minute over a medium heat. Take off the heat, add achiote seeds and swirl until oil turns red, about 30 seconds. Strain and set aside.

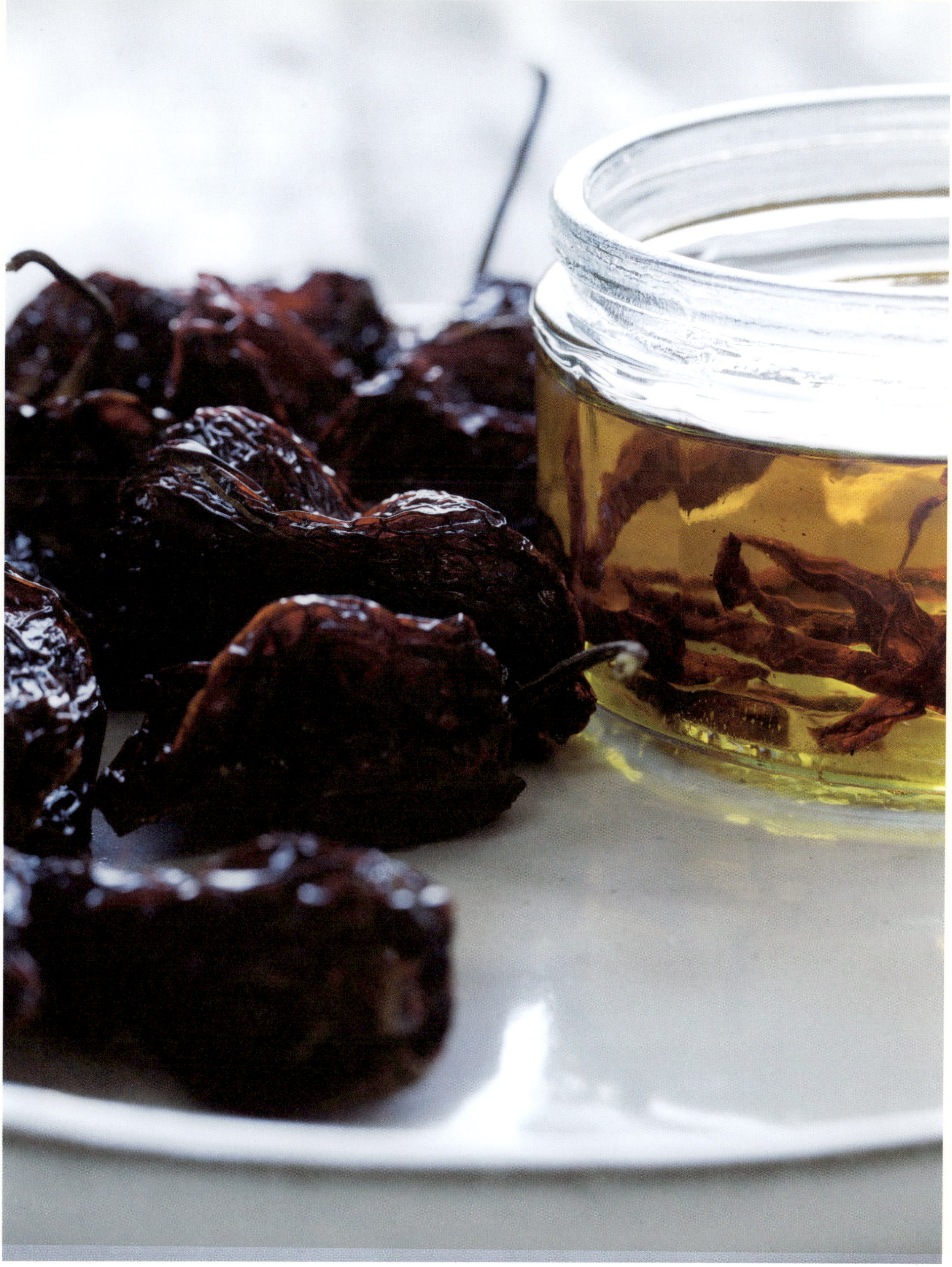

All countries

MAYONESA

Basic Mayonnaise

GF

2 egg yolks
1 tsp Dijon mustard
4 tsp lemon juice
1 cup rice bran oil

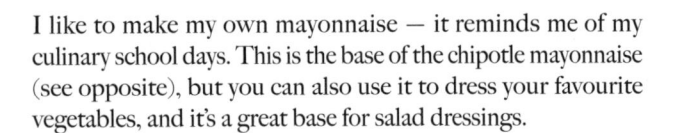

I like to make my own mayonnaise — it reminds me of my culinary school days. This is the base of the chipotle mayonnaise (see opposite), but you can also use it to dress your favourite vegetables, and it's a great base for salad dressings.

Prepare: 5 minutes
Makes: approx. ½ cup

Place egg yolks, mustard and lemon juice in a blender or food processor. Pulse until well combined. With the motor running, add oil in a slow, steady stream. The mixture will become thick and emulsified. Season to taste with salt and freshly ground black pepper.

Refrigerate in an airtight container for up to 1 week.

Chef's note: If the mixture starts to separate (oil rises to the top), add a few drops of ice-cold water. Whip it for about 10 seconds, then start adding oil again.

Mexico

MAYONESA CON CHILE CHIPOTLE

Chipotle Mayonnaise

GF

¼ cup home-made mayonnaise (see opposite) or store-bought mayonnaise
approx. 1 tbsp chipotles, roughly chopped in adobo sauce
zest of 1 lime
1 tbsp lime juice
½ tsp flaky sea salt

Chipotle is a smoked dried jalapeño, very commonly used, with a mild and smoky heat. Use this versatile mayonnaise for coleslaw, street corn (see page 172), fish tacos, to mix with prawns or as a dip for your favourite veggies.

Prepare: 5 minutes
Makes: ¼ cup

Blend all ingredients in a food processor, or whisk everything together, until well combined. Store in an airtight container for up to 1 week.

Chef's note: Use more of the chipotles if you want more heat and flavour.

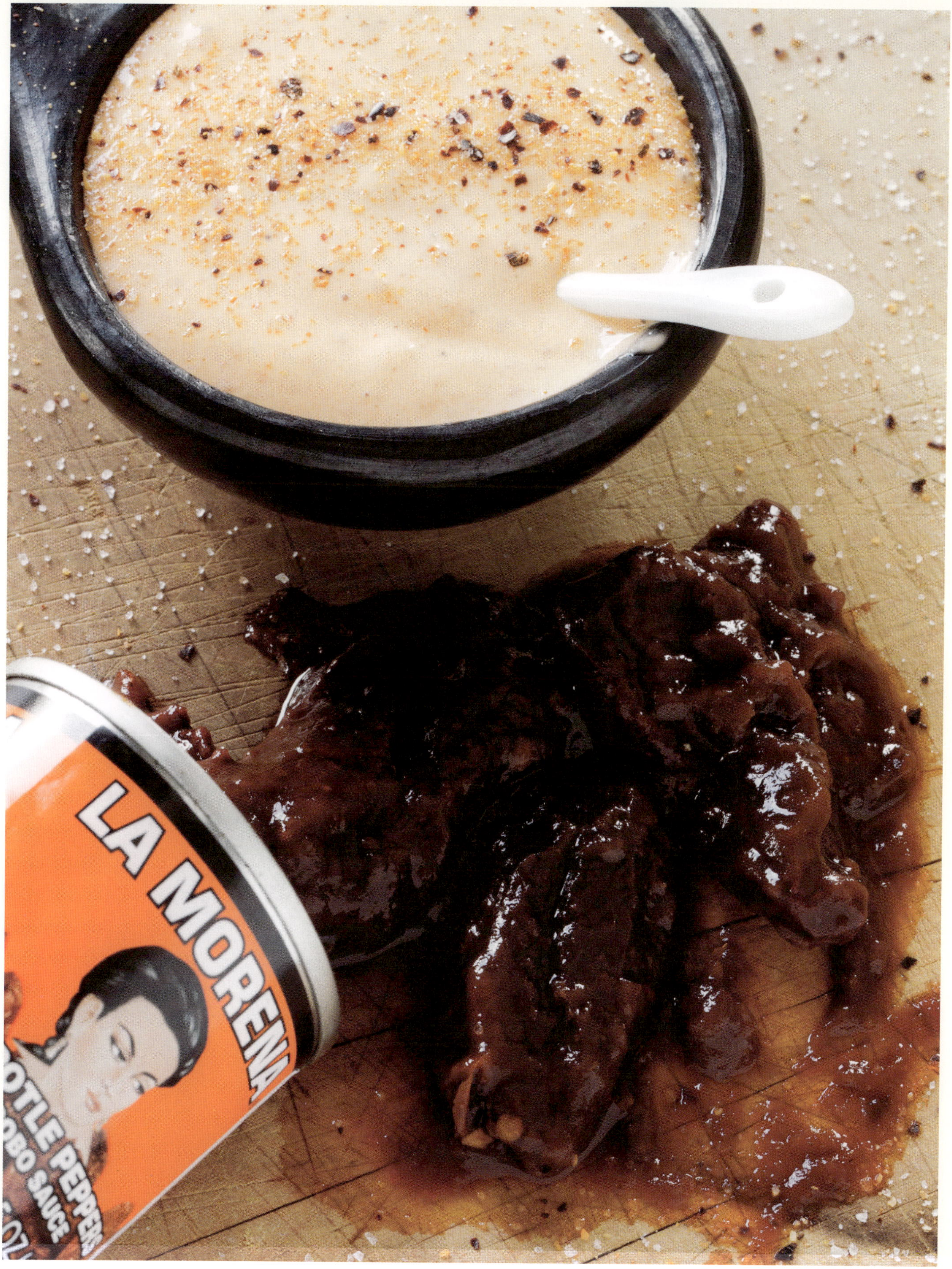
LA MORENA

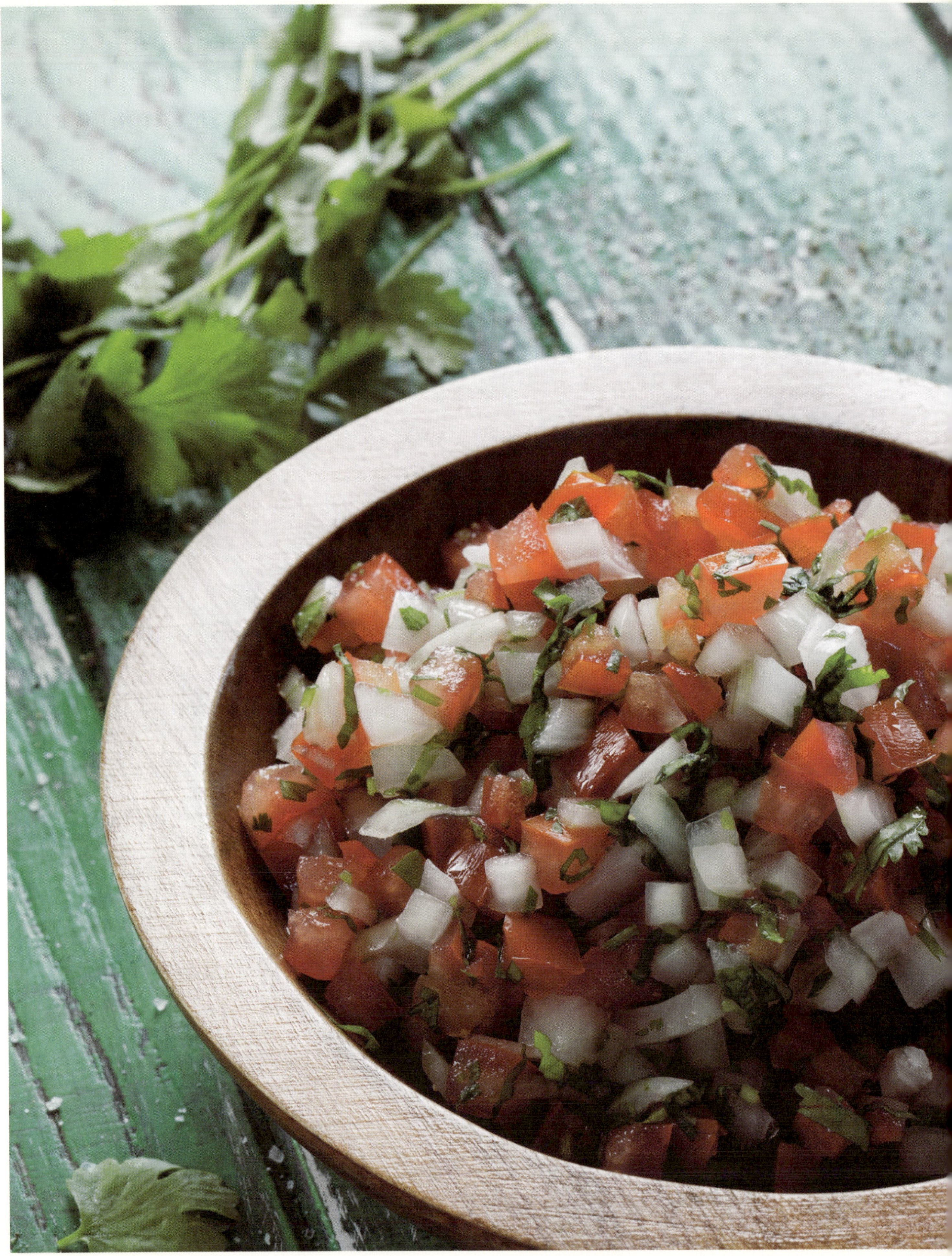

Mexico

PICO DE GALLO

Fresh Chopped Tomato Salad

GF

4 tomatoes, cored, de-seeded
    and finely chopped
1 bunch fresh coriander,
    finely chopped
1 serrano, jalapeño or habanero
    chilli, minced (optional)
½ cup diced onion
2 tbsp lime juice
1 tbsp olive oil
flaky sea salt

This is another versatile, easy-to-use, easy-to-make, tasty and fresh sauce or condiment. Put it on your fish tacos, have it as a side to eat with chips or to complement a grilled chicken breast. Also known as salsa fresca, it's often called salsa Mexicana or salsa bandera (flag sauce) because the colours of the red tomato, white onion, coriander and green chilli are reminiscent of the Mexican flag.

Prepare: 10 minutes; chill: 30 minutes
Serves: 4–6

Mix all the ingredients together and add salt and freshly ground black pepper to taste. Cover and chill for at least 30 minutes to let the flavours blend.

    Chef's note: This salsa can be made in advance and will keep fresh for up to 4 hours. You can also add steamed or charred sweetcorn kernels or chopped mango, fresh chopped pineapple and jicama (Mexican yam) if desired.

Mexico

SAL CON CHILE

Chilli Salt

GF

4 tsp dried guajillo chillies,
    roughly chopped with seeds
1 tsp rock salt

Fun, yum and festive! Just looking at this gorgeous chilli salt brings a smile to my face. It is a perfect way to incorporate life, flavour and spice into your daily dishes and drinks. The guajillo, pronounced 'wha-hee-oh', literally translates to 'little gourd' — for the rattling sound the seeds make when shaking the dried pods. It is the second most popular chilli in Mexico after the ancho and, like the ancho, it looks like it could kill you with its heat and power; very intimidating. But the truth is that it just has a bit of heat; it's slightly fruity with lots of earthy, tart-berry undertones. Guajillos are often combined with other dried chillies like anchos and pasillas in Mexican moles.

Prepare: 5 minutes
Makes: 2 tablespoons

In a food processor, blender or spice grinder, pulse chilli and seeds about three times, then add rock salt. Pulse twice more. Store in an airtight container for up to 2 weeks. Use as a garnish for huevos verde (see page 37), margaritas (see page 252), tostaditas de pulpo (see page 68) and more.

Mexico

SALSA VERDE

Charred Tomatillo Sauce

GF

4 green tomatoes, quartered, or 340 g can tomatillos
½ onion, peeled
1 bunch coriander
2 serrano chillies, or 3 fresh New Zealand chillies, stems removed, or 5 slices pickled jalapeño (amount of heat is optional)
juice of 1 lemon
¼ cup water, or as needed
flaky sea salt

Like salsa roja, salsa verde is a Mexican staple. Charring the onion until caramelised isn't traditional, but this gives the salsa a great smoky but sweet flavour, plus beautiful specks.

Prepare: 10 minutes; cook: 30 minutes
Makes: approx. 1 cup

If using fresh green tomatoes, remove the cores. If using canned tomatillos, drain off the brine and don't char.

Heat a cast-iron pan or griddle pan with no oil over a medium-high heat. Place onion in cut side down, and char the flat side of the onion until caramelised; about 10 minutes. At the same time, if using fresh, dry-roast tomatoes in the same pan. When black spots start to appear, rotate the tomatoes so that they become evenly charred.

Add coriander to a blender with the rest of the ingredients. Pulse until smooth and season to taste with flaky sea salt.

Mexico

SALSA ROJA DE MOLCAJETE

Red 'Pestle & Mortar' Sauce

GF

2 ripe medium-sized plum tomatoes, cored
2 serrano chillies, or 3 fresh New Zealand chillies, stems removed, or 5 slices pickled jalapeño (the amount of heat is optional)
1 garlic clove, peeled

Salsa roja and salsa verde are 'must have' basic Mexican sauces, and you'll find a variation of these in every Mexican home, restaurant, taco stand or truck. Molcajete means 'pestle and mortar', as this was traditionally used to make the sauce; nowadays, most people toss all the ingredients in a blender or food processor.

Prepare: 10 minutes; cook: 30 minutes
Makes: ½ cup

Using a cast-iron pan or griddle with no oil over a medium heat, roast the tomatoes, fresh chillies and garlic. When black spots start to appear, rotate until you get an even char on all sides. (Only char whole chillies, not slices.)

If using a pestle and mortar, start by mashing the garlic until smooth, followed by the chillies and lastly the tomatoes. Season with flaky sea salt and freshly ground black pepper. If using a blender, put all the ingredients in the blender with seasoning and pulse until smooth.

Leave in the refrigerator for a couple of hours before serving.

Chef's note: I encourage people to make this sauce in larger batches and store it in the fridge — it always tastes better the next day. As well as all its other uses, it's the perfect sauce for huevos divorciados (see page 41). Be careful with the heat; it's better to start with just a few chillies and build up — you don't want to burn your guests' palates on their first bite!

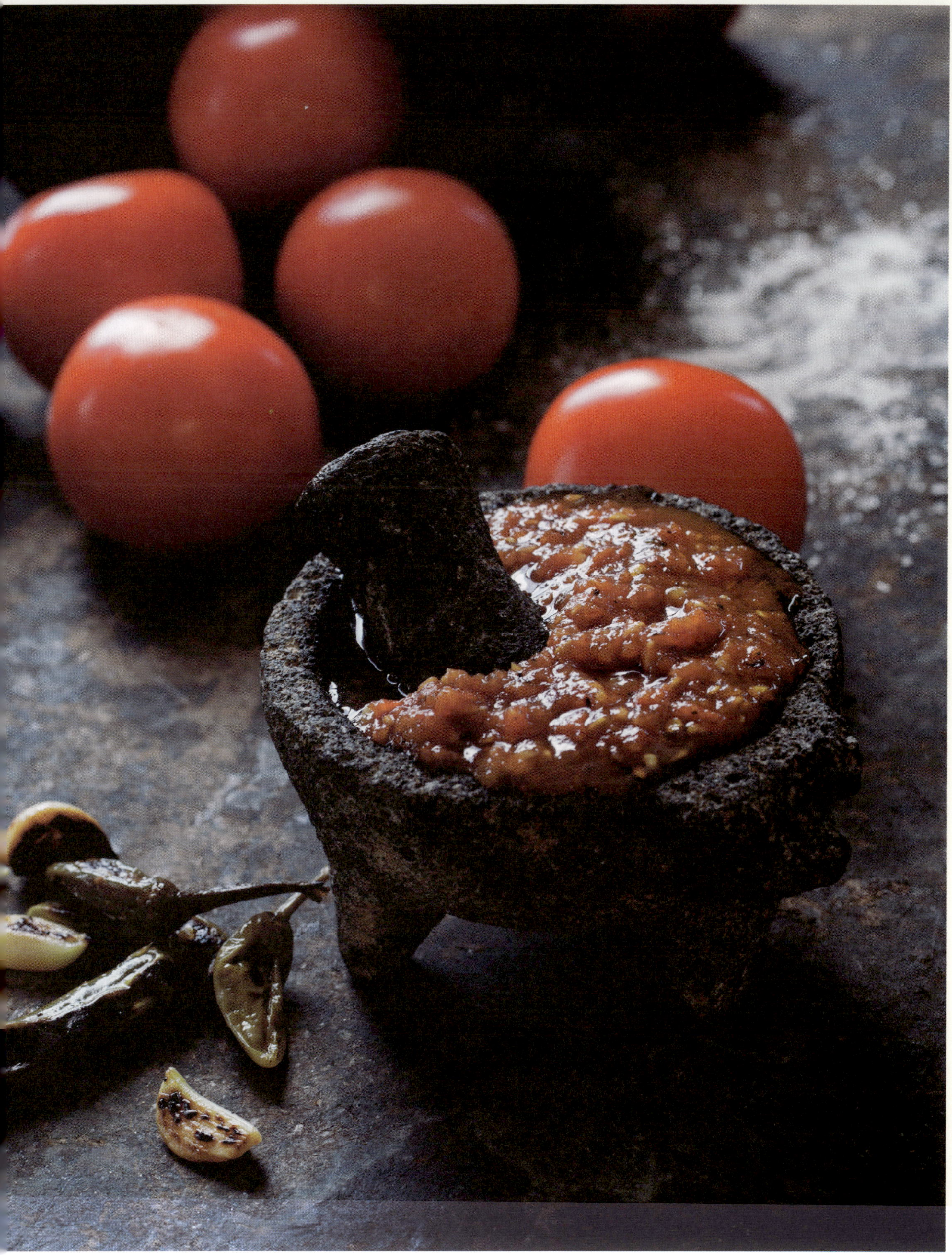

Mexico

GUACAMOLE

GF

2 ripe avocados
½ red onion, peeled and diced (about ¼ cup)
1 jalapeño, serrano or other chilli, minced (optional)
2 tbsp finely chopped coriander leaves, plus extra for garnish
1 tbsp fresh lime or lemon juice
coarse pink Himalayan salt (or flaky sea salt), to taste

Garnish
1 tbsp pomegranate seeds
1 tsp black sesame or toasted sesame seeds

I still haven't met a single person who doesn't go nuts for guacamole. I personally eat guac on toast or a bagel for breakfast at least three times a week before working out. My guests say that my guacamole is exceptionally good. I just tell them, 'I don't really know why, except that it is made with lots of love.' Here is my attempt to crack the code: it's very, very simple as long as a few things are done right. Good avocados equal good guacamole. Always check for ripeness by gently pressing the avocado: it should be firm but with a little give, but it shouldn't feel mushy. But go the extra mile for your perfect guac — once you've got a good avocado candidate, take a peak at what's inside. Flick the dry stem off — if the fruit right under the stem is bright yellow-green, you have a winner; your avocado will be great. If all you see is brown under the stem, put it back because it will be brown inside.

Prepare: 10 minutes
Serves: 4

Halve the avocados. Remove seed and scoop flesh out, putting it in a mixing bowl. Using a fork, mash the avocado, adding some lemon juice to prevent oxidation. Add onion, chilli (if using), coriander and lime or lemon juice, and season with salt and freshly ground black pepper to taste. Keep the pomegranate and toasted sesame seeds separate until ready to serve. Just before serving, finish by garnishing with pomegranate and sesame seeds, some extra coriander leaves and coarse or flaky salt.

To prevent oxidation (browning), put the avocado stone in the middle of the guacamole. Acid also prevents oxidation, so feel free to add a thin layer of lemon or lime juice on top, folding this through just before serving.

If you need to refrigerate your guac (up to 2 days), put it in a bowl that has a tight-fitting lid. Pack the guacamole tightly in the bowl, pressing out any air bubbles. Dribble in some lukewarm water, making sure that the water covers the surface of the guacamole to about 1 cm deep. Put some plastic wrap directly over the guac, then put the lid on and refrigerate. When ready to eat, take the lid off and and gently pour out the water. Stir the guacamole to incorporate any extra moisture.

Chef's note: Do not over-mash your guacamole; leave it a bit chunky. It will have more texture and better taste. Chillies vary individually in their hotness. Start with half of one, and taste. Be careful when handling chillies — wash your hands and do not rub your eyes! If it is not pomegranate season, you can substitute tomatoes in the guacamole. De-seed them first, or the guacamole will be watery.

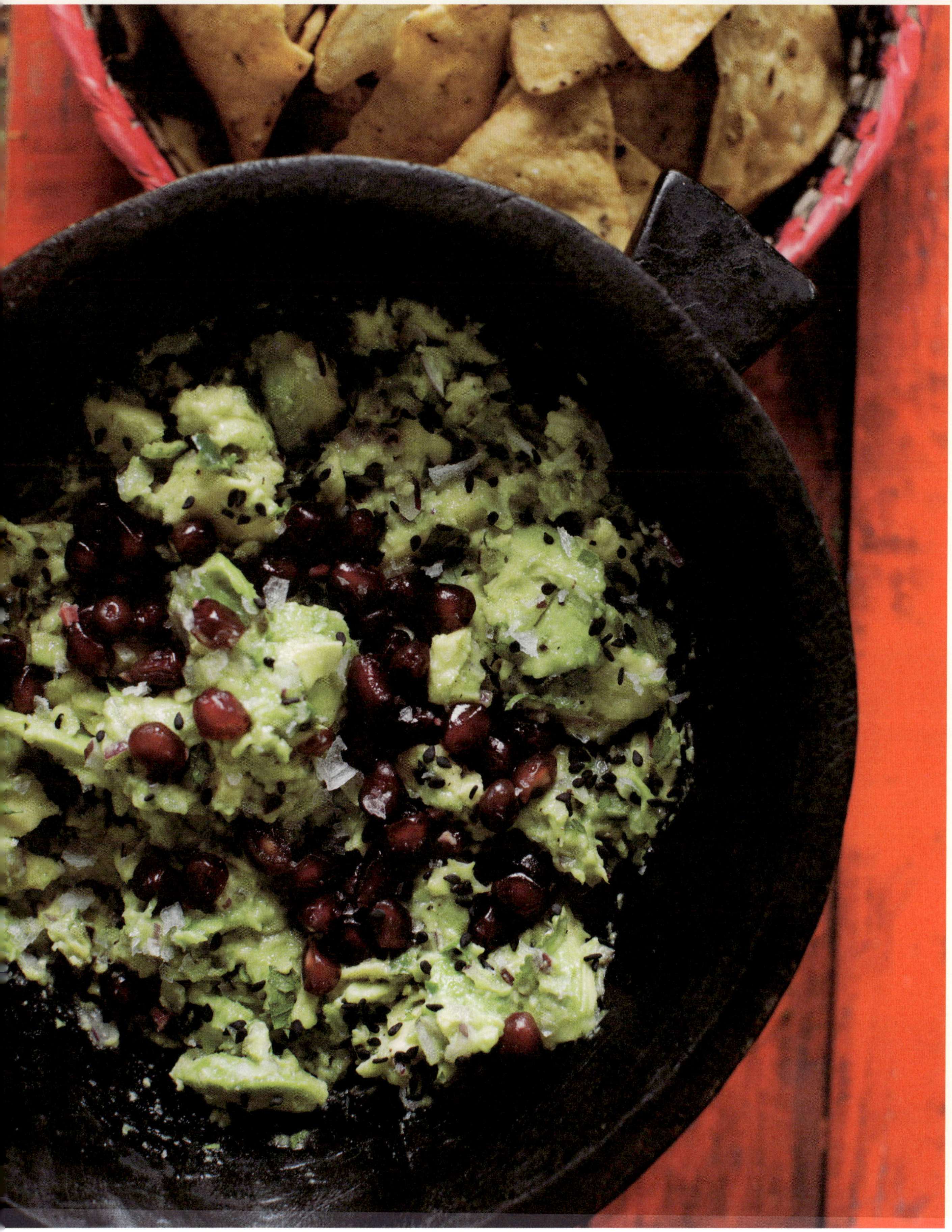

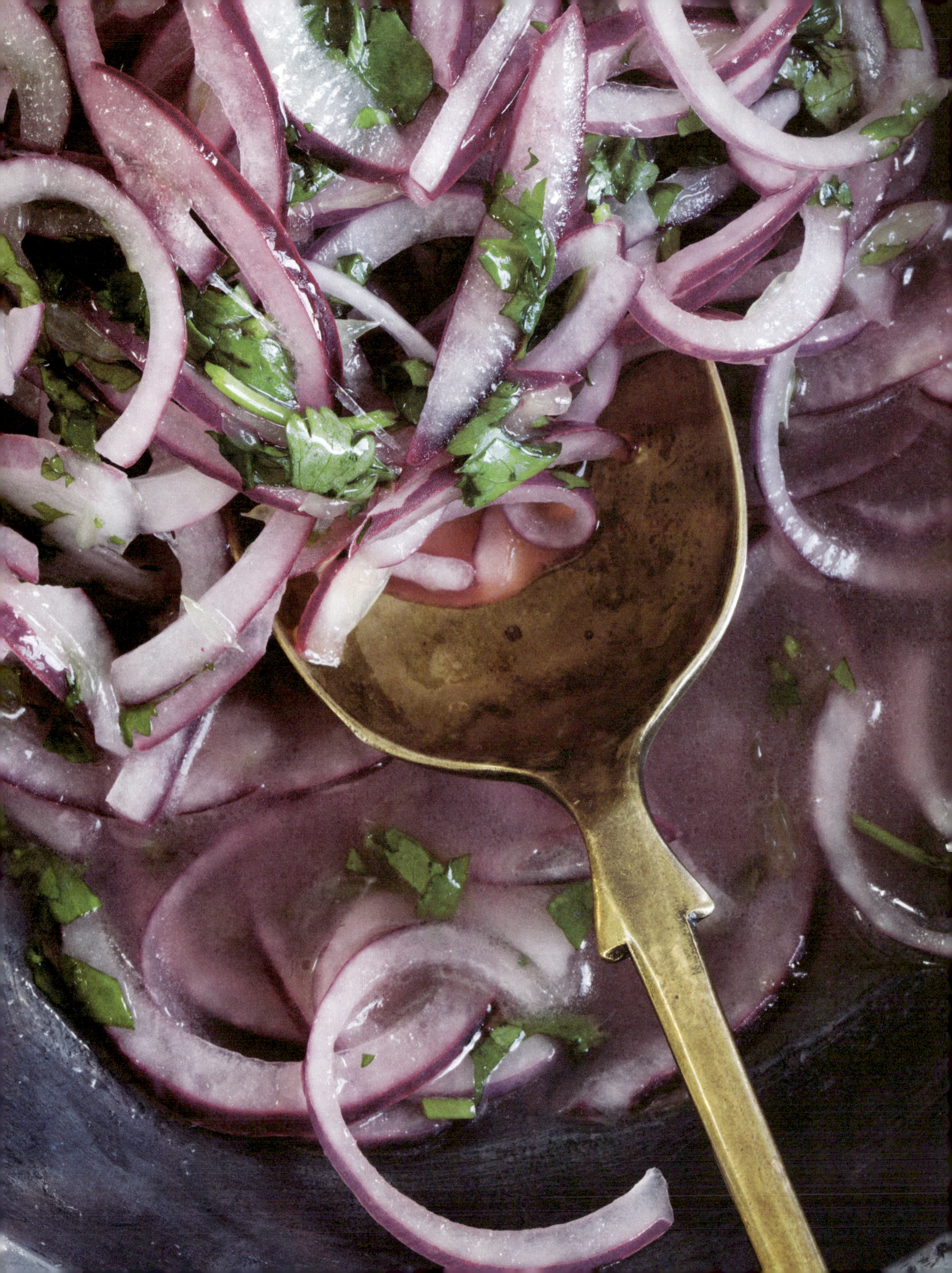

Peru

SALSA CRIOLLA

Peruvian Salsa

GF

1 small red onion, thinly sliced
2 tbsp salt
2 tbsp chopped coriander
    or parsley
½ cup lime juice (from
    about 2 limes)
2 tbsp olive oil
1 fresh chilli (optional)

Peruvians love red onions, and this celebrated salsa is used in countless recipes, inside sandwiches or on top of chicharrón (pork crackling), fish and meats. It's perfect with the jalea mixta (see page 73). It's very simple, but adds life and vivid colours to even the most ordinary dish.

Prepare: 10 minutes
Makes: approx. 1 cup

In a bowl, cover onions with warm water then stir in salt. Leave for about 5 minutes, then rinse with cold water and drain off the liquid. Toss the onions in a clean bowl with coriander or parsley, lime juice, oil, chilli (if using) and a pinch more salt.

Chef's note: Traditionally ají amarillo is used, a type of chilli that is loved and widely used by Peruvians, but you can substitute with your favourite chilli. It doesn't have to be spicy but it will add tons of flavour. For less heat, discard the veins and the seeds of the chilli and chop it very finely. Peruvian's like to soak the onions in warm water and salt to take out the bitterness. They become delicate and sweeter.

Mexico

CEBOLLA MORADA EN VINAGRE

Pickled Red Onions

GF

1 cup vinegar
pinch of salt
1 red onion, thinly sliced

This is also pickled red onion, but different from salsa criolla (opposite). These onions are a great way to add crunch, colour and zest to any dish or protein, and are very popular on top of tacos. The acid 'cooks' the onion and sweetens it.

Prepare: 5 minutes
Serves: 4 as a side

Whisk vinegar and salt together, and pour over the onions to cover, using a non-metallic bowl. Let it stand for at least 30 minutes before serving. Store in an airtight container in the refrigerator for up to 5 days.

Venezuela

GUASACACA

Creamy Avocado & Herb Salsa

GF

4 large garlic cloves, peeled
½ cup olive oil
¼ cup finely chopped flat-leaf parsley with some stems
¼ cup finely chopped coriander with some stems
1 ripe avocado
1 tbsp fresh lemon juice
2 tbsp white vinegar
1 fresh green chilli, or red chilli flakes to taste (optional)
flaky sea salt

Venezuelans use guasacaca like Argentinians use chimichurri (see page 202). Guasacaca is similar to chimichurri but has avocado and coriander in it, making it thicker and creamier in flavour. Both are used as accompaniments to proteins and other dishes. Not one household makes guasacaca the same; some add capsicums, tomatoes, onions and rice bran oil. My version is very simple, and I truly feel I'm not missing a thing. It's a total crowd-pleaser that goes with everything, and you can whip it up in no time before your dinner, lunch or barbecue.

Prepare: 10 minutes
Makes: 1¼ cups

Using a mortar and pestle, crush garlic with a pinch of salt and then muddle it with 2 tablespoons of olive oil. When a paste has formed, add herbs and combine.

Halve avocado, remove stone and scoop out the flesh. Combine with herbs, mashing with a fork. Add lemon juice, vinegar and chilli (if using), and season to taste with flaky sea salt and freshly ground black pepper.

Chef's note: Some people make this in a food processor or blender, but I prefer the chunky, rustic consistency you get from a mortar and pestle.

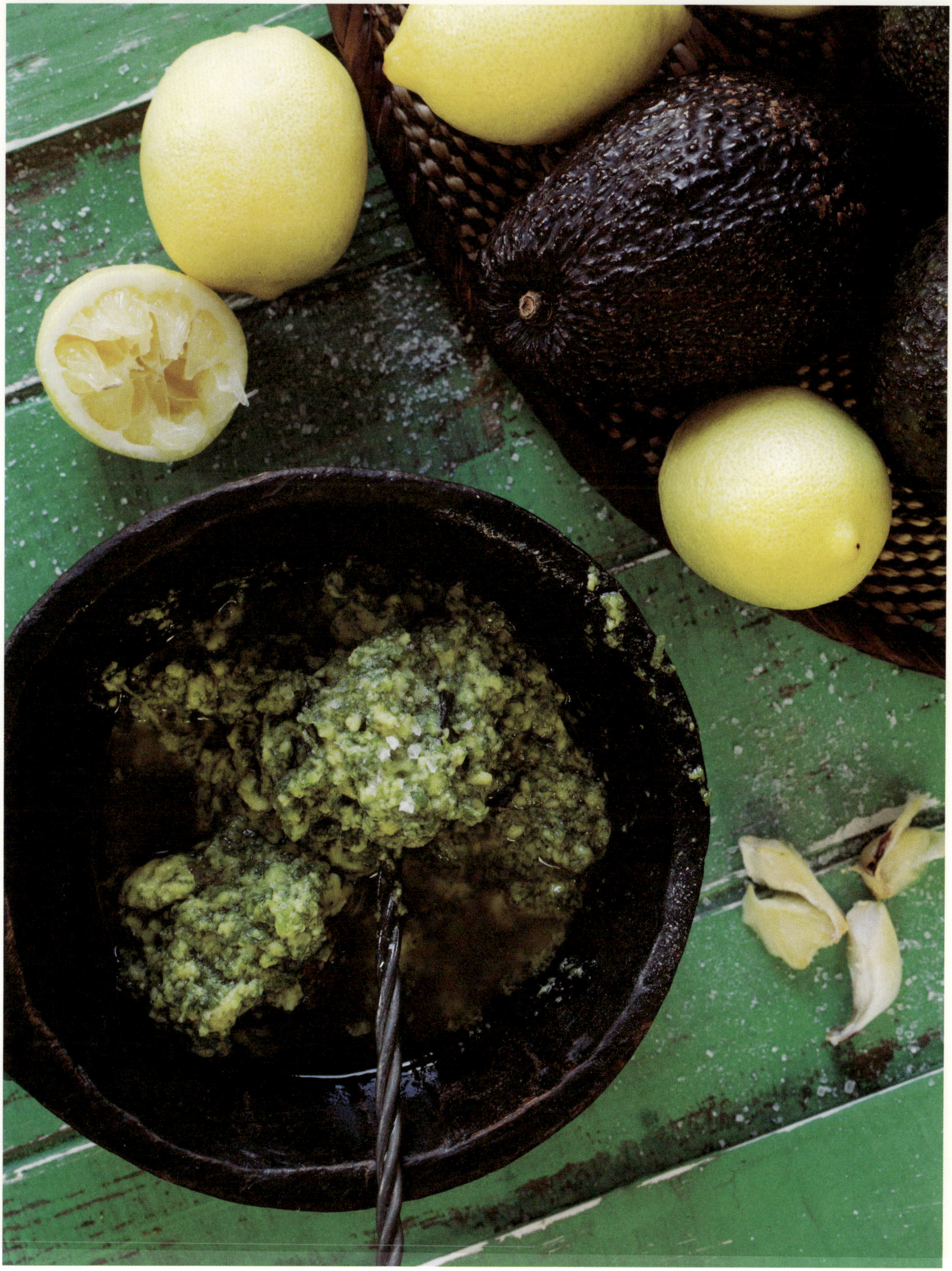

Argentina

CHIMICHURRI

Herby Salsa

GF

½ cup extra virgin olive oil
½ cup very finely chopped flat-leaf parsley
1 tbsp dried oregano, lightly crushed
2 cloves garlic, peeled and finely chopped
½ tsp red chilli flakes
¼ cup white vinegar
flaky sea salt

From gaucho (cowboy) camp-fires to society weddings, you will always find chimichurri in Argentina, and especially served at asados — traditional Argentinean barbecues enjoyed by families and friends every Sunday. The beauty of traditional Argentinean cuisine is that it's mostly unfettered by complicated sauces and preparation techniques. This is especially true in the realm of the asado. Imagine gauchos on horseback, riding over the vast landscape, the Andes rising in the distance, and cooking over a wood fire with little more than salt and a few herbs to season the meat. This is more or less what remains today, and everyone has their own recipe.

Prepare: 10 minutes; rest: 30 minutes
Makes: approx. 1 cup

In a small mixing bowl, whisk (or mix together with a fork) olive oil with herbs, garlic, red chilli flakes and vinegar. Adjust seasoning to taste with flaky sea salt and freshly ground black pepper. Leave to rest for about 30 minutes before serving.

To turn this chimichurri to a mint chimichurri for the lamb recipe on page 95, add ½ cup very finely chopped fresh mint leaves and 1 tablespoon of finely chopped rosemary leaves.

Chef's note: I don't like heavy, over-complicated sauces. Chimichurri is the perfect way to add flavour and freshness to proteins (chicken, beef, fish, pork) without overpowering them. It's also a great way to add freshness and tang to roasted or grilled vegetables, and makes an excellent marinade. You can use red wine vinegar instead of white vinegar. A myth about chimichurri is that it needs to be bright green, but you can add finely chopped tomatoes, paprika and cumin if you like. Another myth is that it needs to be eaten straight away, but this is not true — it keeps in the fridge for up to 5 days.

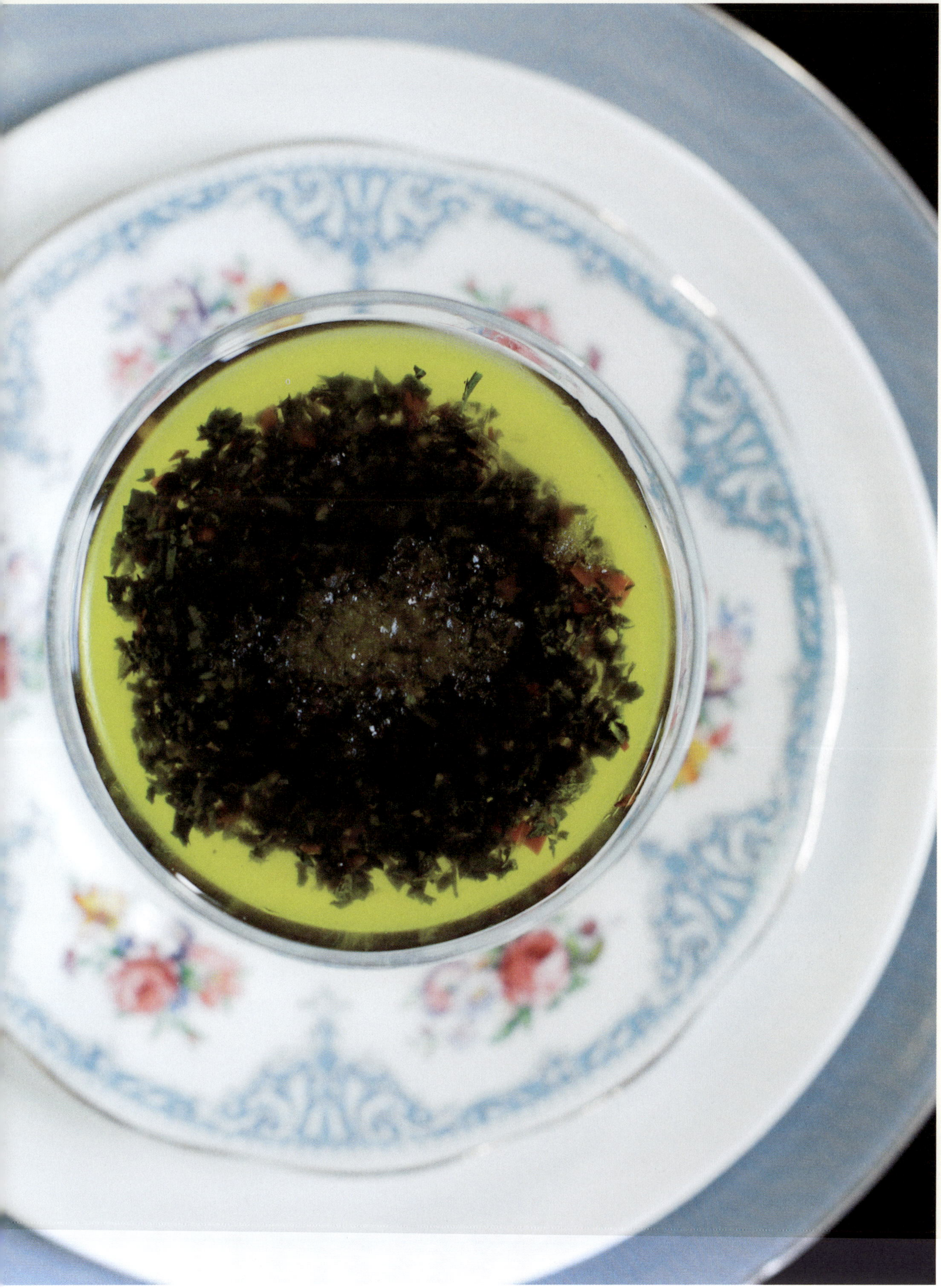

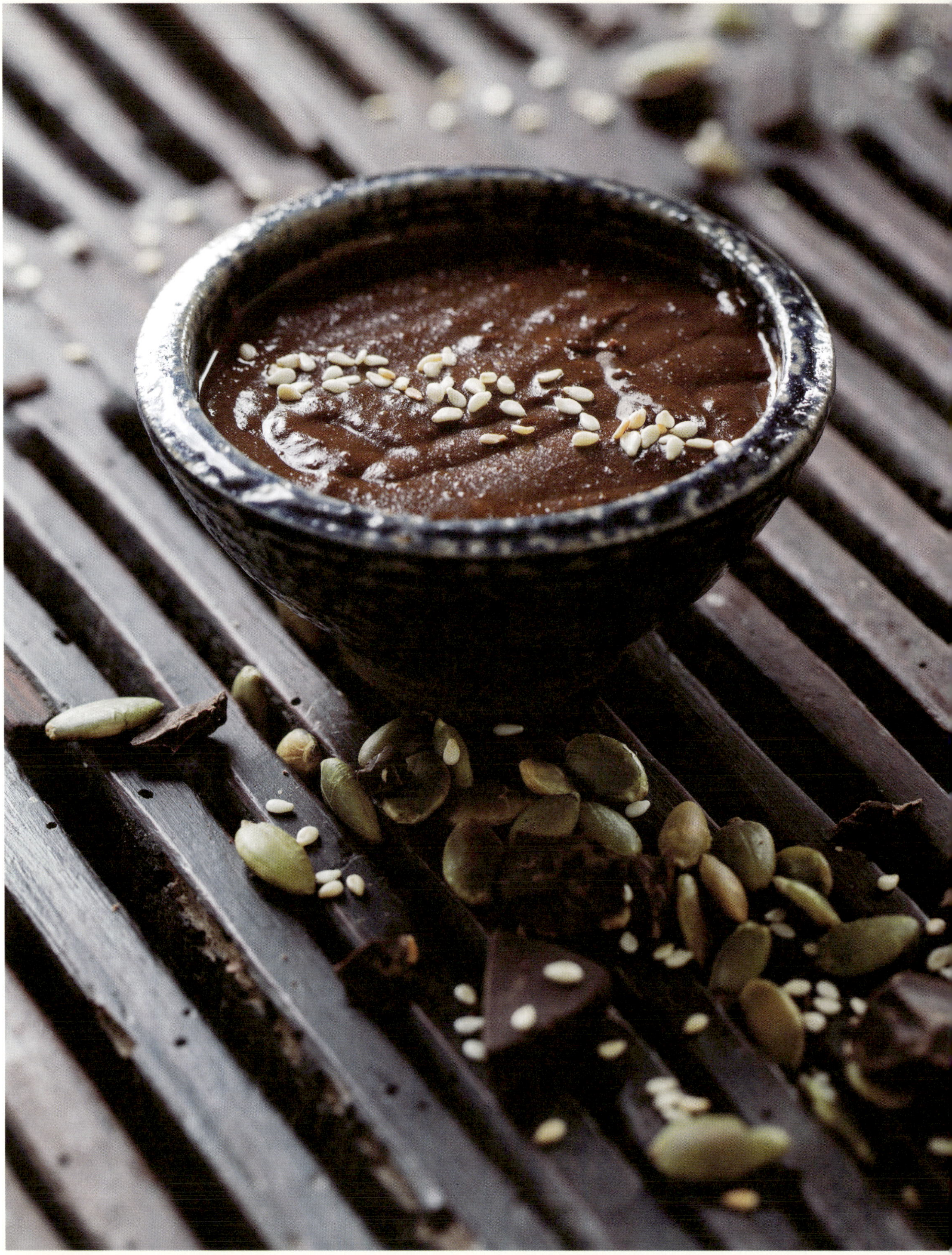

Mexico

MOLE

GF

4 dried mulato chillies
2 dried ancho chillies
3 dried pasilla chillies
2 tbsp raisins
a little cooking oil (optional)
1 tomato, core removed
½ small onion, peeled, cut into four
4 cloves garlic, peeled
1 corn tortilla (see page 115)
¼ cup blanched almonds
1½ tbsp pumpkin seeds
2 tbsp sesame seeds
½ ripe banana, peeled
2 cups chicken stock
¼ tsp ground cloves
pinch of ground anise seed
pinch of ground coriander
pinch of ground allspice berries
1 tbsp butter
1 stick cinnamon
90 g Mexican chocolate (preferably La Abuelita brand)
50 g shaved panela (unrefined cane sugar)

Garnish
toasted sesame and pumpkin seeds
coriander leaves (optional)

The word 'mole' comes from the Aztec word 'molli', meaning 'sauce'. When most people think of mole, they think of the dark chocolate and chilli sauce from Puebla, but each region of Mexico lays claims to its own style of mole — for example, Oaxaca is called the land of the seven moles — and they don't all have chocolate. Because of the number of ingredients and the labour of love involved, moles have the reputation of being difficult and only made for special occasions, birthday parties or weddings. Mole is complex, rich yet delicate, and has a lovely history. It is often traced back to a story about a convent in Puebla and the desire of the nuns to please the bishop who was coming to visit. Having nothing but one roaming turkey and a pantry full of spices and chocolate, they started toasting chillies, frying raisins and grinding almonds and seeds to make a sauce worthy of the bishop. It was truly an immaculate conception.

Prepare: 30 minutes; cook: 1½ hours
Makes: approx. 5 cups

Preheat oven to 200°C.

Devein and de-seed chillies. Bring a pot of water to a boil. Turn off the heat, and put chillies in for 20 minutes to hydrate. Soak raisins in warm water (or fry them gently in a little oil) until they have plumped up.

Meanwhile, prepare the rest of your ingredients. Cover a large baking tray with non-stick paper, and roast tomato, onion and garlic. Set a timer for 5 minutes at a time, and keep an eye on them because they will all roast at different speeds.

While vegetables are roasting, use tongs to hold the tortilla directly over an open flame to toast it, one side at a time, until charred. Toast almonds and seeds, either on separate lined trays in the oven or in turn in a dry frying pan on the stovetop.

Drain chillies and discard the soaking liquid. In a blender, place chillies, tomato, garlic, onion, crumbled tortilla, nuts, seeds, banana and plumped raisins, along with chicken stock. Blend until smooth, and set aside.

Place a stockpot over a medium-high heat and lightly toast the ground spices until fragrant; about 1 minute. Add butter and melt, then pour the blended mixture into the stockpot. Add cinnamon, chocolate and panela. Stir while heating up, to fully incorporate the chocolate and panela. Bring to the boil, then turn down to a simmer, partially cover and reduce until you have a thick and creamy sauce, stirring occasionally so it doesn't stick. If your mole starts becoming too thick and sticking to the bottom, add a little more stock or water. The consistency should be velvety and silky.

Chef's note: This recipe is considered to be a speedy mole, but even though it has its short-cuts, I feel that the tradition, taste and integrity of the sauce is not lost at all. You can add shredded chicken (see page 42), turkey or pork straight into the mole, or plate up a nice chicken/turkey breast or pork medallion and pour the mole over it to give a more elegant presentation. Garnish mole with toasted seeds, and coriander leaves (if using).

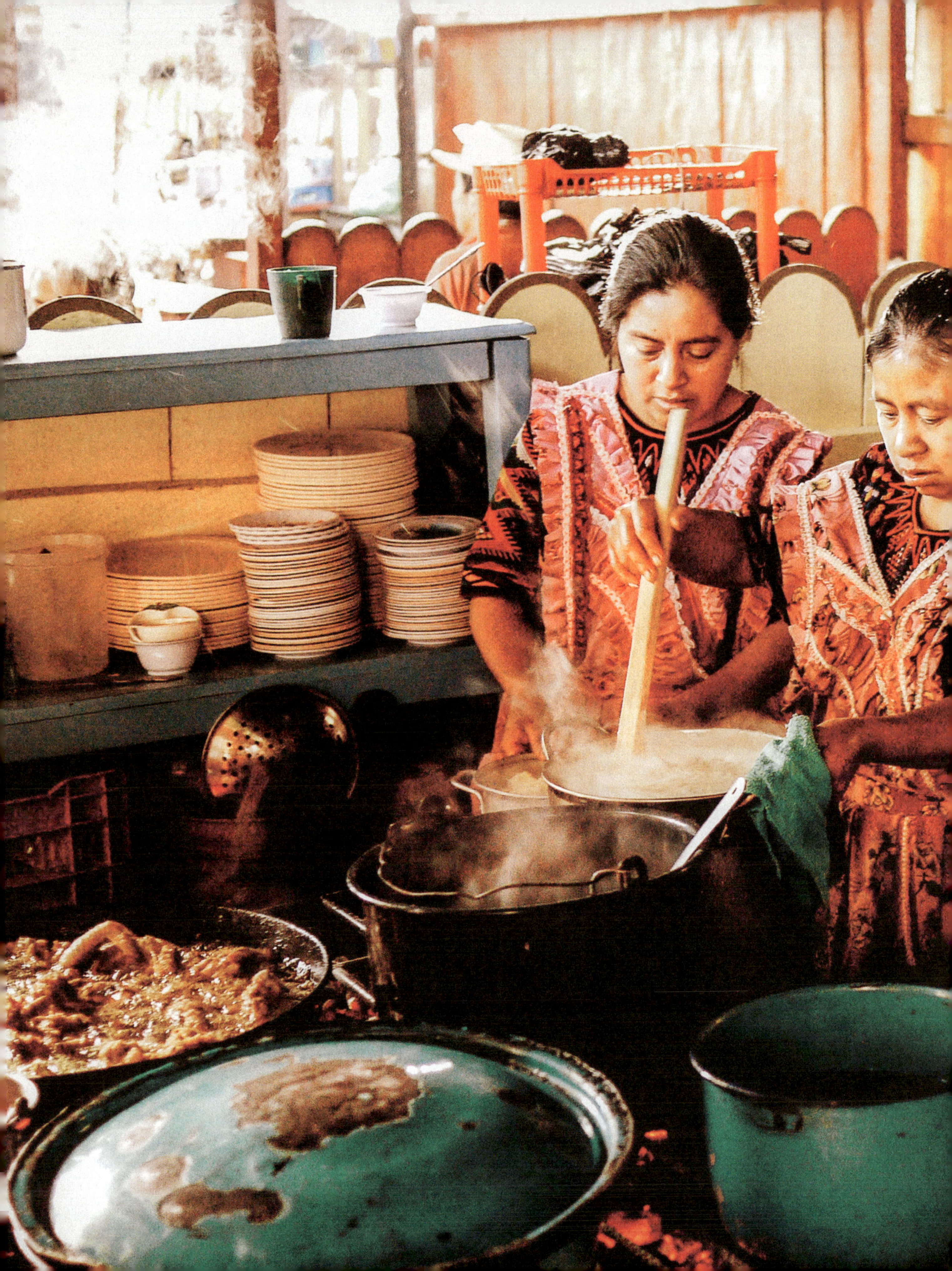

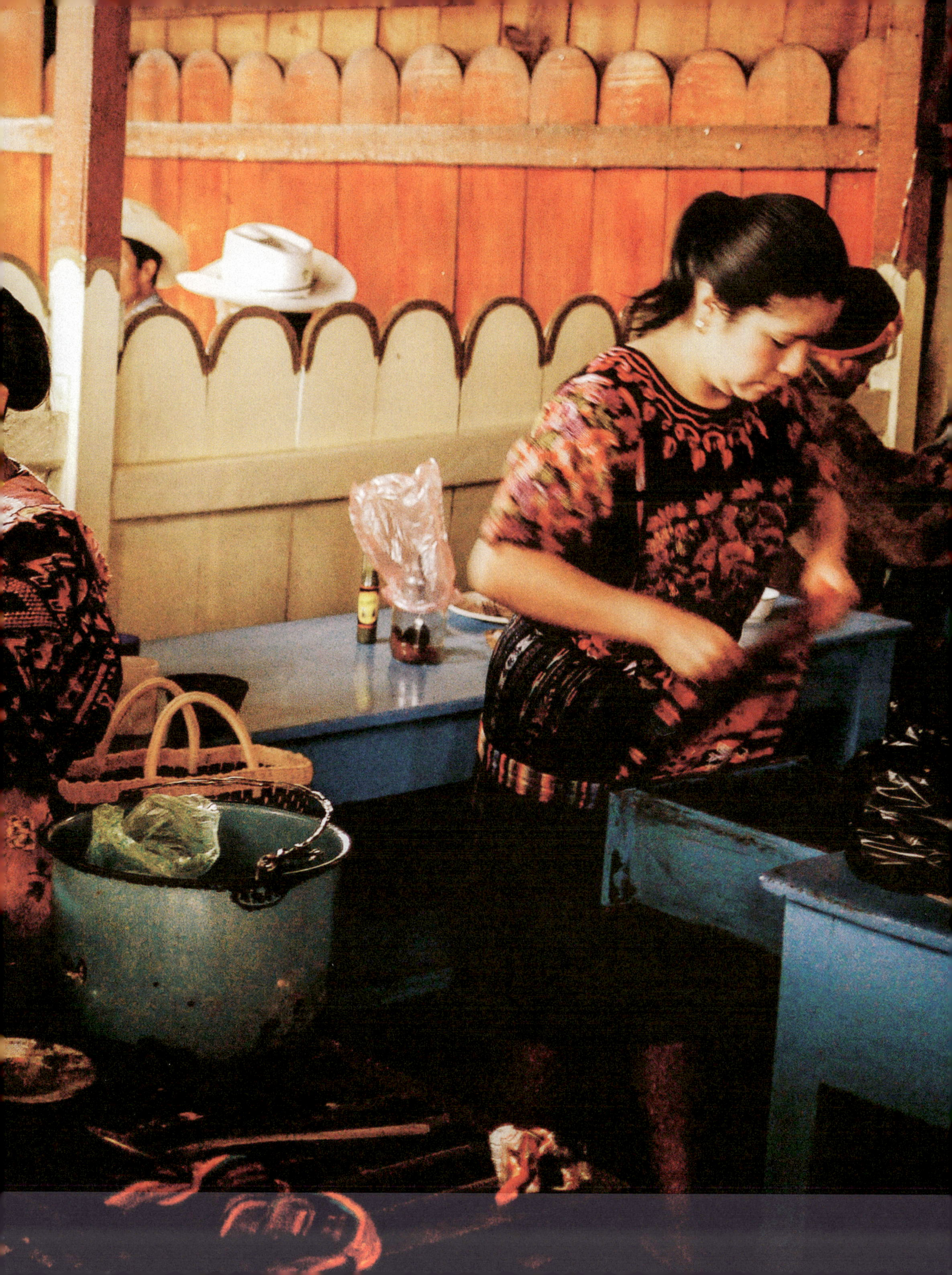

Mexico

QUESO FRESCO

Fresh White Cheese

GF

2 litres full-fat whole milk (such as Anchor silver top)
¼ cup white vinegar
2 tsp salt

Latin America is a culture of dairy lovers, and we have cheeses that I've never tasted anywhere else in the world. In Venezuela, for example, queso Guayanés and queso de año are exquisite cheeses that accompany an arepa or cachapa; queso de año gets used like Parmesan for garnishes and in desserts. Queso fresco is a mild, fresh, milky and bright Mexican cheese, similar to feta and ricotta. It is one of the best cheeses to have on hand to accompany your favourite Mexican dish, summer veggies, huevos (eggs), salads and grilled food.

**Prepare: 5 minutes; cook: 15 minutes; chill: overnight
Serves: 4–6**

Pour the milk into a large saucepan. Heat over a medium-low heat until the milk starts to simmer; a thermometer should register a temperature of 90°C. Stir constantly for 10 minutes with a wooden spoon, making an S movement. This prevents the milk from sticking to the bottom of the pan and keeps the temperature even.

Turn off the heat and pour the vinegar into the milk, stirring constantly. The milk curds will start to separate and the mixture will begin to look grainy and divided.

Pour into a medium sieve lined with cheese-cloth and set over a large empty bowl or pan. Let it drain until the curds look drier, about 5 minutes. Mix salt in.

Transfer the cheesecloth with the mixture to a 1.4 litre rectangular glass dish. Fold the sides of the cheese-cloth over the curds, or place some plastic wrap over. Weight down the cheese with a chopping board with full food cans on top, or anything that is heavy and will fit into the dish (like a milk or fruit juice carton). Refrigerate overnight; the cheese will become firm. Transfer the cheese (without the cheese-cloth) to an airtight container. Keep refrigerated for up to 2 days.

Chef's note: You can also fold a bit of lime juice and zest, chopped red chillies and 1 teaspoon dried ground epazote into your cheese before pressing it. For the perfect snack, heat up a tortilla, add butter, some refried beans and this festive cheese . . . it's mouth-watering just thinking about it.

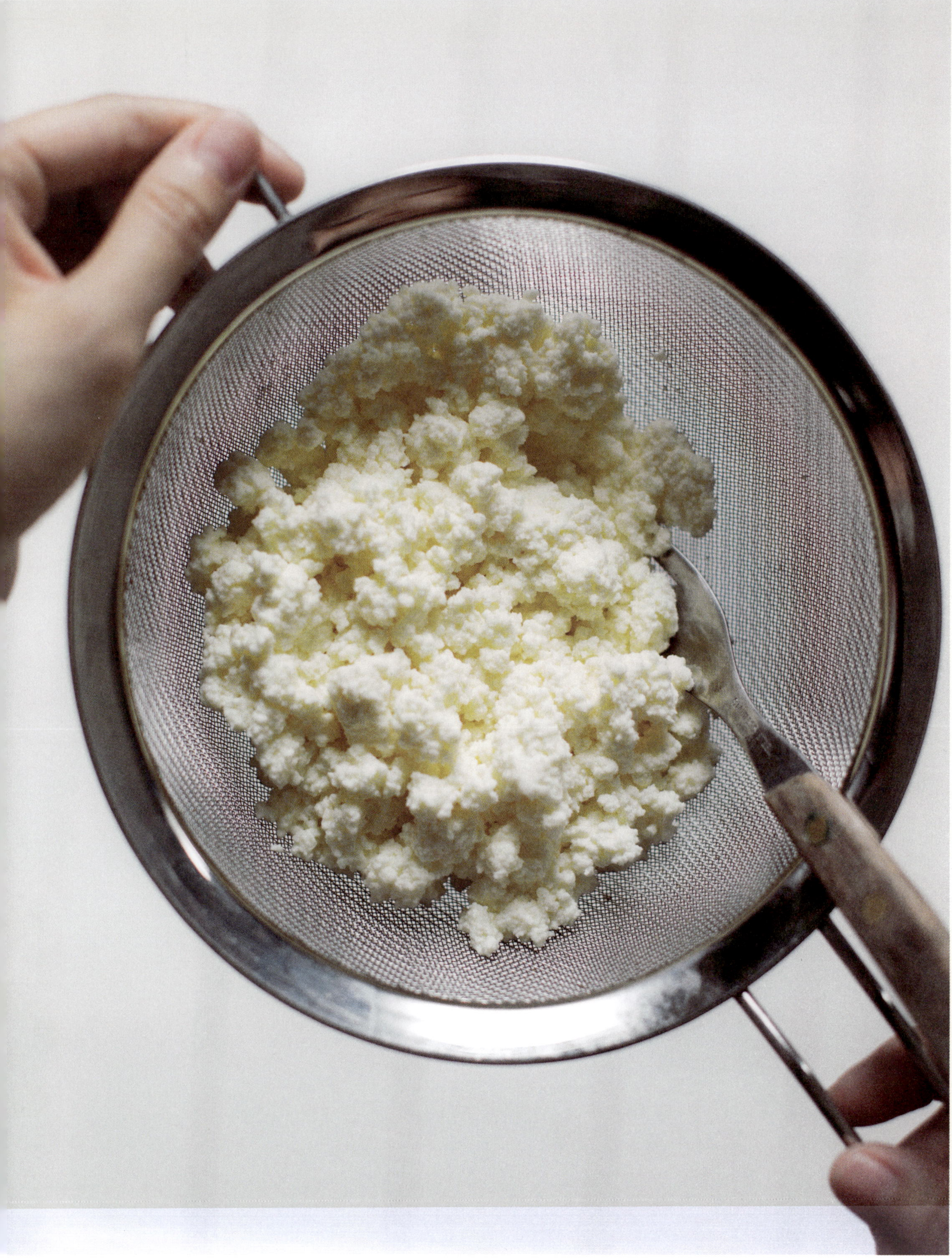

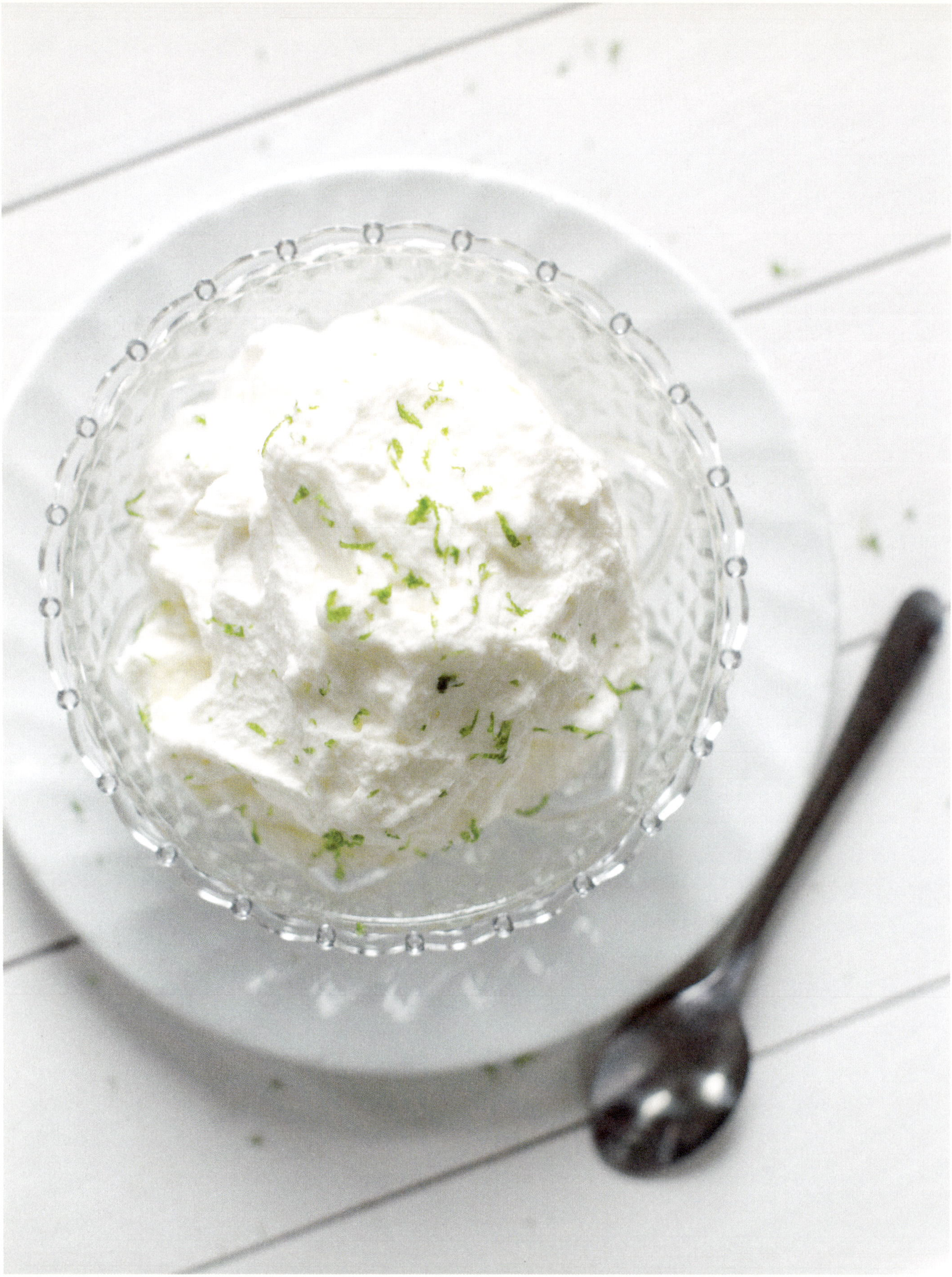

Mexico

CREMA AGRIA

Salty Cream

GF

1 cup cream (I use Anchor Pure Cream)
2 tbsp lime juice (about 1 lime)
½ tsp salt
lime zest (optional)

Crema agria is the most loved, golden child of the sour cream family in Latin America. It will most likely be used rather than sour cream, and it feels lighter and tastier. Every time I make this recipe for dairy lovers, people's eyes light up and they always ask for the recipe. This is my home-made version. Dip your mandocas (see page 133) in it, add it on top of your tacos, quesadillas (see page 139) and chilaquiles (see page 50), or put it inside your arepas (see page 119).

Prepare: 5 minutes; chill: 15 minutes
Makes: 1 cup

Combine cream, lime juice and salt and whip at high speed in a blender until it gets thick and creamy. Taste and add more salt if necessary. Refrigerate for 15 minutes, and there is your crema agria.

Garnish with lime zest if desired and put on the table at your taco party.

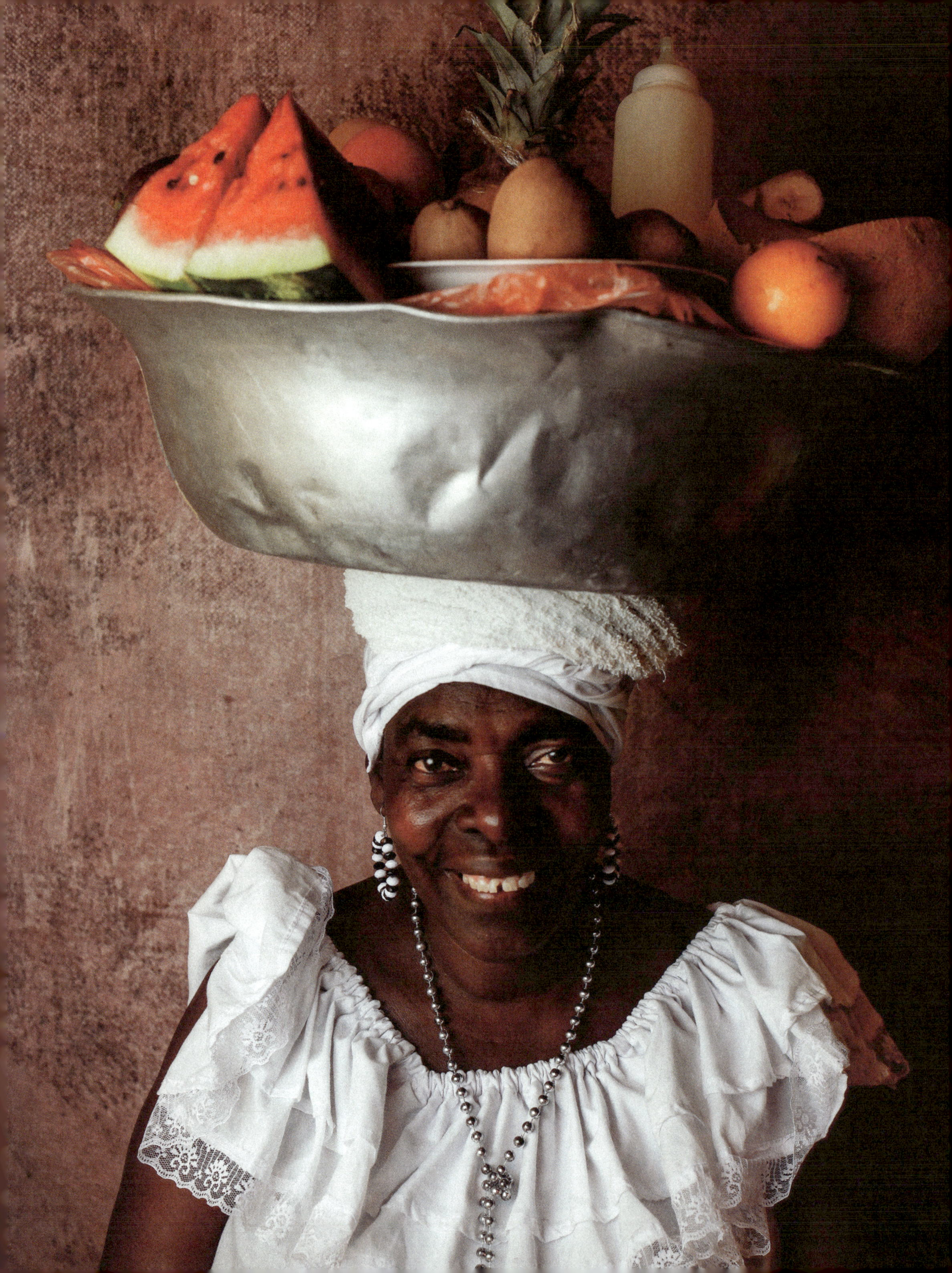

ALGO DULCE

SOMETHING SWEET

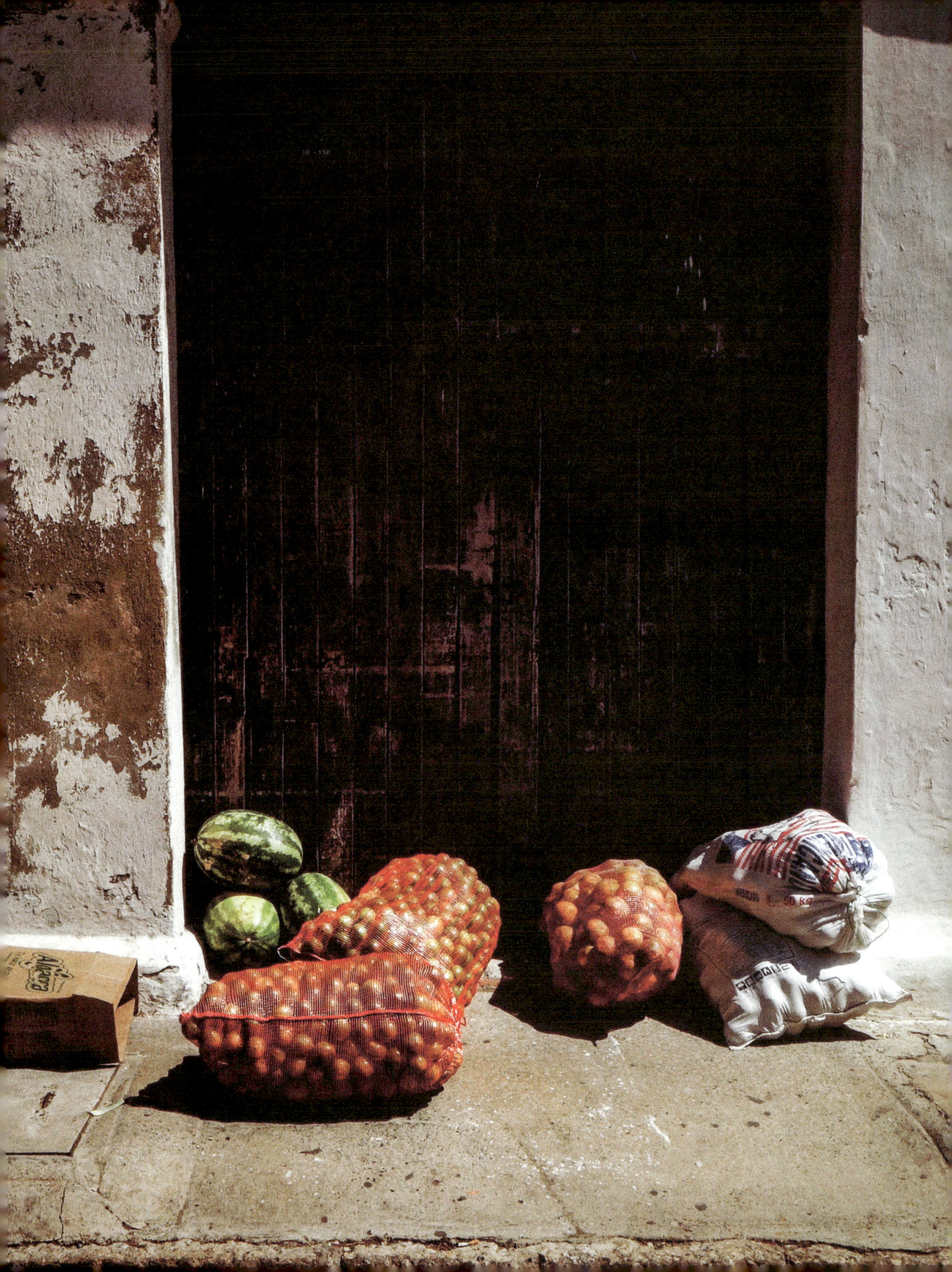

SALPICÓN
Tropical Fruit Salad

MOUSSE DE PARCHITA
Passionfruit Mousse

CRÈME DE PAPAYA CON CASSIS
Papaya Cream with Berry Syrup

FLAN CUBANO
Cuban 'Crème Caramel'

BROWNIES CON CHILE Y NUECES
Flourless Brownies with Spice & Nuts

ARROZ CON LECHE
Rice Pudding

PIE DE LIMÓN CON LECHE CONDENSADA
Condensed-milk Lemon Pie

ALFAJORES
Shortbread Cookie Sandwich with Dulce de Leche

CARAMELO
Spiced Brittle

MERENGÓN
Caramel Meringues

TRES LECHES
Three-milk Cake

BRIGADEIRO
Chocolate Fudge Balls

Colombia

SALPICÓN

Tropical Fruit Salad

GF

1 cup diced mango
1 cup diced watermelon
1 cup diced papaya (pawpaw)
1 cup diced pineapple
1 cup orange, watermelon
 or strawberry juice
1 cup ginger ale

A salpicón is a cross between a tropical fruit salad and a juice, and is craved in Colombia, especially along the coast where it gets 'muy caliente' — really, really hot. Colombians take a simple fruit salad to the next level with salpicón. You can use whatever combination of tropical fruits you choose, and you can include grapes. If using bananas, only add them right before serving to prevent them browning. Here I've added a sparkly touch with ginger ale combined with orange juice, or you can use a San Pellegrino Aranciata. You can also top this with a scoop of vanilla ice cream and/or a tablespoon of condensed milk. Absolutely delicious and refreshing!

Prepare: 10 minutes
Serves: 4

Combine all the diced fruit together, then distribute equally among 4 tall glasses. Pour ¼ cup of juice and ¼ cup of ginger ale into each glass and serve immediately.

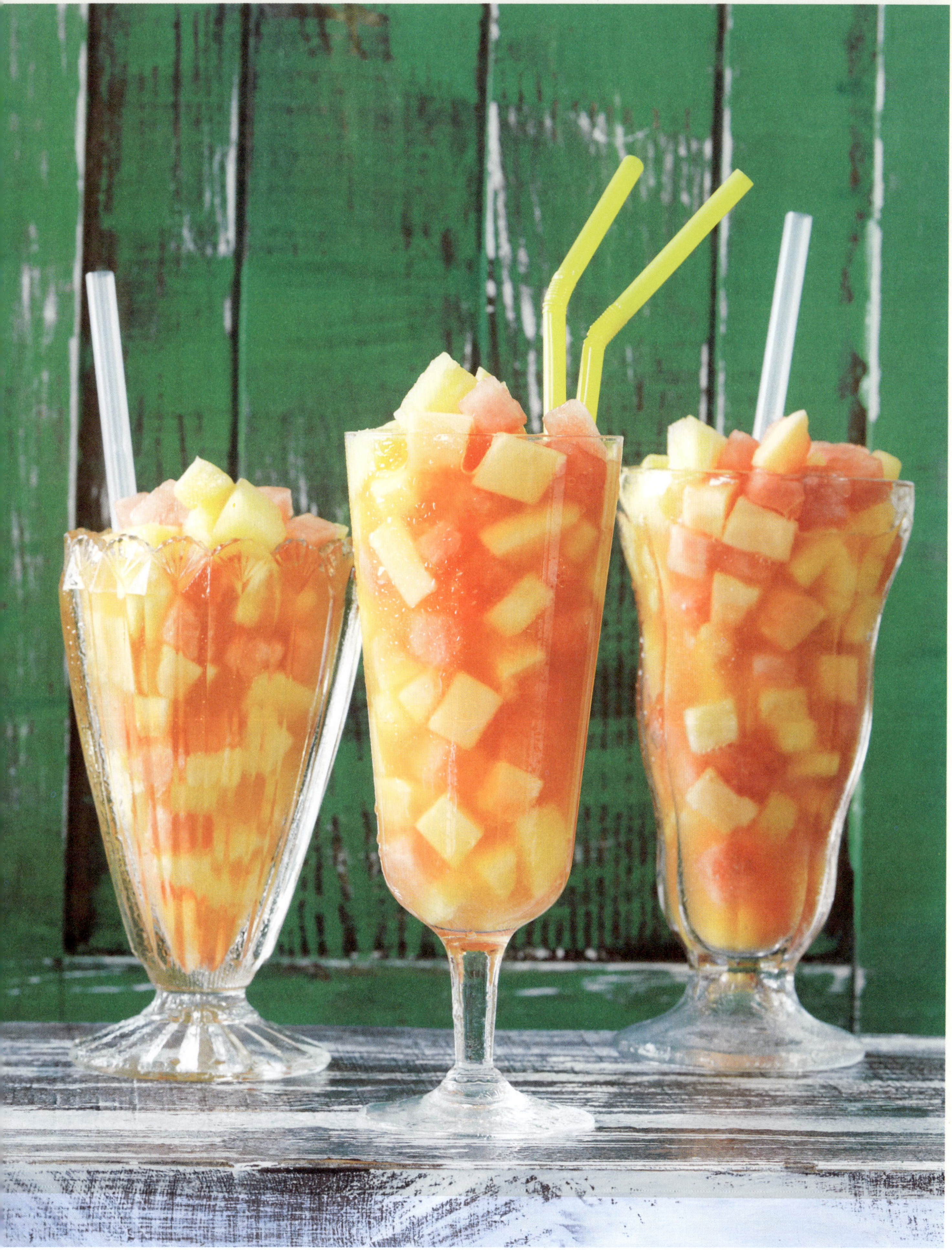

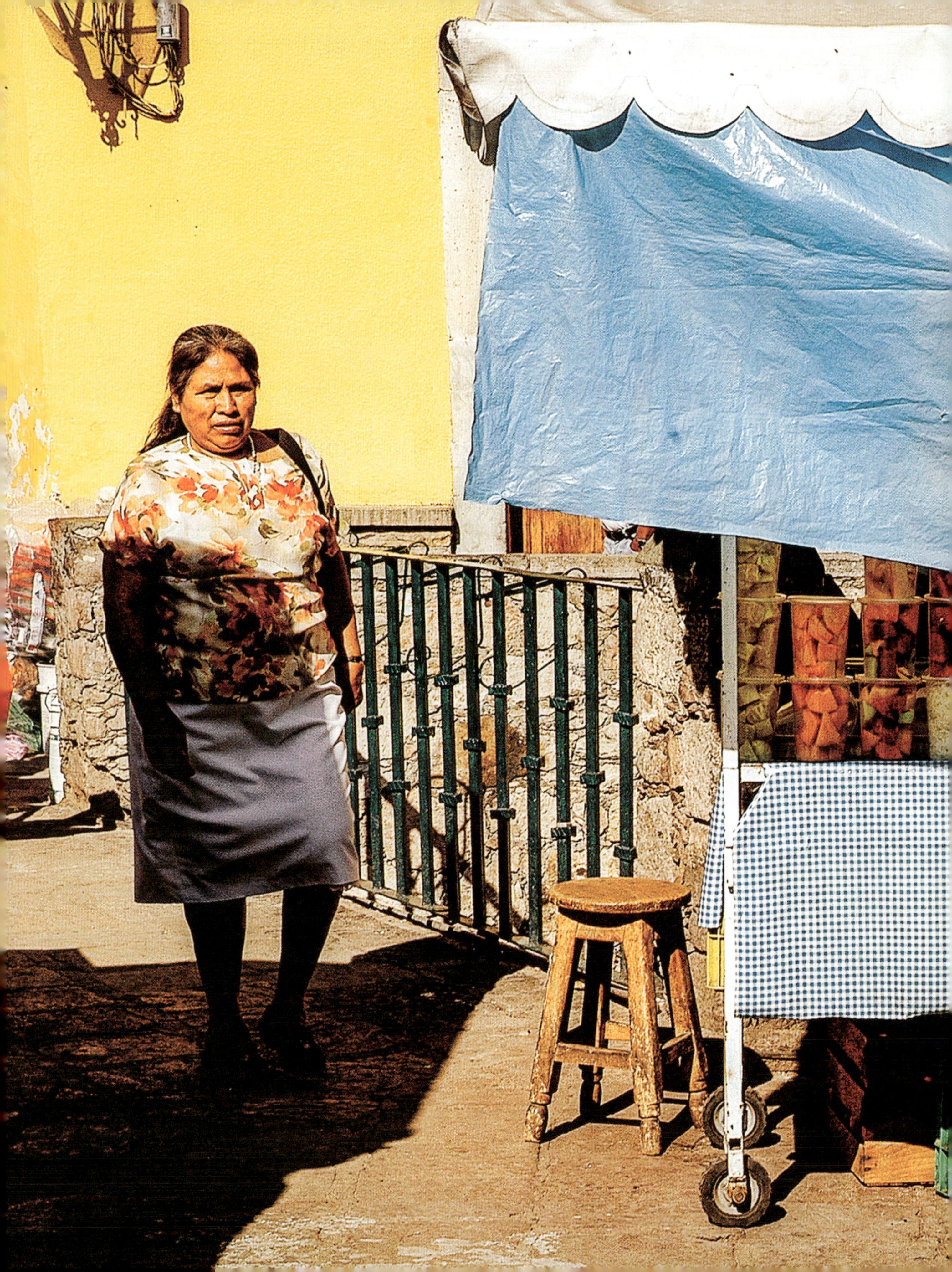

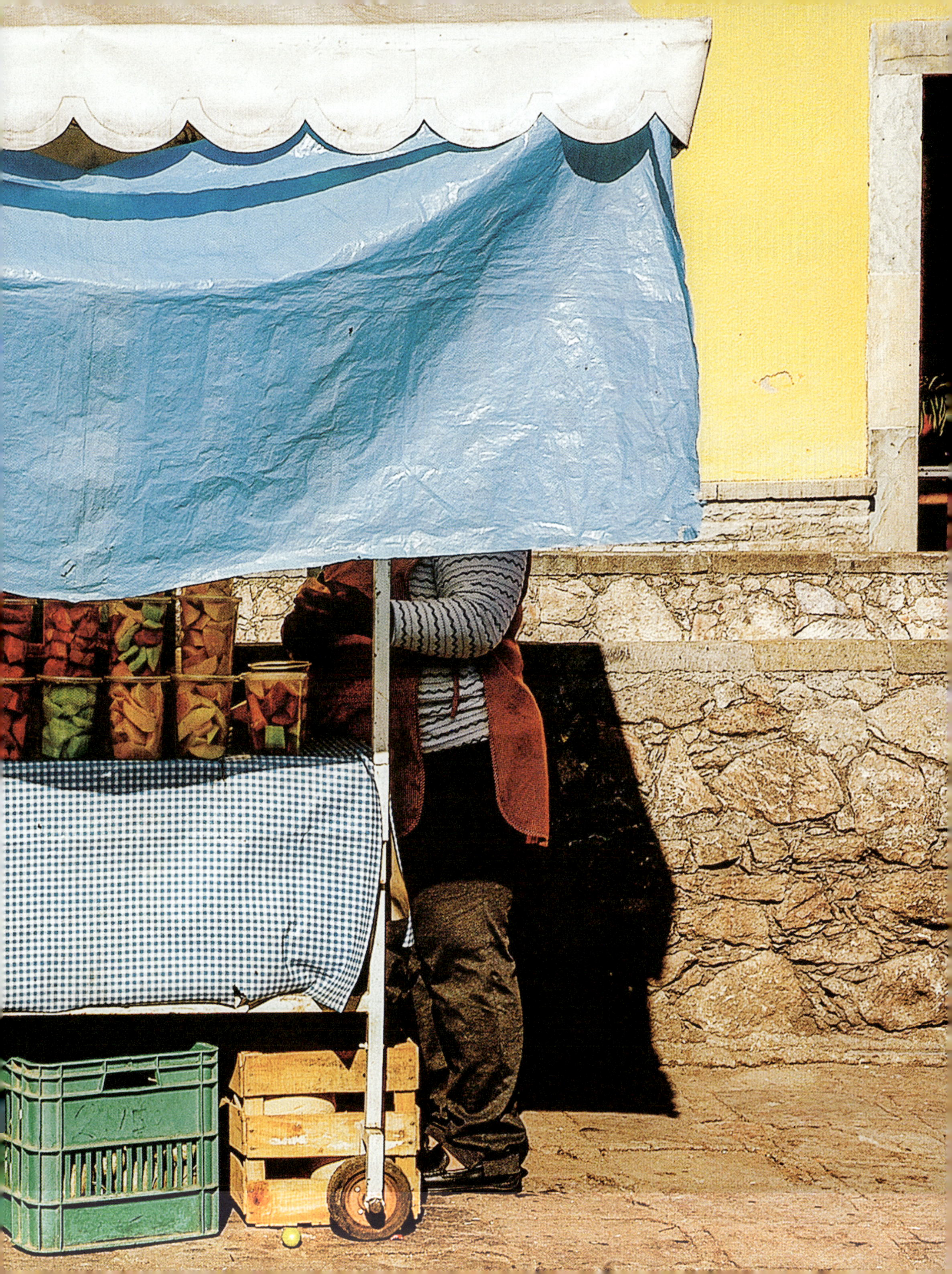

Venezuela

MOUSSE DE PARCHITA

Passionfruit Mousse

GF

½ cup passionfruit syrup,
    plus extra for garnish
3 sheets gelatine
500 ml cream
seasonal fruit, to garnish (optional)

This is a very simple dessert that feels light and refreshing, perfect after a heavy meal or a hot summer day. All the panaderías (bakeries) in Venezuela sell mousse de parchita. Most of them are owned by Portuguese immigrants, so they have a strong European influence and are rather like pâtisseries — they sell petite palmiers, freshly baked baguettes and a variety of éclairs and profiteroles. When we were younger, my cousin Jonathan and I would drool as we looked through the windows of the panadería at the mousses de parchita on spinning pedestal displays, looking like passionfruit-covered cheesecakes. This recipe is a simple version of this beloved mousse.

Preparation: 10 minutes; cook: 5 minutes; chill: 2 hours
Serves: 6

Heat passionfruit syrup in a small saucepan over a low heat for about 5 minutes — do not let it boil. Meanwhile, soften gelatine sheets in cold water. Squeeze excess water from gelatine and add sheets to passionfruit syrup. Place pan over a large bowl filled with ice to cool mixture quickly.

Meanwhile, beat cream just until soft peaks form. Fold cream into passionfruit mixture and pour into serving glasses. Tap the bottom of each glass against a tea towel placed on the work surface to knock out any air pockets. Refrigerate until set, about 2 hours.

Garnish with a thin layer of passionfruit syrup on top of each glass, or top with fresh seasonal fruit.

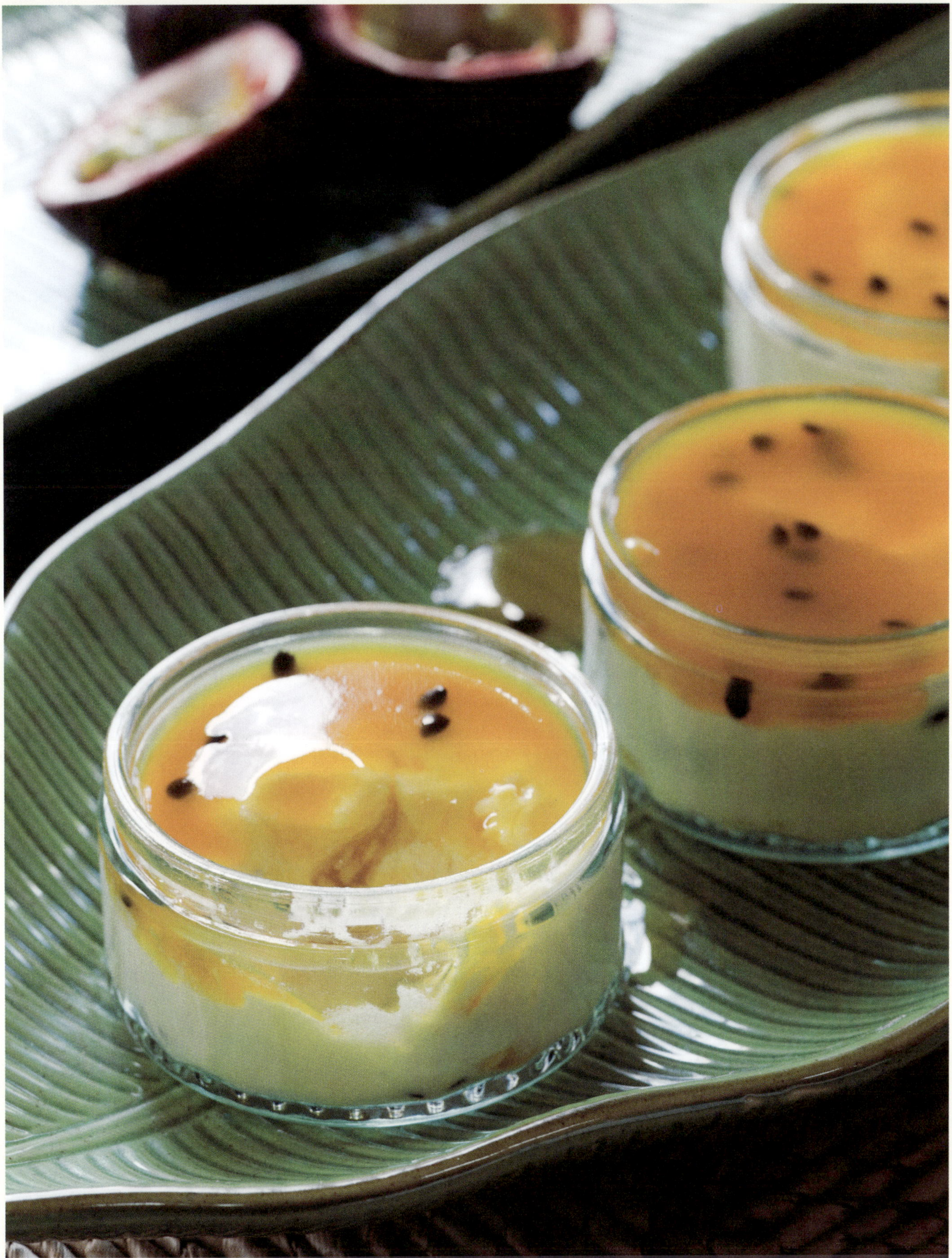

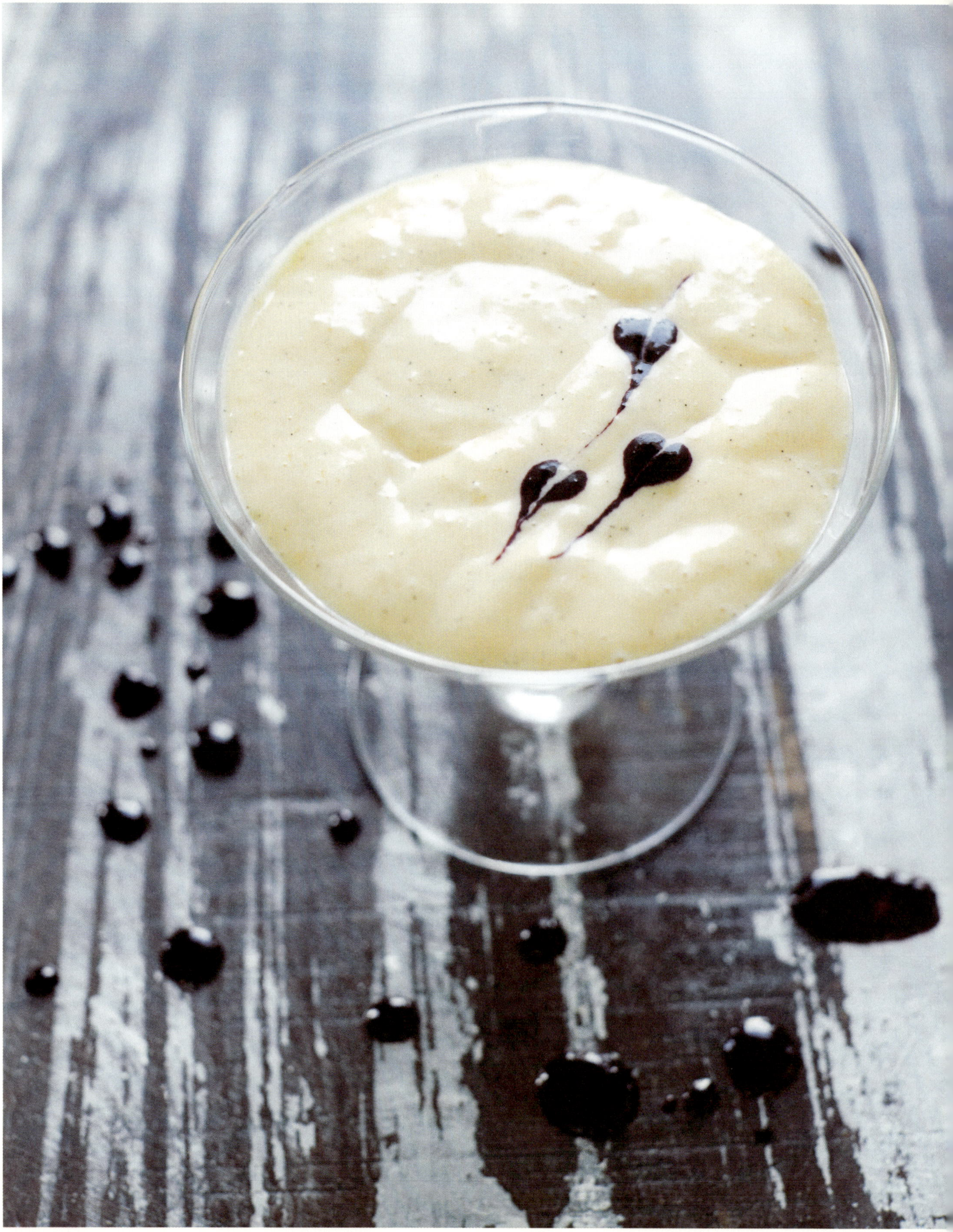

Brazil

CRÈME DE PAPAYA CON CASSIS

Papaya Cream with Berry Syrup

GF

For the berry syrup
⅓ cup blackberries
⅓ cup raspberries
⅓ cup strawberries
4 tbsp sugar
1 cup water
juice of ½ lemon

For the cream
2 cups ripe papaya
   (pawpaw), cubed
3 scoops vanilla ice cream

This really quick and effortless dessert is the perfect way to end a heavy meal. It is thicker than a milkshake but lighter than a pudding. The combination of the papaya, vanilla ice cream and berries is heavenly. It's traditionally served with crème de cassis, a blackcurrant liqueur, but I have replaced this with a non-alcoholic berry syrup.

Prepare: 10 minutes
Serves: 4

Place everything for the berry syrup together in a blender and blend until smooth. Transfer to a saucepan and cook over a medium-low heat until reduced by half. Transfer to a bowl and set aside to cool.

Wash blender. Place papaya in blender and blend until smooth. Add ice cream and blend in. Fold 4 tablespoons of berry syrup in just slightly so that you get some marbling. Pour into serving glasses. Garnish with more syrup and serve immediately.

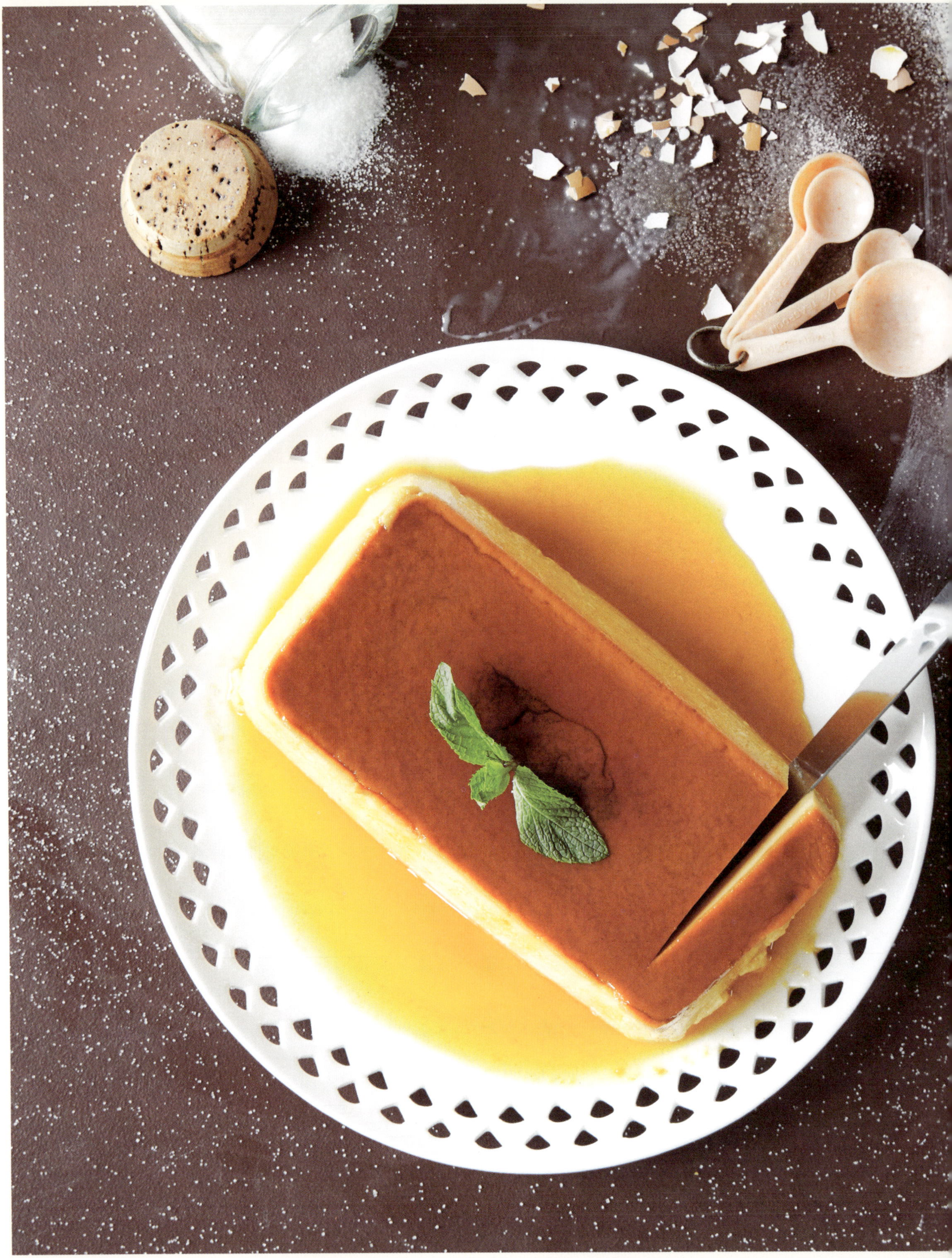

Cuba

FLAN CUBANO

Cuban 'Crème Caramel'

GF

For the caramel
¼ cup water
1 cup sugar

For the custard
5 large or 6 medium eggs
¼ cup granulated sugar
340 g can sweetened condensed milk
1½ cups evaporated milk
seeds from 1 vanilla bean, or 2 tsp vanilla extract

The flan is not really a crème caramel. These dishes are like two cousins, with one growing up in France and the other in the Caribbean; they are obviously going to be a little different. The French crème caramel is light and wobbly, while the flan is dense, richer and creamier. It is a staple at parties in Venezuela and the Dominican Republic, where it is called quesillo (little cheesecake), and my grandpa, the dessert king, makes the best. This is the Cuban version of the flan, which comes from my friend Grettel.

Prepare: 30 minutes; cook: 1½ hours for a 1.4 litre baking dish
Serves: 6–8

Preheat oven to 180°C.

In a heavy-bottomed frying pan or saucepan, place water and sugar over a medium-high heat. Bring to the boil and cook until sugar is completely melted and it has reached a rich medium-brown color (which means it is caramelised). Carefully swirl the pan every few minutes to prevent the sugar crystallising.

Pour caramel into the Pyrex baking dish where you will make your flan, ensuring that the walls of the dish are also covered. Let caramel cool while you prepare the custard.

Beat eggs with a whisk, then add sugar and keep whisking until the sugar is completely incorporated. Add the milks and vanilla seeds or extract. Blend until smooth, then pass through a fine sieve.

Pour custard into the caramel-lined baking dish. Place this in a large glass or ceramic baking dish and fill with boiling water to about 5 cm deep. Cover larger dish with foil and bake for 1-1½ hours, until custard is just set. Check with a knife inserted just to the side of the centre. If the knife comes out clean, it's ready.

Remove and leave to cool. Chill in the refrigerator for at least 2 hours. Invert flan onto a plate, and watch the caramel sauce flow over the custard.

Chef's note: You can also make this in ramekins. Bake them in a similar water bath (bain marie) for 1 hour. The water should come about halfway up the ramekins.

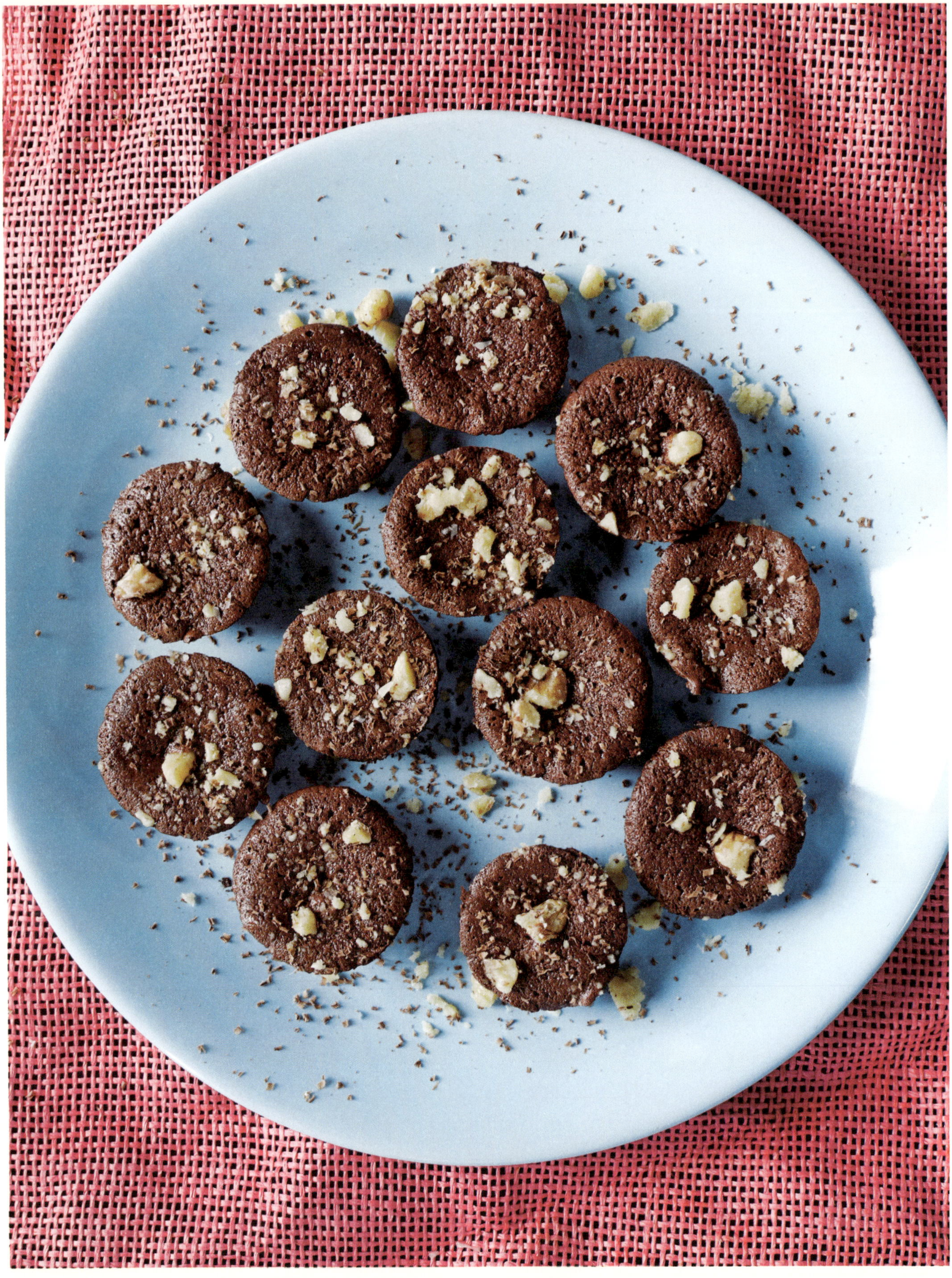

Mexico

BROWNIES CON CHILE Y NUECES

Flourless Brownies with Spice & Nuts

GF

250 g good-quality dark chocolate (minimum 70% cocoa solids)
125 g unsalted butter
¼ tsp cayenne pepper
½ cup raw shelled walnuts or pecans
5 eggs, separated
pinch of salt
125 g sugar

Mexicans love to dress up their chocolate and drinks with spices. This tradition dates back to as early as 1900 BC, when the Mexican Native Americans used to infuse a frothy cacao drink with chilli, spices, wine and even corn purée, to tame its bitterness. Keeping up with tradition, these addictive gluten-free brownies are the perfect gift to take to any dinner party. They have a pleasant kick from the cayenne. Feel free to add seasonal berries and dust with icing sugar for a prettier presentation.

Prepare: 25 minutes; cook: 12–50 minutes, depending on tin size
Serves: 12

Preheat oven to 160°C. Line baking tin with non-stick baking paper, or prepare a mini muffin tin with liners and/or cooking spray.

Break or chop chocolate into small pieces. Melt chocolate with butter in a heatproof bowl set over hot (not boiling) water on the stovetop. Do not let the bowl touch the water. Stir until the chocolate melts, then remove from the heat. Add cayenne pepper and nuts, mix and set aside.

In a stand mixer with whisk attachment, whisk egg yolks with two-thirds of the sugar on high speed until the mixture turns pale yellow and forms a very thick foam; about 3 minutes. Fold egg mixture into chocolate mixture.

Clean the bowl of the stand mixer, then add egg whites. Whisk on high speed, adding a pinch of salt and remaining sugar, until stiff peaks form; about 4-5 minutes.

Carefully fold a third of the whites into the chocolate mixture, followed by the remaining whites. Pour into the prepared tin. For a 22 cm round cake tin, bake for 45-50 minutes. For a 33 cm x 22 cm tin, bake for 20-23 minutes. For mini muffins, fill each hole three-quarters full and bake for 12-14 minutes.

Allow brownie to cool in the tin before transferring to a serving plate. Don't be disappointed that your brownie leaves the oven puffed up and then deflates on cooling; it is meant to do that.

Chef's note: I like to use Whittaker's Dark Ghana 72% chocolate. You can also add your favourite nuts on top instead of inside the batter, or some guajillo chilli flakes and flaky sea salt.

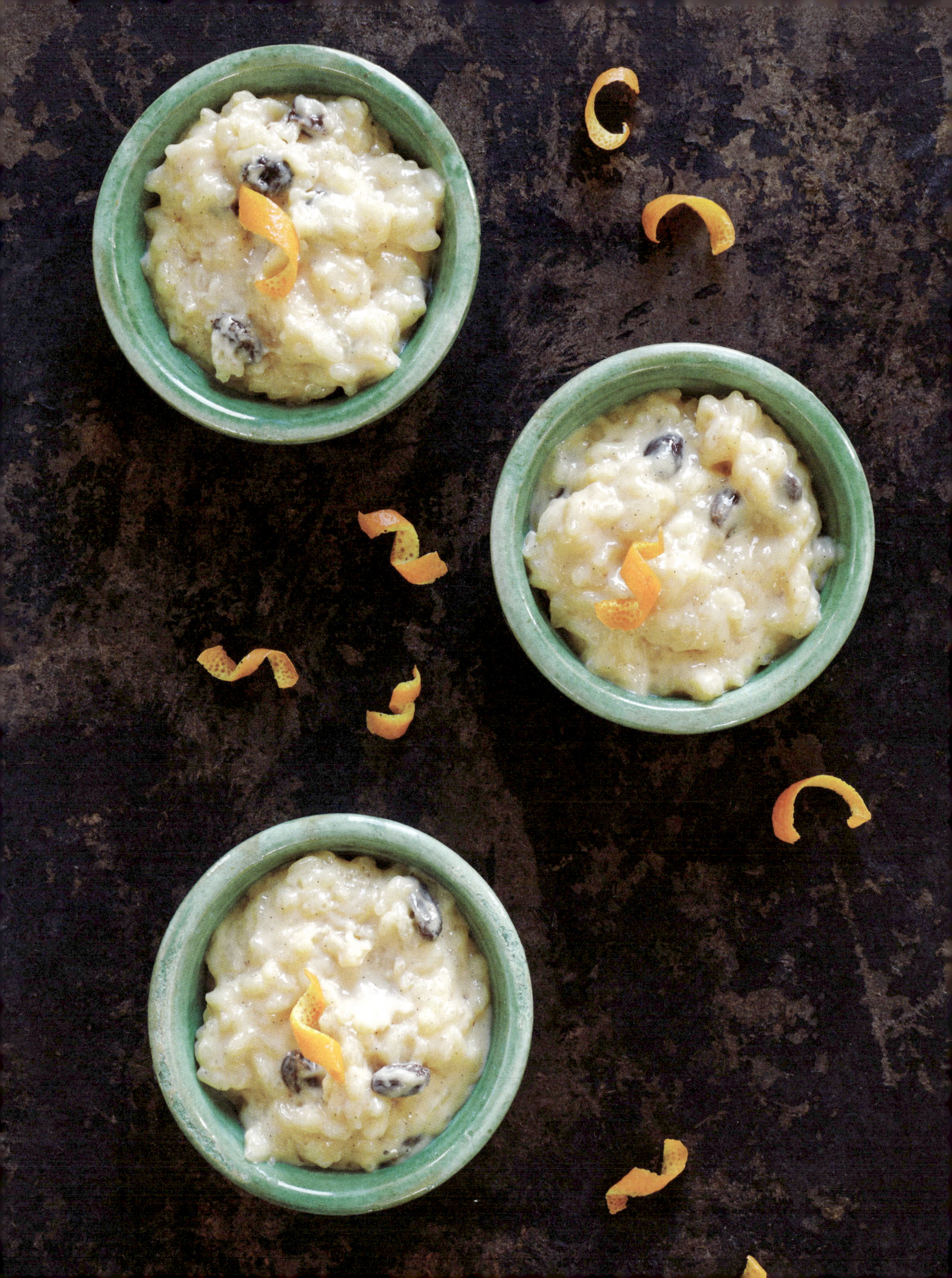

Venezuela

ARROZ CON LECHE

Rice Pudding

GF

2 cups water
2 sticks cinnamon
3 cloves
seeds of ½ vanilla bean
1 cup white long-grain rice
375 ml can evaporated milk
390 g can sweetened
    condensed milk
1 cup whole milk
¾ cup raisins
ground cinnamon, for
    dusting (optional)
orange peel curls, to
    garnish (optional)

This is the quintessential dulce Latino (Latin dessert). Venezuela even has a children's song about rice pudding. Society brainwashes you at an early age, telling you that you must make a good arroz con leche in order to get married! The irony in our family is that my grandmother has always refused to make this dessert; it's always my abuelo, my grandpa, who gets put in charge. Here is my friend Natalia's version. She's passionate about it: the constant stirring leading to the transformation of the rice, and the aromas from the cinnamon, cloves, caramel and vanilla, is indeed pure magic.

Prepare: 10 minutes; cook: 40 minutes
Serves: 4–6

Combine water, cinnamon sticks, cloves and vanilla seeds in a medium-sized non-stick saucepan over a medium-high heat. Bring to the boil, then add rice and lower the heat to medium. Cook rice until tender, about 15 minutes.

Stir in evaporated milk, condensed milk and whole milk. Continue cooking until it comes to the boil, then reduce the heat to low, stirring frequently, for about 20 minutes, until the liquid has evaporated and the mixture is thick. Remove cinnamon sticks and cloves. Stir in raisins, and serve. Dust with ground cinnamon and top with orange peel curls if desired.

Chef's note: Every country has its own version of rice pudding. For this recipe, use the same principle as when making risotto — you must stir and stir, and don't walk away or you'll burn it. Low and slow is the key. You can also make this with any short-grain rice, but note that the starch content will be higher, making it more dense.

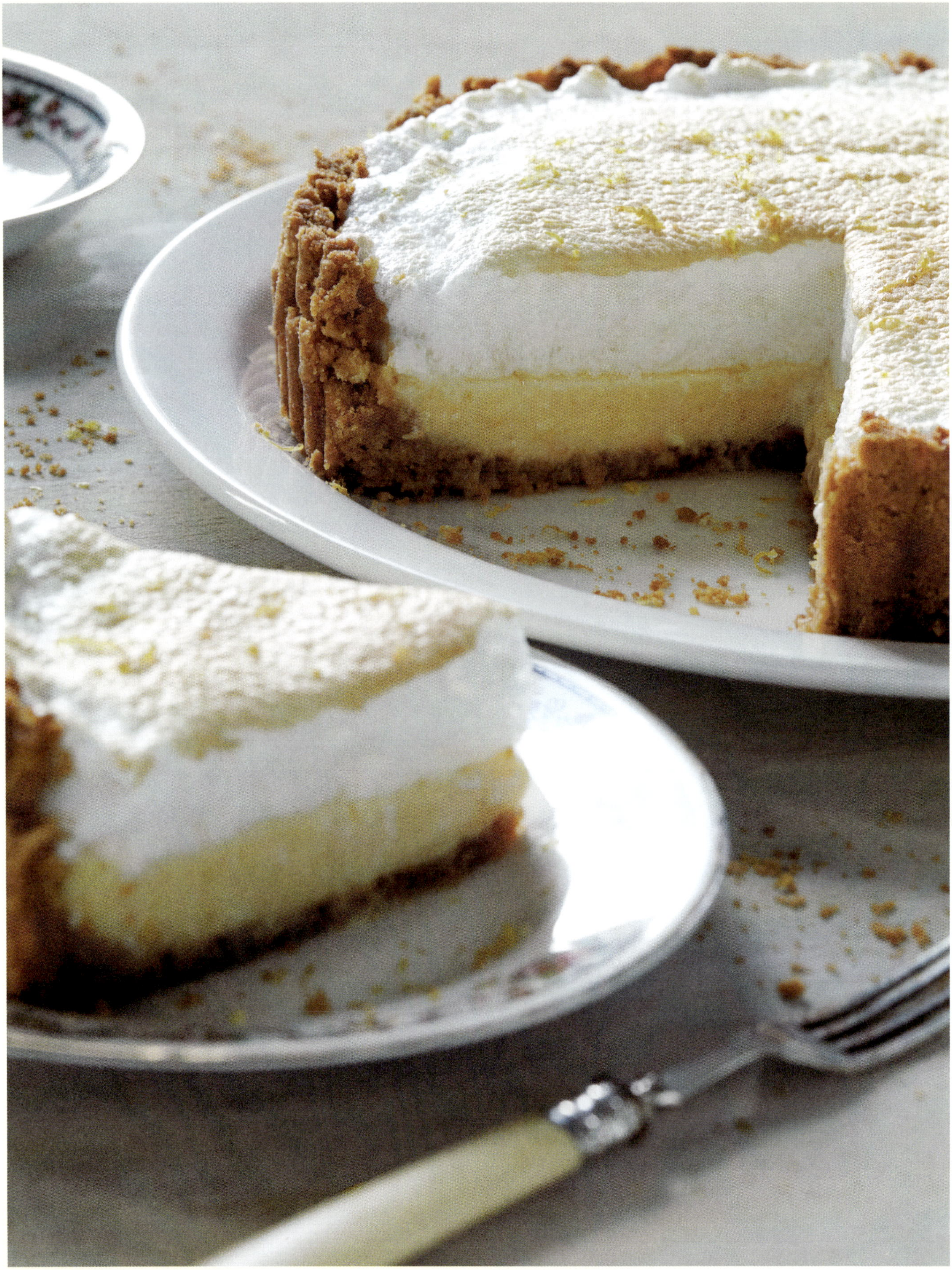

Paraguay

PIE DE LIMÓN CON LECHE CONDENSADA

Condensed-milk Lemon Pie

For the crust
250 g Marie biscuits
3 tbsp soft brown sugar
45 g butter, melted

For the filling
500 ml sweetened condensed milk
2 egg yolks
zest of 2 lemons plus extra to garnish (optional)
juice of 4 lemons

For the meringue
6 egg whites
3 tbsp sugar

This rustic dessert was given to me by Miss Paraguay, Nicole Huber. She is as sweet as the pie, and tells me that this family recipe has been handed down through several generations. What's so special about this pie is love, simplicity and condensed milk. Latinos consider many food products to be traditional to our culture, like the popular biscuit 'galleta María' that is always on hand to drink with our coffee or tea — though it originated in London! This lemon pie is made with 'Maria' cookies (known in New Zealand as Marie biscuits), and is worthy of a true Latina beauty queen.

Prepare: 10 minutes; cook 50 minutes
Serves: 6–8

Preheat oven to 160°C. Butter the bottom and sides of a 20–30 cm tart tin.

Place biscuits in a large sealable bag. Push the air out and seal the bag. Crush biscuits into fine crumbs with a rolling pin. In a medium-sized bowl, combine crumbs with brown sugar and melted butter, stirring until moist clumps form. Press mixture into prepared tin, making sure it goes up the sides. Bake until golden brown and firm to the touch; 10–15 minutes. Turn oven down to 150°C.

Meanwhile, combine condensed milk, egg yolks and lemon zest and juice in a bowl. Pour into pre-baked crust. Return to the oven and bake for 30 minutes. Cool completely before topping with meringue.

Make meringue by beating egg whites until foamy, then gradually adding sugar until stiff peaks form. Spread meringue on top of pie and place under a hot oven grill for 4 minutes (or use a chef's torch), until lightly golden brown on top. Garnish with extra lemon zest, if wished.

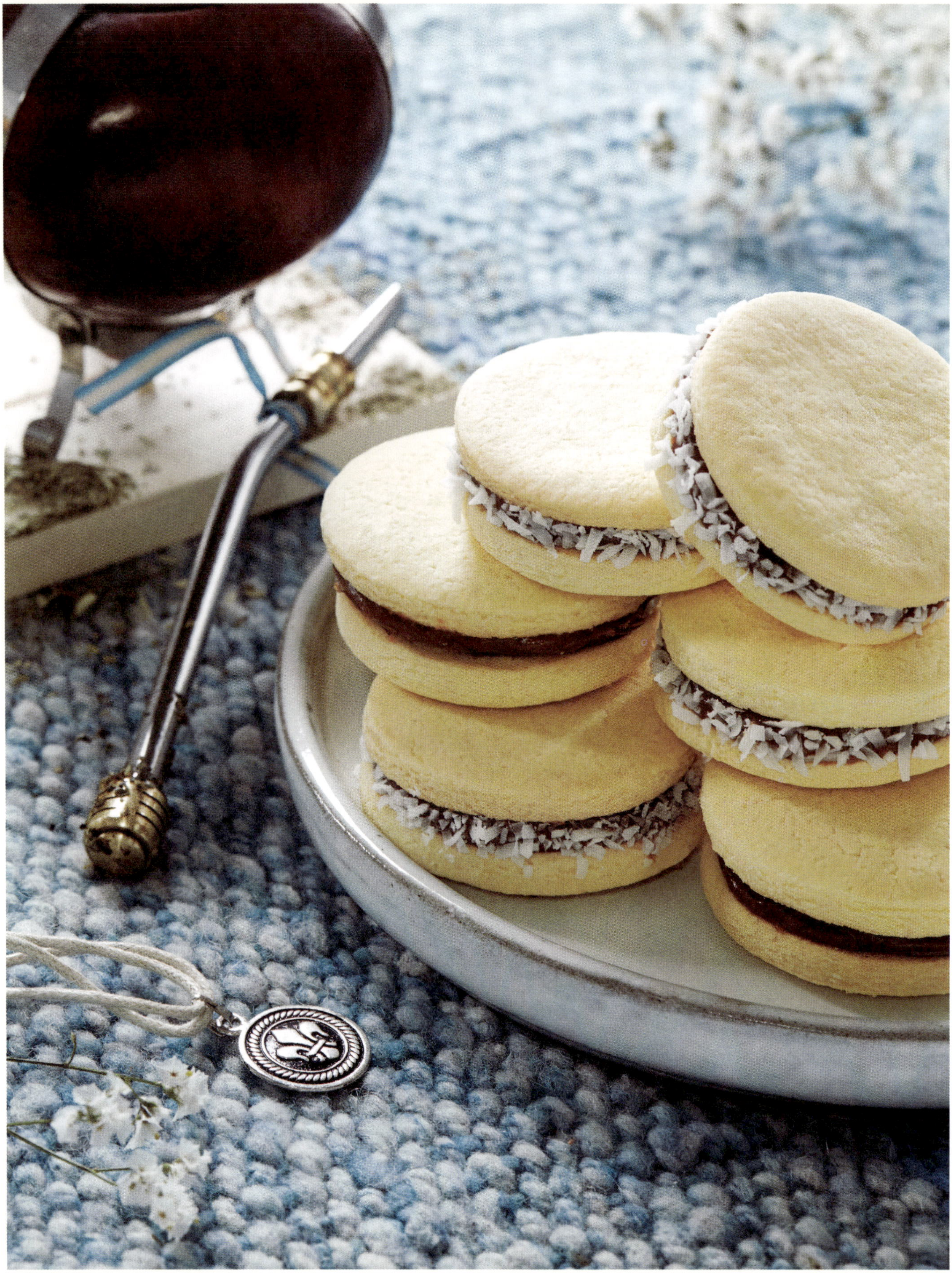

Argentina

ALFAJORES

Shortbread Cookie Sandwich with Dulce de Leche

For the shortbread
1 cup corn starch
¾ cup plain flour, plus extra for dusting
¼ tsp salt
1 tsp baking powder
½ tsp baking soda
115 g unsalted butter, at room temperature
⅓ cup granulated sugar
2 egg yolks
1 tbsp pisco or brandy
½ tsp vanilla extract
¼ cup shredded coconut (optional)

For the dulce de leche (makes 1 cup)
340 g can sweetened condensed milk

At first glance the alfajor is entirely unassuming — one might even pass it up for something with chocolate chips or frosting. This would be a grave mistake. There's good reason that this shortbread cookie defines the café scene in Argentina and Uruguay, with entire establishments devoted to it all across Latin America. It's a melt-in-your-mouth cookie that's sandwiched together with dulce de leche (milk-based caramel). There are many versions of alfajores enjoyed all over Central and South America, but the best ones — in my humble opinion — are those baked with corn starch. Try these alongside mate at your next afternoon tea and be transported to Buenos Aires!

Prepare: 40 minutes; chill: 1 hour; cook: 12 minutes
Makes: 12 sandwiched cookies

In a large bowl, whisk corn starch, plain flour, salt, baking powder and baking soda together until just combined. Set aside.

Place butter and sugar in the bowl of a stand mixer fitted with the paddle attachment. Mix on medium speed, pausing to scrape down the sides of the bowl with a rubber spatula. Mix until light in colour and fluffy; about 3–4 minutes. Add egg yolks, pisco or brandy and vanilla, and mix until incorporated; about 30 seconds.

Turn mixer to low speed and gradually add the flour mixture. Mix until just incorporated; about 30–60 seconds. Remove dough from bowl and form into a smooth round disc. Wrap in plastic wrap and place in the refrigerator for 1 hour until firm.

Meanwhile, make dulce de leche. Pour sweetened condensed milk into the top of a double-boiler pan, and cover. Place over simmering water. Cook over a low heat, stirring occasionally, for 40–50 minutes or until thick and coloured light caramel. Remove from heat and beat with a whisk until smooth. Leave to cool to room temperature.

Preheat oven to 180°C and arrange a rack in the middle. Line two baking trays with non-stick baking paper.

Remove dough from refrigerator, unwrap and place on a lightly floured surface, or between two large pieces of non-stick baking paper. Roll dough out to ½ cm thick, and stamp out 24 rounds using a plain or fluted 58 mm cookie cutter. Re-roll the dough scraps until all of it is used. The dough may crack, but can be easily patched back together.

Place 12 cookies on each baking tray, at least 3 cm apart. Bake until cookies are firm but still pale; 12–14 minutes. Transfer cookies to a wire rack to cool completely before filling.

Flip half the cookies upside down. Spread about 2 teaspoons of dulce de leche on each. Place a second cookie on top and gently press to create a sandwich. If using the shredded coconut, spread on a plate, and roll each cookie sideways through the coconut so that it sticks to the dulce de leche.

Store in an airtight container at room temperature for up to 3 days.

Chef's note: You can use triple sec or extra vanilla extract in place of the pisco or brandy. It's time-consuming making your own dulce de leche as well as the cookies, so you can use store-bought — it's just as good.

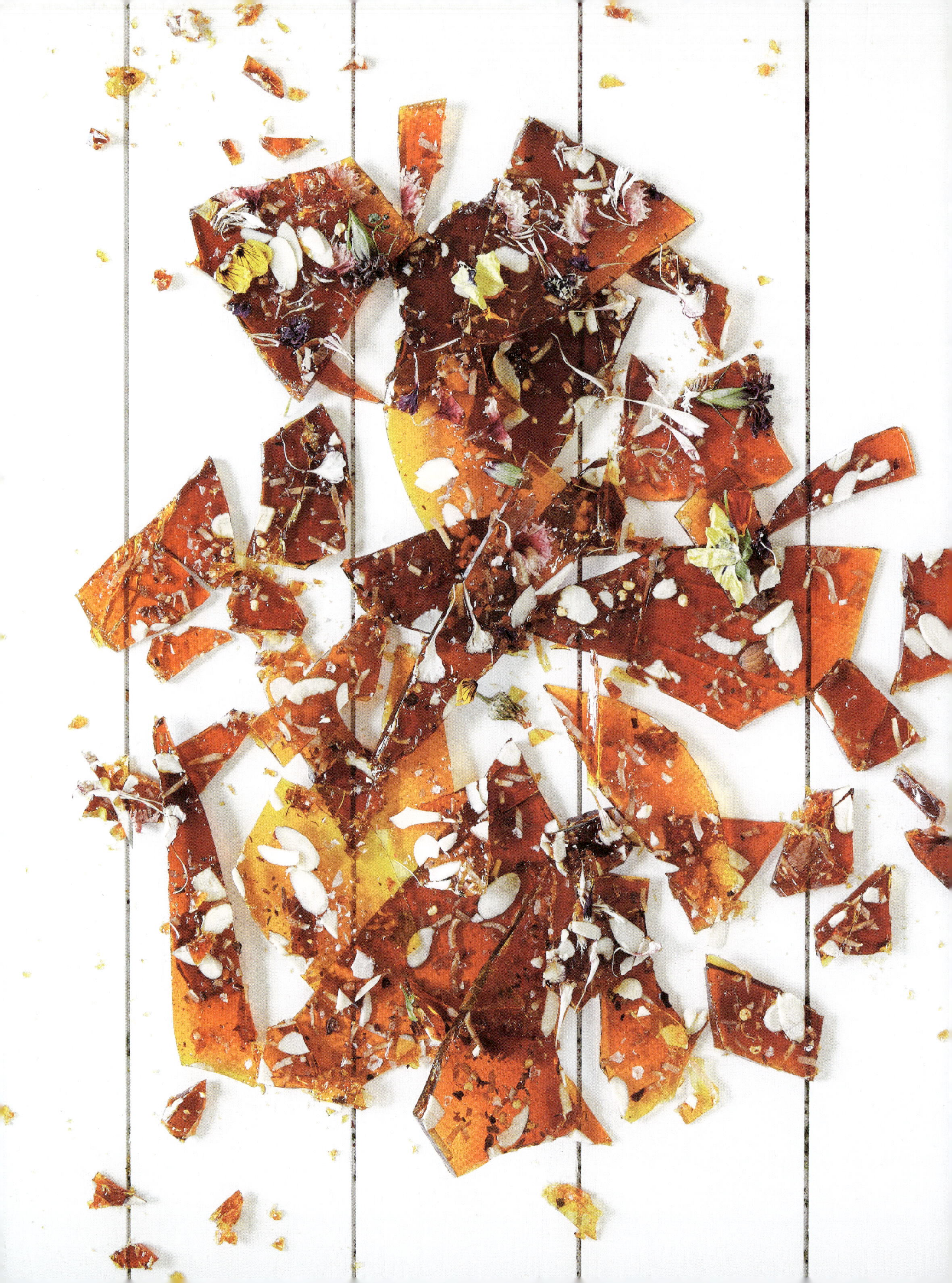

Mexico

CARAMELO

Spiced Brittle

GF

¼ cup water
2 cups sugar
2 tbsp toasted coconut flakes
¼ cup sliced almonds
1 tsp red chilli flakes
1 tbsp flaky sea salt
edible flowers of your choice

This lovely gluten-free snack has been on my mind ever since I tasted something similar in Mexico, called ponteduro (which translates to 'be tough'). Caramelo is a firm caramel filled with textures and tang. The gorgeous edible flowers in this version combine wonderfully well with the sweetness, heat, saltiness and nuttiness, and will have you craving more!

Prepare: 10 minutes; cook: 10 minutes
Makes: one 40 cm x 20 cm slab

Line a baking tray with a silicone mat or non-stick baking paper.

In a small saucepan, combine water and sugar over a medium–high heat. Do not stir, but move the saucepan occassionally until sugar is completely dissolved and caramelised; about 10 minutes. Watch it closely and don't let the caramel burn and turn dark rather than golden (burnt caramel will taste bitter).

Meanwhile, combine coconut, almonds, chilli flakes and sea salt in a small bowl. Set aside.

When caramel is an amber colour, pour it onto the centre of the lined baking tray and let it spread into a thin layer. Quickly sprinkle the coconut and almond mixture over the top of the caramel, then add edible flowers and petals on top. Leave to set and cool to room temperature. Break into smaller pieces with your hands or a mallet. Store in an airtight container at room temperature for up to 3 days.

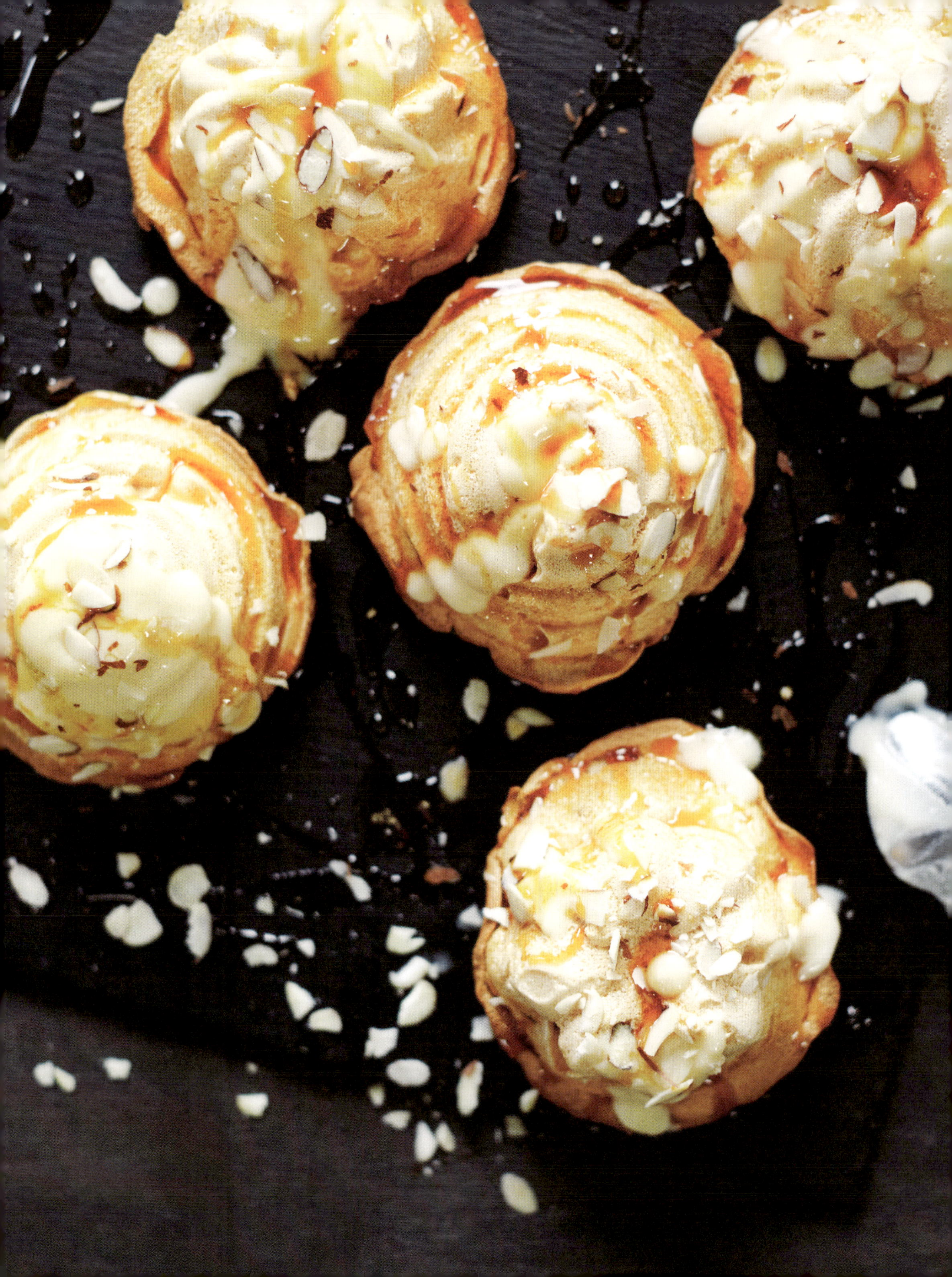

Venezuela

MERENGÓN

Caramel Meringues

GF

For the caramel
¼ cup water
1 cup sugar

For the meringue
8 egg whites (use the yolks for the cream)
1 cup sugar

For the cream
8 tbsp sugar
8 egg yolks
2 tbsp corn starch
2 cups full-fat milk (such as Anchor silver top)
340 g can sweetened condensed milk
1 vanilla bean or 1 tbsp of vanilla extract
1 stick cinnamon
½ tbsp dark rum, brandy or coffee liqueur (optional)

This is Auntie Morela's staple recipe. It's other name, 'isla flotante' means 'floating island'. I had wanted to learn how to make it for years, so when the time came, we made it into a special occasion with family. While this beauty was in the oven puffing up, and the caramel was getting infused into the meringue, we toasted with Champagne as we realised this recipe was being handed over to four generations. It is the perfect marriage between a flan and a pavlova.

Prepare: 30 minutes; cook: up to 1 hour
Serves: 10–12

Preheat the oven to 180°C. Lightly spray (or butter) a large non-stick ring tin or several mini tins.

In a small saucepan, combine water and sugar over a medium-high heat. Do not stir, but move the saucepan occassionally until sugar is completely dissolved and caramelised; about 10 minutes. Watch it closely and don't let the caramel burn and turn dark rather than golden (burnt caramel will taste bitter).

Place egg whites and ¼ cup sugar in the bowl of an electric stand mixer. Whip on medium-high for about 1 minute; then, still whipping, add remaining sugar little by little and whip until firm peaks form.

Once egg whites reach firm peaks, gently fold in caramel. Pour into prepared tin and use a spatula to press meringue down a bit to release any large air pockets. Place tin in a large baking dish and pour hot water into the dish to come two-thirds of the way up the tin. Bake until meringues are double in size and just firm to the touch on top, but with some spring-back. Baking time will vary depending on tin size, 5-7 minutes for small tins and up to 1 hour for a large tin. Remove from oven and cool completely on wire rack before removing from the tin.

While baking, prepare the cream. In a medium-sized heatproof bowl, whisk sugar and egg yolks together. Whisk in corn starch until a smooth paste forms.

In a saucepan, bring milk, condensed milk and vanilla bean (but not extract) to a boil, until it just starts to foam up. Remove milk from heat and add a few tablespoons to egg mixture, whisking constantly to prevent curdling, then continue to whisk while adding remaining milk. If you get a few pieces of curdled egg in the mixture, pour through a strainer. Remove vanilla bean, scrape out seeds, and add seeds to egg mixture and discard bean. Pour egg mixture back into saucepan and cook over medium heat until boiling. Add cinnamon and whisk constantly for about 1 minute until it becomes thick. Remove from heat and immediately whisk in liqueur (if using). Stir in vanilla extract, if using.

Pour cream into a clean bowl, remove cinnamon stick, and immediately cover the surface with plastic wrap to prevent a crust from forming. Cool to room temperature, then drizzle over cooled merengon.

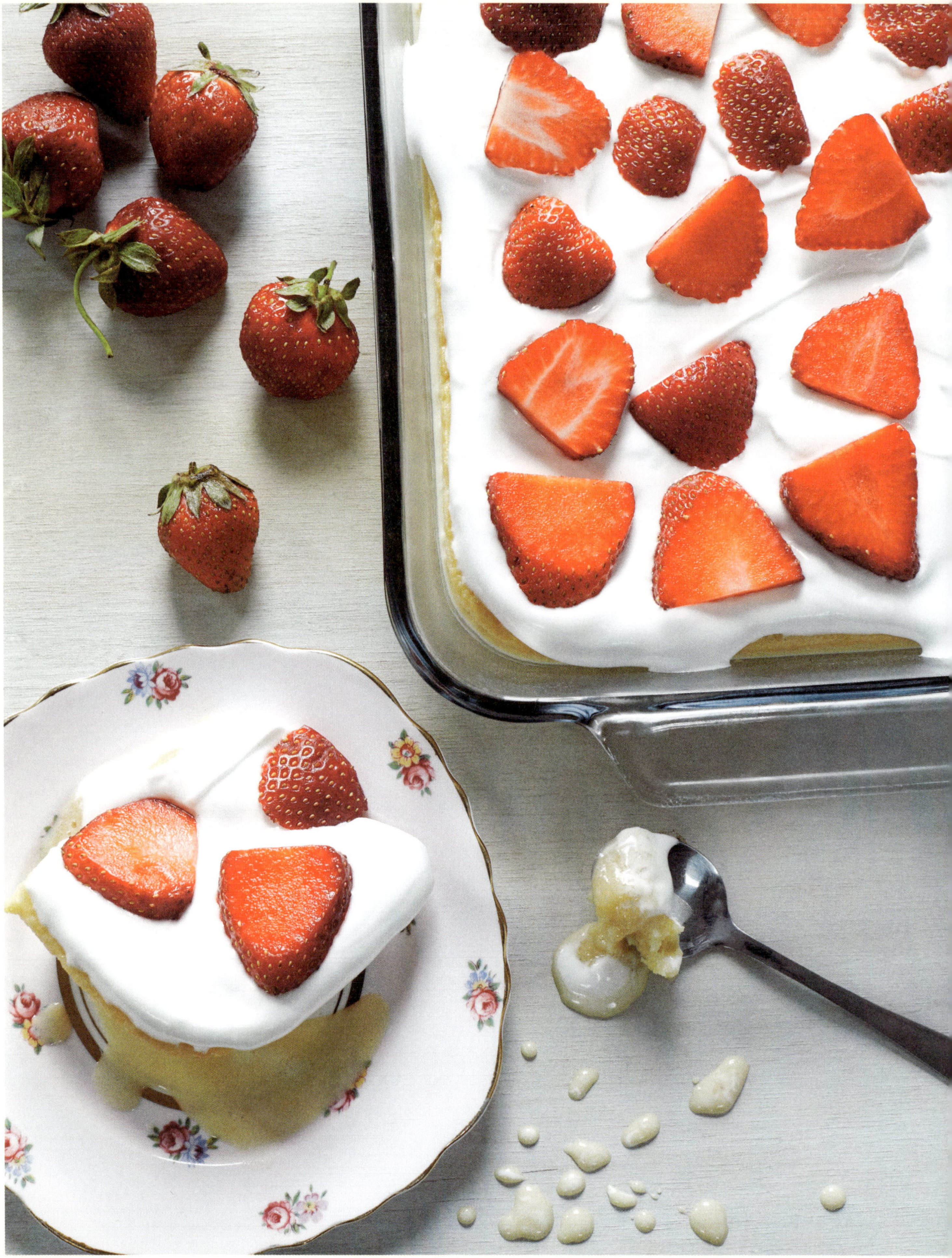

Venezuela, Costa Rica, Nicaragua, Mexico, Ecuador & Cuba

TRES LECHES

Three-milk Cake

For the cake
1 cup plain flour
1 tsp baking powder
4 eggs, separated
1 cup sugar
4 tbsp ice-cold water

For the milk mixture
375 ml can evaporated milk
390 g can condensed milk
500 ml cream

For the swiss meringue
2 egg whites
2/3 cup granulated sugar

Garnish (optional)
ground cinnamon
strawberries

This dessert is so popular that many countries claim it as their own. It's a light cake drenched in a sweet three-milk mixture. The cake absorbs this liquid, and you end up with a moist, sweet cake that's light at the same time. It's one of those classic desserts that never goes out of style. Funnily enough, it originally gained its popularity because of a marketing campaign. Nestlé, who sold sweetened condensed milk, wanted to increase their sales so started putting a tres leches recipe on the back of their cans — and the tres leches craze began.

Prepare: 20 minutes; cook: 25 minutes; chill: 1 hour
Serves: 10

Preheat oven to 160°C. Butter a 28 cm x 18 cm rectangular baking tin.
  Sift flour and baking powder together into a mixing bowl and set aside.
  In a stand mixer at high speed, beat egg whites until they form stiff peaks. While continuing to whisk, add egg yolks one at a time and then slowly pour the sugar in. Turn mixer speed to low and add sifted flour. Lastly, add ice-cold water.
  Pour cake batter into tin and bake for 25 minutes, or until a toothpick comes out clean when inserted. The cake should be a pale colour.
  While cake is cooking, mix both milks with cream in a bowl until thoroughly combined. When cake comes out of the oven, poke holes in cake with a skewer or fork until it's covered with holes. Slowly pour milk mixture over cake while it's still warm, so that it absorbs the mixture. Cool and refrigerate for at least 1 hour before frosting with Swiss meringue.
  To make meringue, combine egg whites with sugar in a double boiler or a heatproof bowl set over a pan of simmering water, until the mixture reaches 45°C or you can see that the sugar is dissolved and the mixture feels warm but not hot when touched. Remove from the heat and immediately start beating; speed up gradually until the bowl is cool and stiff peaks form. Transfer to a piping bag with a spatula.
  Decorate cooled cake with Swiss meringue. If desired, garnish with sprinkled ground cinnamon and strawberries, or gently brown some peaks of meringue with a chef's torch.
  Chef's note: In some countries people hide fruit in between the cake and the meringue; that way you get a nice surprise when you eat it. You can use slices of any favourite fruit, either fresh or canned.

Brazil

BRIGADEIRO

Chocolate Fudge Balls

GF

390 g can sweetened condensed milk
3 tbsp cocoa powder
45 g unsalted butter, plus more for rolling the bonbons
chocolate sprinkles, or other colour of choice
freeze-dried berries, crumbled, to garnish (optional)

In Latin America many French techniques are used in the kitchen — but we must make them our own with unique twists. A brigadeiro is a clear example of this. A simple Brazilian chocolate bonbon made with melt-in-your-mouth condensed milk, it's very popular served as a dessert at birthday parties. The first time I had a brigadeiro, I almost ate the entire tray! The taste of this rich, luscious bonbon will make you eat one after another without realising it — it's dangerous. You have been warned.

Prepare: 35 minutes; cook: 10 minutes; chill: 1 hour
Makes: 30–35 fudge balls

In a medium-sized bowl, combine condensed milk and cocoa powder, stirring with a fork or whisk until cocoa fully dissolves. Meanwhile, melt butter in a small saucepan over a medium-low heat. Add milk and cocoa mixture to the butter, and stir constantly with a wooden spoon or spatula for about 10 minutes, until mixture is very thick — almost fudge-like. Be careful to not let the chocolate crystallise or burn. Pass the chocolate mixture through a fine sieve, onto a plate or baking dish, and cool in the refrigerator for 30 minutes.

Lightly butter your hands. Scoop up rounded teaspoons of chocolate mixture and roll each into a ball. Roll each ball in the sprinkles to cover completely. Place in mini paper cases and return to the refrigerator to cool for another 30 minutes.

Serve at room temperature, sprinkled with freeze-dried berries (if using). They may be stored in the refrigerator in an airtight container for up to 5 days.

Chef's note: This is the traditional brigadeiro recipe, so try this one first. Next time you make it, feel free to add any spices you like to eat with your chocolate, like chilli, cinnamon, allspice . . . anything.

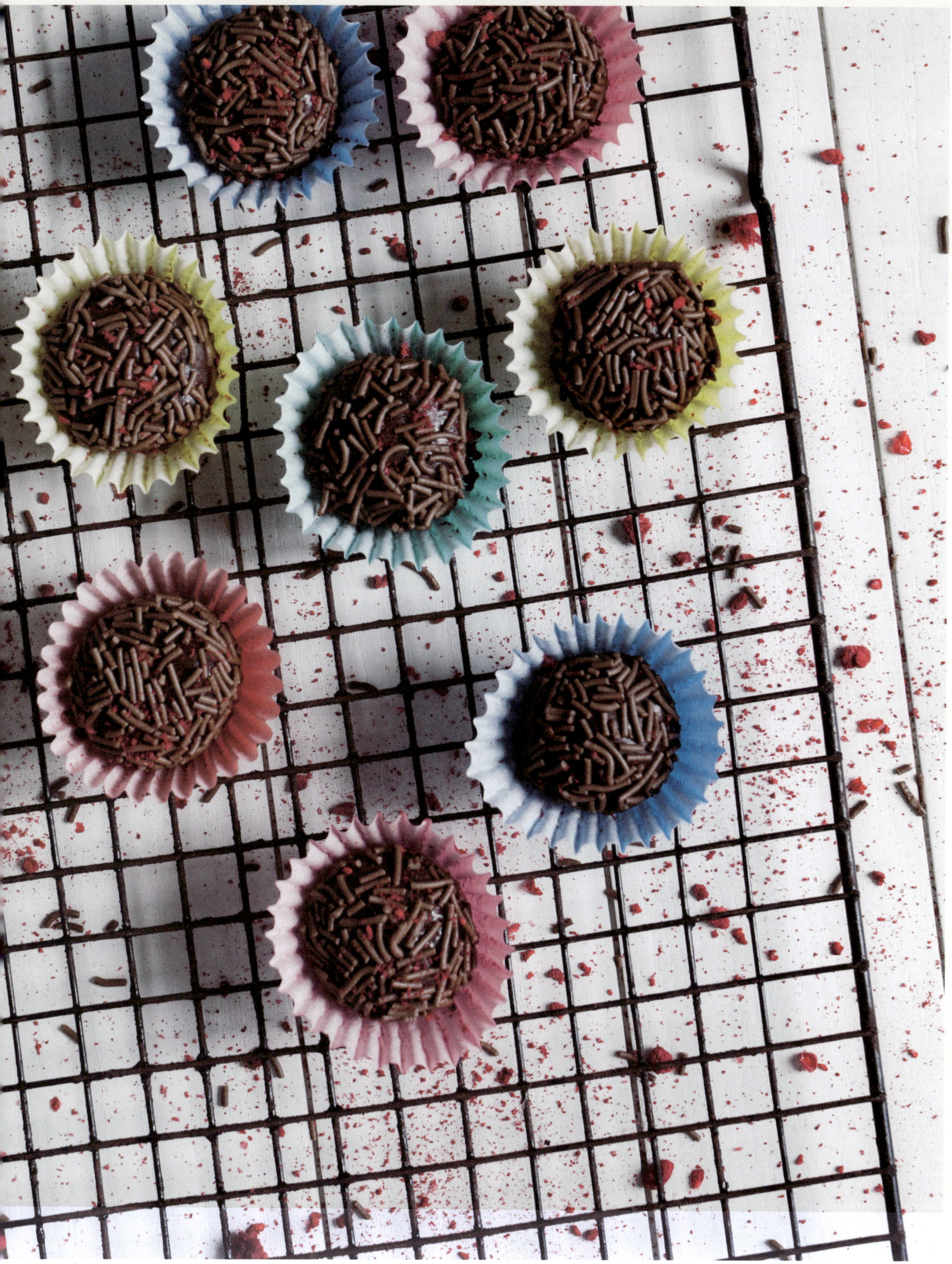

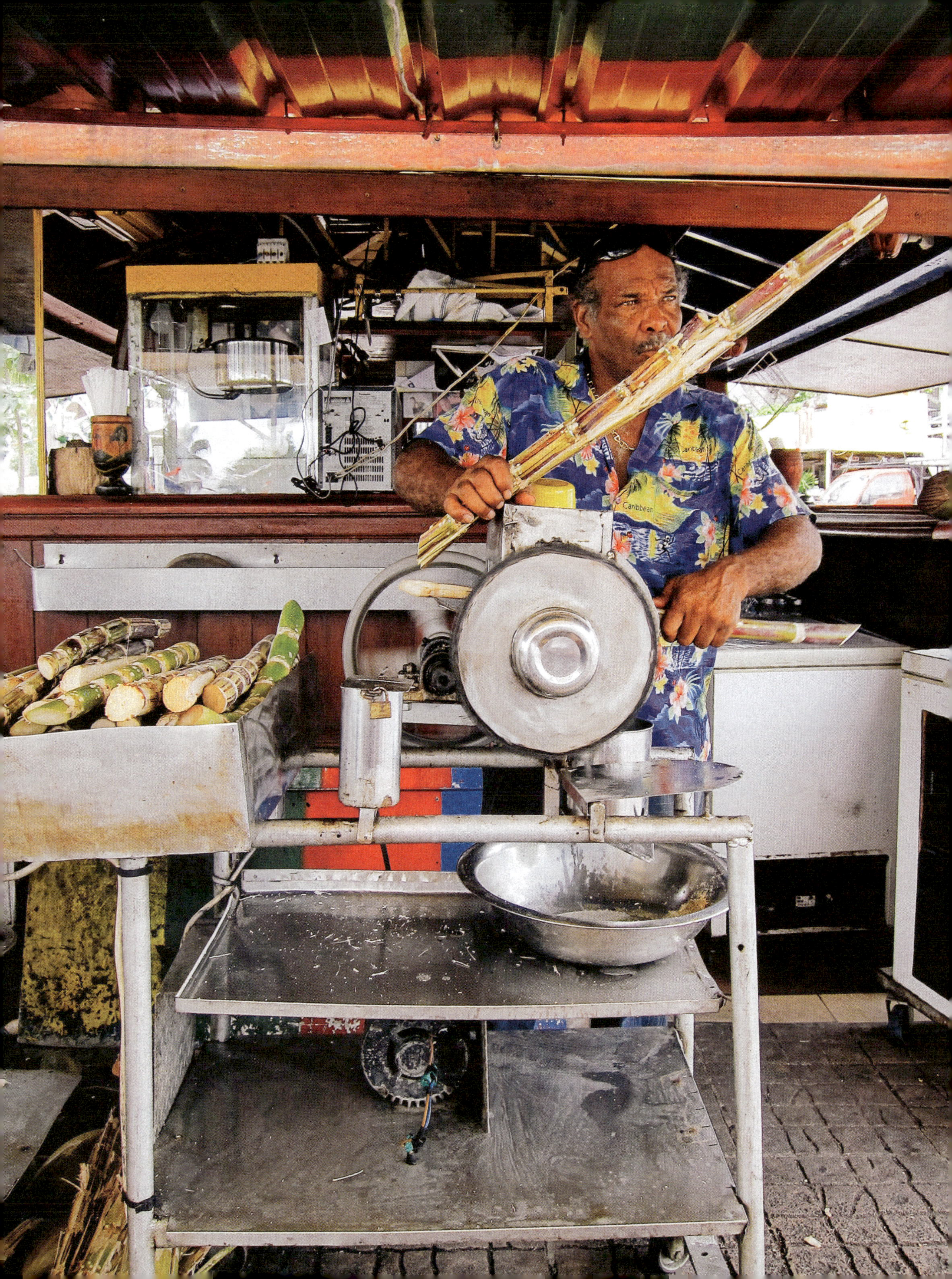

BEBIDAS

DRINKS

Impresiones
Fotocopias
Internet
Certificado Judicial
(D.A.S)
Scanner
Fax
MICRONET

PAPELÓN CON LIMÓN
Sugar Cane Lemonade

AGUA FRESCA DE LIMÓN
Chia and Mint Lemonade

JARABE DE GOMA
Simple Syrup

PISCO SOUR

PIÑA COLADA

MARGARITA

MARGARITA CON FLOR DE JAMAICA
Hibiscus Margarita

SANGRITA
Little Blood

MICHELADAS

MOJITO

CAIPIRINHA

RON CON TORONJA
Zacapa Old Fashioned Cocktail

SANGRÍA

TINTO CAMPESINO
Black Coffee

CAFESITO CON ESPUMITA
Cuban Coffee

Venezuela

PAPELÓN CON LIMÓN

Sugar Cane Lemonade

200 g shaved panela (unrefined
　　cane sugar), or more to taste
1 litre water
juice of 4 limes or lemons
4 cups ice (crushed or cubes)

This is the Venezuelan lemonade, drunk during the hottest hours of the day. This refreshing drink is often served with arepas (see page 119) or cachapas (see page 122). This lemonade is a favourite summer-thirst-quenching tradition in my family.

Prepare: 8 minutes
Serves: 4–6

In a small saucepan over a medium-low heat, melt the panela with 2 tablespoons of water. When melted, add the litre of water, lime or lemon juice and 2 cups of ice. Stir well until fully incorporated, then place in a jug in the refrigerator to chill. Serve in tall glasses with the remaining ice.

Mexico

AGUA FRESCA DE LIMÓN

Chia & Mint Lemonade

2 lemons, juiced
1 lemon, cut into thin rounds
1½ litres water
simple syrup (see page 248),
　　to taste
1 tsp chia seeds
1 whole sprig mint

Agua fresca literally means 'fresh water'. This is a popular Mexican drink made from different kinds of fresh fruit and is often served at the markets in 'vitroleros', huge see-through glass barrels filled with different agua fresca flavours. A jug-full in the centre of your barbecue or taco party will add life to the table. It's refreshing and can be enjoyed by the whole family.

Prepare: 5 minutes
Serves: 4

Place lemon juice, lemon rounds and water in a jug. Mix in simple syrup, to taste. Top with chia seeds and mint sprig.
　　Chef's note: You can use lime in this instead of lemon if you prefer.

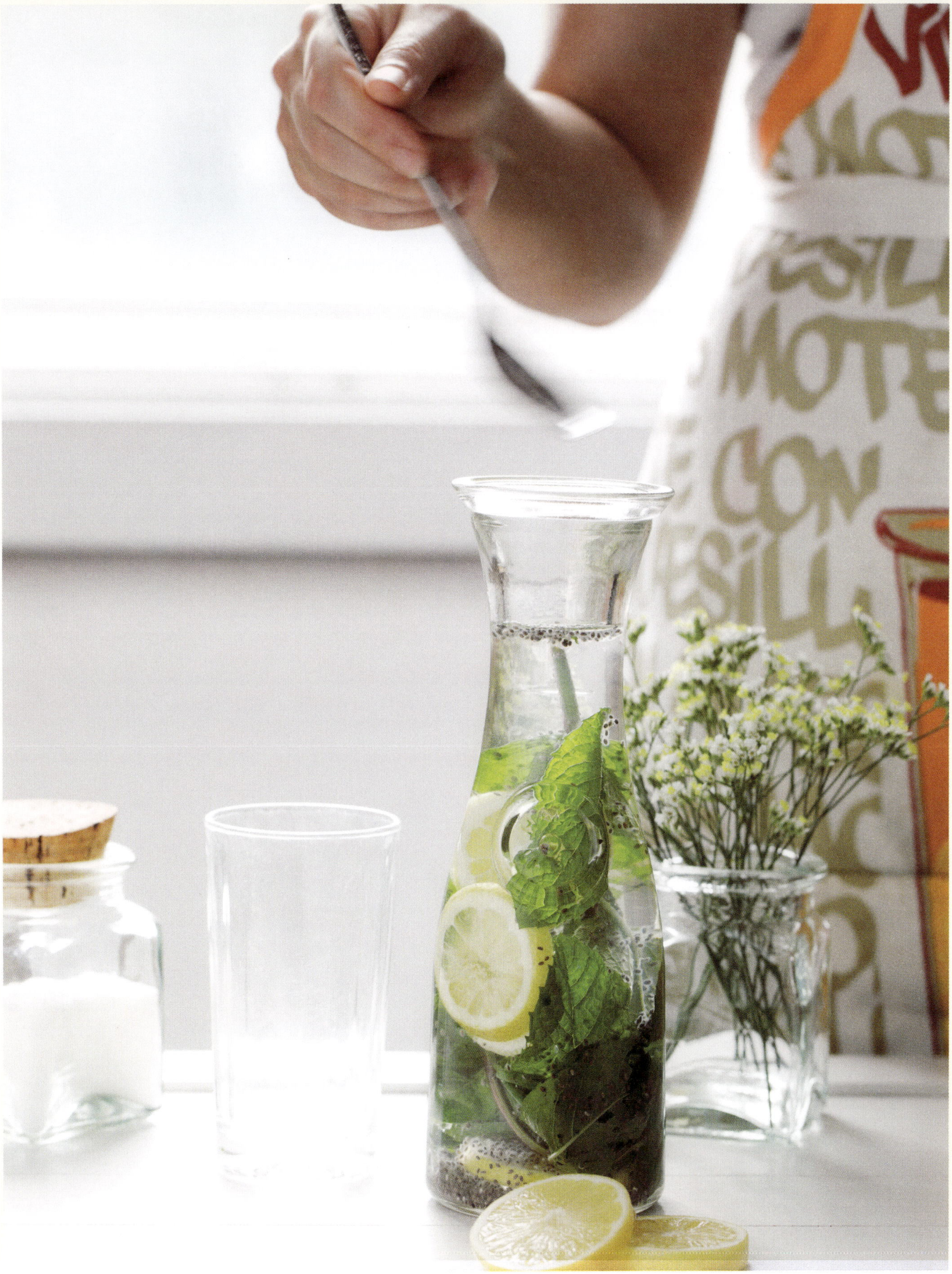

All countries

JARABE DE GOMA

Simple Syrup

2 cups sugar
2 cups water

I like to make this simple syrup in large batches and keep it in the fridge for making cocktails or lemonades. It can easily be doubled for a larger batch.

Prepare: 5 minutes
Makes: 2 cups

Put sugar in a saucepan with water and bring to the boil. Reduce the heat to a simmer and stir for a minute or two until sugar dissolves. Take off the heat and cool to room temperature. Store in a very clean jar; any solid particles may cause crystals to form. Refrigerate, tightly covered, for up to a month.

Peru

PISCO SOUR

juice of 1 lime
2 egg whites
3 tbsp simple syrup (see opposite), or more to taste
½ cup crushed ice
½ cup Peruvian pisco
few drops Angostura bitters

The pisco sour is made with a muscat-grape brandy, similar to grappa. Half the fun of drinking piscos is the heated debate about their origin; both Chile and Peru claim this exotic drink as their national cocktail. Both countries hold a national Pisco Sour Day and celebrate it as their specialty drink, although in fact the dispute has been solved and it is from Peru. While pisco is now very popular and available at most trendy bars, it might be hard to find to make this at home so you can use grappa instead, or white rum or silver tequila.

Prepare: 5 minutes
Serves: 2

In a blender, combine all the ingredients except the Angostura bitters and blend at high speed until frothy. Pour into a glass, add a few drops of Angostura bitters and serve.

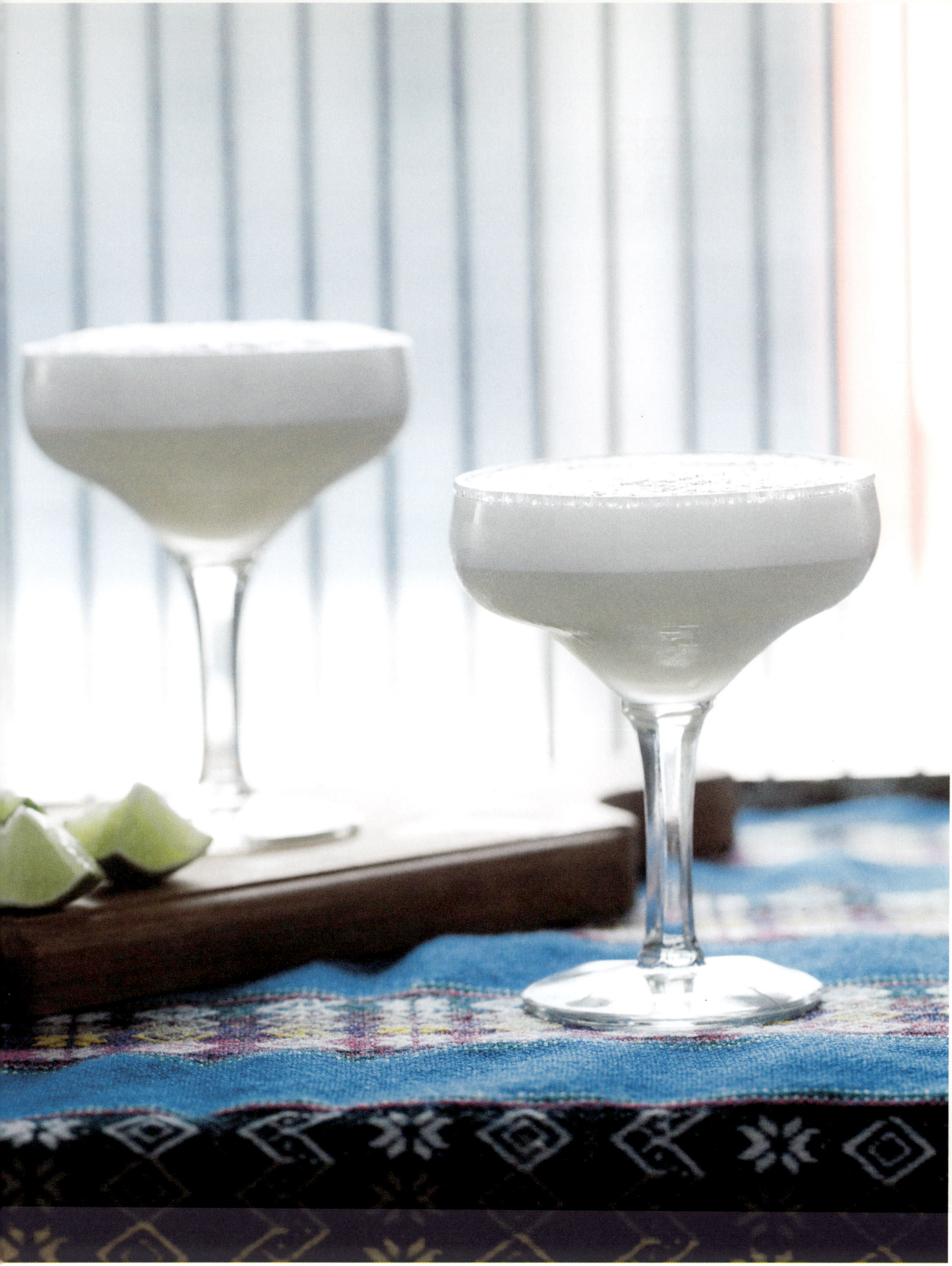

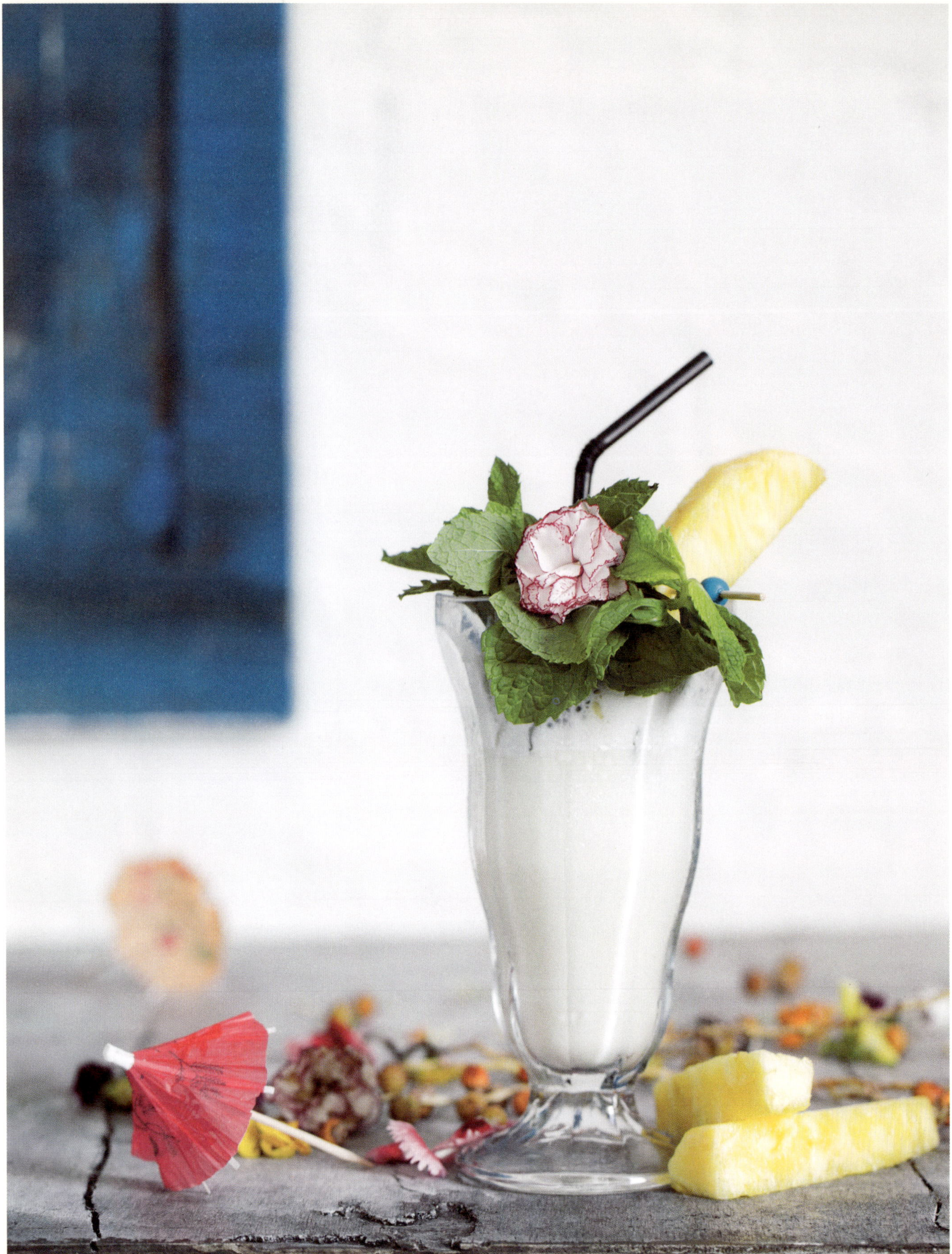

Puerto Rico

PIÑA COLADA

1 cup rum
1 ripe fresh pineapple,
    ½ juiced (about 2 cups)
    and the rest chopped
    lengthwise for garnish
1 tsp lemon juice
1 cup sweetened condensed milk
1 cup coconut cream
simple syrup (see page 248),
    to taste
2 cups ice (crushed or cubes)
mint leaves and edible
    flowers to garnish

Most people don't know that this 'elixir of the gods' comes from the beautiful Caribbean island of Puerto Rico. Piña colada literally means 'strained pineapple', a reference to the freshly pressed and strained pineapple juice used in the drink's preparation. The combination of the sweetness from the pineapple, the sugar-cane taste from the rum and the distinctive creaminess and flavour of the coconut is a match made in heaven. This is a speedy recipe, perfect for a summer party.

Prepare: 10 minutes
Serves: 4–6

Put half the ingredients in a blender and blend until smooth. Repeat with the other half. Combine and serve, garnished with chopped pineapple, mint leaves and edible flowers.

    Chef's note: You can use just simple syrup in place of the sweetened condensed milk; it will just be less creamy.

Mexico

MARGARITA

1 cup tequila blanco
    (white tequila)
½ cup fresh lime juice
½ cup triple sec or cointreau
¼ cup simple syrup
    (see page 248) or
    agave nectar
2 cups ice (crushed or cubes)

Garnish
5 lime wedges
flaky mild salt or
    Himalayan salt
    (optional)

Margaritas are the ultimate gift that Mexicans have given the world. This light, refreshing drink is known worldwide. Part of the fun is in creating your own version with the fruit you have on hand. Here, I've given you a traditional margarita recipe and alongside there's a variation to get you going on the endless possibilities you can have with this drink.

Prepare: 10 minutes
Serves: 4

Pour drink ingredients into a blender and blend until slushy.
    If desired, run 1 lime wedge gently over the rim of each chilled margarita glass to wet it, then dip in salt.
    Pour drink into glasses and garnish with remaining lime wedges.
    Chef's note: Feel free to mix the salt with any freeze-dried fruit powder of your choice. It adds flavour, colour and beauty to each drink.

Mexico

MARGARITA CON FLOR DE JAMAICA

Hibiscus Margarita

Hibiscus water
1 litre water
¼ cup dried hibiscus flowers,
    or 3 hibiscus tea bags

For the rims
1 tbsp chilli salt (see page 193)
2 tsp freeze-dried
    raspberry powder
1 lime wedge

Margaritas
50 ml lime juice
250 ml tequila
100 ml triple sec
250 ml hibiscus water
    (see alongside)
150 ml simple syrup
    (see page 248)
750 ml ice (crushed or cubes)

Hibiscus drinks, with or without alcohol, begin with a beautiful plum-red tea made from dried hibiscus blossoms. Hibiscus brews are fruity with an acidic edge, indicating ample vitamin C on board. That tart flavour says, for my taste buds at least, 'sugar needed'. So sweeten things up just a bit, with sugar, agave nectar or honey.

Prepare: 15 minutes
Serves: 4

Bring water to a soft boil in a medium-sized saucepan. Turn heat off and add dried hibiscus flowers or teabags. Let them infuse for about 10 minutes. Strain into a container. Cool in the refrigerator.
    Combine chilli salt and raspberry powder in a small bowl. Spread onto a small plate. Coat rims of chilled glasses with the juice from the lime wedge. Dip rims into chilli salt/raspberry mixture.
    Combine margarita ingredients in a blender and pulse until smooth, or simply stir together with a wooden spoon. Pour into prepared glasses and serve immediately.
    Chef's note: This recipe makes more hibiscus water than is needed. You can use the extra to make a bigger batch for you and your friends (not a bad option), or keep it in the refrigerator for up to a week, or add lemon and sugar to make a hibiscus lemonade.

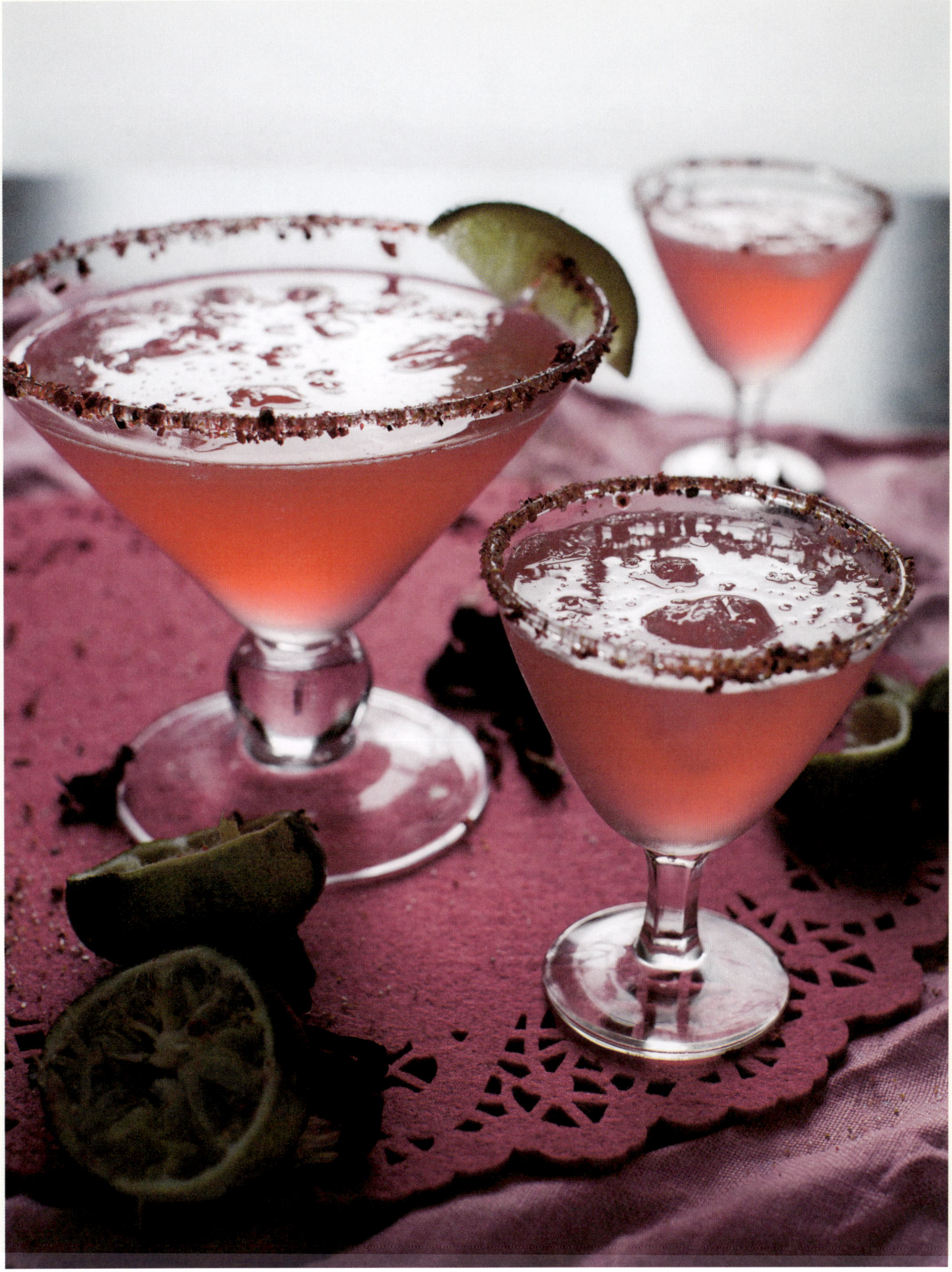

Mexico

SANGRITA

Little Blood

½ cup freshly squeezed orange juice
1 cup tomato juice, chilled
juice of ½ lime
⅓ tsp microplane-grated onion
⅓ tsp Worcestershire sauce
¼ tsp Tabasco sauce
pinch of chilli salt (see page 193)
sprinkle of ground pepper

To serve
a shot of your favorite tequila blanco or sotol

Much like Champagne, a true tequila comes only from the Tequila region. So, when I travelled to Mexico I got introduced to good tequila and other agave spirits rather than the cheap stuff I'd had in college. There are all kinds of blancos, reposados and añejos, and depending on the region you find mezcals and sotol, which comes from Chihuahua. I was also introduced to a sangrita ('little blood') shot alongside a good blanco, but I personally like to sip this alongside my favourite sotol. That's when my love affair with these spirits started. They are much like a good cognac or whisky, with many layers of complexity. The bad rap that they commonly get is slowly changing. Born in Jalisco, the same state as tequila, sangrita is used as a chaser, sipped alternately with the spirit. This is just one version of the sangrita.

Prepare: 5 minutes
Makes: 6 shooters

Combine sangrita ingredients in a cocktail shaker or mixing bowl. Shake without ice, and chill in the refrigerator until ready to serve. Shake well before serving.

When ready to serve, fill one shot glass with tequila or sotol and one shot glass with sangrita. Sip them alternately.

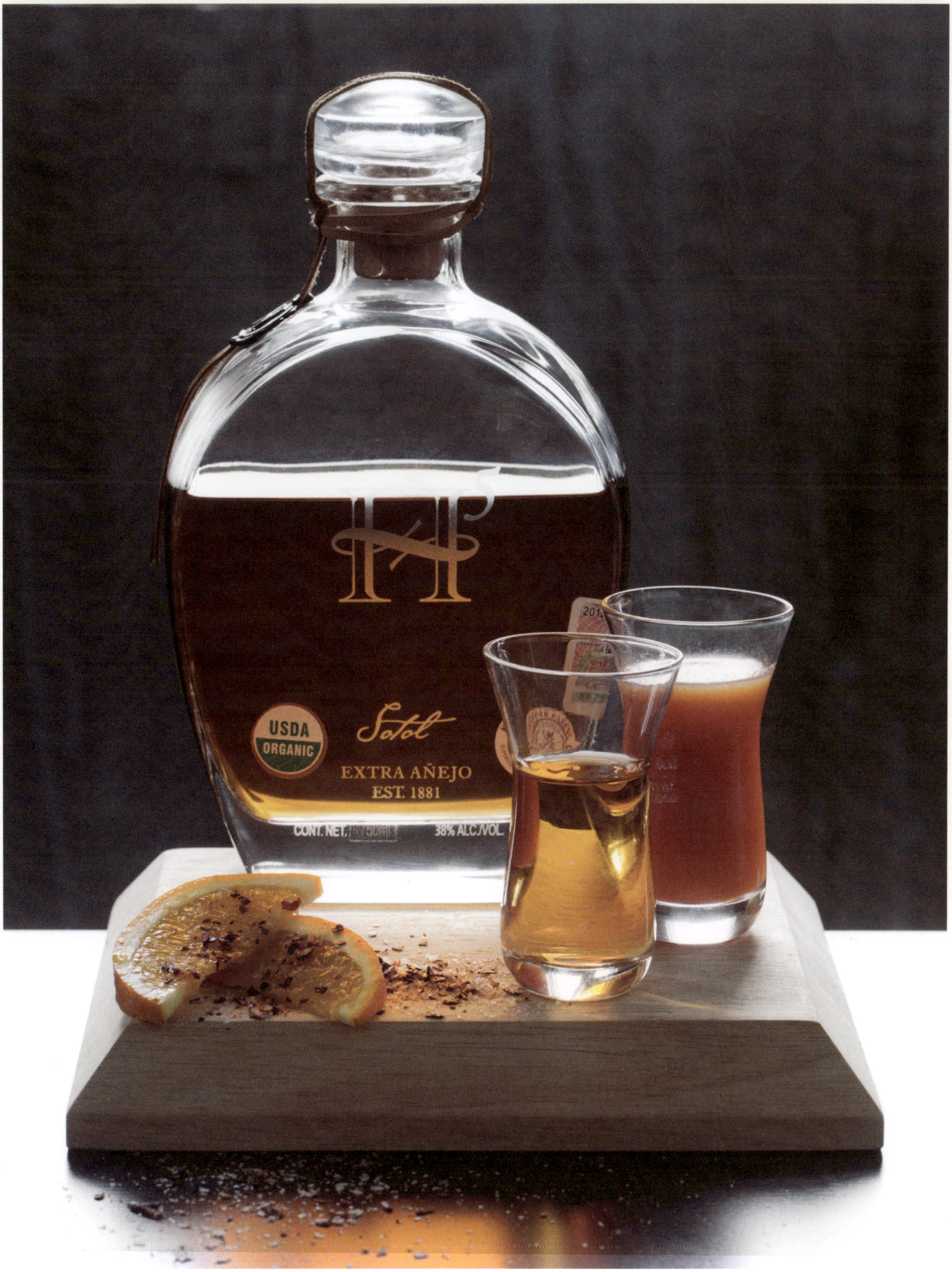

USDA
ORGANIC
Sotol
EXTRA AÑEJO
EST. 1881
CONT. NET.
38% ALC/VOL.

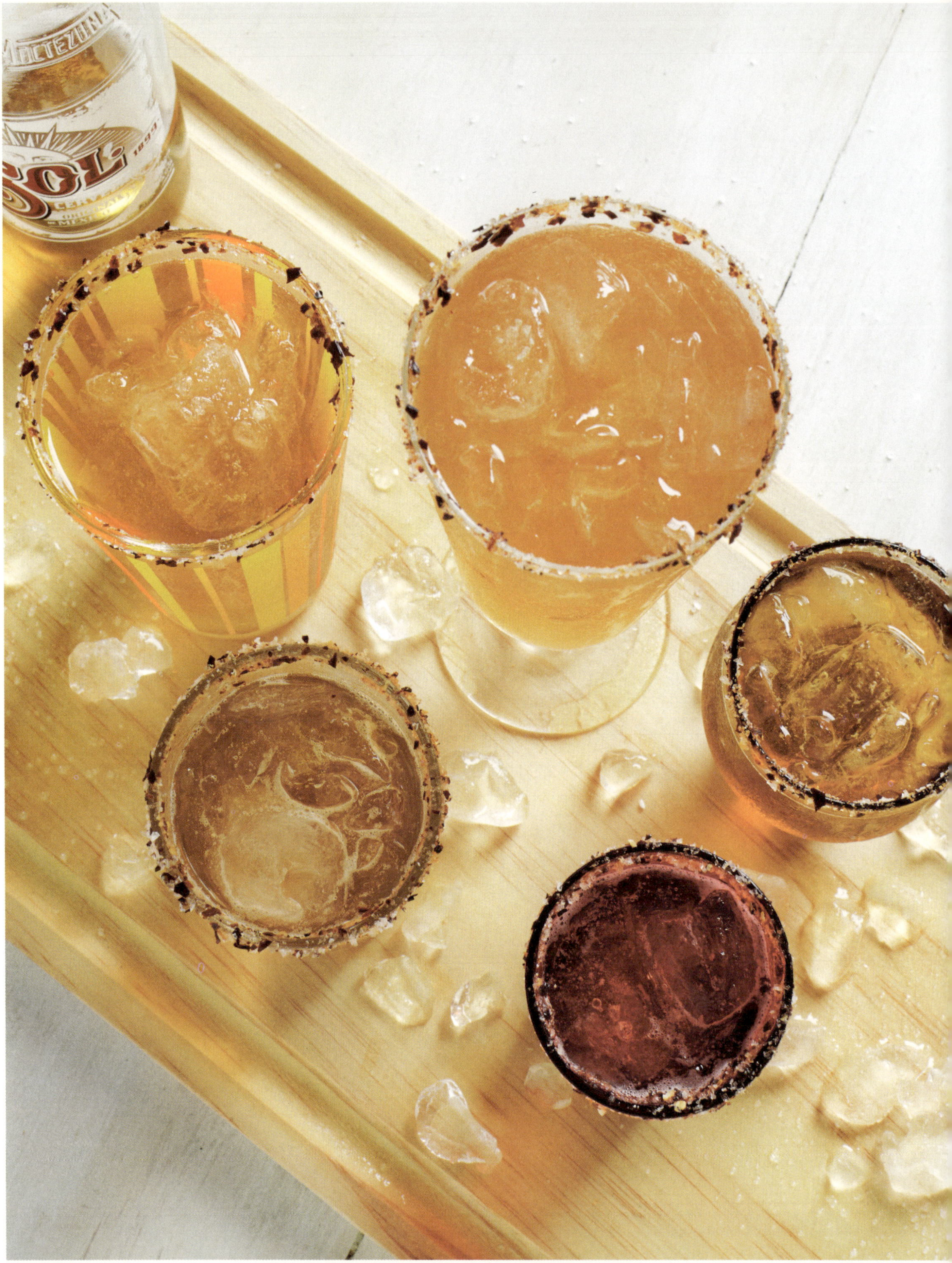
SOL

Mexico

MICHELADAS

juice of ½ lime
¼ tsp Tabasco sauce (or to taste)
¼ tsp Worcestershire
    sauce (or to taste)
pinch of salt
1 cup crushed ice
1 bottle Sol beer
    (a Mexican beer)

For the rims
lime or lemon wedge
chilli salt (see page 193)

'Chela' is slang for beer in Mexico. When you ask for a chela, you're asking for a cold beer. As with anything from Mexico, they love infusing everything with zest and spice. In a michelada, the beer is paired with lime, chilli and Worcestershire sauce and served in a chilled, salt-and-chilli-rimmed glass. Mexicans swear that this cures all hangovers and there are numerous variations of this beverage — some include tomato juice or Clamato (a tomato drink flavoured with spices and clam broth), making it taste like a beer Bloody Mary.

Prepare: 5 minutes
Serves: 1

Get a tall glass and wet the outside rim with the lime or lemon wedge. Fill a saucer or bowl with the chilli salt. Dab the rim into the salt while slowly turning the glass so that only the outer edge is covered.

Add the lime juice to the glass, then add Tabasco, Worcestershire sauce and salt. Fill glass with ice and add Sol beer. Stir and drink immediately.

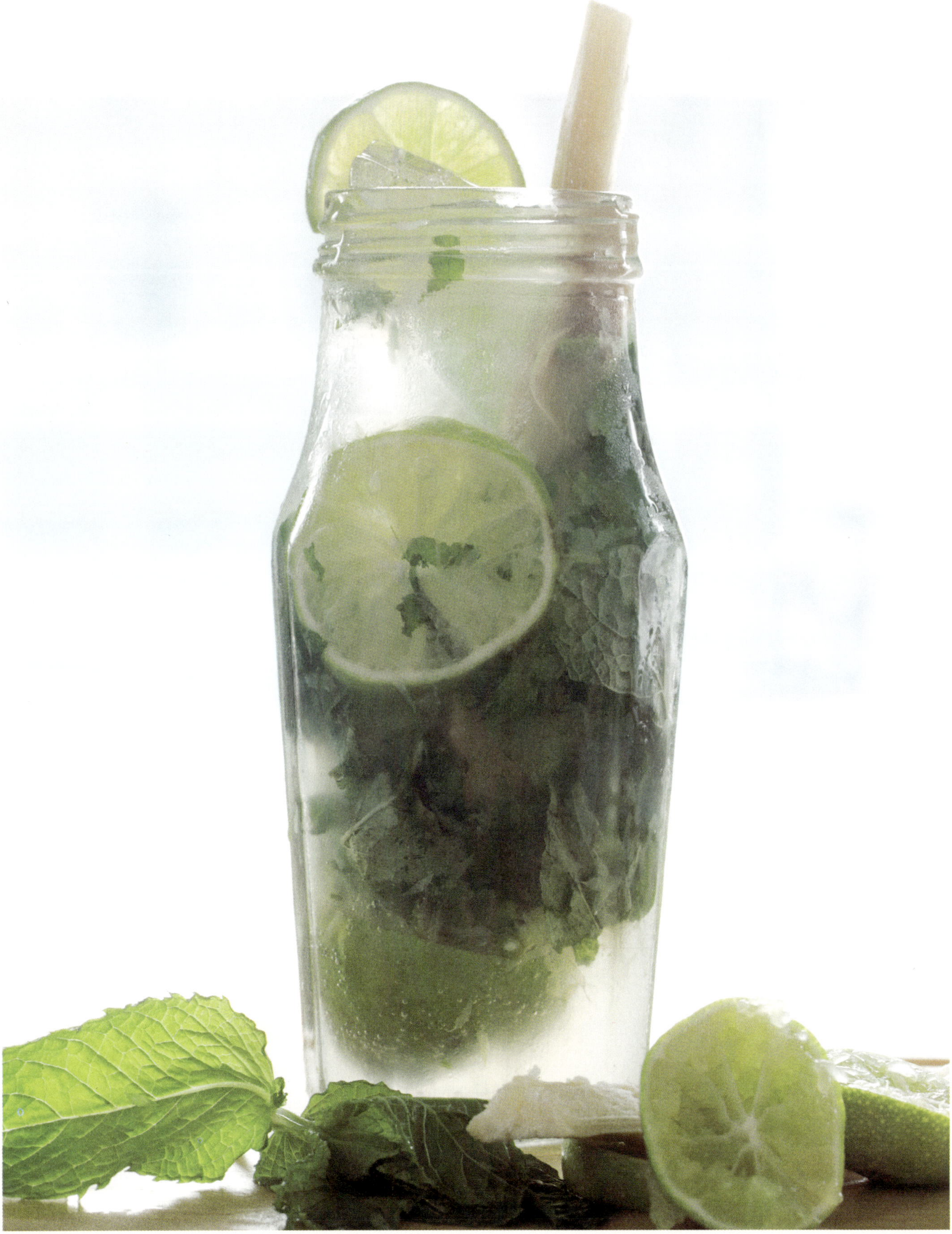

Cuba

MOJITO

½ lime, cut into 4 wedges
    or rounds
2 tsp white sugar
6 mint leaves, plus one
    sprig for garnish
1 cup crushed ice
¼ cup white rum
splash of ginger ale or club soda
sugar cane, to garnish (optional)

The mojito is a deceptively delicious but simple cocktail, traditional to Cuba. Ernest Hemingway raved about this sublime drink. You can have a mojito either with alcohol or virgin — both versions are fresh and divine. It's not difficult to make, but do bruise the mint so that the flavour gets infused into the drink.

Prepare: 5 minutes
Makes: 1

Place lime and sugar in a glass, and use the end of a whisk or the pestle from a mortar and pestle to gently press so that the lime juice is released. Bruise mint leaves by clapping them between your palms, then rub them on the rim of the glass. Press mint down into lime juice. Half-fill the glass with crushed ice, add rum and stir until sugar dissolves. Add a splash of ginger ale or club soda, and garnish with mint sprig and sugar cane (if using).

Brazil

CAIPIRINHA

¼ cup white sugar
3 limes, quartered
2 cups cachaça
½ cup simple syrup (see page 248)
approx. 2 cups crushed ice

Brazil's national drink is made with cachaça, a type of liqueur made from sugar cane. The caipirinha was originally made with lime, garlic and honey and given to patients with Spanish flu! The modern version is a mintless mojito with a kick. It's best to make a large jug and put it in the centre of the table for everyone to enjoy. Also, passionfruit caipirinhas are my favourite, so feel free to stir some passion in there.

Prepare: 10 minutes; marinate: 2–3 minutes
Serves: 4 to 6

Place sugar in a large jug, squeeze in lime quarters and put the quarters in the jug. Add 2 tablespoons of cachaça, mix and leave to marinate for a few minutes.

When ready to serve, add remaining cachaça, simple syrup and ice, stir well, taste and adjust lime or sugar to your liking.

Chef's note: For a passionfruit caipirinha, add the pulp of 1 fresh passionfruit or replace the simple syrup with ¼ cup passionfruit syrup.

Guatemala

RON CON TORONJA

Zacapa Old Fashioned Cocktail

¼ tsp Angostura bitters
1 tbsp simple syrup
    (see page 248)
60 ml Ron Zacapa 23 rum
1 tbsp grapefruit juice
1 cup ice cubes

Garnish
twist of grapefruit peel
grated dark chocolate
(optional)

Some Latin American countries, like Venezuela, Puerto Rico, the Dominican Republic and Cuba are known for their world-class rums. But Guatemala, a beautiful small place in Central America, produces an exceptional one, called Ron Zacapa. Its outstanding taste and wow element are thanks to the unique terroir, their 'above the clouds' ageing process and a fabulous woman, Lorena Vásquez, who is the master blender. Ron Zacapa 23 is ideal for sipping or mixing in cocktails, while Ron Zacapa XO is to be savoured like a fine Cognac.

Prepare: 5 minutes
Serves: 1

Mix bitters, simple syrup, rum and grapefruit juice with ½ cup ice. Stir until chilled, then strain into a double Old Fashioned glass (or lowball) over more ice. Garnish with grapefruit twist and grated dark chocolate (if desired).

Venezuela

SANGRÍA

1 apple, diced
1 peach, sliced
2 cups grapes, halved
1 orange, sliced into rounds
¼ cup sugar
pinch of salt

1½ litres red wine (two
    750 ml bottles)
700 ml ginger ale or
    lemon-lime soda
1 tsp ground cinnamon
½ tsp ground nutmeg

A gift given to us by the Spanish, this red or white wine punch is made with fresh fruit and is perfect for all occasions. Throughout South America it's the perfect accompaniment to our barbecues and festivities. Uruguayans and Argentineans infuse white wine with fruits such as apple and peaches. Chile has a traditional sangría called 'clery' made with sweet wine and stawberries. So you get the point — the fruit combination is up to you!

Prepare: 10 minutes; marinate: 1 hour
Serves: 10–12

In a large jug, marinate fruit with sugar and salt for at least 1 hour. Pour wine and soda over fruit. Add cinnamon and nutmeg, and stir to combine.

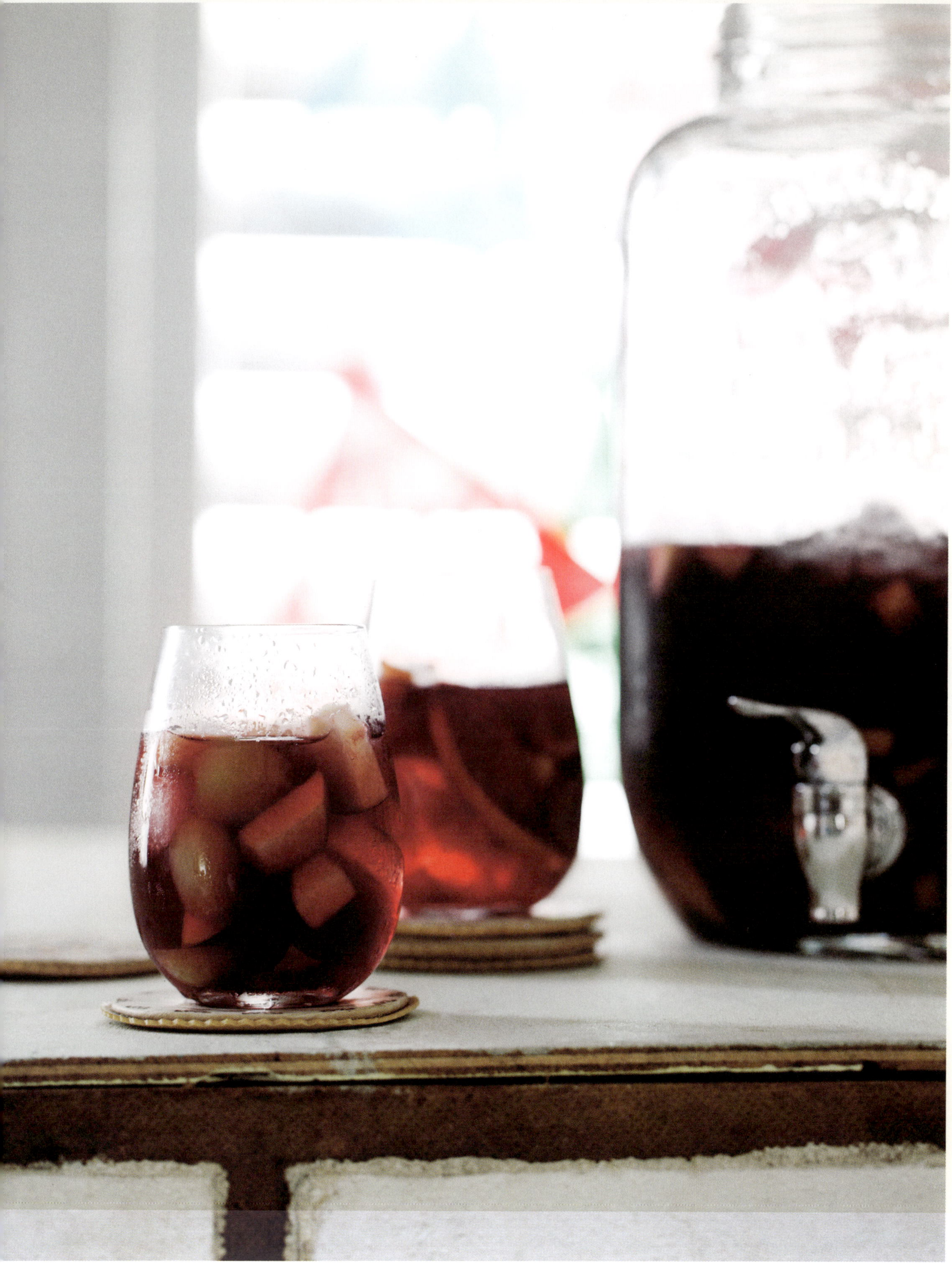

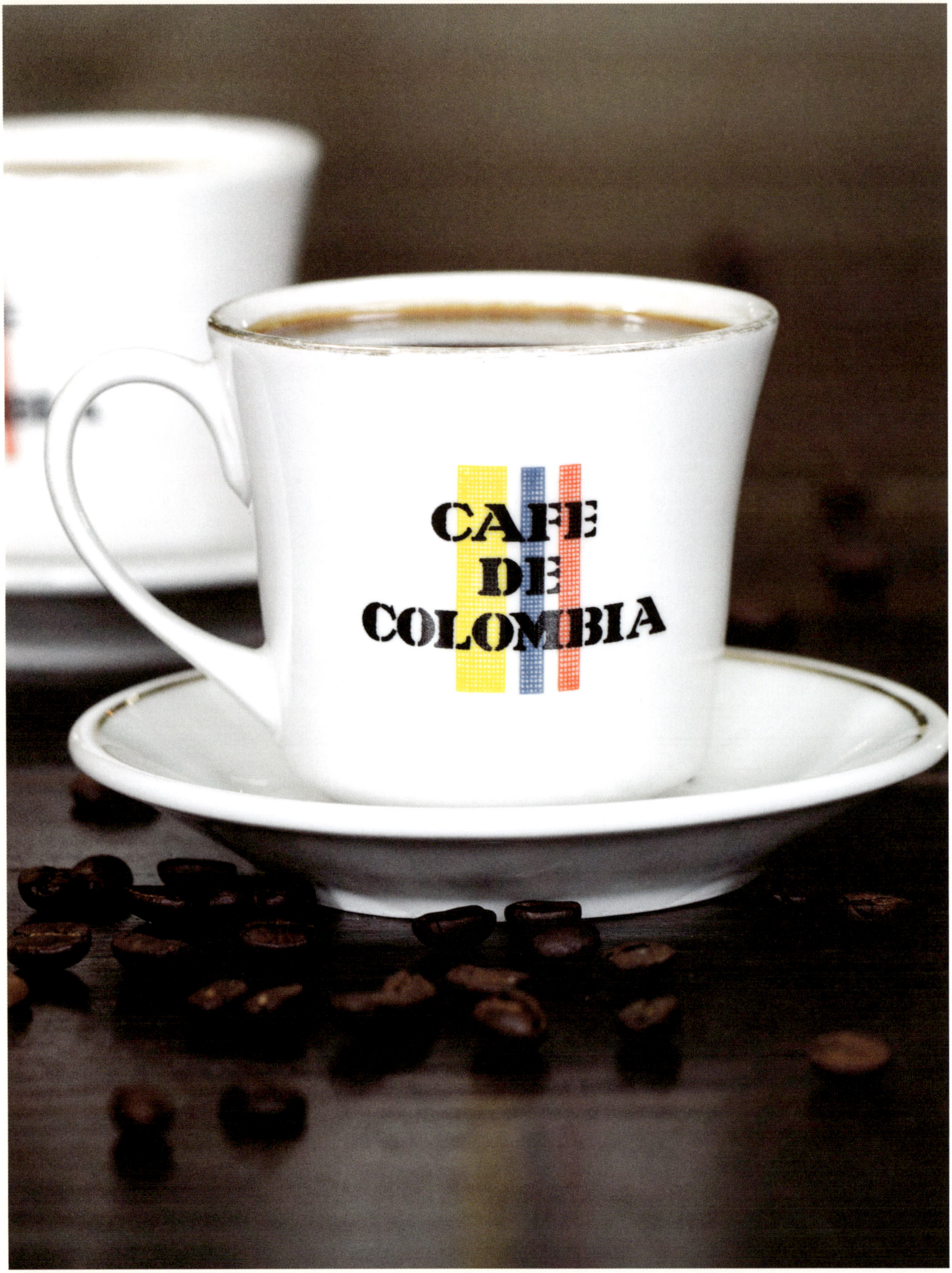
CAFE
DE
COLOMBIA

Colombia

TINTO CAMPESINO

Black Coffee

4 cups water
100 g shaved panela (unrefined cane sugar)
4 tbsp coarsely ground Colombian coffee

Coffee has played a big part in boosting the economies of countries like Brazil and Colombia, as well as smaller Central American countries and islands; single-origin coffees are now immensely popular. When I first got served a tinto, I couldn't believe the taste — so smooth, neither burnt nor bitter; and I was shocked that no filter was needed! Good Colombian coffee is best drunk just like this, by itself with a bit of panela. Like a good wine, you'll be able to taste and smell layers of flavours . . . like dark chocolate, raisins, walnuts, and many more.

Prepare: 10 minutes
Serves: 4

Place water and panela in a small saucepan, ideally one that has an easy-pour lip, and bring water up to 90–96°C — just before it comes to the boil. Take it off the heat immediately and stir, making sure the panela is completely dissolved. The water should never be boiling, or it will burn the coffee. Add coffee and a splash of cold water, cover with a plate and let it sit for about 3 minutes. Do not stir. Pour, leaving the grounds in the saucepan, and enjoy.

Chef's note: If you are feeling sceptical about grittiness, you can use a coffee filter or ultra fine seive!

Cuba

CAFECITO CON ESPUMITA

Cuban Coffee

espresso-ground coffee to fill 4-cup stovetop espresso maker
4 tbsp sugar (1 tbsp per cup)

In Cuban households you drink a LOT of coffee. Even the kids drink coffee, in the form of café con leche — coffee with milk. One of the most important parts of Cuban coffee is the espuma, a foam similar to espresso crema but originating from sugar. It is unlike the frothy foam made from milk, and when made the right way perfectly cuts the acidity of the black coffee beneath. 'Cafecito' — 'little coffee' — refers to an espresso shot which is sweetened with sugar as it is being brewed.

Prepare: 10 minutes
Serves: 4

Fill a 4-cup stovetop espresso maker with correct amount of water and coffee. Place espresso maker over a medium heat.
While coffee is brewing, place sugar in a tall container with a spout, such as a liquid measuring cup. As soon as the coffee starts to fill the reservoir of the espresso maker, pour about 1 tablespoon of coffee over the sugar and return the espresso maker to the heat.
Using a spoon, quickly beat sugar and espresso until the mixture turns a pale beige and most of the sugar granules begin to dissolve; about 1 minute. If too dry, add ½ tablespoon more coffee at a time and keep beating until it comes together and sugar is dissolved. This will create the espuma.
Once all the coffee has been brewed, slowly pour coffee over the creamed sugar. A thin layer of espuma should float on top of the coffee. Pour coffee into espresso cups and serve immediately.

Chef's note: Making the espuma is the technique that defines Cuban coffee. You cannot overbeat the sugar, so err on the side of beating too much. If you accidentally pour too much coffee into the sugar, continue with the beating process, as you will still achieve a sugar foam.

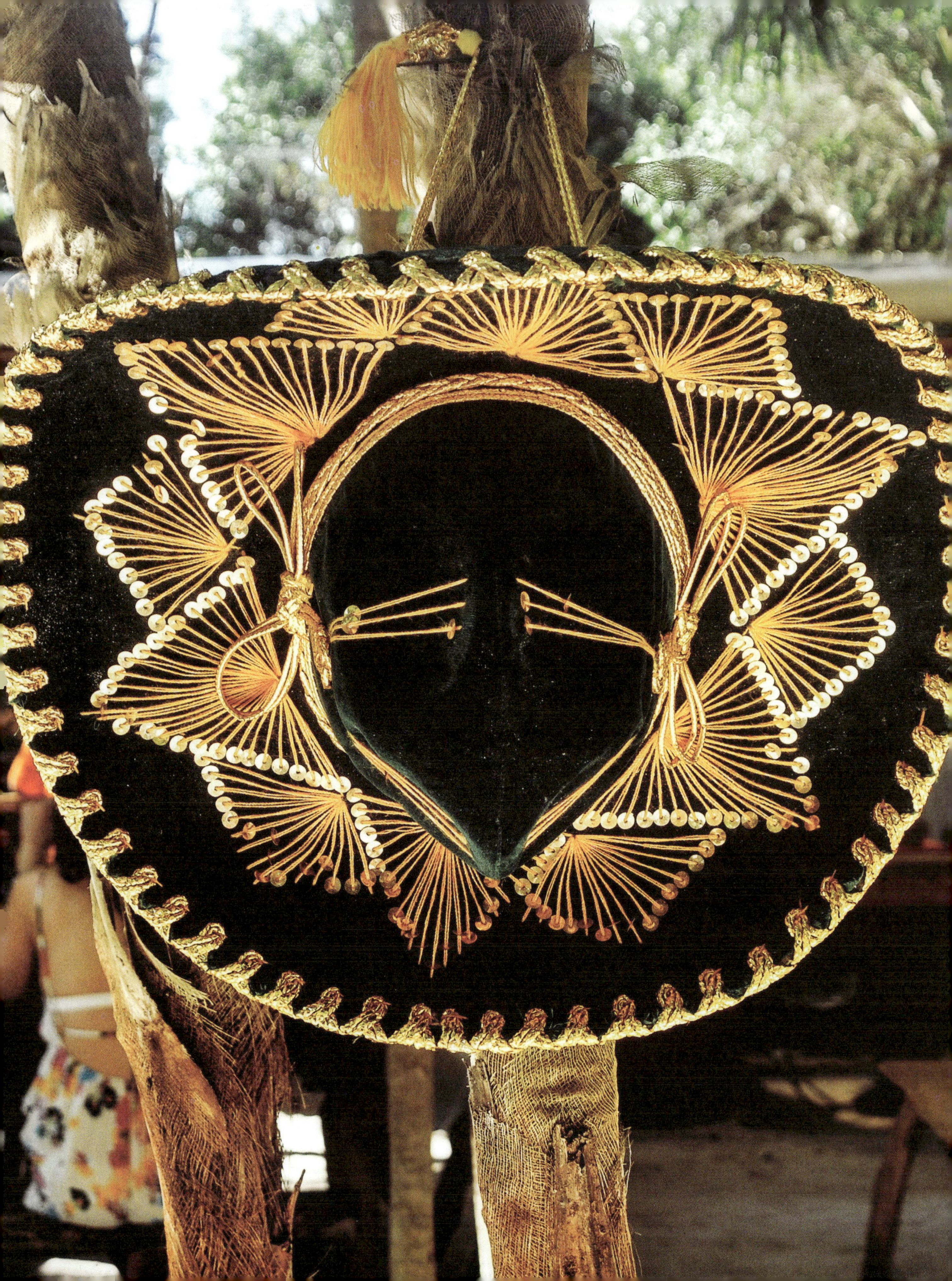

FIESTAS

FEASTS

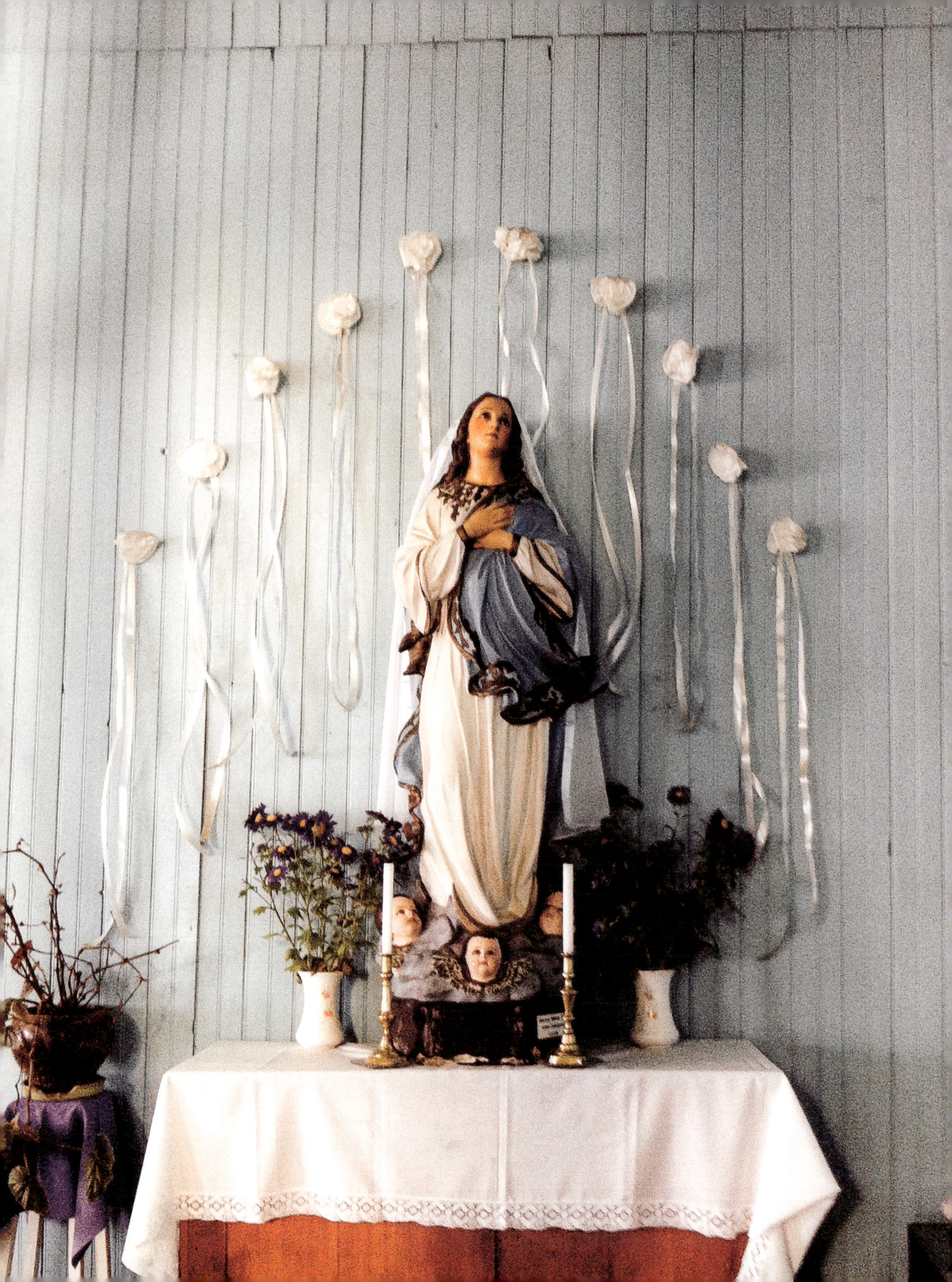

When we think about Latin American cuisine, we think abundance and festiveness. The other thing that comes to mind when we think of Latin food is variety. The term 'fusion cuisine' might have appeared in the seventies, but in Latin America, fusion had been taking place for centuries: Europeans, Africans and Asians brought and preserved many of their traditions and cooking techniques, along with spices, fruits, vegetables and meats, and combined them with the styles that were unique to each specific region long before they arrived. The outcome was, well, a tremendous fusion. Therefore, when food gets placed on the table the cook must think of a balanced meal with the right flavour combinations. Everything is there for a reason and when it is all eaten together it's explosive, a real fiesta in your mouth.

This book is about tradition and the labour of love in the kitchen. A conscious and honest account on each individual spoonful, so make sure that when friends and family come over for dinner, they are part of the entire procedure, from washing dishes, to cutting and chopping, to stirring the sauces and keeping an eye on the meat. Cooking should be one big collaboration that sets the mood for a long and joyful soirée. In Latin America, when you're invited for dinner, dinner is never ready upon arrival. Grandma's manteles (tablecloths) come out, the fanciest vajilla (plates) fill the table, and if ten people are invited, we cook for thirty, in case more people show up, which they always do. Because for us food, and its preparation, is not something to take lightly. And making time to elaborate good hearty dishes is not just therapy for the body and soul, but a cult that brings people together.

After having lived and extensively traveled throughout Latin America, I realised that even in the most modest homes, there is a constant theme of plenty of dishes on the dinner table, and even if the portions are small and the food is simple there always seems to be an abundance of choices. The image of a long table, with so much food on top of it that it seems as if it's bending, is something that lives vividly in my mind and memory, and something that I am constantly attempting to recreate for my friends and family.

With the feasts (illustrated on the following spreads), you can make all of the dishes, or just a few, depending on the size of your party. Get together, have fun, share, and enjoy memorable time with your loved ones!

BREAKFAST FEAST — huevos divorciados/divorced eggs (page 41), cachapas/corn pancakes stuffed with buffalo mozzarella (page 122), arepas (page 119), gallo pinto/Ticos' rice & beans (page 152), perico/colourful scrambled eggs (page 39), mandocas/anise, panela & cheese fritters (page 131), café Colombiano/Colombian coffee, hot sauce, fresh orange juice

LUNCH FEAST — Llapingachos/kumara & cheese patties (page 128), pescado en salsa verde/fish fillets in green sauce (page 76), arroz con coco/coconut rice (page 146), ensalada con sandia y mescal/mezcal watermelon salad (page 168), brigadeiro/chocolate fudge balls (page 240), agua fresca de limón/chia & mint lemonade (page 246)

MEXICAN FEAST — Pollo en adobo de chile ancho/ancho adobo chicken (page 48), camarones con adobo de guajillo/guajillo adobo-marinated prawns (page 66), arroz rojo/Mexican-style red rice (page 148), guacamole (page 196), queso fresco/fresh white cheese (page 208), crema agria/salty cream (page 211), ensalada con mango y maracuya/mango & passionfruit salad (page 170), pico de gallo/fresh chopped tomato salad (page 193), frijoles refritos/refried beans (page 19), carnitas/braised & fried pork (page 88), elote del Mercado/street corn (page 172), margarita con flor de Jamaica /hibiscus margaritas (page 252), Sol beer, brownies con chile y nueces/flourless brownies with spice & nuts (page 227).

DESSERT FEAST — Pie de limón con leche condensada /condensed-milk lemon pie (page 231), tres leches three-milk cake (page 239), flan Cubano/Cuban 'crème caramel' (page 225), merengón/caramel meringues (page 237), alfajores/shortbread cookie sandwich with dulce de leche (page 233) salpicon/tropical fruit salad (page 216), mousse de parchita/passionfruit mousse (page 220), arroz con leche/rice pudding (page 229, caramelo/spiced brittle (page 235), crème de papaya con cassis (papaya cream with berry syrup (page 223)

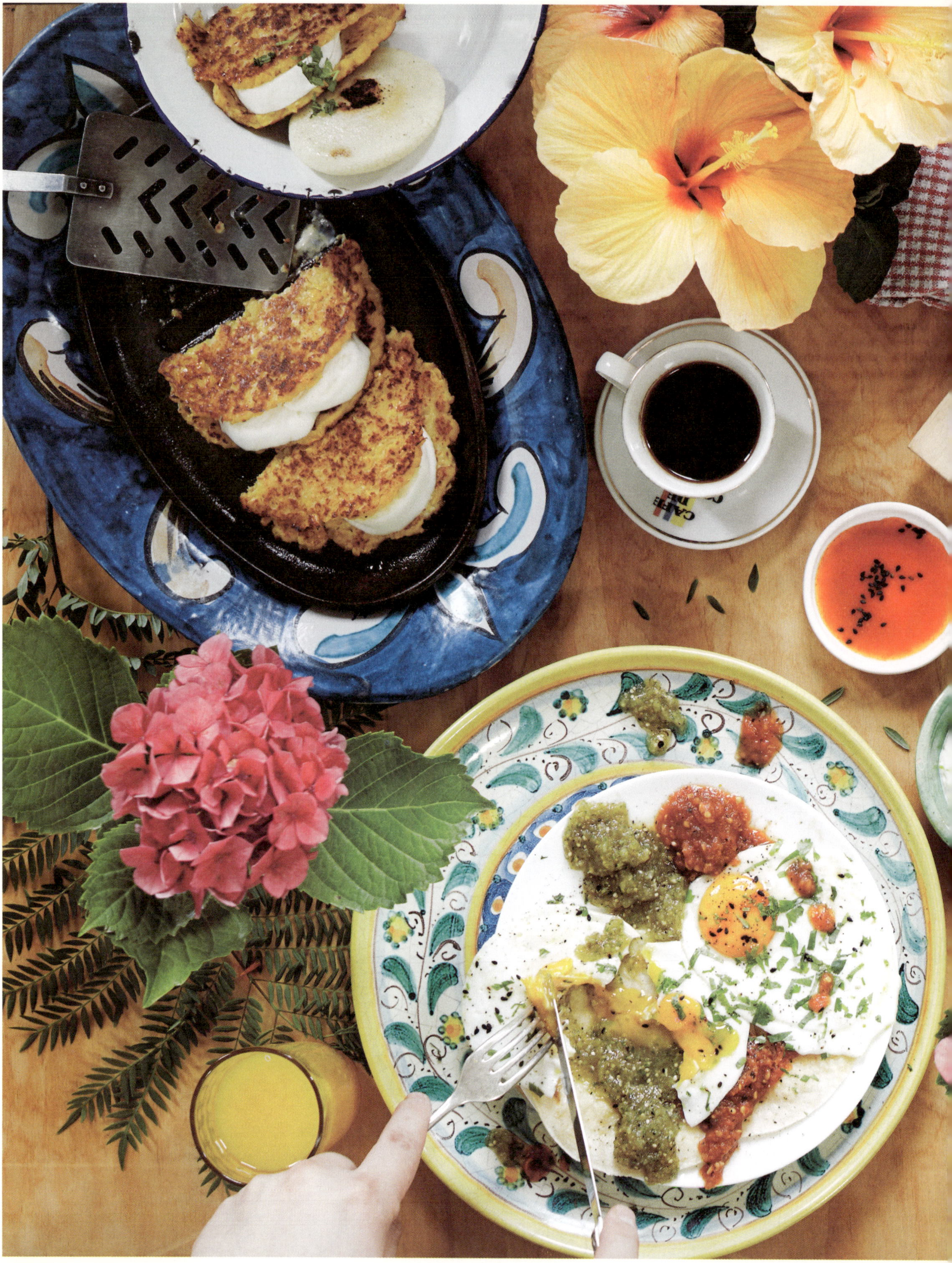

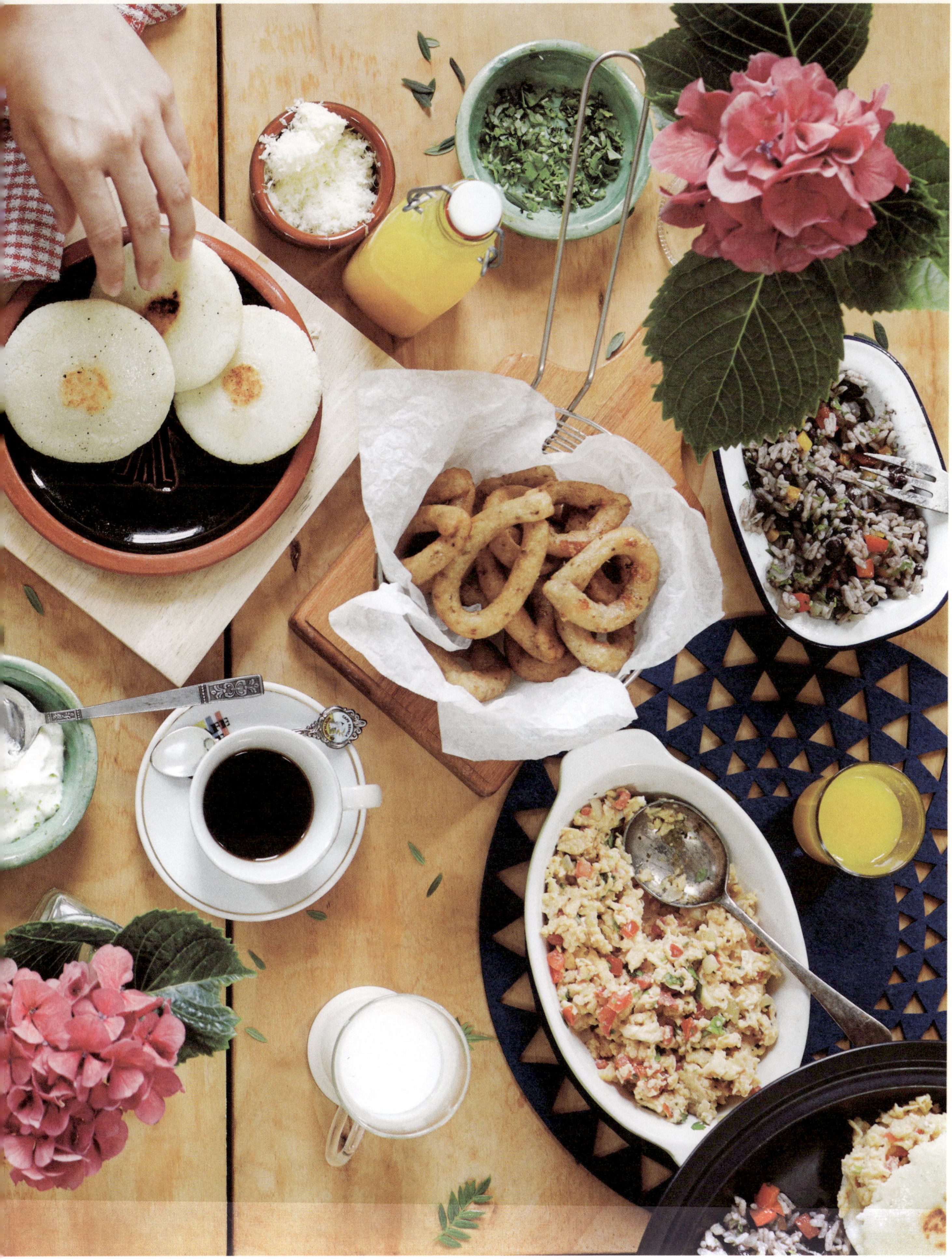

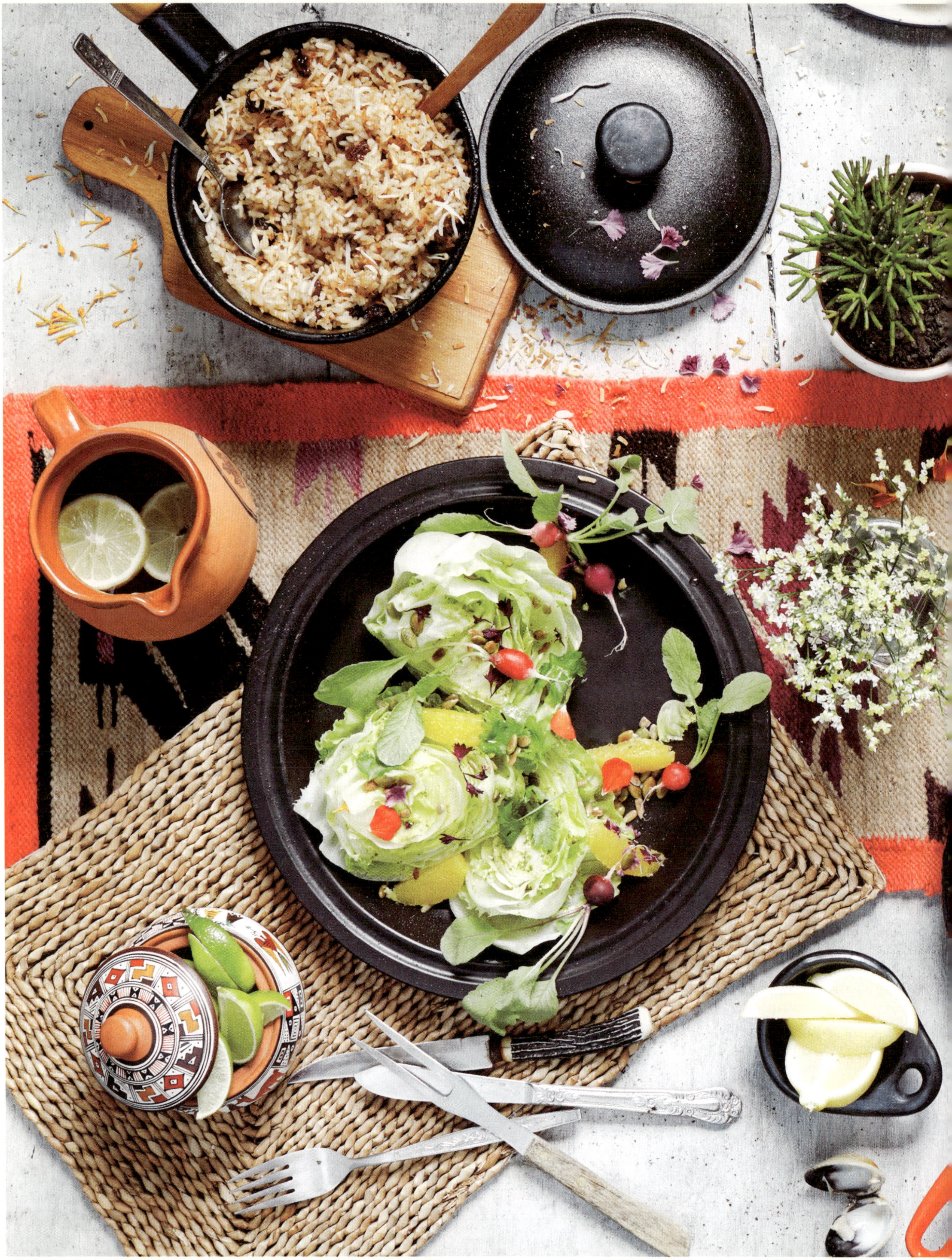

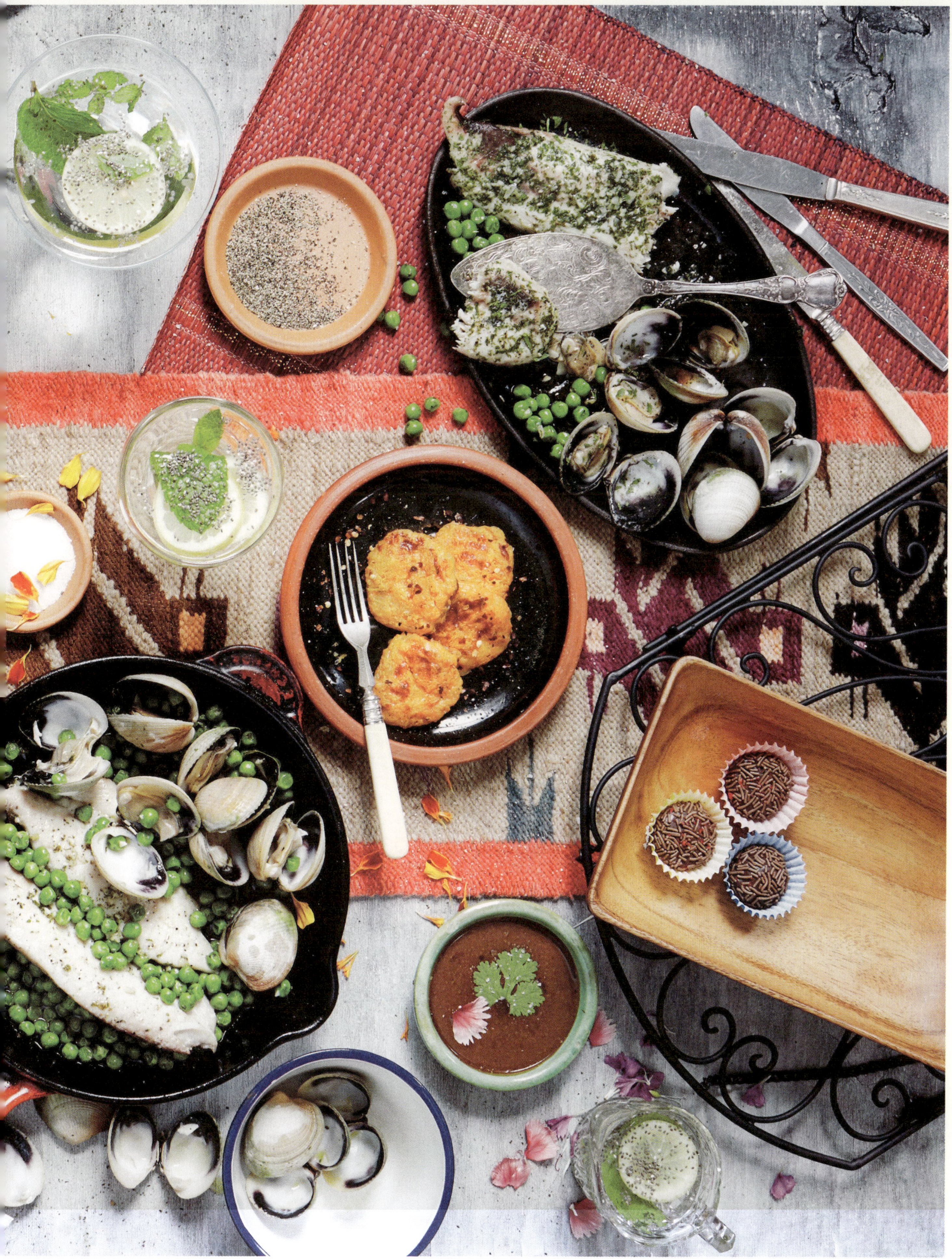

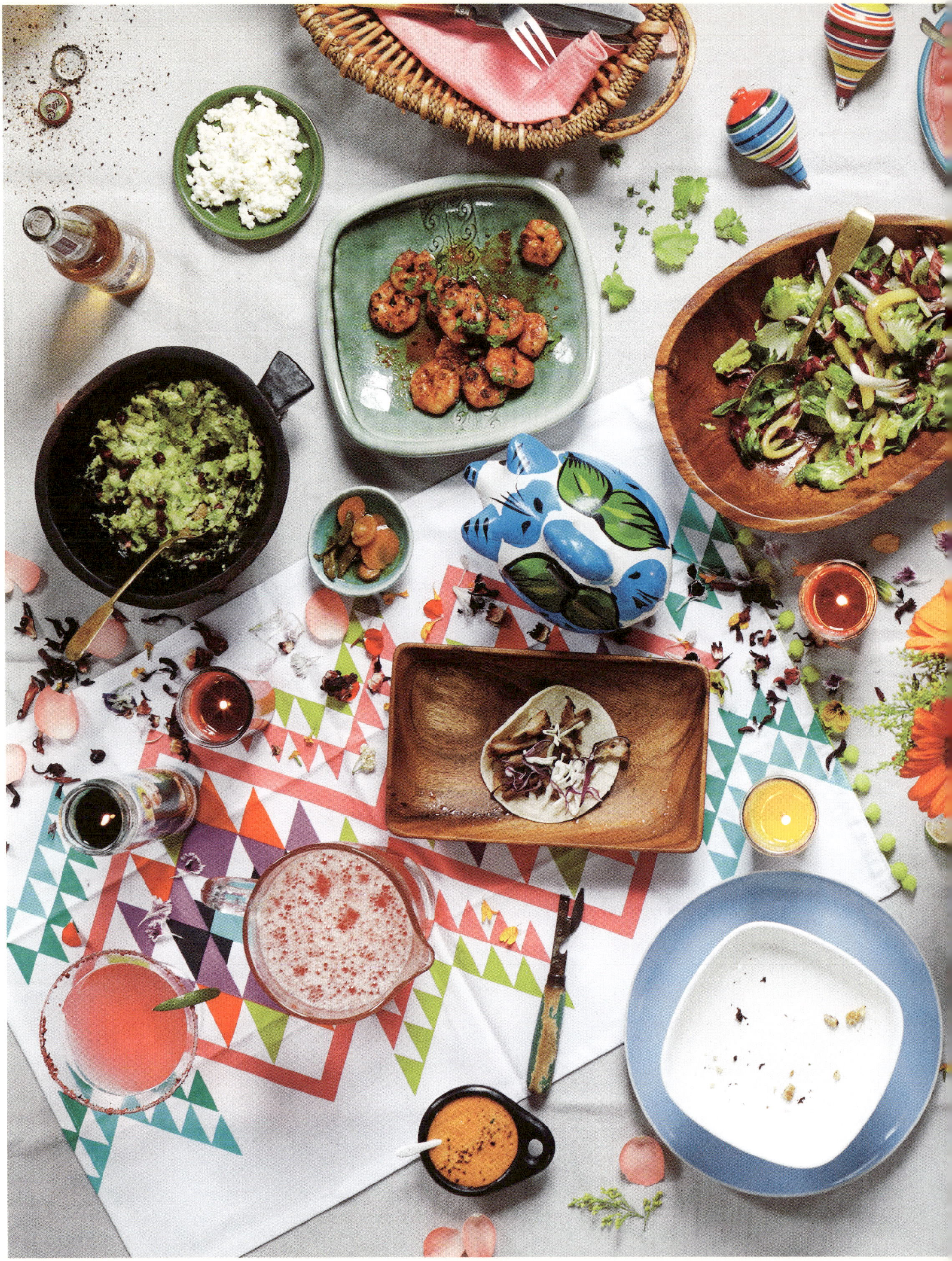

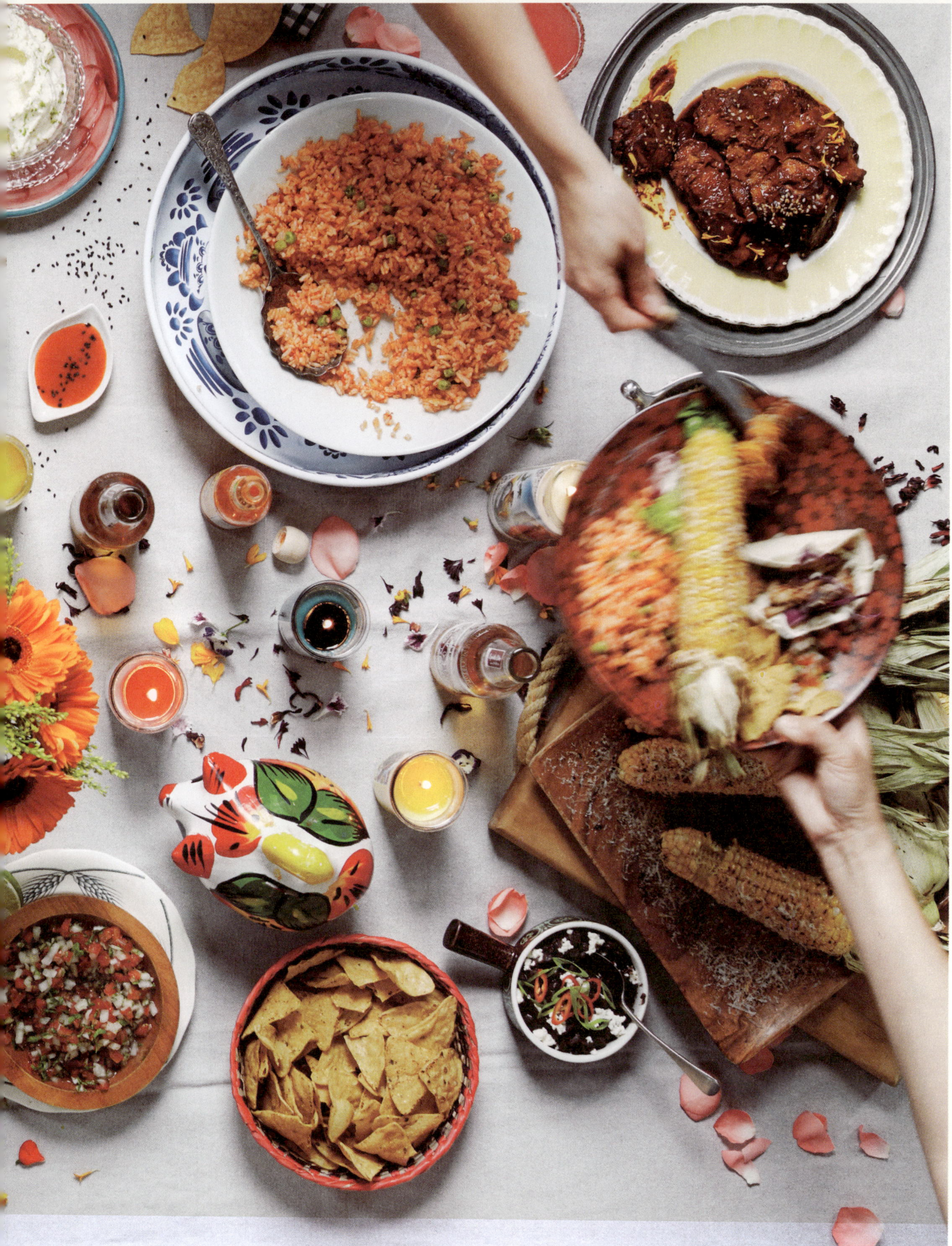

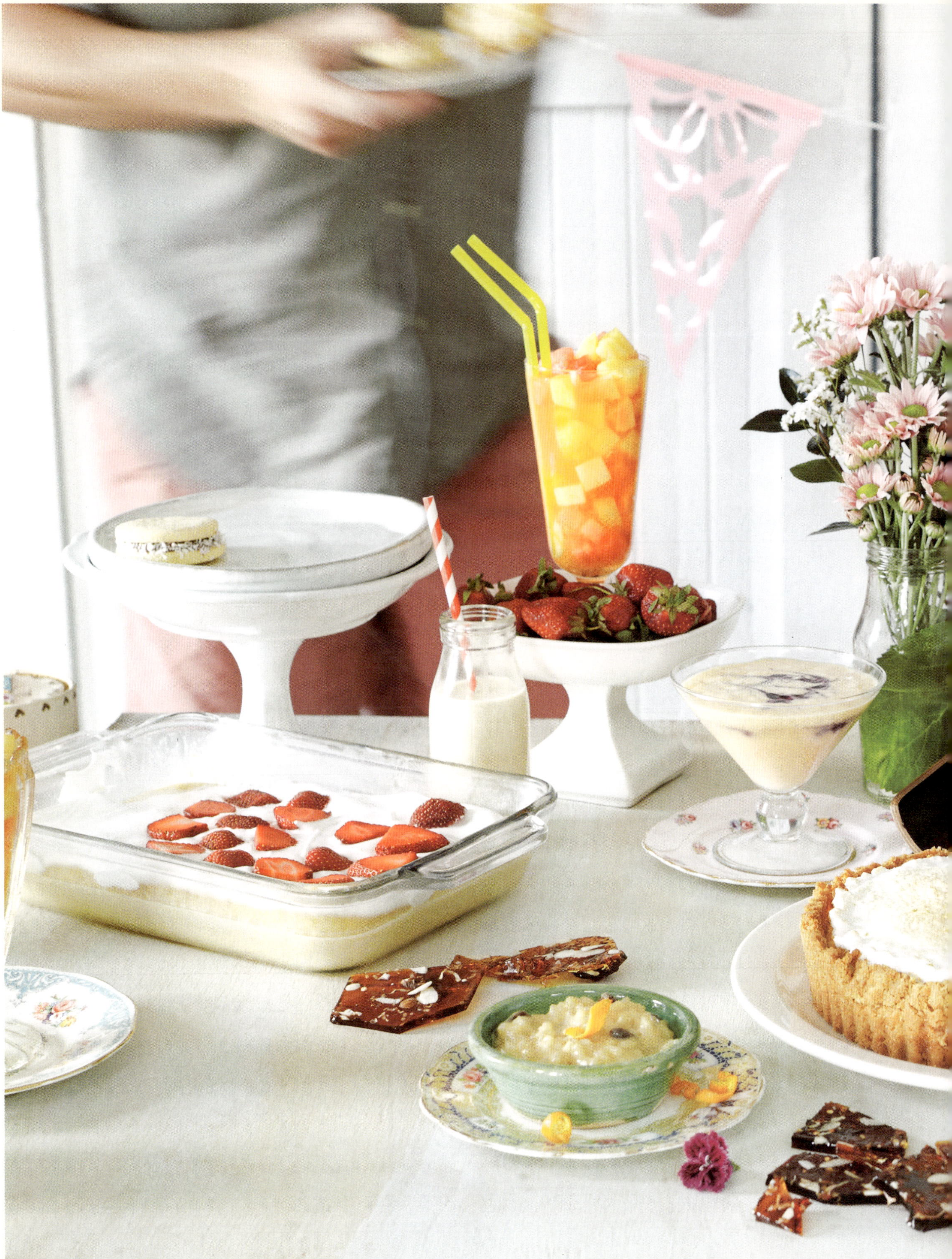

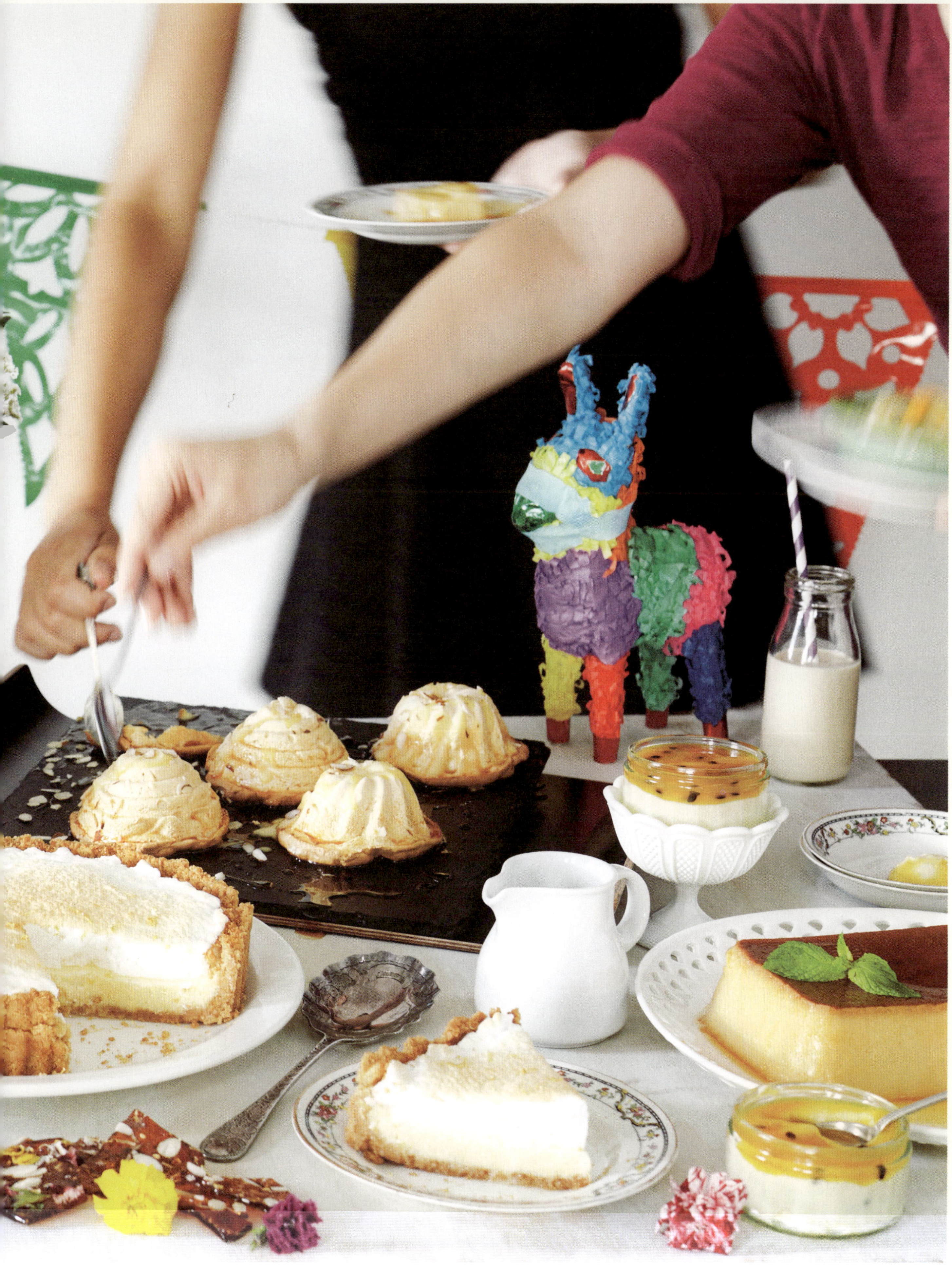

FOOD FROM THE GODS

Gastronomically speaking, since the beginning of time the indigenous people in Latin America have had a very clear belief: the food that nourishes us comes from the gods. Corn, the foundation ingredient, and cacao, the most delicious one, were gifts given to the ancient inhabitants of Mexico by the God Quetzalcoatl, god of life, light and wisdom. This tale is recorded among some of their beautiful fables.

Latin America is vast with several indigenous cultures, thus, these myths not only pertain to the Aztecs. Among the Andean indigenous people of the Inca culture, there is a marvellous legend that explains how men received the food from the gods. In another era, when the Pachamama was still young, a wily fox convinced a condor to fly him to the skies so he could participate in the endless banquets which only the deities enjoyed and which mortals could merely relish the delightful aromas of. The condor took him and the fox was able to sit at the table of the gods and savour their dishes. In his eagerness to taste it all, he forgot time and the condor, tired of waiting, left for the mountains. Feeling more than satisfied with all that food, the fox wanted to go back down to Earth and had to improvise a rope. He was, however, so heavy that the rope broke and the poor animal fell into the void and smashed open when he hit the ground. Men were able to take the heavenly food from his open stomach and in a sort of gastronomic Big Bang, began to recreate such delicacies in the kitchens on earth.

It is no longer a myth but history that centuries later other dishes and ingredients ended up forming a more elaborate, powerful, creative and significant gastronomy, filled with infinite aromas and flavours that came to Latin America from the other side of the ocean — from Europe and Africa. Mexico and Peru have been Latin America's best-known gastronomical locations due to their development in the pre-Columbian culture. However, due to the particular ways in which the indigenous people, Spaniards and Africans related to each other, and because of the immigration patterns of the nineteenth and twentieth centuries, other countries in this vast region developed specific cuisines comprising their own delicious dishes.

Throughout Latin America, people prepare dishes that are similar but retain their local characteristics: some form of cornbread, tortillas or arepas, stewed and refried beans, patties, sauces and an array of delicacies. The tamale, for example, is eaten throughout the region. Its basic elements are corn, vegetable stew and/or meat, wrapped with plantain leaves or corn husks. But in order to explain certain differences in flavour and characteristics, there's a common saying: 'It's the same everywhere, just different.'

In Venezuela, the tamale became the hallaca, a dish of some complexity and sophistication. The hallaca is made with cornmeal dough filled with a stew that combines American and Spanish elements. Its defining feature is the balance between its four flavours: sour, sweet, salty and, importantly, a touch of spice. The hallaca is much more than the traditional dish of Venezuela, it is a ritual — it is our version of turkey on Thanksgiving Day — and it is only made during Christmas.

There are several local stories that tell how the tamale became the hallaca in the city of Caracas. The most well known is linked to a trivial episode that became important to the country's gastronomy. A group of Mantuanos (a term used to refer to the white Creole aristocrat descendants of the founders and rulers of the city) from Caracas were imprisoned by order of the Spanish Captain General. As further punishment, and to inflict more injury to their arrogant characters, they were sentenced to eat the same meals that they served their slaves: slop made of leftovers from the table of their masters mixed with corn, pork lard and any other available ingredient. This mixture was wrapped in banana leaves and then boiled to mix the flavours.

The Mantuana ladies — wives, daughters and relatives of the prisoners — found their own way to comply with the colonial official's order. They prepared the mestizo stir-fry that is common across Latin America: peppers (sweet and spicy), onion, garlic and tomatoes, as the stew base for cooking poultry, pork and beef. They added raisins, olives, capers, pickles, panela (unrefined cane sugar), cubes of cured ham from the Motherland and almonds, and seasoned it with muscatel wine. Wrapped in banana leaves it looked like an ordinary tamale, but the filling was an epicurean, elaborate dish.

The story is enriched with a fictional element that explains why the hallaca is especially eaten during the holidays: these aristocrats were imprisoned at Christmas time, and so the following year a big party was held to celebrate their freedom and the birth of Jesus Christ, and relatives and friends of the former prisoners were invited and were served hallacas and, obviously, plenty of red wine. That was how the hallaca became a gastronomical ritual that binds Venezuelans, both during its preparation, which requires extraordinary diligence, and while enjoying its flavours with family, friends and even with God.

With its truths and fictions, this story also shows one of the distinctive traits of Latin Americans, wherever they may be. A meal is not a mere formality, it is something to celebrate and share, and to prepare it in a rich and tasty manner is a way to honour the generous primitive gods that so kindly gave us that gift.

Francisco Suniaga

INGREDIENTS LIST

GF This symbol at the top of the ingredients list in a recipe denotes a gluten-free dish

Most if not all of the ingredients listed below can be sourced from specialty stores such as Moore Wilsons and Farro Fresh, as well as the following New Zealand-based online stores: mexicanspecialities.co.nz; tiopablo.co.nz; finefoodforyou.co.nz. It's also noted where an ingredient may be available from other specialty grocers.

ANNATTO (OR ACHIOTE)
These names are used interchangeably for the seeds of the achiote tree, used to add a yellow/orange colour and a nutty, sweet, peppery flavour to dishes. Annatto seeds can be bought whole, ground, in oil form or in paste form (also called recado rojo). Puerto Rico's favoured sazón (seasoning) consists of annatto seeds ground together with cumin, coriander, garlic powder and salt.

AGAVE NECTAR (OR AGAVE SYRUP)
A sweetener produced from several species of the agave plant.

AJÍ DULCE
Literally meaning 'chilli sweet' ají dulce is a pepper famously used in the Venezuelan national dish hallaca. It's also used in Puerto Rican sauces and in Brazil, where it's known as rubra or biquinho, it's used to make a sweet jam.

ARRACHERA
Mexican term for skirt steak.

BANANA LEAVES
Being large, flexible, waterproof and decorative, they are widely used in the cuisines of tropical regions for wrapping and serving food. Available in Asian and Pacific Island grocers.

BEEF EYE OF ROUND
The back section of the upper leg of the cow. It's a tougher cut and should be braised slowly until tender.

CHICKPEA FLOUR
Available in Indian grocers, wholefoods stores and the gluten-free section of some supermarkets.

CHILLIES (OR CHILES)
Many varieties are used in Latin American cooking, either fresh or dried and sometimes smoked, each with specific flavour and heat profiles and therefore used specifically to flavour dishes. Different names may be given to the same variety depending on whether it is sold fresh, at different stages of ripeness, or dried/smoked. Some of the chillies important in Latin American cuisine are as follows. Fresh: poblano, jalapeno, chilaca, habanero, serrano, cayenne, ají limo, ají dulce; dried and/or smoked: ancho, mulato, chipotle, habanero, pasilla negro, guajillo, piquillo, chile de árbol.

CHIPOTLE
Smoked dried jalapeno pepper, also made into adobo sauce, blended with paprika, oregano, salt, garlic and vinegar.

CORN HUSKS
Used to wrap and cook food in, particularly tamales. Corn husks not only help secure the food in place, they also keep it moist, seal in flavour, and impart their own flavor and aroma, which varies depending on whether the corn husks are fresh and tender, fresh and mature or dried.

CORNMEAL/CORN FLOUR
Both are made from ground white corn (maize). Corn flour is finer than cornmeal. Not the same as cornflour/corn starch, which is a starch derived from treated corn (in this book we have used the term 'corn starch' to avoid confusion). Look for these brands: Harina P.A.N. — a brand of precooked cornmeal which is used for arepas and cachapas; Maseca — an instant corn flour used to make corn tortillas, tamales and more (called 'instant corn masa flour' on the packaging).

DULCE DE LECHE
A confection of sweetened, caramelised milk that can be made fresh, or bought ready-made from specialty stores.

EDIBLE FLOWERS
Available at Farro Fresh and other specialty stores and some supermarkets.

EPAZOTE
A pungent herb used fresh and to make tea. It's used in Mexican cooking to add a resinous, citrus-like flavour to a range of dishes.

GUAVA PASTE
A sweet jam-like paste made from guava fruit and sugar, with a consistency similar to quince paste, commonly served with cheese or used in desserts. Especially popular in the Caribbean.

HIBISCUS TEA
To make it at home look for 'flor de Jamaica' - deep purple-coloured dried hibiscus flowers, in specialist stores and tea shops.

LARD
Pig fat in both rendered and unrendered forms. Still favoured in many Latin kitchens.

MEXICAN CHOCOLATE
Used to make Mexican-style hot chocolate, also known as chocolate para mesa. Bought as either chocolate tablets or powdered mix in individual packets, La Abuelita and Tio Pablo are brands to look for.

MEZCAL (OR MESCAL)
A spirit distilled from a type of agave plant native to Mexico.

PANELA
The standard name for a type of unrefined cane sugar also called papelon or piloncillo. It may be sold in crystals or in a block or cone from which you shave the amount you require. Available in specialty stores and some wholefoods stores, or you may substitute light muscavado or rapadura.

PINK HIMALAYAN SALT
This salt has a higher mineral content and is particularly good with seafood or to finish dishes.

PLANTAIN LEAVES
These large, fragrant green leaves are often used to wrap savoury or sweet ingredients before baking or steaming. Available in the frozen section of Asian grocers.

POZOLE (OR HOMINY)
Dried, treated white corn kernels, sold in cans, ready to use. Used in a traditional Mexican soup.

QUINOA
A pseudocereal traditionally used in South American cooking and popular in contemporary cooking for its high nutritional value.

SRIRACHA SAUCE
A Thai hot sauce originating in the coastal city of Sri Racha, made from chillies, vinegar, garlic, sugar and salt.

TORTILLA PRESS
Used to make tortillas, a tortilla press is simply two flat iron plates joined with a hinge and a lever to clamp the plates together.

YUCA (OR CASSAVA)
A starchy tuber cultivated in tropical regions, where it is an important staple carbohydrate. Available fresh in some greengrocers, or in the frozen section of Asian and Pacific Island grocers.

PHOTO CREDITS

PAGE 4
Baru, Colombia
William Coupon
williamcoupon.com

PAGE 10
Mérida, Venezuela
Ana Maria Marrero
anamariamarrero.com

PAGE 12
Tepoztlán, Mexico
Ana Maria Marrero
anamariamarrero.com

PAGE 16
Antigua, Guatemala
William Coupon
williamcoupon.com

PAGE 32
Feira Livre da Gávea,
Rio de Janeiro, Brazil
Ricardo Lemes & Wagner
Ziegelmeyer
estudiocria.com.br

PAGE 34
Pereira, Colombia
Natalia Escobar

PAGE 43
Tulum, Mexico
Antonio Navas
symmetrykills.tumblr.com

PAGE 56
Coche Island, Venezuela
Ana Maria Marrero
anamariamarrero.com

PAGE 58
Coche Island, Venezuela
Ana Maria Marrero
anamariamarrero.com

PAGE 80
Salvador da Bahia, Brazil
Cristina Bocaranda
cristinabocaranda.com

PAGE 84
Lujan, Provincia de
Buenos Aires, Argentina
Francisco Odriozola
franodriozola.com.ar

PAGE 86
Havana, Cuba
Jock Mcdonald
jockmcdonald.com

PAGE 93
Lujan, Provincia de
Buenos Aires, Argentina
Francisco Odriozola
franodriozola.com.ar

PAGE 108
Mercado de Hidalgo,
Guanajuato, Mexico
Ana Maria Marrero
anamariamarrero.com

PAGE 110
Mercado de Hidalgo,
Guanajuato, Mexico
Ana Maria Marrero
anamariamarrero.com

PAGE 116-17
Antigua, Guatemala
William Coupon
williamcoupon.com

PAGE 134
Tulum, Mexico
Antonio Navas
symmetrykills.tumblr.com

PAGE 140
Cuzco, Peru
Danilo Alvarez

PAGE 142
Palenque de San Basilio,
Colombia
William Coupon
williamcoupon.com

PAGE 158
Mercado de Hidalgo,
Guanajuato, Mexico
Ana Maria Marrero
anamariamarrero.com

PAGE 160
Mercado de Hidalgo,
Guanajuato, Mexico
Ana Maria Marrero
anamariamarrero.com

PAGE 182
Feira Livre da Gávea,
Rio de Janeiro, Brazil
Ricardo Lemes & Wagner
Ziegelmeyer
estudiocria.com.br

PAGE 184
Mercado de Hidalgo,
Guanajuato, Mexico
Ana Maria Marrero
anamariamarrero.com

PAGE 187
Feira Livre da Gávea,
Rio de Janeiro, Brazil
Ricardo Lemes & Wagner
Ziegelmeyer
estudiocria.com.br

PAGE 206-7
Antigua, Guatemala
William Coupon
williamcoupon.com

PAGE 212
Palenque de San Basilio,
Colombia
William Coupon
williamcoupon.com

PAGE 214
Cartagena, Colombia
William Coupon
williamcoupon.com

PAGE 218-19
Mercado de Hidalgo,
Guanajuato, Mexico
Ana Maria Marrero
anamariamarrero.com

PAGE 242
Margarita Island, Venezuela
Grace Ramirez
chefgraceramirez.com

PAGE 244
Cartagena, Colombia
William Coupon
williamcoupon.com

PAGE 264
Tulum, Mexico
Antonio Navas
symmetrykills.tumblr.com

PAGE 266
Antilhue, Los Lagos, Chile
Charles Brooks
charlesbrooks.info

PAGE 283
General Las Heras,
Provincia de Buenos Aires,
Argentina
Mártin Sigal
martinsigal.com

MEXICO
CUBA
DOMINICAN REPUBLIC
PUERTO RICO
HONDURAS
GUATEMALA
NICARAGUA
VENEZUELA
EL SALVADOR
COSTA RICA
PANAMA
COLOMBIA
ECUADOR
BRAZIL
PERU
BOLIVIA
PARAGUAY
URUGUAY
CHILE
ARGENTINA

ACKNOWLEDGEMENTS

This book is a labour of love and a true collaboration between friends, family and colleagues. I couldn't have done it without all the love, help, support and guidance from some very talented, loving and inspiring people whom I'm so grateful and privileged to have in my life.

First and foremost I have to thank my husband, **Antonio Navas**. No words can express my gratitude. You helped me make this dream come true; you pushed me over and over again to think bigger, and above all, believe in myself. **Mi adorada familia**, you guys are my rock and strength and this is all for you! To Penguin Random House, for believing in me — thank you to **Nicola Legat**, **Debra Millar** and **Tessa King** for giving life to my baby. **Melissa Tung**, I must have done something right in life to deserve you. You have been a gift from Virgin Guadalupe and my right-hand woman on this project. **Kyle Herrman**, you are one skillful chef and a great friend. **Garth Badger**, talented photographer and my good friend, thanks for believing in this passion project, your amazing skills brought to life my vision and made it better than I could have imagined. **Genevieve Senekal**, you always came in at the perfect time. **Nicky Bell**, thanks for persuading us to come to New Zealand — what a rewarding, life-changing adventure this has been. **David** and **Julienne Mclean**, you both are angels sent from above, I couldn't have pulled this off without your kindness and big-heartedness. **Natty Chow**, your smile, big heart and incredible work ethic helped us over and over again in the kitchen when we needed the most help. **Grant Allen**, your gorgeous collection elevated the food and took the look and feel to the next level. **Jimmy Kouratoras**, you are such a talented artist and I'm honored to call you a friend — your light gave life and soul to all those backgrounds. **Maud Meijboom**, you have brought me strength and guidance and your unconditional support means the world to me. **Brian Blake**, what a privilege to call you my mentor. **Kiki** and **Alex Turnbull**, my Brazilian family, thanks for opening the door to your home and for sharing with me your moqueca. You have both always believed in me. **Pip Walls** and **Dave Good**, true friends are always there when you need them the most — thank you. **Carolina** and **Tom Hoare**, I'm so appreciative of our friendship and forever grateful for your generosity and hospitality. **Natalia Escobar** — our shared passion for coffee brought us together and its aroma helped unite us all. **Antonia Baker**, you are my first call. **Karin Williams**, you are one selfless and loving amiga. **Victor Rodger**, you are a genius. Thanks for your guidance in giving life to my introduction to this book. **Dave Sylvester**, gracias brother for your words and thoughtfulness. **Carolina Orozco**, for your empanadas and always carrying your Argentinean heart on your sleeve. **Barbara Chapman**, your graceful power inspires me. Thanks for the encouragement, all those kitchen tools and so much more. **Leanne Moore**, you gave me an opportunity when no one else would. **Julie Christie**, you are an inspiration to me and you've helped me get back on track. **Emily Cablin** and **James Doughty**, for helping me see clear in times when things where blurry. **Adela Smith**, you helped me get through that last challenging phase and gave me one final push. **Natalia Forero**, for all your help and those delicious dulce treats. **Ana María Peña**, you have been like a mother to me. Thanks for being there and for the perfect job translating Francisco Suniaga's history. **Gaby Sanchez**, I love your Mexican passion and your expertise on sotol and agave spirits. **Francisco Suniaga**, te la comistes, gracias. **Herman Sifontes**, gracias compadre. **Helen Lopez**, por tu generosidad. **Isobel Kerrnewell**, brilliant advice. **Anna King Shahab**, my ingredients list partner. The sisterhood — you are my support system. **Lily Neumeyer**, you have been a key part of it all. **Myra Santiago**, you rescued me. **Lissette Decos**, for your magic touch. **Grettel Singer**, for your gift of beautiful words. **Alicia Marin**, I know I can always count on you. **Jessica Higueras**, for your friendship and my gorgeous portraits. To **Norka**, my mother-in-law, thanks for all your wonderful recipes. This story would not have been complete without all the beautiful street photos that capture the essence of our beloved Latin America. For those I thank my husband, who always attracts and surrounds himself with the most talented and generous artists, who I'm honoured to call friends. Thank you to all of you who have donated your gorgeous images to help me tell this story. My dear friends — **Ana Maria, Cristina, Danilo, Francisco, Guillermo, Martin, Natalia, Ricardo, William** . . . I'm forever grateful. **Chris Leskovsek**, gracias amigo for making all those street photos look consistent and like they belong together in the book. To **Nadia Lim** and the My Food Bag team, thanks for lending me the space where we photographed this book. **Tio Pablo**, thanks to you New Zealand has a range of high-quality and traditional Mexican specialties and products. I would not have been able to make so many delicious and authentic recipes if it wasn't for you.

I must acknowledge my sponsors — my dream came true thanks to you. To Sol Beer and DB Breweries, **Maud Meijboom** and **Grant Caunter** — thanks for believing in *La Latina*, cheers to much more! To Fonterra, **Rachel Leeuwenberg** and **Grant Watson** — I can personally and professionally say I am so impressed with your products!

Last but not least, thanks to my **guru** and my **Isha family**, for the gift of consciousness. You have taught me to go inwards and trust my gut, always! You have all inspired me and pushed me to be a better, more loving and giving human being that believes in herself no matter what and for this I'm forever grateful. Gracias.

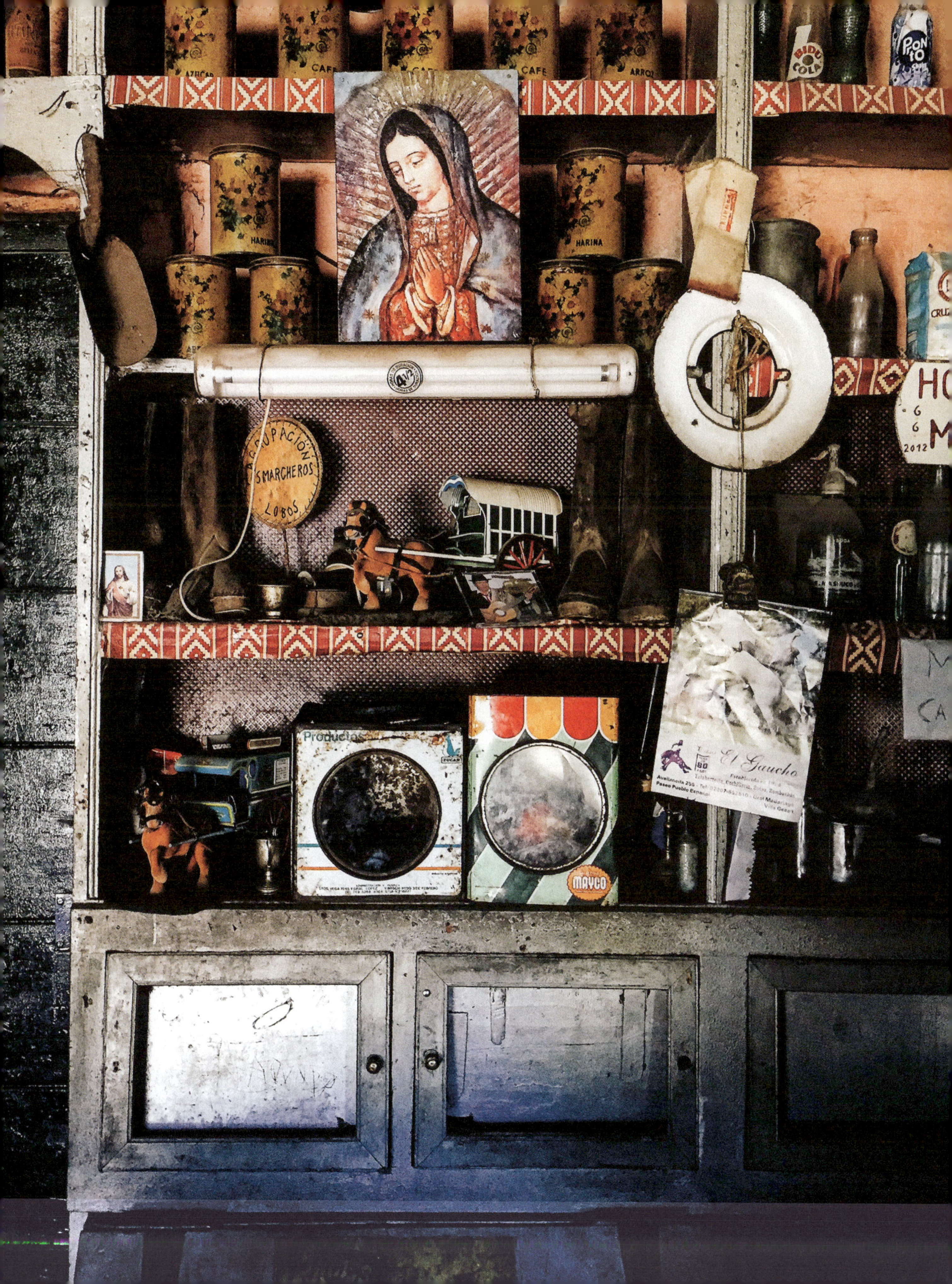
CAFE
HARINA
ARROZ
BIDU COLA
Productos
MAYCO
El Gaucho

INDEX

A

Aceite de achiote 188
Aceite de chile habanero 188
Achiote oil 188
Achiote-rubbed grilled fish wrapped in plantain leaves 75
Adobo 186
Agua fresca de limón 246
Alfajores 233
ancho chillies
   Ancho adobo chicken 48
Anise, panela & cheese fritters 133
Arepas 119
Arrachera 101
Arroz blanco 144
Arroz con coco 146
Arroz con fideos 151
Arroz con leche 229
Arroz con pollo 157
Arroz negro 154
Arroz rojo 148
Arroz verde 144
Asado negro 106
Avocados
   Creamy avocado & herb salsa 200
   Guacamole 196
   The curvy arepa queen 44
   Venison carpaccio with watercress, palm hearts & avocado 166

B

baking *see* cakes, cookies, desserts
Barbecued lamb chops with mint chimichurri 95
Basic mayonnaise 190
beans *see also* beans, black
   Refried beans 19
beans, black
   Black bean & meat stew 17
   Mom's black beans 15
   Refried beans 19
   Ticos' rice & beans 152
beef *see also* beef eye of round, beef, minced, steak
Beef stiry-fry Peruvian-style 102
Beer-marinated skirt steak 101
Shredded beef in tomato sofrito 105
Skirt steak quesadillas 139
beef eye of round
   Panela-braised beef eye of round 106
beef, minced
   Beef-stuffed corn buns 98
   Corn pie with pebre salsa 97
   Empanadas 124
Beer-marinated skirt steak 101
berries
   Duck breast with guava & wild berry sauce 54
   Papaya cream with berry syrup 223
biscuits *see* cookies
Black bean & meat stew 17
Black coffee 263
Black ink rice 154
Bollos pelones 98
Braised & fried pork 88
bread
   Arepas 119
   Chickpea flat-bread 20
   Chipas 120
Brigadeiro 240
brittle
   Spiced brittle 235
brownies
   Flourless brownies with spice & nuts 227
Brownies con chile y nueces 227
butternut squash
   Creamy butternut squash soup 28

C

Cachapas 122
Cafecito con espumita 263
Caipirinha 259
cakes
   Three-milk cake 239
Caldito de pollo de la abuela 30
Camarão na moranga 79
Camarones con adobo de guajillo 66
Caramel meringues 237
Caramelo 235
Caraotas de mi Madre 15
Carne mechada 105
Carnitas 88
Carpaccio de venado con ensalada 166
Casquinha de siri 70
Cassava with garlic & citrus sauce 177
Cebiche de camarones y vieras 63
Cebiche Peruano 60
Cebolla morada en vinagre 199
ceviche
   Peruvian ceviche 60
   Prawn & scallop ceviche 63
Charred tomatillo sauce 194
cheese *see also* mozzarella
   Fresh white cheese 208
Chia & mint lemonade 246
chicken
   Ancho adobo chicken 48
   Chicken & rice 157
   Chicken chilaquiles in green sauce 50
   Golden tacos filled with chicken 46
   Grandmother's chicken soup 30
   Shredded chicken 42
   The curvy arepa queen 44
chickpeas
   Chickpea flat-bread 20
   Spinach with chickpeas & chilli 23
Chilaquiles con pollo 50
Chilli salt 193
chillies *see also* ancho chillies, guajillo chillies, habanero chillies
   Mole 205
   Spinach with chickpeas & chilli 23
Chimichurri 202
Chipas 120
chipotles
   Chipotle & beer mushrooms 179
   Chipotle mayonnaise 190
chocolate
   Chocolate fudge balls 240
   Flourless brownies with spice & nuts 227
Choripàn 91
chorizo
   Black bean & meat stew 17
   Latin sausage rolls 91
Choros a la chalaca 65
chowder *see also* soups
   Prawn chowder 27
Chupe de camarones 27
cocktails *see* drinks
coconut milk
   Seafood stew in coconut milk 81
Coconut rice 146
Codorniz con naranja y arroz verde 53
coffee
   Black coffee 263
   Cuban coffee 263
Colourful scrambled eggs 39
Condensed-milk lemon pie 231
cookies
   Shortbread cookie sandwich with dulce de leche 233
Cordero con chimichurri de menta 95
corn
   Beef-stuffed corn buns 98
   Cheese-filled corn pupusas with curtido slaw 127
   Corn pancakes stuffed with buffalo mozzarella 122
   Corn pie with pebre salsa 97
   Corn tortillas 115
   Open-faced mussels topped with corn & tomato salsa 65
   Red hominy stew 25
   Steamed corn parcels 135

Street corn 172
crab
  Stuffed crab shells 70
cream
  Salty cream 211
Creamy avocado & herb
  salsa 200
Creamy butternut squash
  soup 28
Creamy prawn stew in
  pumpkin 79
Crema agria 211
Crema de auyama 28
Crème de papaya con cassis 223
Crispy seafood salad 73
Cuban coffee 263
Cuban 'crème caramel' 225
Cuban sandwich 130

D

desserts
  Condensed-milk lemon
    pie 231
  Cuban 'crème caramel' 225
  Papaya cream with berry
    syrup 223
  Passionfruit mousse 220
  Rice pudding 229
Divorced eggs 41
dressings
  coriander dressing 165
  Dijon mustard dressing
    166
  lime & orange dressing 168
  passionfruit dressing 170
drinks *see also* lemonades
  Black coffee 263
  Caipirinha 259
  Cuban coffee 263
  Hibiscus margarita 252
  Little blood 254
  Margarita 252
  Micheladas 257
  Mojito 259
  Piña colada 251
  Pisco sour 248
  Sangría 260
  Zacapa old fashioned

    cocktail 260
duck
  Duck breast with guava &
    wild berry sauce 54

E

eggs
  Colourful scrambled eggs
    39
  Divorced eggs 41
  Very green eggs 37
Elote del mercado 172
Empanadas 124
Encurtido hondureño 162
Ensalada con cilantro 165
Ensalada con mango y maracuyá
  170
Ensalada con sandía y mezcal
  168
Espinaca con garbanzo y chile 23

F

Fainá 20
Feijoada 17
fish
  Achiote-rubbed grilled fish
    wrapped in plantain
    leaves 75
  Crispy seafood salad 73
  Fish fillets in green sauce
    76
  Peruvian ceviche 60
  Salmon with caramelised
    shallot & mango salsa
    83
  Seafood stew in coconut
    milk 81
Flan Cubano 225
flat-bread *see* bread
Flour tortillas 113
Flourless brownies with
  spice & nuts 227
Fresh chopped tomato salad
  193
Fresh white cheese 208
Frijoles refritos 19
fritters

Anise, panela & cheese
  fritters 133
fruit salad
  Tropical fruit salad 216

G

Gallo pinto 152
Golden tacos filled with
  chicken 46
Grandmother's chicken soup
  30
Green pesto rice 144
Guacamole 196
guajillo chillies
  Chilli salt 193
  Guajillo adobo-marinated
    prawns 66
Guasacaca 200
guavas
  Duck breast with guava &
    wild berry sauce 54

H

habanero chillies
  Habanero chilli oil 188
Herby salsa 202
Hibiscus margarita 252
Hongos con chipotle 179
Huevos divorciados 41
Huevos verdes 37

J

Jalea mixta 73
Jarabe de goma 248

K

kale
  Very green eggs 37
Kiki's moqueca 81
Kumara & cheese patties
  with peanut sauce 128

L

La reina pepiada 44
lamb
  Barbecued lamb chops
    with mint chimichurri
    95
Latin sausage rolls 91
Lechón con mojo 92
lemonades
  Chia & mint lemonade
    246
  Sugar cane lemonade 246
lemons
  Condensed-milk lemon
    pie 231
  Sugar cane lemonade 246
Little blood 254
Llapingachos 128
Lomo saltado 102

M

Mandocas 131
mangoes
  Mango & passionfruit
    salad 170
  Salmon with caramelised
    shallot & mango salsa
    83
Margarita 252
Margarita con flor de Jamaica
  252
margaritas *see* drinks
marinades
  for beef 101, 102, 106
  for chicken 157
  for pork 92
  for prawns 66, 79
Mayonesa 190
Mayonesa chile chipotle 190
mayonnaise
  Basic mayonnaise 190
  Chipotle mayonnaise 190
meat *see* beef, chorizo, lamb,
  pork, sausages, venison
Merengón 237
meringues
  Caramel meringues 237
Mexican-style red rice 148

Mezcal watermelon salad 168
Micheladas 257
Mojito 259
Mole 205
Mom's black beans 15
mousse
  Passionfruit mousse 220
Mousse de parchita 220
mozzarella
  Anise, panela & cheese fritters 133
  Cheese-filled corn pupusas with curtido slaw 127
  Corn pancakes stuffed with buffalo mozzarella 122
  Kumara & cheese patties with peanut sauce 128
mushrooms
  Chipotle & beer mushrooms 179
mussels
  Crispy seafood salad 73
  Open-faced mussels topped with corn & tomato salsa 65

N

noodles
  Rice & noodles 151

O

Octopus tostaditas (two ways) 68
Open-faced mussels topped with corn & tomato salsa 65
oranges
  Stuffed quail with green rice & oranges 53

P

palm hearts
  Venison carpaccio with watercress, palm hearts & avocado 166

pancakes *see also* tortillas
  Corn pancakes stuffed with buffalo mozzarella 122
panela
  Anise, panela & cheese fritters 133
  Panela-braised beef eye of round 106
Papas a la huancaina 180
Papaya cream with berry syrup 223
Papelón con limón 246
Passionfruit mousse 220
Pastel de choclo con pebre 97
Pato en salsa de guayaba 54
Perfect white rice 144
Perico 39
Peruvian ceviche 60
Peruvian salsa 199
Pescado en hoja de plátano 75
Pescado en salsa verde 76
pesto 144
Pickled red onions 199
Pickled vegetables 162
Pico de gallo 193
Pie de limón con leche condensada 231
pies
  Condensed-milk lemon pie 231
  Corn pie with pebre salsa 97
Piña colada 251
Pisco sour 248
plantain leaves
  Achiote-rubbed grilled fish wrapped in plantain leaves 75
Pollo desmenuzado 42
Pollo en adobo de chile ancho 48
pork
  Black bean & meat stew 17
  Braised & fried pork 88
  Pork roast with garlic 92
  Red hominy stew 25
Potatoes in huancaina sauce 180
poultry *see* chicken, duck, quail
Pozole rojo 25

Prawns
  Creamy prawn stew in pumpkin 79
  Crispy seafood salad 73
  Guajillo adobo-marinated prawns 66
  Prawn & scallop ceviche 63
  Prawn chowder 27
  Seafood stew in coconut milk 81
puddings *see* desserts
Puerto Rican cooking base 186
pumpkin *see also* butternut squash
  Creamy prawn stew in pumpkin 79
Pupusas con curtido 127

Q

quail
  Stuffed quail with green rice & oranges 53
quesadillas
  Skirt steak quesadillas 139
Quesadillas de arrachera 139
Queso fresco 208
quinoa
  Tomatoes stuffed with quinoa 174

R

Red hominy stew 25
red onions
  Peruvian salsa 199
  Pickled red onions 199
  Red 'pestle & mortar' sauce 194
Refried beans 19
rice
  Black ink rice 154
  Chicken & rice 157
  Coconut rice 146
  Green pesto rice 144
  Mexican-style red rice 148
  Perfect white rice 144

Rice & noodles 151
Rice pudding 229
Ron con toronja 260

S

Sal con chile 193
salads
  Crispy seafood salad 73
  curtido slaw 127
  Fresh chopped tomato salad 193
  Mango & passionfruit salad 170
  Mezcal watermelon salad 168
  Wedge salad with coriander dressing 165
Salmon with caramelised shallot & mango salsa 83
Salmón con salsa de mango 83
Salpicón 216
Salsa criolla 199
Salsa roja de molcajete 194
Salsa verde 194
salsas
  caramelised shallot & mango salsa 83
  Charred tomatillo sauce 194
  Creamy avocado & herb salsa 200
  Fresh chopped tomato salad 193
  Herby salsa 202
  pebre salsa 97
  Peruvian salsa 199
  Red 'pestle & mortar' sauce 194
Salty cream 211
sandwich
  Cuban sandwich 130
Sandwich Cubano 130
Sangría 260
Sangrita 254
sauces *see also* dressings, salsas
  Basic mayonnaise 190

Chipotle mayonnaise 190
Mole 205
peanut sauce 128
sausage rolls
   Latin sausage rolls 91
sausages *see also* chorizo
   Latin sausage rolls 91
seafood *see also* fish
   Black ink rice 154
   Creamy prawn stew in pumpkin 79
   Crispy seafood salad 73
   Guajillo adobo-marinated prawns 66
   Octopus tostaditas (two ways) 68
   Open-faced mussels topped with corn & tomato salsa 65
   Prawn & scallop ceviche 63
   Prawn chowder 27
   Seafood stew in coconut milk 81
   Stuffed crab shells 70
scallops
   Prawn & scallop ceviche 63
shallots
   Salmon with caramelised shallot & mango salsa 83
Shortbread cookie sandwich with dulce de leche 233
Shredded beef in tomato sofrito 105
Shredded chicken 42
Simple syrup 248
Skirt steak quesadillas 139
Sofrito 186
soups *see also* chowder
   Creamy butternut squash soup 28
   Grandmother's chicken soup 30
spice rub 186
Spiced brittle 235
spinach
   Spinach with chickpeas & chilli 23

Very green eggs 37
squid
   Black ink rice 154
   Crispy seafood salad 73
steak
   Beer-marinated skirt steak 101
   Skirt steak quesadillas 139
   Steamed corn parcels 135
stews
   Black bean & meat stew 17
   Creamy prawn stew in pumpkin 79
   Red hominy stew 25
   Seafood stew in coconut milk 81
stir-fries
   Beef stiry-fry Peruvian-style 102
Street corn 172
Stuffed crab shells 70
Stuffed quail with green rice & oranges 53
Sugar cane lemonade 246

T

tacos
   Golden tacos filled with chicken 46
Tacos dorados de pollo 46
Tamales 135
The curvy arepa queen 44
Three-milk cake 239
Ticos' rice & beans 152
Tinto campesino 263
Tomates rellenos 174
tomatillos
   Charred tomatillo sauce 194
tomatoes
   Fresh chopped tomato salad 193
   Open-faced mussels topped with corn & tomato salsa 65
   Shredded beef in tomato sofrito 105
   Tomatoes stuffed with quinoa 174

tortillas *see also* quesadillas, tacos
   Corn tortillas 115
   Flour tortillas 113
Tortillas de harina 113
Tortillas de maíz 115
Tostaditas de pulpo 68
Tres leches 239
Tropical fruit salad 216
turtle beans *see* beans, black

V

venison
   Venison carpaccio with watercress, palm hearts & avocado 166
Very green eggs 37

W

watercress
   Venison carpaccio with watercress, palm hearts & avocado 166
watermelon
   Mezcal watermelon salad 168
Wedge salad with coriander dressing 165

Y

Yuca con mojo 177

Z

Zacapa old fashioned cocktail 260

Random House

UK | USA | Canada | Ireland | Australia
India | New Zealand | South Africa | China

Random House is an imprint of the Penguin Random House group of companies, whose addresses can be found at global.penguinrandomhouse.com.

Penguin Random House New Zealand

First published by
Penguin Random House New Zealand, 2015

1 3 5 7 9 10 8 6 4 2

Text copyright © Grace Ramirez, 2015
Photographs copyright © Garth Badger, 2015,
except for photographs listed on page 280

The moral right of the author has been asserted.

All rights reserved. Without limiting the rights under copyright reserved above, no part of this publication may be reproduced, stored in or introduced into a retrieval system, or transmitted, in any form or by any means (electronic, mechanical, photocopying, recording or otherwise), without the prior written permission of both the copyright owner and the above publisher of this book.

Cover and text design by Starblock Limited
© Penguin Random House New Zealand
Cover illustration by Starblock Limited © Starblock Limited
Author photograph on page 7 by Jessica Higueras (jessicaphotography.co.nz)
Map on page 281 by Megan van Staden
Typeset in Big Caslon, Futura, ITC Caslon 224
Colour separation by Image Centre Limited
Printed and bound in China by 1010 Printing

A catalogue record for this book is available from
the National Library of New Zealand.

ISBN 978-1-77553-814-1

penguinrandomhouse.co.nz